# Engaged Classrooms:
The Art and Craft of Reaching and Teaching All Learners

Supporting Middle and High School Students' Academic Achievement
and Social-Emotional Learning and Development

*Engaged Classrooms: The Art and Craft of Reaching and Teaching All Learners*
*Supporting Middle and High School Students' Academic Achievement*
*and Social-Emotional Learning and Development*

By Carol Miller Lieber, Michele Tissiere, Sarah Bialek, and Donna Mehle

**Engaging SCHOOLS**

©2019 Engaging Schools
Engaging Schools
23 Garden Street
Cambridge MA 02138
www.engagingschools.org

All rights reserved. No part of this book may be reproduced in any form or by any electronic or mechanical means without permission in writing from the publisher.

Project Editor: Denise Wolk
Copy Editor: Julie Clark

Book design by Walter Zekanoski / WZ DESIGN
Classroom Illustration: Nalia Santiago

Silhouette Images:
Illustration 7006212 ©2019 Kirsty Pargeter - Dreamstime.com
Illustration 51964712 ©2019 Whiteisthecolor - Dreamstime.com

10 9 8 7 6 5 4 3 2
Printed in the United States of America
ISBN: 978-0-942349-36-8
Library of Congress Control Number: 2019906019

# Engaged Classrooms:
The Art and Craft of Reaching and Teaching All Learners

Supporting Middle and High School Students' Academic Achievement and Social-Emotional Learning and Development

*Engaging Schools is deeply grateful to the NoVo Foundation, the Lippincott Foundation, and an anonymous donor for the financial support that made this publication possible.*

**Carol Miller Lieber**
**Michele Tissiere**
**Sarah Bialek**
**Donna Mehle**

**Engaging SCHOOLS**
Connect • Collaborate • Learn

# Table of Contents

Foreword – by Sonia Nieto . . . . . . . . . . . . . . . . . . . . . . . . . . . . . . . . . . . . . . . . . . . . . . . .v

Preface – by Larry Dieringer . . . . . . . . . . . . . . . . . . . . . . . . . . . . . . . . . . . . . . . . . . . . vii

Acknowledgements . . . . . . . . . . . . . . . . . . . . . . . . . . . . . . . . . . . . . . . . . . . . . . . . . . . . ix

Letter to the Reader . . . . . . . . . . . . . . . . . . . . . . . . . . . . . . . . . . . . . . . . . . . . . . . . . . . .x

**Section I**     **Making the Case**

Chapter 1     Frameworks that Support the Engaged Classroom . . . . . . . . . . . . . .3

Chapter 2     Six Conditions for Academic Engagement . . . . . . . . . . . . . . . . . . . . 17

Chapter 3     Domains of the Engaged Classroom . . . . . . . . . . . . . . . . . . . . . . . . . 29

**Section II**     **Practices and Strategies that Promote Academic Engagement**

Chapter 4     Positive Personal Relationships . . . . . . . . . . . . . . . . . . . . . . . . . . . . 43

Chapter 5     Organizing the Learning Environment . . . . . . . . . . . . . . . . . . . . . . 61

Chapter 6     Content Design, Learning Tasks, and Protocols . . . . . . . . . . . . . . . 81

Chapter 7     Academic Support. . . . . . . . . . . . . . . . . . . . . . . . . . . . . . . . . . . . . . . 109

Chapter 8     Restorative and Accountable Discipline and Behavior Support . . . . . . . 139

**Section III**     **Pulling it Together**

Chapter 9     Planning Engaging Units and Purposeful, Well-Paced Lessons . . . . . . . 173

Chapter 10     Collaborative Teaming for Ramping up Academic Engagement and Student Achievement . . . . . . . . . . . . . . . . . . . . . . . . . . . . . . . . . . . . . . 183

Chapter 11     The Value of Teacher-Family Partnerships . . . . . . . . . . . . . . . . . . . . 203

**Section IV**

Appendices . . . . . . . . . . . . . . . . . . . . . . . . . . . . . . . . . . . . . . . . . . . . . . . . . . . . . . . . . 219

Index . . . . . . . . . . . . . . . . . . . . . . . . . . . . . . . . . . . . . . . . . . . . . . . . . . . . . . . . . . . . . . 321

About the Authors. . . . . . . . . . . . . . . . . . . . . . . . . . . . . . . . . . . . . . . . . . . . . . . . . . . 348

About Engaging Schools . . . . . . . . . . . . . . . . . . . . . . . . . . . . . . . . . . . . . . . . . . . . . 350

# Foreword

**By Sonia Nieto**

As a long-time supporter and national advisory board member of Engaging Schools — and before that, Educators for Social Responsibility — I've seen it grow from a small grassroots group of committed and passionate educators to a well-known and highly respected organization that provides thoughtful professional development expertise and valuable resources to teachers, administrators, and other educators around the nation and beyond. But neither growth nor time have diminished its passion nor its commitment to working towards equitable and relevant education for the young people it serves. That is certainly also evident in this volume.

Engaging Schools has a long and notable history of promoting social and emotional learning, starting long before this aspect of teaching and learning was taken seriously in most teacher education and professional development circles. The issue of equitable education, which is at the heart of giving all students the emotional and social support they need, has also marked the organization from its beginnings. In its newest iteration, restorative practices — which the authors term "restorative and accountable discipline" — are defined as more than just a trendy mantra and instead include the need to understand students both culturally and developmentally. In *Engaged Classrooms*, culturally responsive education is not promoted as a way to add what I've called "cultural tidbits" to the curriculum and pedagogy; it is instead a way to honor the histories, experiences, and identities of all students and their families and communities while also tackling the tremendous disparities in educational outcomes among students of color and students living in poverty. One way to do so is to engage not only students and teachers, but also families, and the authors provide many examples of doing so.

The commitment to provide an excellent and high-quality education to all young people means engaging them in rigorous learning that will prepare them for consequential lives. It assumes that teachers, administrators, teacher educators, and policymakers need to develop the tools to help them accomplish the goal of making school a place where young people want to be, and where they feel they truly belong. Thus, in addition to the focus on social and emotional learning, for more than 35 years Engaging Schools has explored how schools might become more academically stimulating spaces for all students. The underlying assumption in doing so is that teachers and administrators have to be at the center of change in schools and classrooms. This implies that teachers need to be constantly immersed in learning and relearning their craft, and that administrators need to find innovative ways to promote the professional development of teachers and other educators. Another significant focus of this book is that teachers and administrators benefit when they work together in the service of student learning.

Though the focus of Engaging Schools has often been on practices that make schools more welcoming spaces for a wider range of students — and that is clearly the case in the current volume as well — this is no simple guidebook. That is, rather than simply a "how-to" book, it is also a "why-to" book that emphasizes theoretical understandings, proven practices, and compelling examples. While the authors offer numerous examples based on their extensive experience with real classrooms and schools, they stay away from offering mindless quick fixes. From mindsets to protocols to tasks and assessments, the authors, all seasoned educators with a deep commitment to equity and learning, have put together a veritable treasure trove of ideas and strategies to help educators create the kind of warm, nurturing, and exciting learning environments that all students deserve. By functioning as a writing collaborative, the authors model the importance of the practice of teamwork.

In the end, *Engaged Classrooms* is fundamentally about learning, not only for students but also for teachers and administrators. As the authors assert, "Learning is one of the most beautiful, gratifying parts of the human experience." As such, no one should be denied the excitement and fulfillment of learning. Yet, many schools are places of disengagement and frustration for both students and teachers. As a result, too many students experience schools as places of unimaginative pedagogy and irrelevant curricula, and too many teachers experience professional development as numbing their creativity and insulting their intelligence. *Engaged Classrooms* aims to change this situation by honoring the knowledge and experience that teachers bring to their work as well as by a core belief that all students want to experience the sheer joy of learning.

Of course, no book can overlook the tremendous inequities that define public education today: appalling segregation, undemocratic funding, a senseless focus on high-stakes testing, discriminatory disciplinary policies, uninspired curricula, and the blatant disrespect experienced by many teachers, among other conditions. All of these are especially onerous in Black, Latinx, Indigenous, and poor White communities. Nevertheless, in spite of the larger sociopolitical issues that characterize so many of our public schools today, *Engaged Classrooms* gives us a vision of what they can become. While it is true that as a society, we need to work to eliminate these disparities, we also need to create individual classrooms and schools that energize and engage students. This book will be a source of hope and support for educators who believe that our schools can be more than what they are.

I wish *Engaged Classrooms* had been around when I walked into my first teaching job at an intermediate school in Brooklyn, New York some 50 years ago. It would have saved me countless hours of frustration, indecision, even heartache as I faced the first students I taught. In my case, I had to learn without the wise guidance offered in the pages of this book, and I improved. Fortunately for the new crop of teachers today — and even for seasoned veterans — it is a goldmine of insights and strategies that they will come back to again and again.

Sonia Nieto
*Professor Emerita, Language, Literacy, and Culture*
*College of Education, University of Massachusetts*
*Member, National Academy of Education*

# Preface

What are the teaching practices and strategies that support academic, social and emotional learning and development, and school success for each and every middle and high school student? That is the question that *Engaged Classrooms: The Art and Craft of Reaching and Teaching All Learners* answers. It follows a long Engaging Schools tradition of producing resources for teachers that are highly practical, while at the same time rooted in theory and research about what works.

As the term Engaged Classrooms suggests, we place student engagement at the heart of this book. Perspectives from researchers and experts, and data from a variety of sources support the need to focus on and better understand the nature of engagement. For example:

- The 2017 Gallup poll of fifth through twelfth graders found that 53% of students are not engaged or are actively disengaged.[1]

- The University of Chicago Consortium on School Research, in *Supporting Social, Emotional, & Academic Development: Research Implications for Educators*, says that "engaging students in learning is an educator's most critical task…It is essential that all students fully participate in learning to reach goals around equity"[2] and to experience school success in the fullest sense of the word. In addition to interfering with academic success, disengagement likely contributes to classroom management and attendance problems. According to the Consortium, attendance and effort, which follow when students are motivated and engaged, are "the main drivers of students' course grades, grade point averages, course failure, high school graduation, and college readiness."

- *A Nation at Hope: Recommendations from the National Commission on Social, Emotional, and Academic Development* tells us that "more than two decades of research across a range of disciplines—psychology, social science, brain science—demonstrates that the social, emotional, and cognitive dimensions of learning are deeply linked."[3]

We recognize this interrelationship and introduce a schema that defines engagement as having social, emotional, and cognitive dimensions and that explores the conditions that support engagement.

Engaging Schools holds a deep commitment to equity, one of our core values, and *Engaged Classrooms* reflects this. A commitment to educational equity begins with the belief that all young people can learn and deserve a high-quality education. Schools can help to level the playing field of opportunity for young people in our society. Equitable schools identify and eliminate biases and barriers to students' healthy development and academic achievement. Equitable schools recognize, normalize, and value differences across and within groups, and do not allow those differences to predict student outcomes. Equitable schools create access to high quality educational experiences and supports for all students. Staff members communicate high expectations and provide high support for each and every student. Equitable schools understand and actively work to close achievement and opportunity gaps.

What we refer to as the *Engaged Classrooms* approach, which is embodied in the book, supports teachers to provide an equitable education in several important ways. First, it supports every student to experience a safe, caring, inclusive, engaging, and challenging learning environment. Second, it directly engages teachers in practices that support developmentally appropriate and culturally responsive teaching. Third, it helps all students gain understandings and learn behaviors that enhance their capacity to succeed in school, career, and life. Finally, the approach incorporates a restorative and accountable approach to discipline, in contrast to a punitive and exclusionary approach that disproportionately impacts students of color, special education groups, and other subgroups.

*Engaged Classrooms* builds upon a white paper released previously by Engaging Schools on *Embedding Social and Emotional Learning in High School Classrooms* and years of work supporting schools to create more engaging learning environments. Recognizing the overlap of competencies associated with social and emotional learning, academic development, and postsecondary readiness, the book presents a synthesis of these competencies. *Engaged Classrooms* provides a framework that shows the dynamic relationships among student mindsets, skill sets, specific competencies, and desired target behaviors.

*Engaged Classrooms* provides the tools for integrating academic, social, and emotional learning and development in the moment-to-moment and day-to-day life of classrooms. The book introduces practices and strategies in various classroom learning domains that cover the terrain of personalized relationships, instruction, classroom management, discipline, academic and behavior supports and interventions, and family engagement. The approach embraces the idea that social, emotional, and academic skill sets and competencies can be modeled, taught, practiced, assessed, learned, and strengthened over time.

*Engaged Classrooms* reflects a commitment to a Multi-Tiered System of Supports as an important model for supporting teacher effectiveness and equity. There are two key underlying beliefs: (1) All students are capable of achieving their personal best academically, and when necessary improving their behavior with guidance, instruction, support, and coaching; and (2) Different students need different kinds and amounts of time, attention, instruction, and support to behave responsibly and succeed academically. The book maps out Tier 1 supports that can be taught and provided to all students. It also lays out Tier 2 practices and strategies that can be implemented with individuals or groups of students who have different needs, life experiences, and backgrounds.

*Engaged Classrooms* aligns with the growing understanding that "focusing only on the content of instruction and students' tested achievement is insufficient to improve educational outcomes and address issues of equity" and that "the role of teacher is more akin to that of a coach and facilitator."[4] This book is about how to teach, not what (content) to teach, and thus the audience for the book is middle and high school teachers of any subject, and instructional leaders. *Engaged Classrooms* will support teachers to re-focus on engagement and shift from "not only identifying how well students are meeting expectations…, to also figuring out why students are falling behind…, [and] working to get all students to meet those expectations."

I am grateful to Michele, Donna, Carol, Sarah, and the other contributors to this book. The authors bring to their thinking and writing many years of collective experience as secondary school teachers, administrators, and instructional leaders. They are also program leaders and education consultants with Engaging Schools. They have provided professional learning and served as coaches for schools and districts, especially in urban communities. Many are previous authors. They draw upon more than 30 years of Engaging Schools' collaboration with many hundreds of middle and high schools and thousands of teachers across the country. The authors have worked together in a learning community, in which they have shared reflections, challenges, successes, and inspiration.

I hold the deepest respect for teachers, and recognize the complexity of the art and craft of teaching. I am confident that this book will make an important contribution to the efficacy and success of teachers in creating the conditions and providing the learning opportunities that enable each and every student to connect, collaborate, achieve, thrive, and excel.

Larry Dieringer
*Engaging Schools, Executive Director*

[1] *School Engagement Is More Than Just Talk* accessed online at: https://www.gallup.com/education/244022/school-engagement-talk.aspx

[2] Allensworth, E.M., Farrington, C.A., Gordon, M.F., Johnson, D.W., Klein, K., McDaniel, B., & Nagaoka, J. (2018). *Supporting social, emotional, & academic development: Research implications for educators.* Chicago, IL: University of Chicago Consortium on School Research.

[3] *A Nation at Hope: Recommendations from the National Commission on Social, Emotional, and Academic Development* (2019). The Aspen Institute National Commission on Social, Emotional, and Academic Development. Accessed online at http://nationathope.org/

[4] Ibid. University of Chicago Consortium on School Research.

# Acknowledgements

This book revolves around a deep belief that teachers are the cornerstone for reaching and engaging each and every student in their care. Each year teachers are tasked with refining their practice to meet the needs of a range of learners, and incorporating key learnings from their experiences. Teachers are responsible for creating the conditions for high performing classroom communities where all students can grow socially, emotionally and academically. Our goal in writing this book was to identify pathways for reaching and engaging every adolescent learner. A lofty goal perhaps, and one we wouldn't have attempted as we embarked on this learning journey without the help and support of so many knowledgeable, committed, and inspiring educators in our company.

Thank you to Engaging Schools for inviting us to take part in the envisioning and writing of this book. Engaging Schools gathered the resources necessary for this project to come to fruition. Perhaps even more importantly, Engaging Schools brought together a group of staff members and consultants who are wholeheartedly committed to supporting teachers and the students whom they inspire. This project was a collaborative effort, both in its conception and in its production. We thank Larry Dierienger for supporting our vision to bring this book to fruition.

Thank you to MJ Austin, Naomi Migliacci, and Jess Miller, who generously shared fine thinking in the initial stages of the book, through writing and conversation. Their efforts, experience, and ideas helped push our thinking, and their generosity of heart and mind enhanced this work. We also express deep gratitude and great appreciation for Nicole Frazier for her graphic design skills to help us visually represent our thinking, making information more compelling and more approachable for the reader. Thank you to Sara Adelmann for her faithful and unwavering support and talent in navigating multiple authors and helping to prepare the manuscript of this book.

We appreciate the importance, perspective and graciousness of the many people who reviewed and commented on portions of the manuscript. We benefitted from their knowledge and wisdom, which motivated us to read, re-read, rethink, and reconsider. Our reviewers included:

- Heather Cabrera, New York City Department of Education
- Jane Ellison, The Thinking Collaborative
- Deidre Farmby, CASEL consultant
- Ann Scharf, Denver Public Schools
- Lee Teitel, Harvard Graduate School of Education

Thanks to Sonia Nieto for writing the foreword to our book. Her words serve as an inspiration to all of us doing the work of improving equity and access to excellent education for all students.

Our sincere gratitude goes to the Engaging Schools' staff and work-study students from Harvard University. They tirelessly tracked down citations, and read and re-read chapters.

And of course, no book can be published without the folks behind the scenes; a huge thanks to our production team:

- Julie Ann Clark, Copy Editor
- Patricia Tanalski, Proofreader
- Denise Wolk, Editorial Project Manager
- Walter Zekanoski, WZ DESIGN

A special thanks to Nalia Santiago, a student who attends George Washington High School in Denver, Colorado for creating the classroom illustration in Appendix 5.1.

We'd like to thank our colleagues throughout the country — district leaders, school leaders, and teachers — whose work in schools on behalf of young people have inspired this book. Your dedication to your work and your students gives us hope for the future.

Lastly, we would like to thank our families and friends for their ongoing support of our daytime and midnight toil to engage in work that matters.

# Letter to the Reader

### Who is the audience for this book?
Supporting adolescents' academic success and social and emotional growth is at the heart of this book. It is written for educators interested in refining the art and craft of reaching, teaching, and engaging each and every middle and high school student. And we do mean every student — all backgrounds, all groups, all learner profiles. We believe classroom teachers, teacher leaders, instructional coaches, administrators, and pre-service educational instructors will find this book to be a useful tool that supports teachers' professional growth and development.

### Who are the writers?
Our writing collaborative at Engaging Schools includes seven women who have, collectively, taught Math, Science, English, Social Studies, and Humanities for 75 years, served as school leaders for 40 years, taught pre-service and graduate education students for 25 years, and authored more than 25 books, white papers, and articles. Through our combined 90 years of consulting work with Engaging Schools, we have had the opportunity to work with thousands of teachers, student support teams, and administrators in dozens of urban districts, mid-size cities, and small towns. Our years in education span across six decades. So, what keeps us inspired? We still love learning and teaching, we still love adolescents and making a difference in young people's lives.

### Why did we write the book?
In an era, when teachers are under intense public scrutiny, they still hold the power where it matters most — in the classroom. We have great respect for the teachers we meet every day who want to do right by every student. Their commitment prompted the authors to live with this question, "What exactly are the frameworks, strategies, and mindsets that maximize teachers' capacity to reach and engage every adolescent learner?"

Research tells us that all teaching practices do not have an equal impact on student learning. Given the urgency of closing academic and disciplinary disparities among student groups, decisions about how to teach and engage all students more effectively take on even more importance. This book presents a compelling set of evidence-based strategies that we know increase academic engagement, build high performing classroom communities, improve academic achievement, and strengthen the learning and life competencies so essential to living a successful and productive life during and after high school. This resource combines our best collective thinking, direct experiences, and observational insights with a rich research base drawn from the fields of learning and behavioral sciences, educational equity, youth development, and social and emotional learning. We have incorporated twelve practices in five domains of the Engaged Classroom. We believe these domains do, in fact, capture the important work we are called to do in secondary classrooms.

We also wanted to write a book that highlights the traits and behaviors so beloved by those who have been taught by great teachers: authenticity; respect for young people; an unwavering commitment to know and care for individual students; rigorous, yet supportive expectations; a passion to make what matters interesting and relevant; and a call for excellence and students' ownership of their learning and creativity, humor, and a sense of fun.

### What do we believe about teachers and teaching?
A strong set of beliefs grounds our writing and frames the lenses through which we view teachers and the profession of teaching.

**We know teachers are agents of change and have the power to influence the trajectory of young people's lives.** In what other profession do you have the opportunity to light a fire and ignite a person's passion; to truly listen empathically to a student's story in a way that jumpstarts her academic turn-around; to become an ally to a student who felt silenced and invisible; to witness a class's growing capacity to think, problem-solve, and express themselves right in front of you?

**We know teachers have the power to foster students' sense of agency and self-direction.** In the next decade, nearly 40% of workers will be part of the "gig" economy and most people will be working in small entrepreneurial and organizational settings rather than large corporations. Getting a good job and keeping it will demand a level of personal confidence, initiative, and self-management never before required of just about everyone in the work force. Every time you encourage student voice and choice, student leadership, and student-driven learning tasks, you are punching a student's entry ticket to a rewarding future.

**We know a teacher's role and guidance matters in a technology-saturated environment.** The effectiveness of computer assisted instruction is inconclusive. Internet and electronic learning platforms have little learning value without a teacher's probing questions and mediated conversations to guide their application. Adolescent use of social media is rife with cautionary tales. More than ever, we celebrate teachers' efforts to model the messy give and take of face-to-face relationships that cultivate meaningful communication and deep learning.

**We know teachers are smarter, more creative and effective when they collaborate with colleagues.** Sharing your thinking and observations about your practice with peers generates a common vision and purpose, clearer standards of quality instruction and quality student work, and the excitement of discovering a new idea, a better strategy, or a different perspective. In turn, these collective efforts foster trusting relationships and intellectual engagement. Most importantly, teacher collaboration is a contributing factor to improved academic outcomes. Students win and you do, too.

**We know students learn as much from who teachers are as they learn from what is taught.** Never forget that when students remember you years later, they will remember what you cared about, how you treated them, what you stood for, and the goofy things you did to get them to love what you love, even if the magic lasted for just one period. Never forget that you may be the one teacher in a student's life whose kindness, attention, and encouragement opened the door to the life that student lives today.

Our heartfelt hope is that this book can serve as a beacon that reaffirms the joy, satisfaction, and honor of helping young people navigate their way to a bright and meaningful future.

We send you good wishes on your own educational journey.

Carol Miller Lieber, Michele Tissiere, Sarah Bialek, and Donna Mehle

# Section I

# Making the Case

# CHAPTER 1

## Frameworks that Support the Engaged Classroom

**Chapter Outline**
- Introduction
- Equity-Centered Classrooms: Culturally Responsive and Developmentally Informed
- Multi-Tiered System of Supports
- Learning and Life Competencies (Social and Emotional Learning)
- Closing

**Essential Question**
What are the pedagogical frameworks that make "The Engaged Classroom" a reality?

## Introduction

Teaching is complex. Every year we encounter new students, and we continually refine our practices, mostly informed by our own experience, to meet students' needs. We struggle at times when we encounter new situations and are unsure of the pathway forward. As teachers, we know that the holistic development of adolescents academically, socially, and emotionally is at the heart of our work. We also know that as the standards for student learning have increased for all students, the range of students we teach requires us to have a deep bench of knowledge and skills. In this chapter, we offer three key frameworks for classrooms that increase equity and the academic success and achievement of each and every student:

1. **Equity-Centered Classrooms** emphasize *culturally responsive* and *developmentally informed* practices that affirm students' multiple identities, their cultural experiences, and the range of their developmental needs and interests. These practices aim to counter social and developmental barriers that cause disparities in student outcomes so that students across all groups experience high levels of achievement and social and academic efficacy.

2. **Multi-Tiered System of Supports (MTSS)** provides a strategic and scaffolded approach for teachers to reach and engage diverse groups of learners through the implementation of universal promotion and prevention practices for all students and teacher-facilitated interventions for students who are struggling academically and/or behaviorally.

3. **Learning and Life Competencies (LLC)**, which fall under the umbrella of social and emotional learning (SEL), are linked to academic achievement and college, career, and life success.[1] Knowing how to nuance and integrate Learning and Life Competencies into learning tasks; classroom procedures, rituals, and routines; and learning protocols is essential to supporting sustained academic engagement. This results in an increase in students' self-awareness, self-management, social efficacy, and academic efficacy.

Six Conditions for Academic Engagement (Chapter 2) and Domains of the Engaged Classroom (Chapter 3) are two additional frameworks of the engaged classroom. These five frameworks empower teachers to cultivate every student's capacity to learn and reach higher levels of engagement and academic achievement (Figure 1.1). To further explore an *Empowered Teacher Presence*, please see Chapter 3.

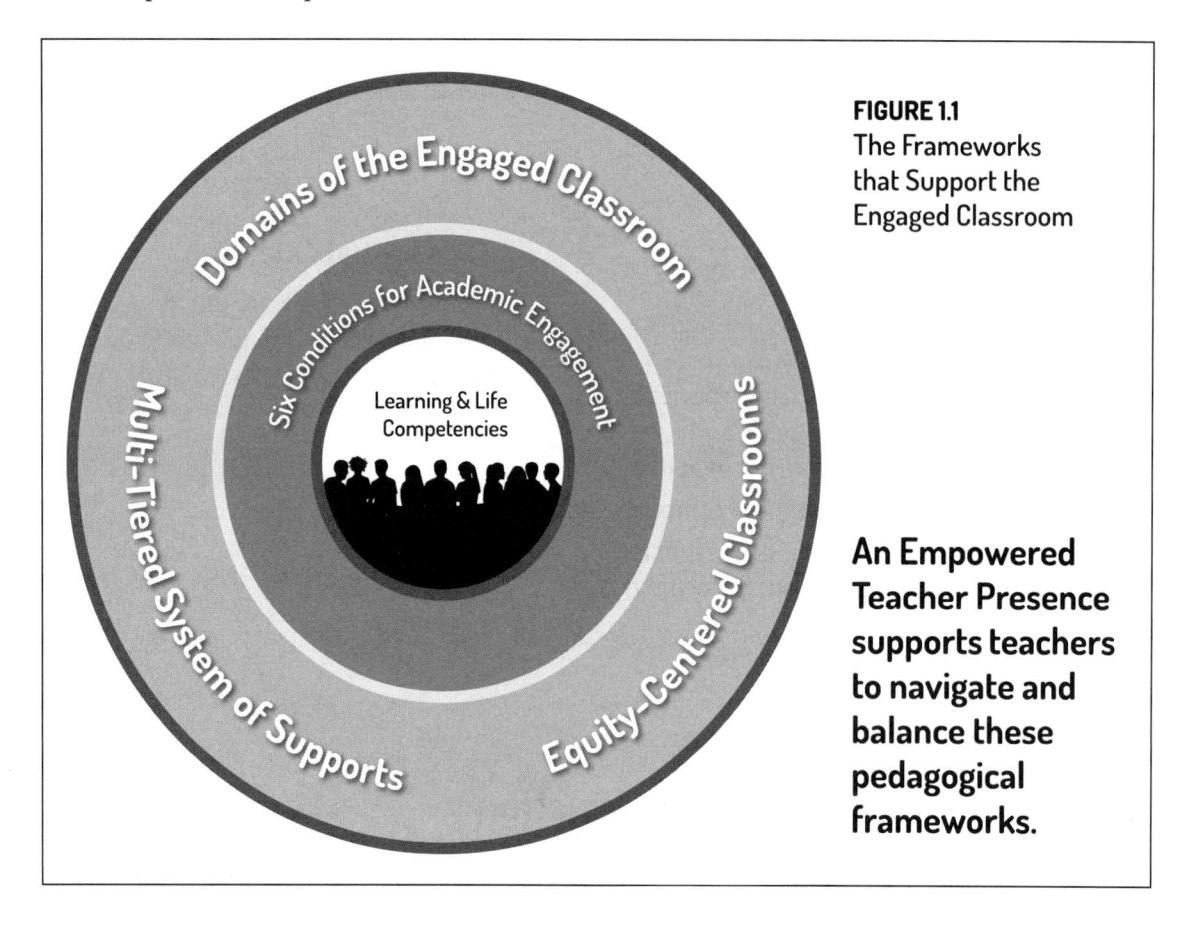

**FIGURE 1.1**
The Frameworks that Support the Engaged Classroom

(Concentric circles diagram showing: Domains of the Engaged Classroom / Multi-Tiered System of Supports / Equity-Centered Classrooms / Six Conditions for Academic Engagement / Learning & Life Competencies at center)

**An Empowered Teacher Presence supports teachers to navigate and balance these pedagogical frameworks.**

## Equity-Centered Classrooms:
## Culturally Responsive and Developmentally Informed

In simple terms, educational equity involves the analysis, processes, and strategies used to achieve equal outcomes across different groups. Equity serves as the remedy when measures of equality are absent for a specific group, whether that measure is equal treatment, equal opportunity, equal resources, or equal outcomes. At the district, school community, and classroom level, this calls for vigilant efforts to examine and address persistent patterns of unequal opportunities and outcomes that impact individuals who identify with a particular race, gender, ethnicity, class, religion, degree of able-ness, or other significant identity difference. Pursuing equity means interrupting systems, structures, policies, and practices that discriminate against some student groups while privileging others. To be clear, the end goal of equity strategies is to achieve equal outcomes for all groups within the same classification, such as race, gender, class, or religion. Outcomes for individuals within and across groups will always vary given the vast spectrum of human differences. Increasing equitable outcomes across groups begins with believing that every student is capable of success and recognizes the uniqueness and strengths of each student, allowing for differences in time, attention, instruction, and support.

In Figure 1.2 we offer examples from districts and schools with whom we have partnered that identified equity concerns and implemented initiatives to address those concerns.

> **Practices and strategies that promote equity are intended to ensure fairness by:**
>
> 1. Countering biased behaviors that cause harm to specific groups;
> 2. Countering unfair policies, programs, practices that consistently result in negative outcomes for groups who are disadvantaged by these actions; and
> 3. Negotiating, re-allocating and sometimes re-imagining resources, opportunities, and supports when the equal distribution of these things (one size fits all) results in unequal outcomes that do not adequately meet specific needs and interests of all groups of students.

**FIGURE 1.2** What Educational Equity Initiatives Look Like

| Inequality of Outcomes for Groups Within the Same Classification | The Equity Initiative Goals and Activities |
|---|---|
| *District Level:* Suspension is three times higher for Black students in comparison to White students. | • Unpack biases and other root causes that contribute to the current reality.<br>• Change policies and practices in ways that will reduce disproportionality (e.g., decrease office referrals by training teachers in strategies to respond to low-impact behaviors).<br>• Increase restorative interventions that strengthen social efficacy and increase opportunities for students to develop a positive attachment to school and peers. |
| *School Level:* 90% of the students who participate in clubs, sports, and extra-curricular activities after school live in just two of seven zip codes of students who attend the school. | • Unpack biases and other root causes that contribute to the current reality.<br>• Reconfigure the school day to include a designated period for extra-curricular activities open to all students.<br>• Set an initial target outcome of at least 40% of students from every zip code participating in an extracurricular activity. |
| *School and Classroom Level:* Over 40% of all students in 9th grade are failing at least one course, and 25% of all 9th graders are failing two or more courses. Failing students comprise a disproportionate percentage of boys, students of color, and students with disabilities. | • Unpack biases and other root causes that contribute to the current reality.<br>• Reduce the overall failure rate by 30% by the end of two years through changes in classroom and schoolwide academic support practices, structures, and interventions.<br>• Examine and monitor student grades and GPAs systematically at regularly scheduled times during the year. |
| *Classroom Level:* Twice as many girls as boys earn As and Bs. | • Unpack biases and other root causes that contribute to the current reality.<br>• Engage in research and professional learning to build an understanding of boys' developmental needs.<br>• Implement practices that align with the developmental needs of boys. |

### Equity-Centered Classrooms

This book is focused on equity-centered classrooms that are culturally responsive and developmentally informed. *The Equity-Centered Classroom* communicates, "I believe in you and your ability to be successful, and I will support you to navigate the complexities of rigorous and meaningful learning and social experiences." When teachers consider how cultural background, race, religion, ethnicity, socio-economic status, gender, gender identification, sexual orientation, language, learning preferences, and ability/disability impact students' learning, students feel affirmed; their voices are heard and honored. When teachers acknowledge and respond to the ways in which adolescents are beginning to establish their own identities, become more intimate with peers, and grow their sense of autonomy, control, and mastery in the world, students are better able to engage cognitively, behaviorally, and emotionally.

As curators of *Equity-Centered Classrooms*, we:

1. Embrace the range of developmental and cultural differences among adolescents with curiosity, creativity, and passion. These differences include the ones we are born with, the ones connected to our family background and culture, and the ones shaped by our preferences and experiences.

2. Create a culture that is simultaneously rigorous and safe intellectually, socially, and emotionally; emphasizes relationships, relational trust, and caring communication; includes relevant content and student work; values student voice and choice; accommodates diverse learning strategies; and scaffolds learning that meets students where they are and pushes them to excel.

3. Are mindful of how personal biases shape our interactions with different groups of learners, our choice of learning strategies and learning tasks, and our approach to discipline and student support.[2]

4. Aim to directly counter racial, cultural, behavioral, and developmental biases with explicit practices that help reduce favoritism, preferential treatment, and discriminatory behaviors.

We invite the readers of this book to hold two questions: (1) In the face of structural and systemic racism, and other prejudices based on gender, class, culture, religion, and able-ness: In what ways might I model a way of being that communicates my commitment to be an advocate and ally to all students and their families? and (2) For the many adolescents who come to me already impacted by prejudicial experiences that have shaped their perceptions of and their performance at school: How will I incorporate culturally responsive and developmentally informed practices that interrupt cycles of prejudice and academic struggle to help students re-capture a vision of themselves as successful learners?

## Culturally Responsive Classrooms

The practices and strategies described in the Domains of the Engaged Classroom in Chapters 4 through 8 include many "best practices" associated with culturally responsive teaching.[3] Here we would like to highlight six practices recommended by prominent thought leaders in the field of culturally responsive teaching:[4]

1. Affirm students' multiple identities (See Chapter 6);[5]
2. Support and guide students for how to "do school" by learning the "cultural capital" of school success (See Chapter 7);[6]
3. Introduce stories, texts, people, places, and visible symbols that reflect the cultural heritage of different ethnic groups (See Chapter 6);
4. Make connections between content topics and students' lived experiences, families, peers, neighborhoods, and cultures and invite students to think critically about the social-racial-political context of their own realities (See Chapter 6);[7]
5. Create opportunities for students to work together in mixed groups (See Chapter 6);[8] and
6. Counter disproportional disciplinary practices by reframing discipline problems into teaching-learning opportunities (See Chapter 8).[9]

For a deeper look at how cultural competency supports an *Empowered Teacher Presence*, please see Chapter 3. For a comprehensive and extremely accessible resource on culturally responsive teaching, we recommend downloading "Culturally Responsive Teaching: A Guide to Evidence-Based Practices for Teaching All Students Equitably" from the Equity Center Education Northwest.[10]

## Developmentally Informed Classrooms

In *Developmentally Informed Classrooms*, principles of positive youth development drive day-to-day interactions between students and teachers. We are mindful of how we provide a saturation of opportunities and supports that foster three benchmarks of the adolescent experience: **Being**—defining who I am; **Belonging**—finding my place in school, with peers, and family; and **Becoming**—achieving my personal goals, hopes, and aspirations. Helping to grow happy, healthy, and successful young people is informed by what we know about adolescent development. This includes the phases and stages of adolescents' physical, emotional, social, cognitive, ethical, and spiritual growth and maturity, and the conditions that enable adolescents to thrive.[11]

The concept of resiliency is a key lever for embedding youth development into everyday classroom practices. Resiliency is the capacity to bounce back from adversity, recover from loss and personal setbacks, and adjust to new challenges in ways that help young people achieve positive outcomes and life chances. Resilience reflects the "self-righting tendencies that move children toward normal adult development under all but the most persistent adverse circumstances"[12] (See Figure 1.3 Fostering Resiliency).

**FIGURE 1.3** Fostering Resiliency

| Four personal strengths foster resiliency: | Three protective factors (in schools, at home, and in the community) support the development of these personal strengths: |
|---|---|
| 1. Social competence;<br>2. Problem-solving;<br>3. Autonomy (positive identity, internal locus of control, self-efficacy, and mastery); and<br>4. Sense of purpose (goal direction, achievement motivation, hope in the future, and optimism). | 1. Caring relationships;<br>2. High expectations and consistent boundaries; and<br>3. Opportunities to participate and contribute. |

Developmentally informed teachers build students' assets, strengths, and resiliency through social, emotional, cognitive, physical, and moral development. They adjust and differentiate instruction in ways that consider students' learning readiness, personal preferences and interests, prior knowledge, and developmental maturity. They provide a saturation of opportunities and supports to meet the needs and interests of different learners. See Appendix 1.1 – Adolescent Development Essentials.

*Equity-Centered Classrooms* that are culturally responsive and developmentally informed provide opportunities for adolescents to:

1. See themselves and their lives and communities in the curriculum content;
2. See the relevance of what they are learning in relation to their growing and changing sense of identity;
3. Construct knowledge socially through cooperative, experiential, and interactive learning;
4. Construct knowledge through mediated conversations with adults that push their learning beyond what they already know and can do;
5. Challenge rules and assumptions by critically examining the arguments of others, making their own, and discovering the "grey" areas on a given issue;
6. Make meaning of abstract concepts in the concrete contexts of their life experience;
7. Use their evolving ability to reason in order to examine and take on multiple perspectives;
8. Experience choice and develop their capacity to make responsible decisions about their own learning; and
9. Experience a sense of mastery and efficacy in their learning.[13]

## Multi-Tiered System of Supports (MTSS)

A *Multi-Tiered System of Supports (MTSS)* allows teachers to be agile and flexible, integrate universal practices and strategies, adapt to the changing needs of students, diagnose academic and behavioral issues, and organize and distribute resources where they are most needed. Through effective and timely formative assessment systems, teacher dialogue, and regular analysis of student data, teachers can prioritize those students who need immediate interventions. While students' needs fluctuate, the system to identify and respond to these needs remains steadily in place. Standardized structures and protocols enable teachers to implement targeted and timely promotion, prevention, and intervention strategies to maximize success for most of their students.

A classroom teacher who believes in and understands the importance of an MTSS integrates universal strategies that support the growth of all students. Teachers anticipate that many students, at some point, will encounter academic, social, and emotional challenges in their middle and high school experience. Empowered teachers are prepared to facilitate interventions for students who need additional support. This framework reinforces a student-centered view of our classrooms.

> **Promotion, Prevention, and Intervention at the Classroom Level**
>
> **Promotion:** Teachers promote positive behaviors and academic growth for all students through universal classroom practices that they model, teach, practice, and assess.
>
> **Prevention:** Teachers intervene early at the first signs of academic struggle or off-track behaviors to avoid major problems.
>
> **Intervention:** Teachers provide interventions for students who are experiencing persistent academic and behavioral challenges that match students' academic, social, and emotional needs.

## Multi-Tiered System of Supports

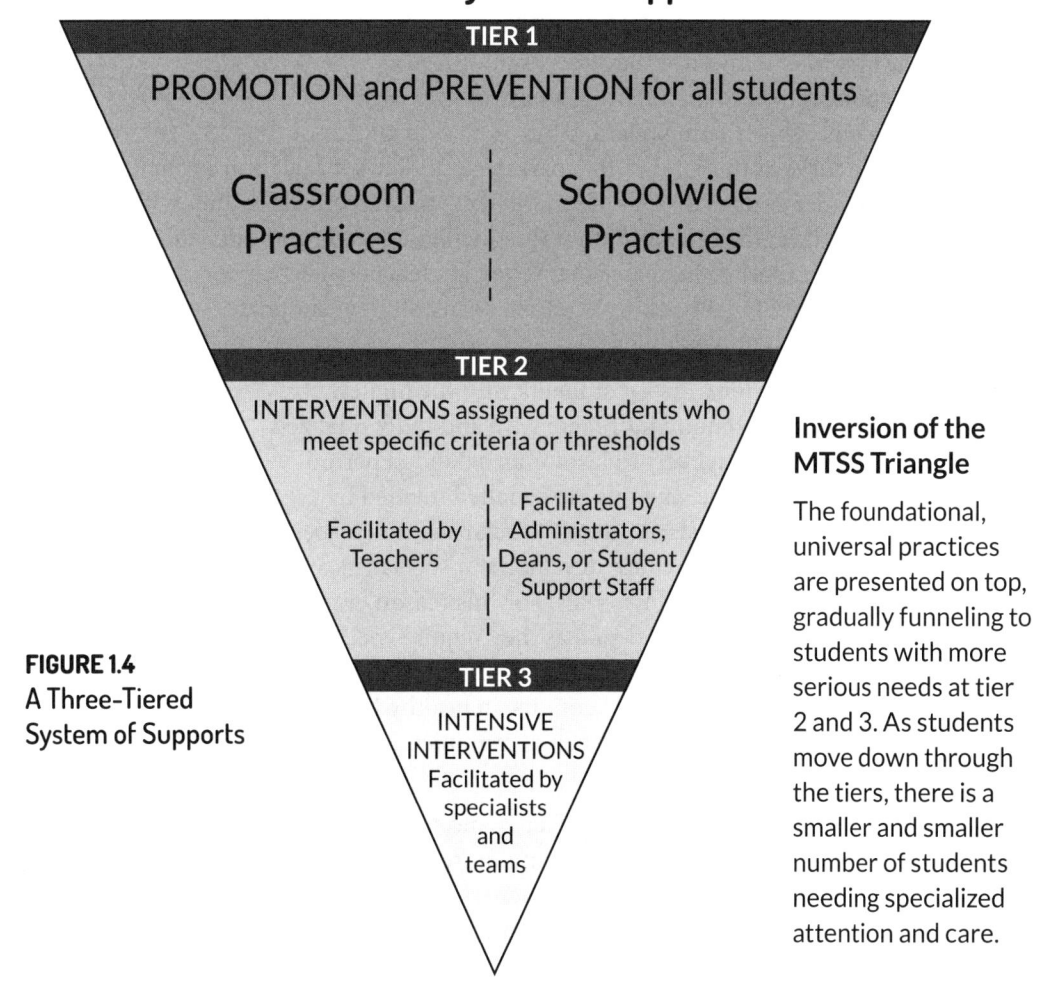

**TIER 1**
PROMOTION and PREVENTION for all students
Classroom Practices | Schoolwide Practices

**TIER 2**
INTERVENTIONS assigned to students who meet specific criteria or thresholds
Facilitated by Teachers | Facilitated by Administrators, Deans, or Student Support Staff

**TIER 3**
INTENSIVE INTERVENTIONS
Facilitated by specialists and teams

**FIGURE 1.4**
A Three-Tiered System of Supports

**Inversion of the MTSS Triangle**

The foundational, universal practices are presented on top, gradually funneling to students with more serious needs at tier 2 and 3. As students move down through the tiers, there is a smaller and smaller number of students needing specialized attention and care.

**Tier 1** Classroom practices focus on *promotion* of students' emotional, cognitive, and behavioral engagement and *prevention* of academic disengagement and unwanted behaviors. These practices are used universally throughout the school; they establish positive relationships, rigorous and meaningful learning tasks, common classroom procedures, critical learning protocols, and high expectations for every student. *Promotion* efforts foster students' self-awareness, self-management, and social and academic efficacy. *Prevention* efforts in the classroom enable teachers to intervene early, support students who experience academic difficulties, and defuse behavioral challenges before they become unmanageable. We call Tier 1 supports "hands-on" as it is the teacher's responsibility to model, teach, practice, and assess the behaviors and mindsets that support each student's success in the classroom.

**TIER 1**
PROMOTION and PREVENTION for all students
Classroom Practices | Schoolwide Practices

**Tier 2** Classroom *interventions* are provided for students who need additional academic, behavioral, and/or emotional support. We know from experience that some students will need targeted interventions to reach the levels of learning and engagement we hold for every student in the class. Yet, it is often unclear whose role and responsibility it is to implement these interventions. Teachers are the experts who know their students best, and consequently, teacher-facilitated interventions are often more effective than those delivered by outside support specialists. When teachers serve as the first interventionist, they are communicating their commitment to maintaining a partnership with the student. This trusting relationship, built over time, can often serve as the catalyst for sparking a student's motivation to change. Students requiring Tier 2 interventions are more likely to overcome learning or behavioral challenges when the intervention is timely, aligned, and monitored. Sometimes, when students are experiencing persistent struggles, teachers participate in a "hands-joined" Tier 2 intervention with administrators, deans, student support staff, learning specialists, or mental health professionals.

**TIER 2**
INTERVENTIONS assigned to students who meet specific criteria or thresholds
Facilitated by Teachers | Facilitated by Administrators, Deans, or Student Support Staff

**Tier 3** Intensive *interventions* are for students with the highest level of need, who require more intensive and individualized interventions that are likely to last for an extended period. Interventions for these students are usually provided by counselors, psychologists, academic specialists/tutors, social workers, case managers, youth development specialists, or other trained mental health professionals. For this reason, we refer to this tier of supports as "hand-off," as they require specialized skills outside of a teacher's role, responsibilities, and expertise. While teachers may not be directly involved in these interventions, in healthy MTSS systems, they are kept informed of the student's progress so they can communicate their support for the goals of the intervention to the student.

**TIER 3**
INTENSIVE INTERVENTIONS Facilitated by specialists and teams

Supporting students directly at Tier 1 and Tier 2, and from a close distance at Tier 3, allows teachers to develop a deeper understanding and more holistic view of their students when they hit the inevitable bumps in the road. When teachers' comfort and skillfulness to intervene early becomes intuitive and habitual, administrators and student support staff can direct their time and attention to students requiring more intensive interventions.

## Learning and Life Competencies (Social-Emotional Learning)

It has become increasingly clear to educators that content knowledge alone is not what prepares students to succeed in school, work, and life. Learning to regulate emotions, set and achieve goals, empathize with others, develop positive relationships, and make responsible decisions are considered as critical to adult success as academic achievement. These competencies help students successfully navigate across culture, settings, and communities. While social and emotional learning (SEL) research focused on adolescents is less robust than SEL research involving younger children, a few studies show a corollary link between social-emotional skills and adult outcomes. Intrapersonal and interpersonal competencies such as flexibility, initiative, appreciation of diversity, metacognition, communication, collaboration, responsibility, and conflict resolution are "highly correlated with desirable educational, career, and health outcomes."[14] SEL is also being championed as necessary for success in today's economy.[15]

Secondary schools are brimming with lists variously identified as college and career readiness skills, life skills, 21st-century soft skills, noncognitive competencies, and habits of learning. Our cross-walk of these lists inspired us to develop a set of competencies, skills, and target behaviors that align with the developmental and cultural needs of secondary students, mirror the academic and behavioral expectations held by secondary teachers, and live naturally in the classroom setting. We call these "Learning and Life Competencies for School, College, and Career Success," referred to hereafter as *Learning and Life Competencies (LLCs)*.

> **Competency:** the ability an individual grows over time and can use fluidly and flexibly in varied contexts, drawing from knowledge, practice, and experience
>
> **Skill:** A specific ability an individual demonstrates within a competency
>
> **Target Behaviors:** Discrete observable behaviors that an individual uses in school, work, and life

LLCs encompass four competencies: self-awareness, self-management, social efficacy, and academic efficacy. Each competency includes associated skills and specific target behaviors that demonstrate students' growing mastery of these competencies over time. Students' capacity to strengthen and refine self-awareness, self-management, social efficacy, and academic efficacy is positively related to course grades, graduation rates, and college and career readiness and success.[16] These LLCs directly build students' capacities to learn, to interact productively in classroom settings, and to grow increasingly efficacious—personally, interpersonally, and academically (See Figure 1.5).

**FIGURE 1.5** Learning and Life Competencies for School, College, and Career Success

| Competency | Skill | Target Behaviors |
|---|---|---|
| Self-Awareness | I know myself. | I am aware that my mindsets and emotions impact my capacity to learn and be skillful. |
| | | I can accurately assess my feelings, behavior, interests, values, and strengths through my experiences. |
| | | I know when I have done the right thing and when I make mistakes. |
| | | I know when I bother others or upset them. |
| | I am aware of skills, behaviors, and attitudes that help me. | I can name and describe the benefits of skills, behaviors, and mindsets that help me be a good student and a good person. |
| | | I know what motivates me. |
| | | I know when it is important to follow the rules, procedures, and norms of acceptable behavior. |
| Self-Management | I identify, express, and manage emotions. | I name and assess emotions accurately. |
| | | I express emotions skillfully even when I feel angry, frustrated, or disrespected. |
| | | I manage my emotions by using strategies to cool down and regain my balance. |
| | I exhibit self-regulation. | I sustain my focus and pay attention throughout an activity or task. |
| | | I work silently without bothering others. |
| | | I accept help, feedback, correction, or consequences with goodwill. |
| | | I follow instructions, procedures, and rules. |
| | I demonstrate perseverance and resiliency. | I persist in my effort until I "get it" and finish the task. |
| | | I pursue and sustain efforts to complete long-term tasks and achieve long-term goals related to my future. |
| | | I can right myself and bounce back even when I experience temporary setbacks, failure, or adversity. |
| Social Efficacy | I communicate and problem-solve effectively. | I focus my attention on people who are speaking to me. |
| | | I listen respectfully and paraphrase/summarize or question before speaking. |
| | | I use school-appropriate language and project appropriate body language. |
| | | I use problem-solving strategies to work things out. |
| | | I resolve interpersonal conflicts constructively. |
| | I demonstrate empathy and respect. | I make an effort to understand the emotions, words, and actions of others. |
| | | I respect the dignity of each person and their rights to be heard, to be valued, and to learn in a safe classroom. |
| | | I accept other viewpoints respectfully and appreciate individual and group similarities and differences. |
| | | I stand up for people whose rights, identity, or dignity have been violated. |
| | | I interrupt or call attention to incidents of bullying, harassment, prejudice, or teasing. |

| Competency | Skill | Target Behaviors |
|---|---|---|
| **Social Efficacy** | I foster healthy relationships. | I greet and talk to people in a friendly manner.<br>I use words of common courtesy like please and thank you, excuse me, sorry about that.<br>I am dependable and follow through on what I say I am going to do.<br>I help and support others. |
| | I am assertive and I self-advocate. | I use neutral, non-aggressive language to express myself.<br>I can verbalize and present my ideas, my values, and my needs to others.<br>I take the initiative to seek help.<br>I can navigate across different settings in order to present my best self to others. |
| | I cooperate and participate. | I work effectively with different students.<br>I take on various roles and responsibilities to complete the learning task.<br>I take turns, listen to and encourage others, and do my fair share. |
| | I demonstrate civic responsibility. | I volunteer to take on leadership roles or extended responsibilities in a group.<br>I do positive things to make the class a good place to learn.<br>I take responsibility for my words and actions and acknowledge the impact of my behavior on the community.<br>I make responsible decisions. |
| **Academic Efficacy** | I invest in quality work. | I attempt each part of the question, task, assignment, or test.<br>I revise, edit/proof, and correct for quality and accuracy.<br>I push myself to take academic risks.<br>I complete assigned tasks regularly.<br>I engage in critical, reflective, and creative thinking. |
| | I organize to learn and study. | I attend class every day and arrive to class on time.<br>I organize myself and manage my materials.<br>I prioritize and manage my time and tasks.<br>I figure out the instructions before I begin a task.<br>I use a range of study strategies to remember and apply key knowledge, skills, and understandings. |
| | I set goals and self-assess. | I make sure that I know the criteria for high-quality work.<br>I set specific learning goals and identify and adjust action steps to improve my grade.<br>I monitor my academic progress through written and oral self-reflection and conferencing.<br>I can identify the evidence that shows my effort to meet my goal. |

Empowered teachers integrate LLCs into their daily instruction by making intentional efforts to Model, Teach, Practice, and Assess target behaviors in the classroom. Students are more willing to practice academic and social behaviors that may at first feel awkward in a climate where growth is a goal, and mistakes and missteps are normalized. Over time, students begin to recognize that their efforts result in greater academic engagement and make learning feel more authentic. For a snapshot of what integrating LLCs look like in engaged classrooms, please see Appendix 1.2 – Learning and Life Competencies: Classroom Snapshot. For a lesson on how to directly teach LLCs and have students perform self-assessments, please see Appendix 1.3 – LLC Sample Mini-Lesson and Appendix 1.4 – LLC Self-Assessment and Reflection Tool.

> A mindset is a predominant attitude informed by a set of deeply held assumptions and beliefs that reinforces our current habits, choices, and preferred way of doing things.

One of our responsibilities as teachers is to encourage students to develop positive mindsets about themselves that, in turn, set the stage for academic engagement and the desire to master LLCs (Figure 1.6). Self-identification with the values of schooling and the roles of a learner will influence the attitudes and perceptions a student holds about his/her learning and academic performance. When students feel that school and school work have value, when they feel a sense of belonging in the classroom, and they approach learning tasks with positive expectations, they can sustain their effort over time and express their curiosity, enthusiasm, and personal interest in what they are learning. This boosts students' confidence in their day-to-day experiences and fires up their hope in a positive future.

**FIGURE 1.6** Student Mindsets

**Mindsets** set the stage for academic engagement and developing Learning and Life Competencies. Self-identification with the values of schooling and the roles of a learner will influence the attitudes and perceptions a student holds in relation to his/her learning and academic performance. When students feel that school and school work have value, when they feel a sense of belonging in the classroom, and they approach learning tasks with positive expectations, they have a capacity to sustain their effort over time and express their curiosity, enthusiasm, and personal interest in what they are learning. This boosts students' confidence about their day-to-day experiences and fires up hope in their future. The examples cited provide a range of entry points for conversations with students.

**EXAMPLES:**
- School and school work have value for me.
- I belong to an academic community.
- I approach tasks with positive expectations and an open mind.
- I accept challenges, take academic risks, and push myself to excel.
- My ability and competence grow with my effort.
- I express curiosity, enthusiasm, or personal interest in what I am learning.
- I cultivate personal talents, values, and positive qualities of character.
- I have hope in a positive future I can make for myself.

Learning and strengthening four key **COMPETENCIES**
1. Self-Awareness
2. Self-Management
3. Social Efficacy
4. Academic Efficacy

That incorporate specific **SKILLS**

Aligned to specific **DESIRED TARGET BEHAVIORS** that strengthen positive **MINDSETS**

## Closing

We hope the frameworks presented in this chapter: *Equity-Centered Classrooms*, a *Multi-Tiered System of Supports*, and *Learning and Life Competencies* offer a solid foundation on which to continually refine your classroom practice. Imagine a generation of students who graduate from schools where the application of these three frameworks is commonplace and result in:

- Students whose academic engagement and achievement flourished because of their experiences in equity-centered classrooms;
- Students whose academic and behavioral needs were attended to through a clearly articulated and viable Multi-Tiered System of Supports; and
- Students who developed personal knowledge of themselves and strengthened their social and academic efficacy through teachers' continual cultivation of these skill sets.

Making this a reality begins one teacher at a time; it is within your power and control as teachers and instructional leaders.

---

[1] Conley, D. *Four keys to college and career readiness*. (2011). Education Policy Task Force, Council of State Governments.

[2] Gorski, P., & Swalwell, K., Equity literacy for all, *Educational Leadership*, March, 2015, Alexandria, VA: ASCD.

[3] Krasof, B. (2016). *Culturally responsive teaching: A guide to evidence-based practices for teaching all students equitably.* Portland, Oregon: Region X Equity Assistance Center Education Northwest.

[4] Ladson-Billings, G. (2009). *The dreamkeepers: Successful teachers of African American children* (2nd ed.). San Francisco, CA: Jossey-Bass.

[5] Nakkula, M. & Toshalis E., (2006). *Understanding youth: Adolescent development for educators.* Cambridge, MA: Harvard Education Press.

[6] Gay, G. (2010). *Culturally responsive teaching: Theory, research, and practice* (2nd ed.). New York, NY: Teachers College Press.

[7] Nieto, S. & Bode, P. (2018). *Affirming diversity: the sociopolitical context of multicultural education* (7th ed.). New York, NY: Pearson.

[8] Banks, C. A. M., & Banks, J. A. (1995). Equity pedagogy: An essential component of multicultural education. *Theory Into Practice*, 34(3), 152–158.

[9] Noguera, P. A. (2007). How listening to students can help schools to improve. *Theory Into Practice*, 46, 205-211.

[10] Krasof, B. (2016). *Culturally responsive teaching: A guide to evidence-based practices for teaching all students equitably.* Portland, OR: Region X Equity Assistance Center Education Northwest. Accessed online at: https://educationnorthwest.org/resources/culturally-responsive-teaching-guide-evidence-based-practices-teaching-all-students.

[11] Lerner, R. M. (2005). *Promoting positive youth development: Theoretical and empirical bases.* Somerville, MA: Institute for Applied Research in Youth Development Tufts University.

[12] Benard, B. (2004). *Resilience: What we have learned.* Los Alamitos, CA: West Ed.

[13] Lieber, C. (2009). *Making learning REAL: Reaching and engaging all learners in secondary classrooms.* Cambridge, MA: Engaging Schools.

[14] Pellegrina, J.W. & Hilton, M.L. (2012). *Education for Life and Work: Developing transferable knowledge and skills in the 21st century.* National Research Council.

[15] American Enterprise Institute for Public Policy Research (2015). *Opportunity, Responsibility, and Security: A consensus plan for reducing poverty and restoring the American dream.*

[16] Nagaoka, J., Farrington, C.A., Ehrlich, S.B., & Heath, R.D. (2015). *Foundations for young adult success: A developmental framework.* Chicago, IL: The University of Chicago Consortium on School Research.

# CHAPTER 2

## Six Conditions for Academic Engagement

**Chapter Outline**
- Introduction
- Six Conditions for Academic Engagement
- Closing
- Why Does Academic Engagement Matter? What the Research Says

**Essential Question**
What are the reasons academic engagement is so critical to each and every student's success in school, work, and life?

# Introduction

We know it when we see it — students are leaning in, contemplating, reading, writing, calculating, discussing, laughing, smiling, maybe even tearing up — in essence, they are immersed in the experience, and they are learning. What are the keys to eliciting and sustaining this type of academic engagement? Learning is one of the most beautiful, gratifying parts of the human experience. Being learners ourselves, most of us can describe a time in which we were deeply engaged and how this positively impacted our learning and lives. Intuitively, we know engagement is critical to learning, which is why, when we encounter students whom we feel lack motivation and do not engage, we can become stymied as educators, racking our brains for ways to engage classrooms full of adolescents with wide-ranging interests and diverse personal, social, educational, and cultural backgrounds.

Before choosing to engage in the cognitive, behavioral, and emotional work of learning, students are exploring three questions in each new learning situation based on their past experiences with learning: (1) How important is this knowledge to me? (2) Will I be successful? and (3) How do I feel about doing this task?[1] The ways in which students answer these questions relate to their academic mindsets: the core assumptions and beliefs that drive their behavior and create powerful incentives to sustain prior habits, choices, and their preferred ways of doing things. The University of Chicago Consortium on School Research has found that academically successful students hold these core beliefs: (1) I belong in this academic community, (2) My ability and my competence grow with my effort, (3) I can succeed at this, and (4) This work has value for me. These internal beliefs lead to academic behaviors, academic perseverance, learning strategies, and positive social skills that reinforce these positive academic mindsets over time.[2] When we engage each and every student in our course, we support students in developing this positive feedback loop, strengthening their learning strategies (study skills, metacognitive strategies, self-regulated learning, and goal-setting) and Learning and Life Competencies (interpersonal skills, empathy, cooperation, assertion, and responsibility) through each successful attempt at learning.

We define academic engagement as sustained learning that involves students emotionally, cognitively, and behaviorally.

- Behavioral engagement is the positive conduct (i.e., following the rules, routines, and procedures) and physical participation that supports learning and academic tasks (i.e., writing, reading, speaking, drawing, presenting).

- Emotional engagement refers to students' positive affective state during learning stemming from an overall sense of belonging and engaging one's mind in a compelling task. Emotional engagement may look like happiness, excitement, interest, or relaxed alertness.

- Cognitive engagement is the investment a student makes in his or her learning resulting in critical, creative, and reflective thinking.[3]

As teachers, we can help students reshape their views of themselves as more competent, autonomous, and connected to their teachers and peers, by increasing engagement, learning, and achievement.[4] While students are internally assessing their motivation to engage, we have the opportunity to structure our classrooms and instruction to create the conditions that will support students' cultural and developmental needs, deepen their engagement, and reshape their academic mindsets over the course of a school year. We call these the Six Conditions for Academic Engagement. See the final section of this chapter — Why Does Academic Engagement Matter? What the Research Says – to learn more about the impact of engagement on student achievement.

## Six Conditions for Academic Engagement

We have researched and explored six conditions that lead to academic engagement and support students in building positive academic mindsets: goodwill, participation, attention, effort, interest, and commitment.[5] Cultivating these six conditions in our students requires deep, personal, and sustained relationships with students. When students feel known, cared for, trusted, and respected, they are more likely to engage with their peer group and with us. As teachers, we have the capacity to create conditions in our classrooms that result in sustained learning that involves students emotionally, cognitively, and behaviorally.

### Goodwill (I Trust)

Building a cohesive community is at the heart of school improvement and academic engagement. Thomas Sergiovanni, who has written extensively about school culture and leadership, suggests that a community must have, among other elements, trust and respect.[6] In this context, students' goodwill and trust show up in behaviors that align with sentiments such as, *"Okay, I'll go with you. You're on my side. You understand me. I'll put in the effort for you even if I don't like some of the learning tasks."*

Trust emerges when teachers cultivate relationships with and among students and when they support and maintain them through dependability, predictability, genuineness, honesty, curiosity, competence, integrity, consistency, and personalization.[7] This sense of trust deepens when students feel safe and are confident that if the boundaries of safety are broken, violations will not be ignored.[8] Because our adolescents are developing their sense of identity through the series of social interactions they have in the myriad of cultural contexts they navigate, the development of trust is a collective concern rooted in the peer culture developed in the classroom.[9] By supporting the development of a trusting peer culture, students can count on each other day in and day out. Adolescents need to be able to rely on us time after time and trust that we are working with their best interests in mind. This sense of deep connection and security will lead to student engagement and a classroom where voices, experiences, and living histories are welcome and honored.

Trust is cultivated by communicating a deep respect for young people. Respect begins by developing an appreciation for each other's uniqueness and what we individually bring to the classroom. It is nurtured by personal, educational, and cultural sensitivity. Positively welcoming, noticing, and learning about the diversity of our students and honoring their experiences through classroom design, and authentic and rich learning experiences cultivates respect. A climate of mutual respect is also supported through the courtesy of asking, inviting, requesting, and by listening to understand before judgment or consequences. A respectful classroom is a place where students feel empowered, have a voice, and feel socially, emotionally, and intellectually safe. Teachers are mindful of using a tone of voice and words that communicate that each person has dignity and each student has contributions to strengthen the classroom culture.

**FIGURE 2.1** Six Conditions for Academic Engagement

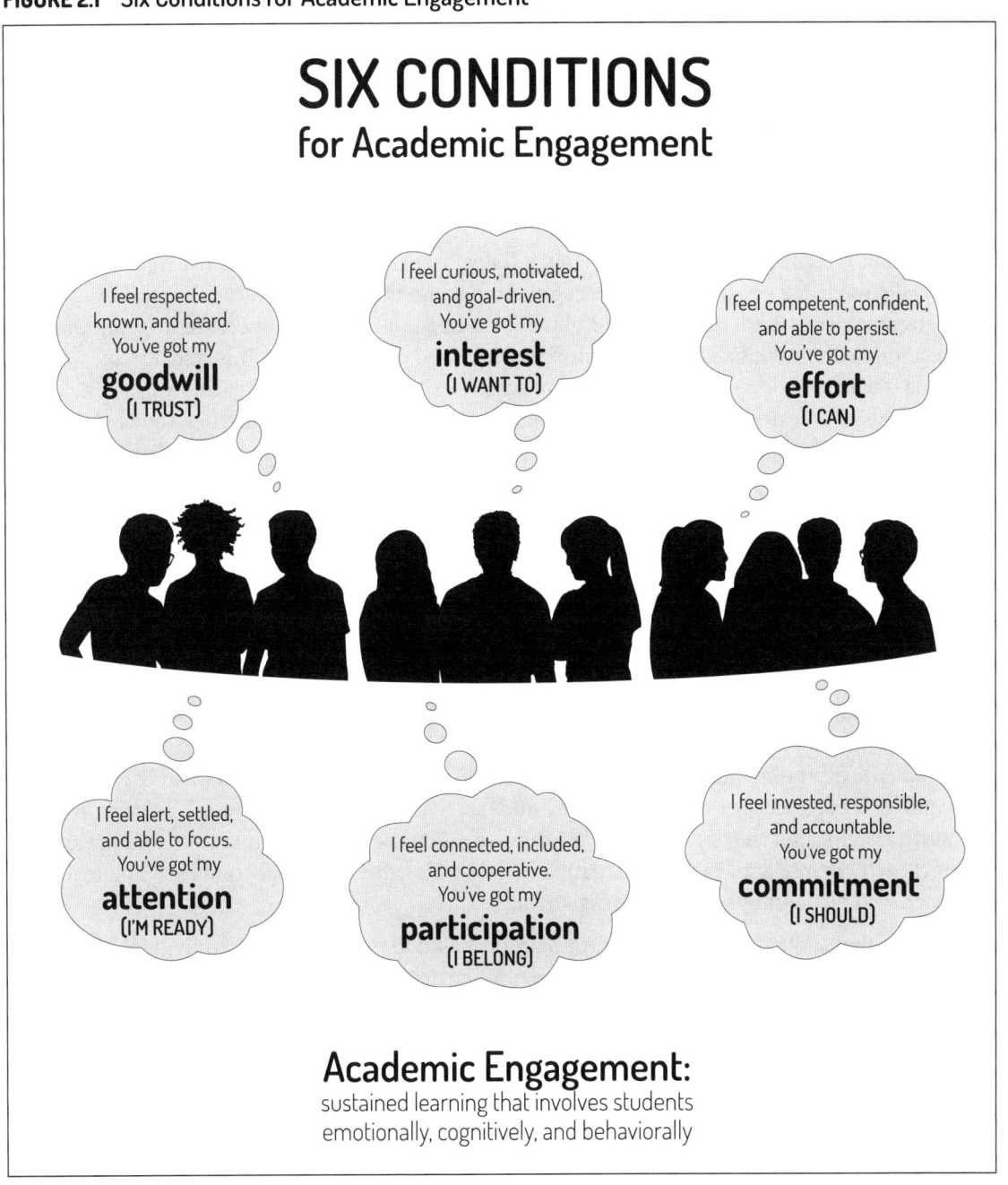

## SIX CONDITIONS
### for Academic Engagement

I feel respected, known, and heard. You've got my
**goodwill**
(I TRUST)

I feel curious, motivated, and goal-driven. You've got my
**interest**
(I WANT TO)

I feel competent, confident, and able to persist. You've got my
**effort**
(I CAN)

I feel alert, settled, and able to focus. You've got my
**attention**
(I'M READY)

I feel connected, included, and cooperative. You've got my
**participation**
(I BELONG)

I feel invested, responsible, and accountable. You've got my
**commitment**
(I SHOULD)

### Academic Engagement:
sustained learning that involves students emotionally, cognitively, and behaviorally

Adolescents benefit tremendously from opportunities to construct knowledge through mediated conversations with adults that push their learning beyond what they already know and can do. Developing a level of intellectual trust that supports students to think and reflect deeply about themselves requires that we be prepared to be on the other side of our students' emotions in order to help them navigate their thinking. Adolescents are developing their capacity to be self-aware and self-managing. As caring adults in their lives, we can play the role of coach to grow the skill sets of self-awareness and self-management by asking questions that push students to identify their strengths and areas of growth. These questions require vulnerability on the student's part to truly reflect, a vulnerability that can only be garnered through the establishment of goodwill.

### Participation (I Belong)

*"Good relationships between teachers and students have been associated with students' increased motivation, academic achievement, high rates of attendance, and attitudes towards school."*[10] Developing good relationships with and among students supports the development of the academic mindset, "I belong in this academic community." In a study of teacher-student relationships in urban high schools, it is worth noting that teachers saw the value of relationships in both supporting instruction and positive behavior; however, teachers also stated that they tended not to invest time in helping students who "failed to make an effort."[11] These are the students who have been given repeated feedback that they "do not belong in this academic community." We have an opportunity to interrupt this negative mindset by identifying this core group of students who struggle the most in academic environments and support their sense of belonging.

Participation is facilitated through an ongoing dialogue between learners and teachers. Learning is a socially mediated process; the teacher's role is to scaffold the students' learning and bridge the gap between current understanding and potential understanding (zone of proximal development) by engaging with students relationally through structured dialogue.[12] It is this structured dialogue—where students can share their current understanding, and the teacher can offer observations and/or deepen thinking—in which students and teachers construct knowledge and make meaning side-by-side.[13] This shared and reciprocal process supports students' engagement in learning. We measure students' participation by asking, "How much dialogue did students engage in today?" and, "What information am I able to glean from this to inform our ongoing learning process?"

Facilitating a sense of group cohesion *among* students can accelerate student learning and deepen student engagement. Adolescents are social creatures, and most young people want to develop knowledge through interaction and discussion with each other. Cooperation provides a social incentive structure in which the only way group members can attain their personal goals is if the group is successful. *"To meet their personal goals, group members must both help their groupmates do whatever enables the group to succeed and, perhaps even more important, to encourage their groupmates to exert maximum efforts."* In competitive classrooms, one student's win is another student's loss, but in cooperative classrooms, students who work together toward a common goal are motivated to align themselves with the norms of academic achievement and encourage and support each other to achieve.[14] Participation in group dialogue is as important as dialogue with the teacher in facilitating academic engagement.

Remember that adolescents are developing a group-based identity, as well as individual mindsets, values, and their own unique identities. In order to participate fully and in ways that support these developmental tasks, adolescents need opportunities to make connections between their in-school and out-of-school experiences, to learn through purposeful social interaction, and to make connections to the broader purpose of their learning whether educational, civic, or career oriented. The marriage of peer culture, personal interest, and academic content create learning experiences that are more relevant and meaningful and thus garner increased participation.[15]

## Attention (I'm Ready)

Brain-based research confirms the causal relationship between emotions and learning.[16] How students feel will determine whether they are ready to learn, whether they use their emotional energy to listen or to move attention somewhere else.

**FIGURE 2.2** The Feeling-Learning Connection

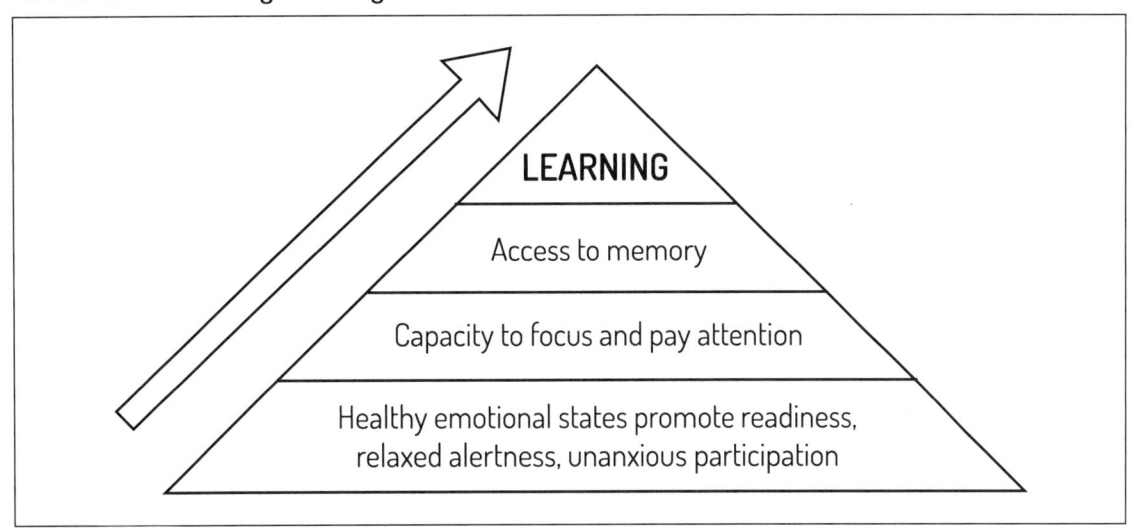

*Pyramid diagram with an upward arrow, showing from bottom to top:*
- Healthy emotional states promote readiness, relaxed alertness, unanxious participation
- Capacity to focus and pay attention
- Access to memory
- LEARNING

When students feel safe, settled, calm, and purposeful, they can balance their feelings with their ability to think. This optimal state of equilibrium, sometimes called relaxed alertness or unanxious anticipation, allows students to use emotional energy to focus and pay attention. Students must be able to focus in order to remember. Moreover, without access to memory, students are unable to learn.

For adolescents, this is no easy task in the best of circumstances, and there is an irony here; by educating their hearts, by welcoming their feelings and emotional energy into the room, we are better able to educate their minds. On the other hand, when students are out of balance and feel emotionally flooded, it is hard for them to focus on anything except the unsettled feelings they are experiencing. When students' emotional needs are ignored or trivialized, their feelings of anger, hurt, hostility, and resistance are going to rule the day. Embracing this aspect of teaching requires the courage, honesty, and generosity to see adolescents as they really are, not as adults would wish them to be to meet their own needs of comfort and convenience. This also means accepting that adolescence is messy, for both the student who is experiencing it and the adults who are supporting students through this stage in their lives. Students want to believe that you are on their side; that you are there for them, especially when they are having a tough time.

By nature of the design of most secondary schools, adolescents see six to eight teachers per day or week. This means six to eight sets of procedures around how students ought to engage in tasks. The uncertainty around how procedures will differ from one class to the next can cause emotional stress for students. It can affect their ability to focus and pay attention to the content they need to learn. When students understand what to expect and what is expected of them, they become ready to learn. By supporting transitions to help students shift gears and get "brain ready" for learning, we help them reach the ideal state for learning—relaxed alertness.

The adolescent brain is undergoing incredible changes. This affects many facets of their demeanor, behavior, and decision-making. This brain development also impacts attention—adolescents' grey matter peaks right at puberty or early adolescence. Throughout the remainder of adolescence, there is an ongoing decline in grey matter as synapses are being pruned; synapses that are being used are being strengthened, while synapses that are not being used are pruned away. This process fine-tunes adolescents' brains to their environments.[17,18] As the neural pathways that are used are the ones that are strengthened, eliciting attention is a critical practice that promotes student learning. Attention is sustained through the limitation of distractions, a student's heightened sense of readiness, and overall energy directed to the task. The more we can support students to engage in the daily ritualized habits of effective learners, the more hardwired these habits will become, and the more they will be able to sustain focus and attention.

### Effort (I Can)

In her book *Mindset*, Carol Dweck elaborated on the concept of fixed and growth mindsets. A fixed *mindset* is that of a student who believes his or her intelligence is fixed, whereas a growth mindset is that of a student who believes his or her intelligence can be developed. In Dweck's studies, students with a growth mindset tended to be excited by challenges and put in higher levels of effort to learn than their fixed mindset peers.[19] In the same studies, Dweck was able to show that students can shift from a fixed to a growth mindset through incremental messages about intelligence being malleable, something one can grow. This message can influence students' theories about themselves and thus their goals. *"Those who are led to believe their intelligence is a malleable quality begin to take on challenging learning tasks and begin to take advantage of the skill-improvement opportunities that come their way."*[20] When we ask students to identify the specific evidence of the efforts that contributed to their success for performance tasks, we grow their self-awareness (metacognitive capacity) to link their efforts to their results. By offering students these opportunities to deconstruct their effort, they begin to more accurately assess the exact skills, learning strategies and habits, and personal attributes that led to their success, so they can recreate these success conditions in new contexts. The road to academic success becomes transparent and attainable.

In our extensive review of the literature, the focus on effort-based learning and growth mindsets has been interpreted by some to imply that students of color, "just need to put in more effort and then achievement gaps will vanish." In our experience in the field, we hear a similar perspective about our students with complex/special academic needs. Dweck has responded by saying that the growth mindset is not just about effort, but also about being offered new strategies for success and reaching out to others for help when students are stuck. It is about the skills and habits students learn to use in schools and classrooms that promote students' understanding and reflection on their effort.[21]

In a recent assessment of the growth mindset, Dr. J. Luke Wood of San Diego State University has put forward the idea that exclusively praising effort without also validating students' abilities could be particularly damaging to underserved groups of students. He contends that when students have experienced racism that has repeatedly implied distrust, disdain, and disregard of their academic abilities, students need to know that we as teachers believe in their ability to complete challenging work.[22] Stereotype threat is defined by the Glossary of Education Reform as, "the risk of confirming negative stereotypes about an individual's racial, ethnic, gender, or cultural group." In a study by Steele and Aronson, when African American students were reminded before an assessment that their racial group tended to perform worse than White peers, this became a self-fulfilling prophecy that resulted in an achievement gap. When African American students were not reminded of their race, this achievement gap all but disappeared.[23] As authors, we would like to extend on this idea. We believe any group that experiences stereotype threat should be supported through validation of their ability in addition to praising their effort. For example, a teacher observes a student's effort, "I noticed you rewrote and illustrated your notes for the upcoming unit test," and then remind the student of their high degree of confidence in the student's ability, "I know you are going to do well!"

Effort is context driven; students will engage when we offer them incremental messages that while they are not yet there, they will achieve and meet their targets. We must hold a sense of optimism about every one of our students. Optimism begins by holding a positive image of human beings as able and capable. We step into an aspirational stance and convey our optimism by valuing an individual's efforts, in addition to his or her ability. We hold high hopes in life for every student. From personal connection and immediate formative feedback to personal check-ins, we let students know that we are confident in their capacities to learn, grow, and change. We believe that students can succeed and do not downplay small successes. In fact, we encourage students to see mistakes, missteps, and setbacks as opportunities to imagine different choices and possibilities. Above all, we do everything we can to let young people know they have the power within to choose the kind of human beings they want to be in a future of their own making. We will know we have accomplished this when we see students practicing, rehearsing, using study strategies, revising, editing, proofing, correcting, and persisting overall in their academic work.

### Interest (I Want To)

Student interest has great potential to increase learning and academic engagement. We believe that promoting interest in the classroom results in a student saying, "I want to do this. I am excited about this topic! I am interested in learning more." A student's interest is critical to encoding memories and thus learning. Interest can be classified into two main categories: (1) personal interest and (2) situational interest.

*Personal interest* is about what students are learning. It is activated internally and is a function of individual preferences and characteristics. With personal interest, students place a value in the course content. A truly interested student is more likely to focus on the topic or activity more fully, to work at it for longer periods, to use more thoughtful strategies in learning and to enjoy doing so.[24] As a result, personal interest often leads to an individual's sustained engagement in a topic over time and can influence academic success.

*Situational interest* is about how students are learning—the practices and strategies we use and the mode of learning to both capture and sustain students' engagement. It is interest elicited by a particular situation that piques an individual's curiosity in the moment. Garnering situational interest requires that we identify and ritualize developmentally informed and culturally responsive learning strategies and processes that align with the learning task at hand. As teachers, we cannot always depend on every student's personal interest in our course content, but we can control the conditions that lead to situational interest to some degree by using instructional strategies that connect to the way students prefer to learn.

A few strategies that garner situational interest include systematically embedding small group work; hands-on learning experiences; simulations; an engaging text; role-plays, games, and technologies that support and deepen a learning experience; and small and large group discussion protocols. In order for students to confidently step into the "how" I am going to learn, it is important to offer student choice, plan rigorous and meaningful learning tasks, make sure that the resources are culturally relevant and developmentally informed, and that we have tapped into students' background knowledge to support their scaffolding of new knowledge.[25]

Maintaining situational interest over a sustained period of time is critical to student learning due to the nature of memory. Students can store a near-complete record of what has happened in short snippets of time in their sensory memory (the shortest form of human memory); however, without maintained situational interest, this information is never processed in a student's working memory where more permanent memories are made.[26]

## Commitment (I Should)

Garnering commitment is one of the most elusive of the six conditions and very much depends on the other five conditions being in place. It is the voice in students' minds that says: "I am a learner. I am a member of this class community, and I am committed to working hard. I feel a responsibility to my fellow students and will work in the spirit of supporting my class, my teacher, and my peers. Doing well in school will result in a more successful school, life, and work experience. I see how my efforts will impact my future." As adolescents move developmentally toward young adulthood, they are better able to analyze the costs and benefits to themselves when the work gets harder, and the going gets tougher. They can broaden their view beyond the value of one task to the value of their education as a whole. On the other hand, early adolescents' level of commitment is deeply related to the academic mindset, "This work has value for me," and this value may need to be made more tangible and transparent. When students feel committed, they are better able to stick with a task and do the work because they are taking the long view.

Identifying with the culture of school, even when it feels disconnected from the world of home and peers, empowers students to navigate and negotiate across cultural divides and expands life and learning opportunities. Some earlier theorists explained the academic failure and disengagement of urban minority youth as a reaction to perceived limits to opportunities to succeed in school and a peer culture that rejects doing well in school.[27] This line of thinking has been largely discredited by more recent work that has examined minority youth who do succeed. In *Young Gifted and Black*, Theresa Perry writes,

> "The most important thing schools, families, and communities can do is to figure out how to develop among African-American children and youth identities of achievement…the most powerful location for this work is in the context of the peer group…if the entire school community is organized around a culture of achievement, if the culture is sufficiently strong, and if African-American students are seen as full members of these communities, these schools seem to be able to counter the larger society's ideology about the intellectual incompetence of African Americans."[28]

It is these communities of learning that exist outside the broader social context, in which students experience high expectations and the absence of stereotype threat that minority students thrive along with their White peers.

> **Coercive Compliance vs. Committed Compliance:**
>
> When we consider how to support young people to engage in behaviors that help establish safe, orderly, and respectful schools and classrooms, we think it is critical to distinguish between the use of coercive versus committed compliance. <u>Coercive compliance</u> uses force, fear, sanctions, rudimentary demands, and punitive threats to control the group. We believe schools should aim for <u>committed or normative compliance</u>, a system of control that rests on an individual's self-identification with the shared values and purpose of the community. From students' perspectives, committed compliance emerges when students understand the interests behind rules, norms, and instructional tasks and procedures, self-identify as learners, value their experience at school, and feel a sense of belonging within the school and classroom communities. Committed compliance helps students move from "You're making me do this" to "I should do this because…"

Helping students see the ways in which learning is about their personal empowerment and development of personal agency is critical to developing commitment in students who may have developed negative academic mindsets in response to staff members and school experiences that have not supported them culturally or developmentally. Knowing our students and expressing interest in understanding their unique experiences and how these differences influence how they learn and what they want to learn is directly linked to their commitment to themselves, their peers, and the success of their class community. Additionally, knowing ourselves, our biases, and our mental models (and we all have them) are critical internal explorations to better develop the commitment of our students that we communicate through our end behaviors in the classroom. This, in turn, communicates to students whether we believe they have the capacity to learn, whether we truly see them as part of the learning community.

## Closing

Lasting learning, the kind that sticks with us and informs the next iteration of our intellectual and personal development, depends on academic engagement. If our goals for education include graduating young people who have discovered their passions and areas of social and academic efficacy, who feel honored for their unique cultural backgrounds and histories, who have developed personal knowledge about themselves, their talents and their skill sets for working with others, then we must inspire goodwill, cultivate participation, garner attention, support student effort, offer topics and experiences of interest, and foster commitment. In Chapter 3, we offer an introduction to the Domains of the Engaged Classroom in which teachers will find myriad ways to facilitate these six conditions in their classroom.

## Why Does Academic Engagement Matter? What the Research Says:

| Engagement Supports Academic Success |
| --- |
| Having a sense of belonging in school and the classroom has a large body of evidence to support its effects on student academic performance. *"Individuals are born with an innate desire to connect to others;"* relatedness, or a student's sense of belonging, has a measurable impact on their emotional engagement in school.[29] On a personal level, we know we are much more likely to go above and beyond when we feel a sense of belonging, versus when we feel like an outsider. Engaging students by deepening their sense of belonging is foundational to increasing students' academic success. |
| Engaging students by showing them the ways in which they get "smarter" by investing their effort has a direct link to their academic success. "Notably, across the empirical literature, one's beliefs about intelligence and attributions for academic success or failure are more strongly associated with school performance than is one's actual measured ability (i.e., test scores)."[30] In his 2008 publication of *Visible Learning: A Synthesis of Over 800 Meta-Analyses Relating to Achievement*, John Hattie developed a list of high-impact practices from nearly all available research on teacher practice. At the top of his list of practices was "student self-reported grades" with a size effect of d = 1.44. An effect size of d =1.0 is associated with advancing achievement by two to three years. This practice involved teachers asking students about their expectations for themselves on an upcoming performance task and then supporting these learners to exceed these expectations. When students outperformed against their expectations, they gained confidence in their ability, leading to increased academic effort.[31] |
| Engaging students through a series of successful learning encounters has a direct impact on their academic perseverance. By showing students the connection between their efforts and their abilities, we grow their confidence that they will be successful going forward. We tend to avoid activities that we think we cannot be successful in and engage in activities we think we can complete with a measure of success.[32] |

| Engagement Is Critical to Keeping Students in School Through Graduation |
|---|
| Students who hold negative academic mindsets are less likely to feel that academic knowledge is important, that they can be successful, or have positive emotional responses to academic tasks; thus, they show little motivation to engage in learning. These negative internal beliefs lead to negative academic behaviors, lack of perseverance, nonuse of learning strategies, and negative social skills that reinforce these negative academic mindsets over time.[33] As teachers we can observe academic behaviors, and sometimes we can glean insight into students' learning strategies, social skills, and overall perseverance; however, academic mindsets are largely hidden from us. Many of our students may come to us having repeatedly experienced this negative feedback-loop, and their behaviors look to us like lack of interest, motivation, and engagement. |
| For students who hold the mindset, "I do not belong in this academic community," school becomes an increasingly painful place to remain throughout adolescence. In an analysis of 2012 graduation rates the National Center for Education Statistics found that nationally, 80% of students graduate on time with their original 9th-grade cohort of students, meaning one in five freshmen will not graduate on time or at all. The average for White students was 86%, while the graduation rate for Native American, Black, and Hispanic students fell well below the national average at 67%, 69%, and 73% respectively. Equally troublesome is the persistent gender gap among high school graduates: 85% of female students graduate, compared with 78% of male students.[34] |
| In a comprehensive study conducted by the University of Chicago Consortium on School Research (2006), researchers concluded that good attendance and decent grades (GPA) the first-time students take a course are the greatest predictors for high school graduation. When freshmen fall behind in credits, their chances of dropping out are four times more likely. Findings revealed that course pass rates are primarily determined by attendance. In extensive interviews, students cited three factors that affected both grades and attendance: the lack or presence of strong supportive student-teacher relationships, the degree to which school felt important to their future, and the degree to which classwork was relevant and meaningful.[35] |
| The current high school dropout rate of 5.9% (2015) is at its lowest point since it was originally recorded in 1960.[36] Still, dropout rates for Hispanic (9.2%) and black (6.5%) students are higher than those of White students (4.6%).[37] In *The Silent Epidemic: Perspectives of High School Dropouts*, a report from the Bill & Melinda Gates Foundation (2006), it was reported that 88% of students have passing grades when they drop out. Boredom, restlessness, and irrelevance were more often associated with school leaving than academic difficulties.[38] Students who have developed negative academic mindsets can only experience limited academic success in the absence of engagement. |

---

[1] Marzano, R., & Kendall, J. (2007). *The new taxonomy of educational objective.* Thousand Oaks, CA: Corwin Press.

[2] Farrington, C.A., Roderick, M., Allensworth, E., Nagaoka, J., Keyes, T.S., Johnson, D.W., & Beechum, N.O. (2012). *Teaching adolescents to become learners: The role of noncognitive factors in shaping school performance: A critical literature review.* Chicago, IL: University of Chicago Consortium on Chicago School Research.

[3] Fredericks, J.A., Blumenfeld, P.C., & Paris, A.H. (2004). School engagement: Potential of the concept, state of the evidence. *Review of Educational Research*, 74(1), 59–109.

[4] Skinner, E., Furrer, C., Marchand, G., & Kinderman, T. (2008). Engagement and disaffection in the classroom: Part of a larger motivational dynamic? *Journal of Education Psychology*, 100(4), 765–781.

[5] National Research Council and Institute of Medicine. (2004). *Engaging schools: Fostering high school students' motivation to learn.* Committee on Increasing High School Students' Engagement and Motivation to Learn. Board on Children, Youth, and Families, Division of Behavioral and Social Sciences and Education. Washington, DC: The National Academies Press.

[6] Sergiovanni, T. (1999). *Building community in schools.* San Francisco, CA: Jossey-Bass.

[7] Tschannen-Moran, M. & Hoy, W. K. (2000). A multidisciplinary analysis of the nature, meaning, and measurement of trust. *Review of Educational Research*, 70(4), 547–593.

[8] Ferguson, R. F., Phillips, S. F., Rowley, J. F. S., & Friedlander, J. W. (2015). *The influence of teaching: Beyond standardized test scores: Engagement, mindsets, and agency.* Retrieved from http://www.agi.harvard.edu/projects/TeachingandAgency.pdf

[9] Bryk, A. S., & Schneider, B. (2004). *Trust in schools: A core resource for improvement.* New York, NY: Russell Sage Foundation.

[10] Wilkins, J. (2014). Good teacher-student relationships: Perspectives of teachers in urban high schools. *American Secondary Education*, 43(1), p. 52 – 68.

[11] Ibid.

[12] Vygotsky, L. (1978). *Mind and society: The development of higher mental processes.* Cambridge, MA: Harvard University Press.

[13] Palmer, P.J. (2000). *Let your life speak: Listening for the voice of vocation.* San Francisco, CA: Jossey-Bass.

[14] Slavin, R., Hurley, E. & Chamberlain, A. (2003). Cooperative learning and achievement: Theory and research. In *Handbook of Psychology, Educational Psychology*, (p. 177 – 198). Hoboken, NJ: John Wiley & Sons.

[15] Nagaoka, J. Farrington, C. A., Ehrlich, S. B. & Heath, R. D. (2015). *Foundations for young adult success: A developmental framework.* Chicago, IL: Consortium on Chicago School Research at the University of Chicago.

[16] Bandura, A. (1997). *Self-efficacy: The exercise of control.* New York, NY: Freeman.

[17] Blakemore, S.J. (2012, June). *The mysterious working of the adolescent brain* [video file]. Retrieved from: https://www.ted.com/talks/sarah_jayne_blakemore_the_mysterious_workings_of_the_adolescent_brain?language=en#t-260788

[18] Domontheil, I. (2014). Development of abstract thinking during childhood and adolescence: The role of rostrolateral prefrontal cortex. *Developmental Cognitive Neuroscience*, 10, p. 57 – 76.

[19] Dweck, C. (2006). *Mindset: The new psychology of success.* New York, NY: Ballantine Books.

[20] Dweck, C. (2000). *Self-Theories: Their role in motivation, personality and development.* New York, NY: Psychology Press. Taylor & Francis Group.

[21] Dweck, C. (2015). Carol Dweck Revisits the 'Growth Mindset'. *Education Week.* Retrieved from http://www.edweek.org/ew/articles/2015/09/23/carol-dweck-revisits-the-growth-mindset.html

[22] KPBS (2017). *SDSU professor challenges concept widely embraced by educators.* Guest. Dr. J. Luke Wood. Retrieved from: http://www.kpbs.org/audioclips/37509/#transcript

[23] Steele, C. & Aronson, J. (1995) Stereotype Threat and the Intellectual Test Performance of African Americans. *Journal of Personality and Social Psychology.* Vol.69, No. 5, pp. 797-811.

[24] Hidi, S., & Renninger, K.A. (2006). The four-phase model of interest Development. Educational Psychologist, 41, 111–127. Hidi, S. (2000). An interest researcher's perspective: The effects of extrinsic and intrinsic factors on motivation. In Sansone, C. & Harackiewicz, J. M. (eds.) (2006) *Intrinsic and extrinsic motivation: The search for optimal motivation and performance* (pp. 311–342). New York, NY: Academic Press.

[25] Schraw, G., Flowerday, T., & Lehman, S. (2001). Increasing situational interest in the classroom. *Educational Psychology Review*, 13(3).

[26] Marzano, R. & Pickering D. (2011). *The highly engaged classroom.* Bloomington, IN: Marzano Research Laboratory.

[27] Fordham, S., & Ogbu, J. (1986). Black students' success: Coping with the burden of 'acting White'. *Urban Review* 18, p. 1–31.

[28] Perry, T., Steele, C., & Hillard, A. (2003) *Young, gifted, and black: Promoting high achievement among African-American students.* New York, NY: Beacon Press.

[29] Skinner, E., Furrer, C., Marchand, G., & Kinderman, T. (2008). Engagement and disaffection in the classroom: Part of a larger motivational dynamic? *Journal of Education Psychology*, 100(4), p. 765 – 781.

[30] Farrington, C.A., Roderick, M., Allensworth, E., Nagaoka, J., Keyes, T.S., Johnson, D.W., & Beechum, N.O. (2012). *Teaching adolescents to become learners. The role of noncognitive factors in shaping school performance: A critical literature review.* Chicago, IL: University of Chicago Consortium on Chicago School Research.

[31] Hattie, John A. C. (2009). *Visible learning: A Synthesis of over 800 meta-analyses relating to achievement.* New York, NY: Routledge.

[32] Bandura, A. (1986). *Social foundations of thought and action: A social cognitive theory.* Englewood Cliffs, NJ: Prentice Hall.

[33] Farrington, C.A., Roderick, M., Allensworth, E., Nagaoka, J., Keyes, T.S., Johnson, D.W., & Beechum, N.O. (2012). *Teaching adolescents to become learners. The role of noncognitive factors in shaping school performance: A critical literature review.* Chicago, IL: University of Chicago Consortium on Chicago School Research.

[34] Stetser, M., & Stillwell, R. (2014). *Public high school four-year on-time graduation rates and event dropout rates: School years 2010-11 and 2011-12.* First Look (NCES 2014-391). U.S. Department of Education. Washington, DC: National Center for Education Statistics. Retrieved from https://nces.ed.gov/pubs2014/2014391.pdf

[35] Allensworth, E. & Easton, J. (2006). *What matters for staying on-track and graduating in Chicago Public Schools.* Chicago, IL: Consortium on Chicago School Research at the University of Chicago.

[36] National Center for Educational Statistics. (2017). *Fast Facts: Dropout Rates.* Retrieved 09/04/2017 from https://nces.ed.gov/programs/digest/d16/tables/dt16_219.70.asp?current=yes

[37] National Center for Educational Statistics. (2017). *Status Dropout Rates.* Retrieved 09/05/2017 from https://nces.ed.gov/programs/coe/indicator_coj.asp

[38] Bridgeland, J., DiJulio, J. & Morison, K. (2006). *The silent epidemic: Perspectives of high school dropouts.* Washington, D.C.: Civic Enterprises, LLC.

# CHAPTER 3

## Domains of the Engaged Classroom

**Chapter Outline**
- Introduction
- Domains of the Engaged Classroom
- An Empowered Teacher Presence
- Closing

**Essential Question**
What are the practices and strategies that ramp up academic engagement and ensure each and every student's academic success?

## Introduction

Reflect on a time when you had the full academic engagement of your students. Take a moment to consider two questions in the T-chart below:

| What were students saying or doing that let you know they were academically engaged — truly immersed in the experience? | What were some of the things you intentionally planned, did, or said to facilitate this engagement? |
|---|---|
| | |

Your list will probably include both your established and emerging practices and strategies that support academic engagement. Most teachers can name a lesson they taught that was highly engaging and describe what they did to make it so. These events are memorable, as we have hit the elusive mark and students are maximizing their learning. What are the myriad ways we make these experiences the normal, everyday business of our classrooms? We aim to support educators, no matter where they may be in their career, in developing and/or deepening these tried and true practices and strategies for their students. We have identified five *Domains of the Engaged Classroom* that support teachers to construct classrooms, units, and lessons that support, inspire, challenge, and engage students. Whether you are seeking strategic ways to deepen relationships with and among students, improve physical and instructional design in your classroom for maximized engagement, increase your use of learning protocols, or support the academic and behavioral engagement of each and every one of your students, we trust that you will recognize practices you already use within the five Domains and have an opportunity to deepen these and learn new ones.

## Domains of the Engaged Classroom

In Chapter 1, we introduced three key frameworks that support improved student outcomes: (1) Equity-Centered Classrooms, (2) Multi-Tiered System of Supports, and (3) Learning and Life Competencies. In Chapter 2, we discussed the multiple ways in which academic engagement is directly linked to student learning and academic success. The *Domains of the Engaged Classroom* are the translation of these frameworks into the high-impact practices and strategies that teachers can implement daily to realize increased equity in the classroom, increased support to every student, increased social, emotional, and academic efficacy, and increased engagement in learning (Figure 3.1).

> We define high-impact practices and strategies as those with a greater size effect. *Size effect* is a statistical term that is the quantitative measure of the magnitude of any given phenomena. A greater size effect for any given practice or strategy means that when compared to other practices and strategies more student learning occurred over the same period using this high-impact practice. Also, we believe that these high-impact practices directly support students' development of self-awareness, self-management, social and academic efficacy thereby increasing student agency and capacity to navigate their learning over time.

The body of research from Evertson and Weinstein's 1,300-page *Handbook of Classroom Management: Research, Practices, and Contemporary Issues* confirm that effective teachers and classroom managers:

1. "Develop caring, supportive relationships with and among students;
2. organize and implement instruction in ways that optimize students' access to learning;
3. use group management methods that encourage students' engagement in academic tasks;
4. promote the development of students' social skills and self-regulation; and
5. use appropriate interventions to assist students with behavior and academic problems."[1]

The domains are drawn directly from these characteristics of effective teaching. Each domain has research-based practices and accompanying strategies that support its implementation. While this list of strategies is in no way exhaustive, it provides a starting point from which to begin integrating social, emotional, and academic practices into the secondary classroom in support of academic engagement.

| Domain | A defined area of pedagogical knowledge |
|---|---|
| Practice | A method that has a high level of agreed upon effectiveness |
| Strategy | A specific action teachers take to support students in completing a learning task or meeting an outcome or goal |

### Domain #1 – Positive Personal Relationships: Chapter 4

Positive personal relationships are the bedrock of academic engagement. Without them students make the inevitable decision at best to simply comply and survive, and at worst, not to engage in learning and exhibit disruptive behaviors. When students feel known and cared for by their teachers, they attend class, connect with the teacher, put forth steady effort, and engage cooperatively with their peers. Feeling known and cared for can result in students being invested in the classroom community and accountable to their peers. They are more likely to align themselves with the academic and behavioral expectations of the classroom.

### Domain #2 – Organizing the Learning Environment: Chapter 5

We have identified two factors that support a student's readiness and preparation to learn and engage: the physical environment and instructional organization. By purposefully arranging the learning environment, we can offer spaces that are primed for creativity, communication, collaboration, and academic support, thereby increasing students' ability to be more self-directed and focused on the task.[2] By making our classroom procedures transparent, we increase the likelihood of students feeling cooperative and meeting our academic and behavioral expectations, particularly when they are trying to navigate six or more classrooms in a single day.

### Domain #3 – Content Design, Learning Tasks, and Protocols: Chapter 6

Content design is the "what" and learning protocols are the "how" of student learning and engagement. For adolescents to feel welcome and have a sense of "I belong here" they need to see their cultural selves represented in the content. Adolescents by nature are curious and passionate about themselves and their place in the world. They want course content to be relevant to who they are and to today's issues. They seek content that is compelling, provocative, inspirational, and challenging. We have an awesome responsibility and opportunity to intentionally design content that support students' ability to see shades of grey in conflicts, articulate nuanced opinions, seek out multiple points of view, collaborate to explore complex issues, and express themselves with care and attention for those around them. Supporting students to engage in such levels of thinking requires systematic participation in an array of diverse learning experiences that range from independent reflection to cognitively rigorous experiences and meaningful social interactions.

### Domain #4 – Academic Support: Chapter 7

Academic supports are the range of instructional practices, strategies, and interventions teachers systematically implement to provide ample opportunities for students to engage in their learning. These varied strategies and interventions intend to enable every student to meet high academic expectations and standards and complete high-quality work. These practices support students in (1) academic reflection, goal-setting, and progress tracking (academic efficacy), (2) engaging in mediative conversations to mitigate "in the moment" learning challenges (self-awareness), (3) feedback for self-correction toward continuous improvement (self-management), and (4) problem-solving with others to overcome learning obstacles (self-management). In a classroom where academic support is intentionally planned, students are active participants in monitoring their learning. These practices help teachers see the depth of student understanding, and as a result, they can make timely and targeted adjustments in their strategies and interventions, so all students can maximize their learning.

**FIGURE 3.1** Domains of the Engaged Classroom

# Domains of the Engaged Classroom

| Domains | Practices and Strategies | |
|---|---|---|
| **Positive Personal Relationships**<br><br>*How do I foster and sustain strong and supportive personal relationships?* | **1** Knowing Students and Making them Feel Known<br>☐ Student Names<br>☐ Meet and Greet<br>☐ Student Profile Data<br>☐ Personal Check-ins<br>☐ Value-added Feedback | **2** Creating Group Cohesion<br>☐ Gatherings<br>☐ Anchor Experiences<br>☐ Circle<br>☐ Student Feedback |
| **Organizing the Learning Environment**<br><br>*How do I purposefully organize my learning environment to support academic engagement?* | **3** Organizing the Learning Environment<br>☐ Visual Postings<br>☐ Furniture Arrangement<br>☐ Tools and Resources | **4** Foundational Procedures<br>☐ Starting Class<br>☐ Ending Class<br>☐ Getting Attention<br>☐ Maintaining Silence<br>☐ Clear Instructions<br>☐ Grouping Formats |
| **Content Design, Learning Tasks, and Protocols**<br><br>*How do I ramp up engagement and rigor in order to increase academic achievement?* | **5** Rigorous, Meaningful Learning Tasks<br>☐ Representing to Learn<br>☐ Problematizing a Learning Task<br>☐ Student Voice and Choice<br>☐ End-of-Unit Assessments<br>☐ Developmentally Informed Content<br>☐ Culturally Relevant Content | **6** Learning Protocols<br>☐ Text Protocols<br>☐ Activators<br>☐ Turn and Talk<br>☐ Cooperative Learning<br>☐ Whole Group Discussion |

Domains of the Engaged Classroom 33

## Domains

### Academic Support

*How do I target my academic practices and strategies to meet the range of learners in my classroom?*

### Restorative and Accountable Discipline and Behavior Support

*How do I plan for, respond to, and manage behavior concerns and intervene in high-impact situations?*

## Practices and Strategies

### 7 Academic Press
- [ ] Setting and Monitoring Expectations
- [ ] Academic Reflection, Goal Setting, and Progress Tracking
- [ ] Anticipating and Planning for Learning Gaps
- [ ] Study Strategies
- [ ] Revise, Edit/Proof, and Correct
- [ ] Guided Work Period

### 8 Formative Assessment
- [ ] Academic Check-ins
- [ ] Walk-around Look-fors
- [ ] Feedback For Self-correction
- [ ] Five-minute Assessment Tools

### 9 Academic Interventions
- [ ] Academic Problem-solving and Planning Conference
- [ ] Progress Monitoring
- [ ] Academic Turnaround Plan
- [ ] Academic Coaching

### 10 Planning for Behavior Concerns
- [ ] Classroom Behavior Plan
- [ ] First Response to Behavior Concerns
- [ ] Behavior Check-ins

### 11 Defusing Charged Situations
- [ ] Depersonalization
- [ ] Responding to Disrespectful Behavior
- [ ] Defusing Students who are Upset
- [ ] Defusing Power Struggles
- [ ] Re-set Protocols
- [ ] Interrupting Physical Altercations
- [ ] Responding to Oppositional Behavior

### 12 Behavioral Interventions
- [ ] Restorative Conversations
- [ ] Behavioral Problem-solving and Planning Conferences
- [ ] Progress Monitoring
- [ ] Behavioral Coaching

**Domain #5 – Restorative and Accountable Discipline and Behavior Support: Chapter 8**

In a classroom where a restorative and accountable discipline approach is front and center, students are held accountable for their unskillful, inappropriate, or unacceptable actions, and are invited to re-engage and "make it right" with themselves and with those who might have been harmed. This approach builds trust with students and supports their ongoing academic engagement. Teachers hold a mindset that unwanted student behaviors will surface (because these are adolescents), that these are opportunities for learning, and as such, require a planned response to the unwanted behaviors most common to the classroom. Teachers also maintain and strengthen their relationships with students through their capacity to depersonalize unwanted behaviors, their invitations to re-engage, their skill to defuse student conflict, their ability to handle the student with disruptive behaviors with dignity, and their skillfulness to implement holistic interventions for persistent unwanted behaviors.

As you reach the end of this description of the domains, you may be asking, "So why incorporate these domains, practices, and strategies? In service of what?" In a recent synthesis of research compiled by the Chicago Consortium on School Research, *Supporting Social, Emotional, and Academic Development: Research Implications for Educators*, student grades were singled out as the strongest predictor of student success after high school:

- High school GPAs are largely a reflection of student effort in their courses and are the strongest predictors of both high school and college graduation.
- Effort and attendance are the main factors impacting student grades and GPAs (more so than demographics, test scores, or which courses students take).
- Teacher practice has a direct impact on student engagement and therefore student grades and GPAs.[3]

These five research-based domains, practices, and strategies are the daily actions teachers can implement to increase the number of students in their school who stay and graduate in four years. Additionally, in our experience partnering with schools across the country, these five domains can be easily aligned to state teaching standards. When setting professional goals aligned to your state teaching standards, you may draw strategies directly from the domain chapters, review the research behind the practice and strategy, and design indicators of your students' ongoing successes.

If we want to grow our students' academic mindsets toward believing, "my ability and my competence grow with my effort," as teachers, we need to engage in reflective processes to grow our own belief, "my practice and competence grow with my effort and reflection." Maximizing our capacity to become reflective practitioners enables us to remain fluid, skillful and nimble as we navigate diverse classroom contexts on a day-to-day basis. The process for taking on the identity of a reflective practitioner cannot be prescribed. It is a personal journey that comes through setting aside time for oneself, along with collaboratively thinking with colleagues to problem-solve and question our intentions and actions. We offer an *Empowered Teacher Presence* as a place to begin.

## An Empowered Teacher Presence

Successfully implementing the practices and strategies of the *Domains of the Engaged Classroom* requires teachers to develop or deepen what we call an *Empowered Teacher Presence*. Helping students grow socially, emotionally, and academically requires that we grow our self-awareness, and the knowledge and skills to support all adolescent learners. Empowered teachers see growth and change as natural outcomes of taking a learner stance toward their practice. Empowered teachers:

1. Are energized by their sense of agency;[4]
2. Hold a set of optimistic mindsets;
3. Know how to navigate their authority with adolescents;
4. Exhibit a finely calibrated physical stance and voice; and
5. Are culturally competent.

## Empowered teachers are energized by their sense of agency

Empowered teachers feel a high degree of personal agency to make classroom and instructional decisions that enhance their effectiveness and ensure student success and academic achievement. They are keenly aware of what is within their control and what is not. Their "can do" spirit enables them to:

- Create conditions that increase student engagement in learning;
- Establish cohesive classroom communities built on trust, care, and respect;
- Make course work meaningful and relevant to students' lives and future aspirations.

Empowered teachers marshal their understanding, empathy, and compassion to welcome every student into their classrooms, serving as allies and advocates for the adolescents in their care.

## Empowered teachers hold a set of optimistic mindsets

A mindset is a predominant attitude informed by a set of deeply held assumptions and beliefs that reinforces our current habits, choices, and preferred way of doing things. Mindsets "orient the way we handle situations and sort out what is going on and what we should do. When our mindsets become habitual, they define who we are, and who we can become."[5] In good measure, mindsets explain the rationale behind our instructional decisions, our communication style, and our approach to students. What we believe about students, teaching, and the goals of schooling impacts how we structure learning and provide support to our students. See Appendix 3.1 — Adult Mindsets Aligned to the Domains of the Engaged Classroom.

## Empowered teachers know how to navigate their authority with adolescents

A teacher's authority creates the opportunity to influence, inspire, guide, coach, and shape the behavior of others. For adolescents, some sources of adult power and authority appear to be far more effective than others. *Authoritative* teachers make extensive use of referent power[6] (power through personal relationships and the student's positive identification with the teacher) and expert power (power through special knowledge and skills that students desire or respect). Authoritative teachers use their power to:

- Create learning environments that are first and foremost a safe place for everyone;
- Ensure that all students are supported to learn and achieve;
- Assert that everyone (including the teacher) deserves to be treated with dignity and respect;
- Demonstrate a clarity of purpose, an insistent resolve to meet their goals, and a deep commitment to model respect rather than demand it;[7]
- Become partners with their students, sharing responsibility for learning and shifting the emphasis from "what I am teaching" to "what you are learning";
- Communicate through responsive listening and dialogue, inviting problem-solving, and conveying high support, friendliness, and helpfulness.[8]

In contrast, when teachers take an authoritarian stance, they often rely on officious power (power through "office," title, status, and position) as a primary source of authority. In other words, "I am the teacher; you are the student, and this is the way it's going to be." *Authoritarian* teachers establish order by commanding obedience, demanding respect, relying on the power to threaten and punish, and exhibiting little or no tolerance for student input and inquiry. Many adolescents, especially those with a record of persistent failure, find it difficult to make authentic connections with authoritarian teachers, and consequently, are less likely to fully engage in the course work or fully participate in the classroom community.[9]

### Empowered teachers exhibit a finely calibrated physical presence and voice

Our voice and physical presence play critical roles in building rapport and trust with students. Effective teachers of adolescents make a conscious effort to match their voice and nonverbal communication to an *authoritative* and collaborative teacher presence.

Over 65 percent of communication involves our nonverbal presence, the messages we send through our eyes, facial expression, gestures, and the physical movement and placement of our bodies.[10] Empowered teachers develop a predictable physical presence that serves them well in most classroom situations—eyes receptive, steady, and focused; an interested and pleasant facial expression that avoids emotional extremes of a zero affect or a highly charged state; and a centered and relaxed posture, and limited physical movement. All of these things help communicate self-confidence and self-control. When a more dramatic physical presence is served up sparingly, it holds power to capture students' immediate attention and interest.

Because so much of teaching is coaching, presenting, questioning, discussing, explaining, and encouraging, we cannot overestimate the crucial role that voice plays in a teacher's performance. Teachers do well to cultivate at least two types of teacher voice: *Credible and Approachable*.

1. The *Credible* voice is the voice of authority that we use when we are giving instructions, establishing routines, redirecting students, or explaining critical concepts or skills.[11]

2. The *Approachable* voice is the voice that we use to invite and encourage students and express enthusiasm toward our content and our students.

### Empowered teachers are culturally competent

Cultural competence is a life-long process of developing mindsets and practices that enable educators to participate fully in diverse communities of adults and students and successfully teach all students across a range of cultural backgrounds. Countering unequal treatment of young people requires a holistic effort to address six interdependent aspects of cultural competency.

1. **Understanding My Own Culture:** Unpacking our own cultural identity (i.e., ethnicity, family background, beliefs, values) helps us to examine our assumptions about human diversity, learning, and discipline.

2. **Knowledge, Recognition, and Appreciation of Human Diversity:** By increasing our knowledge of human diversity and student backgrounds, we are better able to recognize that culture can have a profound impact on the way individuals learn and communicate; develop an identity, beliefs, and mindsets; and approach problems.

3. **Understanding the Biases and Dynamics That Shape My Interactions with Others:** *Explicit* and *Implicit* personal, systemic, and institutional cultural biases have the power to influence our impressions of and response to students with different cultural backgrounds from our own. Identifying and building our awareness of these biases supports us to make better daily decisions about the content we teach, the texts we choose, and the way we respond to unwanted behavior.[12] See Chapter 8, Figure 8.3 – Biases That Can Influence How We Teach and Treat Students.

   > **Six Biases that Impact How We Teach and Treat Students**
   > 1. Gender Biases
   > 2. Biases Related to Students' Developmental Delays and Disabilities
   > 3. Learning Biases
   > 4. Racial/Cultural Biases
   > 5. Negativity Bias
   > 6. Aggression/Conflict Aversion Bias

4. **The Courage to Change:** When we courageously commit to moving beyond our personal discomfort, resistance, anger, and/or fear, we expand our flexibility, self-awareness, and consciousness when working with students and colleagues from cultures different than our own.

5. **Implementing Culturally Responsive Practices:** Culturally responsive practice "allows educators to address social barriers that cause disparities in student achievement." By tailoring instruction that is mindful of these barriers, educators help students overcome obstacles and succeed.[13] Culturally responsive teaching validates the cultural knowledge, prior experiences, strengths, and performance styles of diverse students.[14]

6. **Taking an Equity Stance:** Over time, educators become increasingly comfortable as advocates who communicate, "I am on your side." They become allies who choose to work actively to eliminate culturally biased systems, policies, and practices; stand up in support of equitable practices, and interrupt behaviors and incidents that have a prejudicial impact on students and colleagues through respectful and caring conversations and inquiry.[15]

Some aspects of an empowered teacher presence are like a second skin; others require time and practice to hone and implement with authenticity. The ways in which we express our authority, care, and belief in students' capacity to succeed directly impacts how young people respond to us and whether a student will take on the mantle of an engaged learner.

An empowered teacher presence is essential for navigating the frameworks (i.e., Domains of the Engaged Classroom, Multi-Tiered System of Supports, Equity-Centered Classroom, Learning and Life Competencies, Six Conditions for Academic Engagement) to ensure that every student has an opportunity to succeed in school, at work, and in their lives. See Figure 3.2 – Frameworks that Make Engaged Classrooms a Reality.

**FIGURE 3.2** Frameworks that Make Engaged Classrooms a Reality

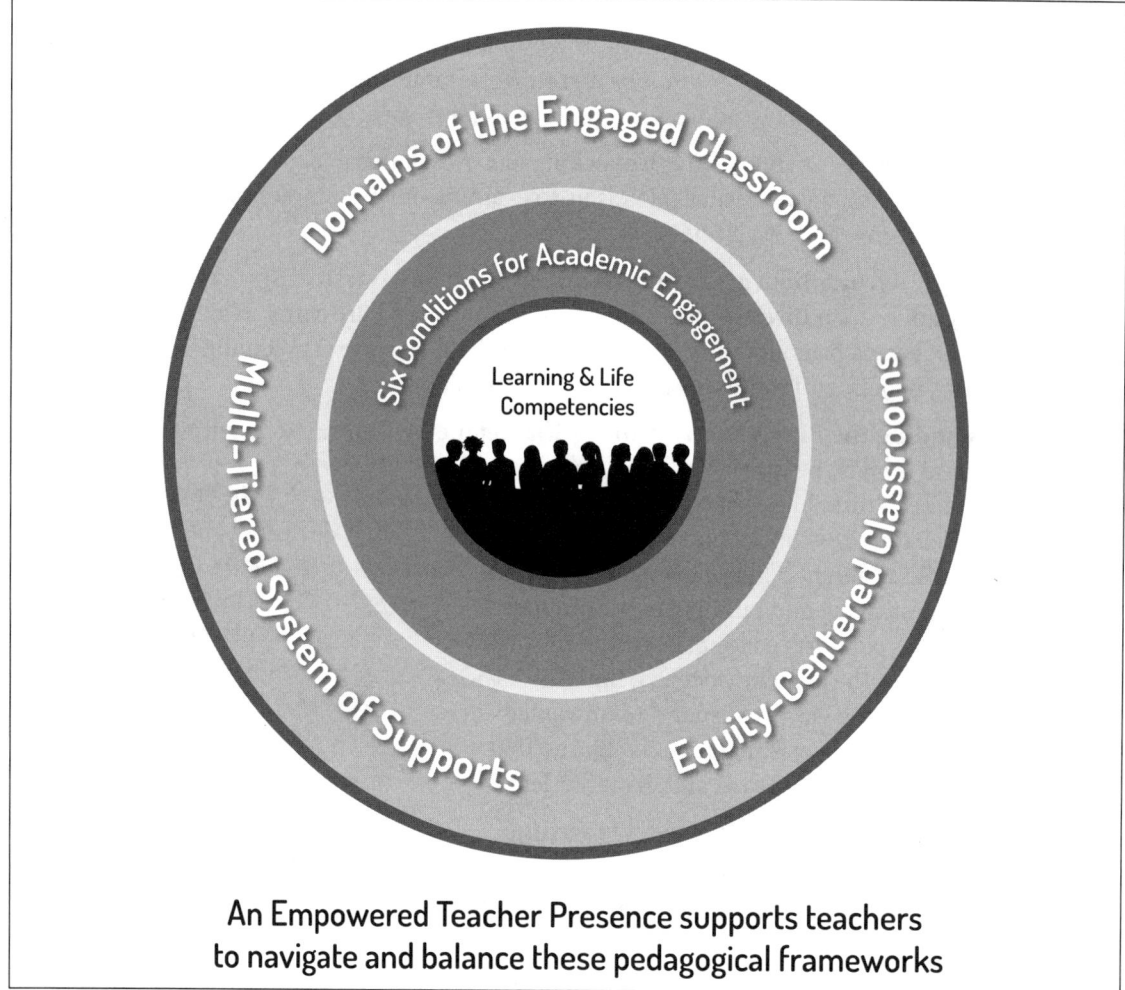

Domains of the Engaged Classroom

Multi-Tiered System of Supports

Equity-Centered Classrooms

Six Conditions for Academic Engagement

Learning & Life Competencies

An Empowered Teacher Presence supports teachers to navigate and balance these pedagogical frameworks

## Closing

Our craft, mindsets, and beliefs have the power to create a classroom culture and climate that embraces every young person in our care. Throughout this book, we invite teachers to examine, question, and rethink their core beliefs with several questions in mind:

- In what ways might ensuring that high-impact practices and strategies are at the heart of my planning and instruction, and support student engagement and academic, social, and emotional growth?

- What is within my power and control around which I can make meaningful change for the benefit of my students?

- What are the core beliefs and mindsets that empower me to reach and engage every student and support student's personal, social, and academic development?

- How do different aspects of my culture and identity influence my instruction and my interactions with students?

> **A Note to the Reader About Technology**
>
> In the descriptions of each of the *Domains of the Engaged Classroom*, you will notice there is no mention of practices that are directly tied to the use of technology as a strategy for student engagement. This is not because as authors we hold a belief that technology should not be used in the classroom or that it does not have a potential role in student engagement. On the contrary, we have all used technology creatively to support student learning in strategic and meaningful ways. In short, technology is used as one more tool in an effective teacher's repertoire of strategies. We see the five *Domains* and their accompanying practices as foundational to developing classrooms that are safe, caring, supportive, and engaging to adolescent learners. While we do not offer strategies corresponding to these practices that use technology, we know they exist and can and should be used in service of deepened student learning.

---

[1] Evertson, C.M., & Weinstein, C.S. (2016). Classroom Management as a Field of Inquiry. In C.M. Evertson & C.S. Weinstein (eds.) *Handbook of classroom management: Research, practice, and contemporary issues* (pp. 1048). Philadelphia, PA: Lawrence Erlbaum Associates.

[2] Granito, V., & Santana, M. (2016). Psychology of learning spaces: Impact on teaching and learning. *Journal of Learning Spaces*, 5(1), 1–8.

[3] Allensworth, E.M., Farrington, C.A., Gordon, M.F., Johnson, D.W., Klein, K., McDaniel, B., & Nagaoka, J. (2018). *Supporting social, emotional, & academic development: Research implications for educators*. Chicago, IL: University of Chicago Consortium on School Research.

[4] Bogler, R. & Somech, A. (2004). Influence of teacher empowerment on teachers' organization and professional commitment and citizenship behavior in schools. *Teaching and Teacher Education*, Volume 20, Issue 3, April, 2004. Amsterdam: Elsevier Press.

[5] Klein, G. Mindsets: What they are and why they matter. May 1, 20016. Retrieved from *Psychology Today*. New York, NY: Sussex Publishers.

[6] Thomas, J. (2002). Leadership effectiveness of referent power as a distinction of personal power. Regent University Center for Leadership Studies, *LEAD605 Foundations of Effective Leadership*, 18-Feb-2002.

[7] Wubbels, T., & Levy, J. (eds.). (1993). *Do you know what you look like?: Interpersonal relationships in education.* London, UK: Falmer Press.

[8] Evertson, C., & Weinstein, C. (2006). Chapter 8. Student-Teacher Perspectives on Classroom Management, pp. 181-219. *Handbook of classroom management: Research, practice, and contemporary issues.* Mahway, N.J.: Lawrence Erlbaum Associates.

[9] Wubbels, T., Levy, J., & Brekelmans, M. (1997). Paying Attention to Relationships. Alexandria, VA: *Educational Leadership* 54 (7), 82-86.

[10] Burgoon, J.K., Buller, D.B., & Woodall, W.G. (1989). *Nonverbal communication: The unspoken dialogue.* New York, NY: Harper and Row.

[11] Powell, W., & Kusuma-Powell, O. (2010.) *Becoming an emotionally intelligent teacher.* Thousand Oaks, CA: Corwin Press.

[12] Gregory, A., Skiba, J., & Noguera, P. (2010). The achievement gap and the discipline gap: Two sides of the same coin? *Educational Researcher* 2010; 39; 59

[13] Goldstein, C. (2017). *Culturally responsive instruction: Best practices and supports.* Chicago, IL: REL Midwest at American Institutes for Research

[14] Retrieved from https://www.iidc.indiana.edu/pages /culturally-responsive

[15] National Center for Cultural Competence. (2018). *Cultural Competence Continuum.* Washington, DC: Georgetown University Center for Child and Human Development.

# Section II

# Practices and Strategies that Promote Academic Engagement

# CHAPTER 4

## Positive Personal Relationships

**Chapter Outline**
- Introduction
- The Big Ideas that Inform Positive Personal Relationships
- Practice #1: Knowing Students and Making Them Feel Known
- Practice #2: Creating Group Cohesion
- Closing

**Essential Question**
How do I foster and sustain strong and supportive personal relationships?

## Introduction

We have all experienced the power of personal relationships in our working lives as educators. Think of a student with whom you strongly connected: the sense of pride, fulfillment, and joy in knowing them and being part of their story. Think of how you experienced their successes, the attention, and care you provided them as individuals, and the ways in which they occupied your mind when they struggled. These types of relationships ground and sustain us. They renew our optimism as we see our students take critical steps to evolve into young adults. Many of us can easily recall memories of those classes and learning environments in which we felt connected with our students, and they felt connected to each other. What conditions were in place? What actions did we take as a teacher to develop such deep rapport with our students? What behaviors did we cultivate in them to support their social efficacy? Creating supportive, welcoming, and trusting environments takes time and an infinite number of small steps to ensure that there is a deep sense of belonging to each other and to the class community.

As teachers, we constantly seek to provide the best possible context for learning for each and every student. For adolescents, an emotional connection with adults is perhaps the single most important factor for fostering positive development, including higher levels of engagement, motivation, and academic performance.[1] There are many young people who enter our classrooms who struggle to make connections with adults and/or peers. They lack the interpersonal skill set enabling them to engage in social interactions that form healthy and sustaining relationships. For some of these students, end behaviors may show up as extremely shy, distant, or detached. For others, they may exhibit behaviors that are angry, aggressive, hostile, edgy, or sarcastic. Often, these students do not know how to assert themselves, advocate for what they need, or connect in ways that are skillful and socially appropriate. There are myriad reasons for students not yet able to form relationships.

Many teachers express difficulty in connecting with these students, as some are very practiced at keeping teachers and/or peers at a distance. It is a charge, of sorts, for us to remain steady, patient, and persistent with these young people in our care. Like those students who are ready to connect and get to know us and their peers, these students also need attention and guidance to develop critical competencies that ensure they are getting the most out of their schooling and relationships to be successful in school and life.

This chapter invites us to reflect on, discuss with colleagues, and consider two key practices that enable teachers to cultivate classroom cultures where quality relationships are a priority and cohesion between students is paramount:

> **Practice #1 – Knowing Students and Making Them Feel Known:** Teachers provide students with systematic experiences that help them feel acknowledged, cared for, and valued.
>
> **Practice #2 – Creating Group Cohesion:** Teachers intentionally embed rituals, routines, and experiences that support students feeling connected and empowered as a group.

These practices help us create a context in which students are primed for learning and develop a sense of shared accountability by demonstrating that they are part of a larger classroom community. The well-being of each student is at the heart of a healthy class culture, and in the interest of making our classroom communities stronger, we are called to study our students, their assets, the resources they bring to the class, and their talents. We have a rich opportunity as teachers to explore with our students what we can create together, and this evolves from knowing our students deeply. "The future is created one room at a time, one gathering at a time. To build community we seek conversations where people show up by invitation rather than mandate, and experience an intimate and authentic relatedness."[2]

---

**The Big Ideas that Inform Positive Personal Relationships**

- Effective instruction, discipline, and support for students is formed through positive relationships.
- When students experience a sense of belonging, trust, attachment, caring, and respect from teachers and fellow students, they are more likely to engage.
- Positive relationships with students heighten a teacher's sense of efficacy, professional sustainability, and commitment to the craft of teaching.

### Effective instruction, discipline, and support for students is formed through positive relationships

Forming positive relationships with students automatically communicates that we believe each and every student has value just by virtue of being who they are; that we recognize and acknowledge their innate skills, strengths, and gifts; that we invite their voice, perspective, and expertise into the classroom; and that we make room for multiple ways of being in and knowing the world. Doing so is essential to teaching strategically, being able to manage a classroom effectively, and customizing targeted teacher facilitated interventions for individual students. "In classes with person-centered teachers, there is more engagement, and more respect of self and others. There are fewer resistant behaviors, greater non-directivity (student-initiated and student-regulated activities), and higher achievement outcomes."[3] Multiple researchers have concluded that students who form close and healthy relationships with teachers generally have stronger social skills, fewer externalizing behaviors, and overall higher academic performance.[4,5]

### When students experience a sense of belonging, trust, attachment, caring, and respect from teachers and fellow students, they are more likely to engage.

We know that young people thrive and do better in school when they feel supported, cared for, and valued. There is a particular benefit for students who do not identify with the dominant culture as a result of race, class, language, gender/identity, sexual orientation or learning differences. Students who feel marginalized for these reasons might withdraw, engage in disciplinary incidents, or even drop out because school "isn't for them." Also, students with chronic or situational anxiety, or students who have lived in environments where traumatic stress and chronic traumatic stress is a reality may significantly struggle to perform in school.[6] These students require intense care and strategic support to grow their trust. How we respond to these students can support substantial resilience.[7]

Authentic curiosity about all of the students with whom we work, as whole, complex individuals, with multiple identities, is a culturally responsive practice that fosters the emotional safety necessary for academic success. Poplin and Weeres assert that the relationships students desire are "authentic" ones, wherein they are *"trusted, given responsibility, spoken to honestly and warmly, and treated with dignity and respect."*[8] Children's perceptions of supportive relationships with adults can buffer them against the negative effects of excessive stress and even increase their attachment to school.

### Positive relationships with students heighten a teacher's sense of efficacy, professional sustainability, and commitment to the craft of teaching.

Finally, we believe strongly in the importance of teacher sustainability, satisfaction, and joy in continuing to hone their teaching practice. In our current climate of schooling, teachers face multiple stressors that range from teaching students with complex learning profiles to managing challenging student behaviors, increased accountability measures, curricular mandates, and administrative demands with limited time and support to meet such expectations. Yet, despite all of these hurdles, research points to the main source of stress leading to teacher burnout being negative teacher-student relationships.[9,10] There is, however, a promising corollary: satisfying relationships with students serve as a buffer against teacher stress.[11,12] For so many of us, this is why we became teachers: to explore and discover our own connections with students; and to build trusting relationships in which students feel safe and secure to experiment, try on various roles, to lean in and observe and listen to the world of adults around them and begin to shape a vision of who they might be and how they might lead the life that they envision for themselves.

In this chapter, we will explore *Promotion* and *Prevention* practices and strategies that cultivate trusting relationships and enable students to thrive and flourish as they navigate the day-to-day complexities of school and life. See Figure 4.1 – Positive Personal Relationships.

**FIGURE 4.1**  Positive Personal Relationships

| Promotion and Prevention ||
|---|---|
| Practice 1:<br>Knowing Students and Making them Feel Known | Practice 2:<br>Creating Group Cohesion |
| Strategies:<br>• Student Names<br>• Meet and Greet<br>• Student Profile Data<br>• Personal Check-ins<br>• Value-added Feedback | Strategies:<br>• Gatherings<br>• Anchor Experiences<br>• Circle<br>• Student Feedback |

| The following adult mindsets support the implementation of these practices with integrity and fidelity: |
|---|
| • I believe that all students being known and valued strengthens their identity as a learner, validates a sense of belonging, and increases a students' motivation and effort to succeed in school.<br>• I believe that students connecting with each other will create a culture and climate of trust and engagement, where students feel attached to one another, rely on each other, and persevere through tasks to achieve individually and collectively. |

## PRACTICE 1: Knowing Students and Making Them Feel Known

One of our greatest opportunities for increasing academic outcomes is to know the students with whom we work. *"Our relationships with students can drive and define the meaning of teachers' work and can be pivotal to student success."*[13] It is incumbent upon us to provide experiences that help students get to know us and us to know them. Research from the fields of prevention and resiliency cites the consistent presence and availability of adults who believe in them—who listen, empathize, encourage, push, and probe—as a primary factor in students making the most of their lives and maximizing their performance at school. Adults who serve as both advocates ("I'm on your side!") and coaches ("I'm on your case!") have the most positive influence on young people. Positive relationships with adults create conditions that increase motivation and effort. Put simply, students who feel respected and supported, who feel seen, heard, known, and understood do better in school.[14,15]

> **Benefits of Knowing Students and Making Them Feel Known**
> - Demonstrates care, compassion, and interest in students, resulting in positive personal relationships and relational trust.
> - Fosters positive and welcoming ongoing interactions between the student and the teacher.
> - Supports a continuous dialogue about the interests, needs, past experiences, and future aspirations of our students.
>
> **Learning and Life Competencies Aligned with the Practice**
> - Self-Awareness: I know myself, and I am aware of skills, behaviors, and attitudes that help me.
> - Self-Management: I identify, express, and manage emotions, and I demonstrate perseverance and resiliency.
> - Social Efficacy: I foster healthy relationships.

### The following strategies invite us to consider the power of really knowing students.

**Strategy:** *Student Names*

*"A person's name is, to that person, the sweetest and most important sound in any language."*[16] Our names are central to our sense of identity. There is something incredibly powerful about being called by name—it immediately instills a sense of being known and recognized. Learning how to pronounce a *Student's Name* creates a culture of respect within the class community and can have a lasting impact on each student's success. For students, especially the children of immigrants or those who are English language learners, a teacher who knows their name and can pronounce it correctly signals respect, care, and appreciation and marks a critical step in helping them adjust to school.[17] When we make time to study *Students' Names* and get them right, we demonstrate care for the diversity of names and identities we encounter.

| **What It Looks Like:** *Name Tent* |
| --- |
| Have students make Name Tents and choose what name (full name, nickname, etc.) to write. Name Tents are placed on desks or tables. This visual approach assists the teacher, classmates, and any visitors with learning and remembering names. It also invites newcomers to get to know the group and the group to get to know the student right away. At the end of class have a student collect them and store them in your resource center. Keep blank tents and pens on hand for visitors and newcomers. |

| **What It Looks Like:** *Story of My Name* |
| --- |
| Have students fill out a short questionnaire that includes their full name, nicknames, the origin of their name or nickname, what they prefer to be called, and feelings associated with any of their names. This enables young people the opportunity to select the name they want to identify with, which may differ from what they were assigned at birth.<br><br>*See Appendix 4.1 – The Story of My Name.* |

| **What It Looks Like:** *My Name, Getting it Right* |
| --- |
| To ensure correct pronunciation of students' names, it is important to identify strategies that will support this effort. Print the class roster and consider the following: read through it several times before the first day of class so that names sound familiar when you meet students; identify those names that might be challenging and conduct an Internet search as there are often pronunciation guidelines; as you meet students write in the student's preferred name and pronunciation tips; use a seating chart for the first couple of weeks and explain your interests to the students; ask students to say their name before asking or answering a question. This gives both their classmates and you a chance to learn names and correct inflections. |

### Considerations

1. Invite students to use their peers' names when responding to each other: "I agree with X, because…"
2. Set a goal at the start of the year to learn a few names of students per day. Greet your students by name when they enter the classroom or use their names as you pass back assignments.
3. Check in with students personally and ask them for tips: "it rhymes with…" "The middle sounds more like…" "Think about this when you say it…" Encourage them to correct you when you mispronounce their names.

### Strategy: *Meet and Greet*

A *Meet and Greet* is a ritual in which teachers stand at the classroom door during transitions between class periods or move about the classroom as students enter the room to welcome and greet them by name. This gives teachers a dedicated time to connect with students through brief personalized comments and questions. Students tell us how much it means when teachers greet them by name and make a personal connection before class begins, and before redirecting a student to do the right thing or jumping into business. *Meet and Greets* have the power to set the tone for the class period. They communicate a sense of welcome and inclusion, support us in understanding students' emotional readiness to learn, inspire students to engage in the work ahead, and be accountable to the expectations of the class.

> **What It Looks Like:** *Meet and Greet*
>
> - Present a centered and relaxed posture; make eye contact with students; have an interested and pleasant facial expression; use an invitational and encouraging voice; consider whether you're hoping to get students energized or to calm down a rambunctious group—modulate your stance to match.
> - Say hello or welcome students in different languages.
> - Greet each student by name.
> - Share a quick verbal appreciation, question, or personal connection with some students.
> - Give a handshake, high five, fist bump, dap, or hugs (whatever is appropriate to you, individual students, and your school context).

### Considerations

1. *Meet and Greets* implemented at least three times a week become a ritual that students remember and count on. If it is in your schedule, you are more likely to *Meet and Greet*. In some schools, all teachers *Meet and Greet* at the door to support students to transition to their next class in an organized and timely fashion.

2. Be at the door before students arrive. They will be looking for you.

3. You can *Meet and Greet* in the classroom. Move about the room as students are settling in and briefly connect with students. Go table-to-table or desk-to-desk and make a personal connection and set a positive tone with each individual.

### Strategy: *Student Profile Data*

To teach students well, we need to know them well. To really know our students is to commit to embedding a systematic set of viable processes and structures for collecting critical kinds of student data. Gathering the right information about our students, over time, helps us develop a better sense of our students as whole individuals. When we have a deep understanding of how our students learn, it is easier to diagnose student needs and plan effective developmentally-informed interventions. In the opening days of school, or when new students enter our classrooms, a first priority is to signal to them that we want to get to know them—in all of their complex and intriguing individuality.

| **What It Looks Like:** *Student Contact Card* |
|---|
| Collect basic information on all students that they can fill out independently: Full name, the name they prefer to be called, cell phone number, email address, best contact person, birthday, etc. Emphasize that your interest in collecting data is to be able to support students effectively. This signals to the student that you want to be able to reach them and support them throughout the year.<br><br>See Appendix 4.2 – Personal Contact Card. |

| **What It Looks Like:** *Learner Profile* |
|---|
| Collect critical data that will give you a more comprehensive picture of your students' learning preferences, strengths, and challenges. Think about the information you already have access to and what you still might need to support your students. Design your profile questionnaire to fit the needs of your classroom and school community, and be sure to include some version of these questions:<br><br>1. How do you learn best?<br>2. What has been your best school experience so far? Your hardest?<br>3. What motivates you?<br>4. What things make it most challenging for you to learn?<br>5. What are some things that get in the way of you getting your work done?<br>6. How do your family members view school? Your friends?<br>7. What kind of supports might you need to help you with your academic work?<br>8. What do you like/love to learn about?<br>9. What's an extracurricular activity you really enjoy? |

| **What It Looks Like:** *My Personal Story* |
|---|
| Have students write or visually represent their own story on an 11x17 paper that enables them to answers a series of questions that helps you get to know them personally and lift up the student similarities in the class. This can be filled out over time. Hand this out once a semester, so students can add to it and you can reconnect with students around their story.<br><br>See Appendix 4.3 – My Personal Story. |

## Considerations

1. If you are part of a teaching team and share the same students, have the students fill out various *Student Profile Data* formats over time in one class and copy them for your colleagues, or keep the profile data in one central location. If there are not grade level teams, dedicate a couple of teachers in the grade to take on this process, and store the information in the guidance office, so all teachers have access to the information. Let students know you will be sharing this with your team or grade level teachers and the interests for doing this. Once a term, return these to students to have them updated. This data is critical when teachers come together to discuss students who need additional support. It provides the teachers with a window into the student and can enhance the conversation.

2. Make sure newcomers have an opportunity to fill out *Student Profile Data* formats over time. Appoint a student ambassador to connect with new students to orient them to the process and materials and explain the interests for collecting this information.

3. Depending on the types of information collected, provide opportunities for students to share some of this information with each other to make personal connections and create group cohesion.

Type in "learning preference inventory" to your web browser search bar, and you'll find myriad resources and downloadable templates for students to assess and reflect on their personal learning styles. Check out https://www.edelements.com/blog/the-first-step-to-personalize-learning-is-knowing-your-students for links to example profiles and tips on how to design (and keep track of the results from) your own learner profiles.

### Strategy: *Personal Check-ins*

*Personal Check-ins* combine the power of conferencing as a tool for learning about students with the power of building connections through brief interactions that demonstrate an interest in who the student is and how they are doing in that moment. Systematic implementation of *Personal Check-ins* with students builds rapport and creates a positive and cohesive class culture. As one student put it eloquently, *"I think one thing that really allows me to work hard is knowing that my teacher knows where I am in life at that moment. If they don't know me, I will tend not to work as hard for them."*[18]

---

**What It Looks Like:** *Personal Check-ins*

*Personal Check-ins* can be done during independent work time, at the end of class when students are packing up, as students are exiting class, or during transitions when students are in the hallways or lunchroom.

**Example 1:** Ask a Personalized Question: *"Hi Mike. Good to see you. How are you feeling today?"*

**Example 2:** Make an Individualized Comment or Acknowledgment: *"Hey Maria, I hear from Mr. Tobin that you are quite the athlete. Tell me how soccer tryouts are going."*

---

### Considerations

1. Consider each of your sections. Which students might truly benefit from *Personal Check-ins*? Make a goal for yourself, and consider connecting with at least two to three of these students.

2. Engage in a Whole Group *Personal Check-in* when the energy or vibe seems particularly high or low. "Good Afternoon. So how has everybody's day been so far? Show me on your hand—a five indicates fantastic and a one—really challenging." "Hello, fabulous fifth period. How's everyone feeling as we head into this 3-day weekend?"

3. For students who are really struggling to connect with you and their peers, we offer the following strategy: Appendix 4.4 – 1 Student / 5 Actions / 5 Days.

**Strategy:** *Value-Added Feedback*

*Value-added Feedback* is when a teacher shares a specific, concrete observation of what the student did and names the asset or personal quality that enabled the student to do it. *Value-added Feedback*, when genuine and specific to a student's interaction with a peer or the student's contribution to a lesson, has the power to build rapport and relational trust with the teacher. It reinforces students' positive mindsets about learning, which increases their investment to do well. *Value-added Feedback* also increases academic engagement and the likelihood of the student replicating the behavior and taking additional academic risks. Teachers have multiple opportunities to offer students *Value-added Feedback* throughout a class period. Authentic *Value-added Feedback* promotes goodwill in students; it also increases participation, effort, and focus.

---

**What it Looks Like:** *Value-Added Feedback*

Providing *Value-added Feedback* on the Learning and Life Competencies reinforces key target behaviors that support students day to day in their classes.

1. Social Efficacy: "I noticed you wanted to hear everyone's opinion in your group before making a decision. You really demonstrated your capacity to work cooperatively in your small group."
2. Self-Management: "I noticed how you completed your last three labs. You tackled every part of each lab. That showed real perseverance."
3. Academic Efficacy: "Before you started on your project today, I noticed that you took the time to check the machinery and get all of your tools out before jumping in. That shows me you are organized and responsible. Thank you."
4. Self-awareness and Social Efficacy: "I saw that you were frustrated today when we were graphing linear equations, and you took a break and asked for help. This showed how in touch you are with your emotions and your ability to be your own advocate in order to learn something you find challenging."

---

## Considerations

Providing *Value-added Feedback* when you are teaching multiple sections in classes of 25 or more may feel overwhelming. As a starting point:

- You might begin by giving *Value-added Feedback* to the entire class, which will support a climate and culture of safety, care, and encouragement.
- Identify three to four students you think would really benefit from *Value-added Feedback*.
- Consider providing *Value-added Feedback* to home groups, project teams, or cooperative learning groups.

# PRACTICE #2: Creating Group Cohesion

We live and work primarily in community. The soul of a classroom is the psychological sense of community created among and between the students and the teacher. Howard Adelman and Linda Taylor describe community this way: "People can be together without feeling connected or feeling they belong or feeling responsible for a collective vision or mission. In a school and in a class, a psychological sense of community exists when a critical mass of stakeholders are committed to each other and to the setting's goals and values, and exert effort toward the goals and maintaining relationships with each other."[19] As leaders in the classroom, we have the opportunity to build a high-functioning, cohesive classroom community of learners. Being on a team or a member of a group gives us a sense of belonging and investment. It requires its own set of individual and collective skills. Consider for a moment all of the elements of teamwork that need to be present when a drama production is underway, a basketball team is in the middle of its season, a musical group is performing, or a newspaper is printing its daily publication. With the guidance of a director, coach, leader, or supervisor, teammates inspire, motivate, connect, and care for one another.

> **Benefits of Creating Group Cohesion**
> - Provides structured skill-building around problem-solving, cooperation, collaboration, and communication.
> - Creates opportunities to discover commonalities and shared experiences among students.
> - Develops trust and rapport within the group.
> - Emphasizes student voice and leadership.
>
> **Learning and Life Competencies Aligned with the Practice**
> - Self-awareness: I know myself, and I am aware of the skills, behaviors, and attitudes that help me.
> - Self-management: I demonstrate perseverance and resiliency, and I identify, express, and manage emotions.
> - Social Efficacy: I communicate and problem-solve effectively, demonstrate empathy and respect, and foster healthy relationships. I am assertive and self-advocate, I cooperate and participate, and I demonstrate civic responsibility.

**Strategy:** *Gatherings*

*Gatherings* set the stage for learning by bringing everyone together in a joint exercise, which serves to build community and focus attention. *Gatherings* can be a ritualized way of opening your week or can occur within the context of a *Circle* (see p. 55). *Gatherings* help students transition from public space to the class period and take anywhere from 3-8 minutes to facilitate. They provide critical practice in listening and speaking in ways that demonstrate respect, understanding, empathy, and self-management. In particular, *Gatherings* give quiet students frequent, low-threat practice at speaking, while providing talkative students with an opportunity to practice listening, often resulting in equal participation. *Gatherings* enable teachers to slowly and deliberately build the group's emotional and psychological safety and sense of reciprocal trust—going from simple, low-stakes topics to more complex, personal, higher-stakes experiences and conversations. In *Gatherings*, each person's voice enters the room and provides opportunities for everyone to be acknowledged and heard, modeling that each and every student is important and has something valuable to say. And when each student speaks within the first few minutes of class, they are more likely to engage fully and positively throughout the class period.

**What It Looks Like:** *Table Topics for Teens*

Adolescents have opinions... capitalize on that fact! Table Topics for Teens is an opportunity for students to think about their future, hear multiple perspectives, practice articulating their thoughts, develop their relationships, and connect with their peers.

**Sample Questions:**
1. What are some ways you take care of yourself to support your efforts in school?
2. Where do you like to be alone to study, do your homework, or prepare for "doing school"?
3. Where in this course do you feel most confident? Where might you want support?
4. What is an academic habit you have learned to help you in this class?
5. When you think about this course, what is a change you have made in yourself in the last semester?
6. What strategies do you have to re-enter a learning task or class, when you are feeling down, when you have had a difficult moment in class or received a lower grade than you wanted?

Check out Larry Eckert's book, *If Anybody Asks Me...: 1,001 Focused Questions for Educators, Counselors, And Therapists* (Pocket Prompters Series), for more ideas.

**What It Looks Like:** *How are you feeling? Or, How is your day going?*

Checking in with students about how they are feeling or how their day is going results in the entire class understanding that students are in different places at the start of the class. It increases students' sensitivity and understanding for their peers. The students also appreciate that we care enough to check in with them. This Gathering can be done in a number of ways:

1. **One to Five:** On your hand let us know how you are feeling or how your day is going: 1 (I am struggling a bit.) to 5 (I am good and ready to go.)
2. *How are You Peeling?: Foods with Moods* by Elffers and Freymann has an array of foods with facial expressions. It is a Scholastic picture book that you can cut up, and students can select the food that represents how they are doing.
3. *Weather Cards:* Create a series of cards depicting all kinds of weather, and have students select the one that captures how they are doing or how their day is going. Type "weather card images" into your browser and copy and paste into a word document, print, and cut.

The beauty of all of these samples is they can be used throughout the year as students do not tire of them.

**What It Looks Like:** *Metaphor Object Bag*

Collect a bag of small objects. You are sure to find objects by looking in junk drawers and kitchen drawers, on shelves, and in random places in your home. Set the items out and invite students to pick an object that represents any of the following:

1. The best thing I bring to a group...
2. A personal skill that I bring to working out problems...
3. A part of my personality that helps me...
4. An object that represents my work style in a cooperative group...

This is a *Gathering* that can be repeated throughout the year. Students love it! Ask them to bring in objects to contribute to the bag and have them work in pairs to make up additional metaphor starters/prompts. If you have a large class, create a PowerPoint slide with images. Project the slide, and have students select an image.

> **What It Looks Like:** *Appreciations*
>
> 1. Create randomized groups of four students.
> 2. Hand each student a piece of recycled paper.
> 3. Have students write their name on the top of the paper. Let students know that they will write something they appreciate or admire about each student as they pass the papers around their group. Example: I appreciate the way Gonzalo always helps people with word problems.
> 4. Once this is completed, have students silently read through the appreciations written about themselves.

## Considerations

1. Use topics and questions that all students can address without feeling vulnerable, embarrassed, or defensive. Establishing a culture in your class that is emotionally and intellectually safe will enable you as the teacher to select from a wide variety of questions or prompts. Topics can be personal, or connect to the curriculum, the school, a community issue, or a current event. This is also a great way to harness student voice and thinking by having them come up with questions of their own.

2. When you have a class of 20 or more, it can be impractical to have every student share. Consider using either a whole group or small group format. With whole group *Gatherings*, students share with a partner first, and then four to six partner volunteers are asked to share publically. Keep track of who shares and be sure to ask for new voices the next time around.

3. Use a talking piece or a soft, tossable object to ensure that everyone focuses on the speaker and that there is only one voice at a time. Students should have the option to pass. They are still thinking, and this builds trust with the teacher. If you notice a pattern of passing, engage in a *Personal Check-in* with the student. You can also use a talking piece for groups of four to six if this feels more realistic for implementation.


### Strategy: *Anchor Experiences*

*Anchor Experiences* create enduring learning moments for students that live beyond one single interaction. They provide an "anchor" to come back to again and again as students venture out into new learning waters, grounding all subsequent knowledge and skill in the context of that initial experience. *Anchor Experiences* promote problem-solving and strategic thinking, offer interaction and fun, and build self-management, self-awareness and social and academic efficacy. Because *Anchor Experiences* involve deliberate reflection, they require that students not only actively engage in an interactive experience but also process the knowledge and skills used in order to increase knowledge, develop skills, and clarify values.[20,21] When chosen strategically and implemented at opportune times of the year, *Anchor Experiences* can serve as touchstones for identifying and reflecting on *Expectations* (see p. 113) and Learning and Life Competencies (see p. 12–13). They also support classroom cultures in which students feel integral to their own learning and understand how their learning and their classmates' learning is mutual and reciprocal.

> **What It Looks Like:** *Lava River*
>
> This is an *Anchor Experience* that requires collaboration, communication, listening, commitment, and a willingness to succeed. These are the same elements that are needed to support collaborative groups in our classes.
>
> *See Appendix 4.5 – Lava River Anchor Experience.*

> **What It Looks Like:** *Building The Tallest Tower*
>
> This is a problem-solving activity for groups of four that requires the group to use the information and constraints provided to design a Tall Tower. There is no one right approach, and the problem requires that team members collaborate, cooperate and communicate to meet the outcome successfully. This *Anchor Experience* supports future cooperative learning groups.
>
> *See Appendix 4.6 – Tallest Tower Anchor Experience.*

## Considerations

However fun and engaging these *Anchor Experiences* are to do; it is the reflection questions afterward that make these activities important learning experiences. Intentional reflection results in students increasing their self-awareness about the skills and behaviors they used to accomplish the task. Students begin to make connections about how they learn and work in groups, which can lead to improvements in group processes and transfer of skills to new learning tasks.

## Strategy: *Circle*

*Circles* have a deep history in indigenous practices and have been adapted and used successfully in education and in juvenile justice to build a sense of solidarity and support, to foster empowerment and accountability, and reduce instances of harm.[22,23] *Circles* create the space for students to learn about themselves and each other, build trust, and bring the reality of who and where they are in life into the classroom; they also create the space for groups to respond proactively to challenges or harms, building skills in solving community problems and creating the type of learning environment that works for the group. *Circles* build trust, psychological safety, and class cohesiveness by engaging students in a real dialogue about real issues, encouraging honesty, deep listening, and the sharing and holding of each person's perspective. *Circles* have a very different feel from the typical classroom set-up of desks in rows, or even of small groups of desks or tables. It is very important to have an arrangement where everyone can see each other (e.g., circle, u-shape, square-up, stand around the perimeter of the room). These types of physical arrangements increase accountability because all body language is obvious to everyone."[24] Because the space is structured to be egalitarian, students are given the message that we are equals in this space and that our individual and collective voices are heard and valued.

> **What It Looks Like:** *Community-Building Circles*
>
> The purpose of community-building *Circles* is to support young people to communicate, connect, and care for one another. In this type of *Circle*, students come to know each other more intimately, find similarities, appreciate differences, treat each other with dignity, and find joy in what they have to offer one another. The beliefs, attitudes, and mindsets we create in a community-building *Circle* are what we hope to replicate in the larger school community when students step outside of our classroom.
>
> *See Appendix 4.7 – Community Circle Protocol*

> **What It Looks Like:** *Problem-solving Circles*
>
> The purpose of the problem-solving *Circle* is to build the students' sense of agency to solve problems and issues that surface in their class community. Students in this *Circle* understand that they have the capacity to share perspectives on how to lean on each other to work through problems or conflicts that arise in the classroom.
>
> See Appendix 4.8 – Problem-solving Circle Protocol

## Considerations

1. Keep a clear and consistent structure so that students can take on increasing responsibility within the safety of a known format.

2. Build *Circles* into your schedule. Consider the skills and needs of your group. Do you have a weekly *Circle*? Bi-weekly? Monthly? What is going to be most supportive of your students' growth and development? Think flexibly about the amount of time dedicated to the *Circle*. Depending on the context, they could be 20 to 30 minutes or an entire class period.

3. Skillful facilitators of *Circles* create multiple ways for students to take ownership of the space, from coming up with *Gatherings* and prompts, and taking on facilitation themselves. In high-functioning *Circles*, students take primary responsibility for generating the agenda, raising issues, and solving problems. Teachers can begin by facilitating several *Circles* as a model for what we expect of students, and then transfer facilitation responsibilities to students and serve as a coach as they take on ownership. *See Appendix 4.9 – Circle Facilitation.*

**Strategy:** *Student Feedback*

*"Students are what we do. They are the center of our classroom… Honest feedback from our students will help us level up."*[25] When teachers invite students to give feedback on the course, the learning process, the teacher's performance, or the group's participation, the classroom becomes a more collaborative culture where students partner with the teacher to enhance the learning environment. Students feel valued because the teacher wants to hear from them—their voice, opinions, and interests. The process of sharing *Student Feedback* validates the range of perspectives students bring into the room and can prompt small and large improvements that can make the class a more cohesive, engaging, and personalized place to learn.

> **What It Looks Like:** *Group Process Feedback*
>
> **How students assess small groups or the whole group.**
>
> - Rate how the class is meeting *Expectations*. Print out the *Expectations* and have students work with a partner or trios to discuss the *Expectation* they feel is 90 percent of the class culture. Have them also discuss an *Expectation* they feel needs more intentional effort from the group. Have the students report out and chart their responses. Discuss the patterns and specific next steps.
>
> - Rate your *Cooperative Learning* group's effectiveness according to the four criteria we use: (1) We sustained our focus and met the *Expectations* for the group task; (2) We worked effectively and cooperatively and finished the task; (3) We were respectful, friendly, and supportive to one another; (4) We accepted help, feedback, and others' perspective with goodwill.
>
>    4 = We did it consistently without prompting.
>    3 = We did it sometimes without prompting.
>    2 = We did it sometimes with prompting.
>    1 = We did not do it.
>
> - Rate the group's active collaboration, attentiveness, and helpfulness during a specific learning task. If the rating is low, explore possible reasons and solicit suggestions for how to be more on-point next time.

**What It Looks Like:** *Lesson, Unit, or Course Feedback*

Have students assess their own learning. Consider using a few questions and be sure to revise to meet your context.

- What is something important you learned?
- What activity did you like the most? What are some reasons?
- What activity did you like the least? What are some reasons?
- Name an activity that helped you learn something that was new or challenging for you. How did this activity help you learn?
- Name an activity or task that did not help you to stay engaged and learn. What are some reasons it did not work?
- Identify something the teacher might have done during this unit that would have helped you learn.

**What It Looks Like:** *Appreciative Feedback*

How students support and recognize the efforts, accomplishments, and contributions of individuals, the group, and the teacher.

- What did you appreciate about the group's participation today?
- What is one way you felt supported to make your best effort this week?
- What is something the teacher said or did that helped you learn this week?
- What is something a student did that made the class a good place to be this week?
- What is something the whole group has accomplished that you feel especially proud of?

**What It Looks Like:** *Recognitions, Appreciations/Kudos*

1. Provide feedback to individuals and the class as a whole and create opportunities for the students to acknowledge/appreciate each other's effort and achievement that day. By opening this up to students, we eliminate the power dynamic in which only the teacher can give *Feedback*. It communicates that we are all part of a community that celebrates achievements (both big and small) and we all pay attention to each other's successes.
2. Make this a regular weekly practice, as it will support positive behavior change as students begin to see and get public recognition for incremental progress.
3. Model *Feedback* for particular actions, outcomes, or effort—avoid generalizations.
4. Encourage students to speak from their own observations.

> **What It Looks Like:** *Pluses and Wishes*
>
> 1. Ask students to share at least one "plus" (what worked particularly well about the lesson, unit, or activity) and at least one "wish" (what they would like to see changed for next time or any suggestions for improvements to support their learning). This demonstrates respect for students as 'consumers' of the lesson, whose *Feedback* is valued in making the class the best it can be.
> 2. Students can do this orally, or provide them with two different color sticky notes—"plus" on one color, "wish" on another and have them post on a chart as they leave the room. Look for patterns or have some students volunteer to come at lunch and do this for you. They can type up or write the patterns on a chart for the next class, and you can let students know a change you are considering based on their "wishes."

## Considerations

1. It is always important when collecting *Student Feedback* that you identify the patterns that are surfacing and share the data with the students. It is most powerful to share this data visually via a chart, or PowerPoint presentation. Publicly displaying data validates *Student Feedback* and builds a cohesive and collaborative classroom culture to support instructional next steps.
2. Have students identify the patterns in the data collected and recommend next steps to support your instruction and their learning.

# Closing

"The need to create a structure of belonging grows out of the isolated nature of our lives, our institutions, and our communities."[26] Positive personal relationships between teachers and students and amongst classmates result in classroom learning environments where students feel empowered to show up and explore who they are in relationship to themselves, their peer group, and their school community. Cultivating healthy and trusting relationships is inextricably linked to student success. When students feel safe, supported, cared for, and respected, it results in a communal structure where relatedness, accountability, and commitment are at the heart of each and every interaction.

> What strategies from this chapter align with your classroom context?

> What are the ways these support the 6 Conditions for Engagement?
>
> Attention, Goodwill, Effort, Interest, Participation, Commitment

[1] National Research Council. (2004). *Engaging schools: Fostering high school students' motivation to learn.* Washington, DC: The National Academies Press.

[2] Block, P. (2008). *Community: The structure of belonging.* San Francisco, CA: Berrett-Koehler Publishers.

[3] Hattie, J. (2009). *Visible learning: A synthesis of over 800 meta-analyses relating to achievement.* London: Routledge.

[4] Crosnoe, R.; Johnson, M. K.; & Elder, G. H., Jr. (2004). Intergenerational bonding in school: The behavioral and contextual correlates of student-teacher relationships. *Sociology of Education*, 77(1), 60-81.

[5] Sabol, T. & Pianta, R.C. (2012). Recent trends in research on teacher-child relationships. *Attachment & Human Development*, (14), 213-31.

[6] Blodgett, C., & Lanigan, J. D. (2018). The association between adverse childhood experience (ACE) and school success in elementary school children. *School Psychology Quarterly*, 33(1), 137-146.

[7] Garmezy N. (1991). Resilience in children's adaptation to negative life events and stressed environments. *Pediatric Ann.* Sep; 20(9):459-60, 463-6 Review. Martinez P, Richters JE. (1993) The NIMH community violence project: II. Children's distress symptoms associated with violence exposure. *Psychiatry.* 1993 Feb; 56 (1):22-35.

[8] Poplin, M., & Weeres, J. (1992). *Voices from the inside: A report on schooling from inside the classroom.* Claremont, CA: Institute for Education in Transformation, Claremont Graduate School.

[9] Friedman, I. A. (1995). Student behavior patterns contributing to teacher burnout. *Journal of Educational Research*, 88(5), 281–289.

[10] Phillips, B. N. (1993). *Educational and psychological perspectives on stress in students, teachers, and parents.* Brandon, VT: Clinical Psychology.

[11] Cohen, S., & Wills, T. A. (1985). Stress, social support, and the buffering hypothesis. *Psychological Bulletin*, 98, 310–357.

[12] Gugliemi, Sergio R. & Tatrow, Kristin (1998). Occupational stress, burnout, and health in teachers: A methodological and theoretical analysis. *Review of Educational Research*, 68, 61-99.

[13] Bernstein-Yamashiro, B. & Noam, G. G. (2013). Learning together: Teaching, relationships, and teachers' work. *New Directions for Youth Development*, 2013: 45–56. doi:10.1002/yd.20047

[14] Henderson, N. (2002). *Resiliency in schools: Making it happen for students and educators.* Thousand Oaks CA: Sage Publications.

[15] Benard, B. (2004). *Resiliency: What we have learned.* San Francisco CA: WestEd.

[16] Carnegie, D. (1998). *How to win friends and influence people.* New York: Pocket Books.

[17] Mitchell, C. (2016). A teacher mispronouncing a student's name can have a lasting impact. *Education Week*, May 11, 2016. Vol. 35, Issue 30, Pages 1, 10-11.

[18] Student quote from Doda, N., & Knowles, T. (2008). Listening to the voices of young adolescents. *Middle School Journal*, 39(3), 26-33.

[19] Adelman, H. & Taylor, L. (2001). *Enhancing classroom approaches for addressing barriers to learning.* Los Angeles, CA: UCLA Center for Mental Health in Schools.

[20] Association for Experiential Education. (n.d.) *What is experiential education?* Retrieved September 7, 2004, from http://www.aee2.org/customer/pages.php?pageid=47

[21] Kolb D. G. (1992). The practicality of theory. *Journal of Experiential Education*, 15(2), 24–28.

[22] Booyres-Watson, C., & Pranis, K. (2015). *Circle forward: Building a restorative school community.* St. Paul, MN: Living Justice Press.

[23] Hopkins, B. (2004). *Just schools: A whole school approach to restorative justice.* New York, NY: Jessica Kingsley Publishers.

[24] Ibid: Booyres-Watson & Pranis.

[25] Computer Fundamentals, Computer Science and IT Integrator from Camilla, GA - https://www.edutopia.org/blog/student-feedback-improves-your-teaching-vicki-davis

[26] Block, P. (2008). *Community: The structure of belonging.* San Francisco, CA: Berrett-Koehler Publishers.

# CHAPTER 5

# Organizing the Learning Environment

**Chapter Outline:**
- Introduction
- The Big Ideas That Inform Organizing the Learning Environment
- Practice #3: Organizing the Learning Environment
- Practice #4: Foundational Procedures
- Closing

**Essential Question**
How do I purposefully organize my learning environment to support academic engagement?

## Introduction

We have probably all walked into a classroom where the teacher(s) intentionally designed the learning environment to inspire and support student engagement and accountability. The furniture was arranged to promote ease of movement and cultivate dynamic interactions, quiet reflection, and a sense of community and care. Visual Postings were carefully designed, strategically placed, and aligned with the classroom context and developmental and cultural needs and interests of the students. Resources were strategically organized, easily accessible, and well maintained. We know who these teachers are. They are brimming with passion and heart for their students and their subject, and are keenly aware that considered choices around classroom organization will significantly impact the culture and climate of their room.

The concept of a behavioral setting refers to environments that are designed to influence the behaviors or actions of those who occupy the setting. Therefore, we are called to create classrooms that communicate to students what we expect of them when they enter and settle. The learning environment and clearly articulated classroom procedures promote learning and social environments that are welcoming, predictable, energizing, and hospitable. Choosing to intentionally design your learning environment and embed critical procedures into the classroom influences student readiness to participate, focus, commit, and put forth effort in your daily lessons. When students have a voice in creating the environment, and they understand the rationale behind the arrangement of the space and the procedures to support learning and accountability, it empowers them to meet the *Expectations* for learning and interacting.

This chapter invites us to reflect on, discuss with colleagues, and consider two key practices that (1) enable teachers to design and arrange their learning environments and (2) identify routine procedures to support student self-awareness, self-management, and social and academic efficacy:

**Practice #3 – Organizing the Learning Environment:** Teachers design optimal learning environments to support active learning and teaching.

**Practice #4 – Foundational Procedures:** Teachers put in place transparent procedures that will improve the quality of the learning task and the academic product or performance.

> ### The Big Ideas That Inform Organizing the Learning Environment
>
> - Attending to the "ecology" of the classroom supports student engagement while minimizing disruptions.
> - Procedural Memory is critical to supporting academic success.
> - Model, Teach, Practice, and Assess Procedures for Maximum Success.

### Attending to the "ecology" of the classroom supports student engagement while minimizing disruptions

"Everything a teacher does has implications for classroom management, including creating the setting, decorating the room, arranging the chairs, speaking and responding to students and handling their responses, putting routines in place (and then executing, modifying, and reinstituting them), developing rules, and communicating those rules to the students."[1] Creating and sustaining a learning environment with these conditions in mind means careful planning for the start of the school year and throughout the year. The learning environment must be envisioned as both a physical and cognitive space. The learning environment has the potential to make students feel safe, welcome, inspired, and invested in their learning. In addition to structured routines that support high levels of student involvement, one of the goals of the Ecological Approach to Classroom Management is to use the physical environment "to capture, hold, and sustain students' engagement while minimizing classroom disruptions."[2] In other words, students respond positively to places that are organized, attractive, and cared for, and thus are more likely to do the right thing to help maintain them.

*The Ecological Approach to Classroom Management: the relationship between students and to their physical surroundings.*

### Procedural memory is critical to supporting academic success

Teachers need procedures to help students successfully meet classroom *Expectations*. There is a lot to consider if we want our classes to run smoothly, be free of conflict, and minimize distractions.[3] Clearly articulated procedures that are effectively modeled will help students recognize the patterns of activity within the class and potentially across classrooms. Students must understand the reasons behind the procedure if they are going to invest in it. Once a procedure has been learned, it becomes a part of their procedural memory. Students can access the procedure in a new situation over time and use the procedure automatically.

*"Procedural memory is a part of the long-term memory that is responsible for knowing how to do things, also known as motor skills. As the name implies, procedural memory stores information on*

*how to perform certain procedures. Delving into something in your procedural memory does not involve conscious thought."*[4] Procedural memory is the "knowing how" part of our memory. Motor and cognitive skills are embedded in procedural memory through repeated, saturated practice until they become automatic.[5]

When students grow their procedural memory, they are able to access the procedure and use it across a variety of learning experiences.

### Model, Teach, Practice, and Assess procedures for maximum success

Effective procedures in a classroom shape healthy long-term habits for students and support transferring these habits to similar situations throughout their school day. In order to integrate these procedures into long-term memory, teachers have a responsibility to Model, Teach, Practice, and Assess (MTPA) the procedures. MTPA is a generalized instructional approach for supporting students to develop and use a skill competently. This approach emerges from the mastery learning movement and risk prevention research associated with social skill acquisition.[6,7,8] These steps of MTPA support what it takes for the brain to tune in to new information, process it accurately, and enable new learning to stick in long-term memory. A classroom's rehearsed daily procedures create the backbone of effective classroom management.[9]

In this chapter, we will explore promotion practices and strategies that support the development of procedural memory among students. See Figure 5.1 – Organizing the Learning Environment.

**FIGURE 5.1** Organizing the Learning Environment

| Promotion and Prevention ||
|---|---|
| **Practice 3:** Organizing the Learning Environment | **Practice 4:** Foundational Procedures |
| Strategies:<br>• Visual Postings<br>• Furniture Arrangement<br>• Tools and Resources | Strategies:<br>• Starting Class<br>• Ending class<br>• Getting Attention<br>• Maintaining Silence<br>• Clear Instructions<br>• Grouping Formats |

| The following adult mindsets support the implementation of these practices with integrity and fidelity: |
|---|
| • I believe that supporting academic engagement will require me to intentionally design the learning environment. It will also require me to identify, align, and teach critical procedures to my classroom context.<br>• I believe that when an adolescent enters our learning space, they will make an in-the-moment judgment about the class they are taking, the teacher, and the investment and effort they might be willing to put forth. |

# PRACTICE #3: Organizing the Learning Environment

*"If the goal of classroom design is to enrich academic, psychological, and social growth, how do teachers leverage the learning environment to support active learning and teaching."*[10] In recent years, classroom design has become a critical element for supporting students' attention, participation, interest, effort, investment, and goodwill. *"The way in which teacher(s) organize their learning environment allows them to communicate with their students nonverbally."*[11] Strategically designed and comfortable classrooms promote a sense of well-being, which results in students maintaining their focus and effort on the task at hand.

Given our experience in working in schools throughout the country, we are keenly aware of the limitations many classroom teachers face: poor lighting, desk and chair units screwed to each other, spaces that are too small and crowded, limited wall space to hang things, heating issues, and more. We are also cognizant of the demands on space and that some teachers don't have a home base and others share a classroom. We have met efficacious teachers in these situations who make whatever room they are in as functional and engaging as possible for adolescent learners. They advocate for themselves by setting up meetings with the teachers involved and take on the task of figuring out how to meet the needs of their students and themselves when organizing for learning.

Please know that throughout this practice, we offer several strategies with confidence that will tap into your imagination to mitigate whatever obstacles might present themselves to you. It takes time, creativity, intentionality, and planning to organize an effective learning space. Reaching out to colleagues, thinking with those who have a knack for organizing physical space, and thinking flexibly will help you and your teaching colleagues design optimal learning environments.

---

**Benefits of Organizing the Learning Environment**

- Helps students to stay organized, manage their time, feel productive, and focus on the learning task.
- Creates a setting that is conducive to high levels of student-teacher interaction.
- Increases positive behaviors because students have clarity about how the learning environment works.

**Learning and Life Competencies Aligned with the Practice**

- Self-Awareness: I am aware of the skills, behaviors, and attitudes that help me.
- Self-Management: I exhibit self-regulation.
- Social Efficacy: I demonstrate civic responsibility.
- Academic Efficacy: I organize to learn and study.

---

**Strategy:** *Visual Postings*

Careful selection and design of a limited number of *Visual Postings* and placement of them throughout the classroom have the potential to build students' organizational capacity to learn and study, cooperate and participate, and practice self-management. Limiting postings to ones that are most useful will enable students to focus on those which support learning.[12] Key *Visual Postings* to support academic engagement include: (1) *Expectations*; (2) the unit name, key understandings and skills to be learned, essential questions, and assessments; (3) the agenda and learning outcome for the day; and (4) key procedures. "Students are more likely to engage in learning when the learning intentions—sometimes described as 'learning goals' or 'anticipated outcomes'—are made clear."[13]

We encourage teachers to also find an area in the room to post the school rules, the school schedule, and the school vision to support the students' understanding of "this is how we do things around here." This also helps support the adult to help a student(s) when they begin to engage in off-track behavior. Sharing the purpose behind these *Visual Postings* with students, enlisting some students to design them, and giving them a voice on some of the content will build commitment and maintain engagement with the dialogue of the classroom. See Appendix 5.1 – Sample Learning Environment Layout.

---

**What It Looks Like:** *Unit Name, Essential Question(s), Key Understandings and Skills, Assessments*

- Find a central location that is visible to all students to post the name of the unit, the related essential question(s) to be answered, and what the student will know and be able to do at the end of the unit. This *Visual Posting* will change throughout the year.

---

**What It Looks Like:** *Learning Outcomes for the Lesson*

- Post the learning outcomes where students can review them during a lesson and interact with them throughout a class. This helps students understand what they are responsible for as they navigate the class.

---

**What It Looks Like:** *Check-off Agenda*

- Systematically post the agenda in the same place to support attention.
- Write every other learning task in a different color marker to help students visually track their learning for the class period.
- Check off items that have been completed to sustain attention, interest, effort, and goodwill.

---

**What It Looks Like:** *Procedures*

- *Visual Postings* to support movement, accountability, and responsibility include charts with various furniture arrangements; how to enter, start, end, and exit class; volume level; and grouping formats.

---

## Considerations

1. Consider creating a "Learning Wall" where your critical *Visual Postings* live. This provides a central location that becomes interactive for the students and you. It's a place where you can focus attention and honor what students are doing well, it supports giving clear instructions, helps off-task students to re-engage, and is an opportunity to bring new students into the class culture to see "how things work" in your class.

2. Agendas, learning outcomes, and essential questions respectfully communicate to students where they are headed in a class and promote on-task behavior. They also help late arrivals seamlessly enter the room and support English language learners who are trying to navigate the language of the classroom.

3. If more than one subject is taught in the room, board space can be limited. Meeting with colleagues to discuss how to share and design the space is critical.

**Strategy:** *Furniture Arrangement*

Effectively arranging a learning environment, whether it be in an art studio, science lab, gymnasium, music room, or core content class, is an opportunity and a creative challenge. Good design solves problems.[14] We have met many teachers who take pictures of colleagues' classrooms on their phones, research the Internet for articles and photographs on different furniture configurations, and sketch possibilities on graph paper. They also meet with fellow teachers or instructional leaders who have a knack for organizing and designing space. Ultimately, we need to arrange our classroom furniture to match our learners and the learning task at hand. The mobility of space can create a fresh outlook on what the class might become on any given day.[15]

---

**What it Looks Like:** *Arrange Tables So Everyone Can See Each Other*

This configuration supports whole group instruction, *Circle*, seminar, modeling.

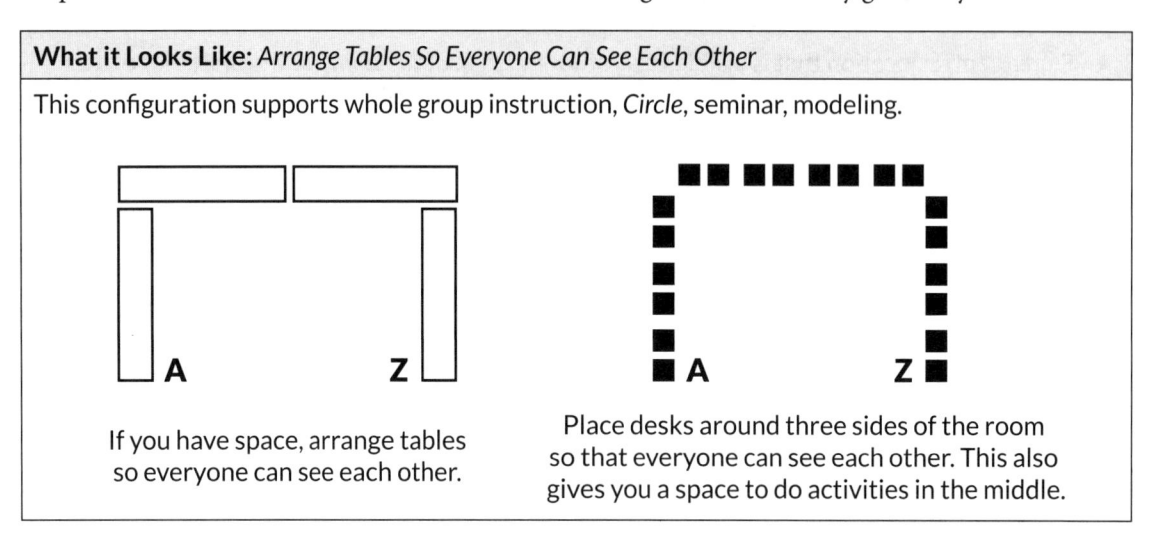

If you have space, arrange tables so everyone can see each other.

Place desks around three sides of the room so that everyone can see each other. This also gives you a space to do activities in the middle.

---

**What it Looks Like:** *Arrange Desks In Rows*

This configuration supports independent work, a mini-lecture format, or a testing environment. Depending on the desks, they could easily be pushed together to form pairs.

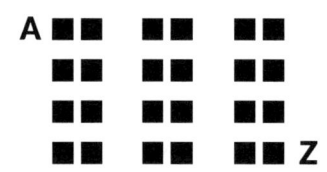

If you need to place students in rows, try placing desks in pairs.

---

**What it Looks Like:** *Arrange Desks In Trios Or Quads*

This configuration supports collaborative group, home groups, teaming exercises, projects, study groups, jigsaw reading, learning clinics, and more.

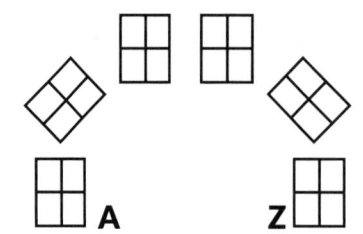

Create working groups of four desks each, so students can turn their chairs around to see each other.

## Organizing the Learning Environment

### Considerations

1. Look at the room holistically and consider designating spaces in the room that align with your classroom context: a conference area, a cool down space, or a resource center.
2. Create a *Visual Posting* with the different configurations you regularly use so you can point and guide students to help you set up the *Furniture Arrangement* for the activity. This is a procedure that takes practice and rehearsal, but once students have this procedure down, room set-up and break-down are efficient. The examples can be clip art or drawings on laminated cards, or actual photographs of the configurations.
3. The layout of the furniture should allow teachers to move freely through the space. Create a floorplan for the different configurations, and MTPA how students navigate the floorplans.
4. If another teacher or teachers are using the space, find a time to meet to agree upon how the room will always be arranged when you enter the room.

### Strategy: *Tools and Resources*

A well-organized classroom can practically run itself and has the potential to create an environment that feels calm, centered, and purposeful. Deep consideration of the *Tools and Resources* needed for our courses, ensures that students will invest, participate, and engage in sustained learning. Students are naturally curious and watch us all the time. How we organize our *Tools and Resources* sends critical messages to them. *She has taken time to select these resources, has provided me with a resource folder/Interactive Notebook, has organized a Resource Center for us to store and take care of our materials. She cares. She believes in me. I will learn well here.* Space and time are at a premium in our secondary classrooms, so prioritizing *Tools and Resources* and how to organize and use them is an essential first step. Having the right *Tools and Resources* at the ready allows for increased participation, interest, and attention, as well as fewer distractions and greater momentum as the task gets underway. Paring down supplies/materials is the very first step to a clutter-free and organized room. What *Tools and Resources* are critical to learning in my class? What can I recycle or donate, and what do I put in the trash? Keep the students at the center of your planning process and choices. Resource management can be the perfect job for a student aide if you are lucky enough to have one who can file, clean out the clutter, and replenish spent supplies. This might also be one of the rituals for *Ending Class* (see p. 68 on Procedures). In the chart below, we offer three examples that have been universally supportive to the secondary teachers we have partnered with over the years. We recognize that choosing and organizing *Tools and Resources* is a personal decision. See Appendix 5.1 – Sample Learning Environment Layout.

---

**What It Looks Like:** *Student Work Folders*

- Crates with hanging folders or an existing empty file cabinet can house student work folders. Color code student hanging folders by class and create labels with each student's name and number.
- **Advantages:** These folders hold critical work in progress and enable the teacher to engage in 1:1, group, and parent conferences. Teachers can spot-check folders with ease for students who might be struggling, and leave a note for the student for the next day.

---

**What It Looks Like:** *Group Supplies Caddies*

- Table/desk caddies have compartments that support an organized toolkit and easy access to what is needed in the moment.
- Supplies such as scissors, glue, tape, paper clips, colored pencils, compasses, sticky notes, pencils, and highlighters can be kept in bins.
- **Advantages:** Having supplies at tables/desk pods minimizes traffic, increases accountability for resources, and helps students develop organizational habits.

> **What It Looks Like:** *Core Classroom Documents*
>
> - Draw organizers/wall mount pocket organizers house syllabi, classroom assignments, homework, vocabulary, project expectations, rubrics, and conventions for writing. Be sure to color code if you are teaching multiple courses so students can easily access their organizers.
> - **Advantages:** This is a dynamic component of the Resource Center that is ever changing depending on the unit design and lesson plan. Students independently gather what they need, and when they have misplaced or lost something, they know where to find it.

### Considerations

1. Create an area in the room and designate it the Resource Center. While some people are blessed with the innate knowledge and skill of how to organize their *Tools and Resources*, many of us welcome support. We encourage you to consult with a colleague who is exceptionally talented in organizing when first creating a Resource Center, especially when you are teaching multiple sections.

2. If you share a room with other colleagues, call a meeting and think together about how to design a Resource Center that will serve the interests and needs of the staff and students collectively.

3. Early on, hold a *Circle* to discuss with students the purpose of the Resource Center, the procedures they will follow, and their role in taking care of it. Consider having your students determine how to organize *Tools and Resources*, as they'll be more empowered to actually follow the procedure(s).

## PRACTICE #4: Foundational Procedures

Effective procedures enable students and the teacher to establish a systematized method for completing the same task consistently time and time again. It is only a procedure if 90% of the students are implementing the procedure systematically and with ease.[16] When we have systematized procedures in place, students know what behaviors are expected and are more self-aware, self-managed, and academically efficacious in the moment. Systematized procedures support more on-task behaviors, reduce disruptions, and can improve the quality of both the learning experience and the academic product or performance.

> **Procedural memory** is a part of the long-term memory that is responsible for knowing how to do things. As the name implies, procedural memory stores information on how to perform certain procedures. Delving into something in your procedural memory does not involve conscious thought.[20]

Sometimes, we hear from middle and high school teachers that they feel their students should already know what the procedural expectations are in a typical class: "I thought they got this in elementary school or middle school." The reality is that each day middle and high school students navigate the varied expectations of six to seven teachers, increasingly complex learning tasks, and more and more intricate social interactions. Thus, it is important for us to identify the procedures critical to our course(s) and Model, Teach, Practice, and Assess (MTPA) them, so they are seamlessly integrated into the classroom culture and embedded in the students' procedural memory.

MTPA provides students with anxiety issues, special learning needs, or limited language proficiency an opportunity to see, not just hear, what the expectation is. We would like students to be successful on the first try and remember the procedure from the first time we reviewed it; however, this is not a realistic expectation and assessing the implementation of the procedure will help everyone know if the procedure is working, or if it needs to be modified in some way. Teachers can provide corrective feedback and hold students accountable once everyone has had a chance to practice. This will result in a classroom that is safe, orderly, productive, and engaging. Procedures that orient students to the way we do things in classes such as science, math, art, social studies, and physical education result in students hardwiring these procedures, which will serve them day-to-day in their classes and their future life and work. When students contribute to the common good of their class, they develop a sense of pride in their classroom—while at the same time encouraging individual responsibility.

> **Benefits of Foundational Procedures**
> - Grounds teachers and students to make steady transitions throughout the class.
> - Creates a sense of calm, order, and structure for students to lean in and participate.
> - Increases academic learning time and time on task.
>
> **Learning and Life Competencies Aligned with the Practice**
> - Self-awareness: I am aware of skills, behaviors, and attitudes that help me.
> - Self-Management: I exhibit self-regulation.
> - Social Efficacy: I communicate and problem-solve effectively, cooperate and participate, and I demonstrate civic responsibility.
> - Academic Efficacy: I organize to learn and study.

**Strategy:** *Starting Class*

Openings matter! How might we use a prompt that has intellectual bite? In what ways might we structure the first eight to ten minutes to have students review content from the previous day or activate knowledge to prepare for the lesson ahead? Intentional and structured openings help students establish a foothold at the start of a class, which enables them to believe that what they are about to tackle is worth their investment.

Getting the absolute most out of the first few moments of class requires careful planning and purposeful implementation.[17] The first eight to ten minutes of class offer us a rich opportunity to ignite interest and capture the attention and energy of students to prepare them for learning. Students often enter our classrooms distracted by their complex emerging lives. We have the charge to bring students' focus to the learning task in front of them. Effective teachers have an established procedure that captures the hearts and minds of students as they cross the threshold of the classroom: (1) they greet students at the door; (2) students move to their assigned learning area; (3) they scan the agenda and learning outcome; (4) they begin the Reflect and Connect that supports them in stepping into the lesson. Students can tell within a minute or two if they plan to invest in the class and you, their teacher, based on this procedural routine.

> **A Reflect and Connect** is a strategy to engage students as soon as they settle into their seats. Students are presented with a prompt (e.g., evocative question, an image, a quotation, or a short video clip) to reflect on, often in writing, and then share their thinking with a peer or the entire class. The prompts ease students into the lesson, get them ready to focus, connect with content from a previous lesson, and activate prior knowledge regarding new content.

> **What It Looks Like:** *Entering the Classroom*
>
> - Meet and Greet students at the door and have them move to their seats and engage in the "Reflect and Connect." See p. 48 for *Meet and Greet* ideas.
> - Create and practice the procedure for how students are to enter the class and settle in.

> **What It Looks Like:** *Reflect*
>
> - Provide students with an opportunity during the first five to eight minutes of class to reflect on a prompt that supports personal relationship building, activates prior knowledge before starting a unit/lesson, or reviews the previous day's lesson. Consider pairing provocative and inspiring photos with your prompt or question. Visuals will hook the student and help them lean into the question. Switch it up, to make sure you sustain the students' interest in this strategy.
> - Post the Reflect and Connect in the same place every day, so students know what to look for and can get down to business once they enter the classroom.
> - Provide quality think time to support the success of student engagement in the Reflect and Connect. This enables students to individually process their thoughts and be emotionally and cognitively prepared for the social interaction that supports deep learning.
> - Use a timer and remind students they have X number of minutes to respond to the prompt in writing.

> **What It Looks Like:** *Connect*
>
> - Students can engage in the "connect" in a variety of ways.
> - *Turn and Talk*: They may interact with a partner to share their reflection.
> - Whole Group: Ask for two to four thoughts from the *Turn and Talk*; two to four student voices if they have reflected silently; or, put your timer on for three minutes and take a number of student responses.
> - Be sure to thank the students for their engagement/participation before transitioning to the lesson.

## Considerations

1. Hold a *Circle* (see p. 55) and discuss with the students the interests behind entering the class in an orderly way and having a Reflect and Connect at the start of class. Explore their role and your role during this eight-to-ten minutes. Create a *Visual Posting* that describes the Reflect and Connect and roles and responsibilities, and hang this visual posting in a prominent place in the classroom.

2. Many school communities open class with a "Do Now." We are intentional about calling this opening a Reflect and Connect because we feel it fosters adolescents' goodwill because students feel "respected, known, and heard." We believe it is important to both provide students with quiet time to tap in and organize their thoughts (reflect) and daily dedicated and structured time (connect) for students to share their thinking to build social efficacy and to send a message to students that we value their voice.

3. It is important that students are aware of how you expect them to respond to a prompt. They may have a section in their Interactive Notebook, binder, or electronic device where they jot down their thinking. Committing their thinking in writing supports accountability to the task and supports deep learning.

**Strategy:** *Ending Class*

Ending a class with intention is as critical as starting a class. We need to abandon the idea of a few more minutes of instruction and instead end each class in a ritualized way in order to support students' in synthesizing their learning and transitioning effectively. It has three distinctive parts. Part One is about closing your lesson, Part Two is about organizing the space for the next group of students (and possibly another teacher who shares the room) and Part Three is about exiting the class.

- **Part One:** Closing a lesson is the vehicle for students to organize, integrate, and make meaning of the learning and experience that just took place. It can function as a formative assessment by providing teachers with a quick "read" on where students are in their thinking. Closing a lesson build students' metacognitive muscles by providing systematic opportunities for students to: (1) solidify their learning; (2) reflect on the learning process; or (3) self-assess the skills or target behaviors they practiced in the lesson.

- **Part Two:** Organizing the space will support your students and you as well as the next group of learners to transition with success. Establishing a routine to help students organize their materials, clean their area, return class resources, and rearrange furniture is critical to the well-being of everyone in the class and the greater school community.

- **Part Three:** Helping students exit the classroom in a calm and orderly way creates the conditions for them to enter their next class in a state of readiness for learning. When students routinely experience this manner of transition, they begin to align their energy with the "exit culture" and learn an important life skill about how to leave a space respecting the individuals in the room and those who are about to enter.

Like the procedural routines at the beginning of class, the routines at the end of class also need to be Modeled, Taught, Practiced, and Assessed (MPTA). All students play a collective role in the end-of-class procedure and need to understand the purpose behind their roles and responsibilities and how to execute them. A *Visual Posting* of this procedure can outline what takes place at the end of class. We recognize that how much time this will entail varies from class to class.

> **What is the signal for re-arranging the furniture?** How do students move furniture responsibly and safely and what *Visual Posting* supports this? What is my plan for how students organize classroom materials and those materials that they are packing up? What makes the most sense for transitioning students out of the class?

---

**What It Looks Like:** *Part One Closing a Lesson*

- MIP (Most Important Point) Ask each student to share what they think is the most important point from the activity, lesson, or unit. If time is an issue, have students first write their thoughts down, then popcorn a few answers out loud and collect the rest. These can be Exit Tickets for the period.

- At the end of the week, a closing could involve the students reflecting on the week's outcomes. Students' consider what they have learned, write and share their key understandings of the week. This enables students to reconnect with the content, build on each-others' thinking, and honor the work accomplished.

> **What It Looks Like:** *Part Two Organizing Your Space*
>
> - Use a sound and/or mantra that lets students know it's time to clean. This creates a procedural routine whereby students stay in work mode until they hear the sound/mantra. Consider the following sequence or adapt it to your style and needs:
>   1. "Please pack, stack, and leave no tracks," or "Clean your space and leave no trace." When students hear this over and over, it becomes a self-mantra, and they say it aloud to their peers to support them.
>   2. Take a look around your workspace and pick up any trash. Please take any items that might need to be placed in the supply caddy or Resource Center.
>   3. Please wait quietly to be dismissed.
>   4. Thank you for your help and coming to class today. I look forward to seeing you tomorrow.

> **What It Looks Like:** *Part Three Exiting the Classroom*
>
> - Move to the door to prepare yourself to make a personal connection with students as they leave your class. High fives, hope you have a nice day, looking forward to seeing you tomorrow.
> - With large class sizes, stagger groups of students leaving: organize your room into quadrants by putting painters tape on the floor and label the groups A-D and dismiss accordingly. This maintains the calm and order you have created at the start of class and helps many students to sustain that as they transition to their next class.
> - Students can stand behind their desks/tables with chairs pushed in, rather than lining up in a classroom, especially a crowded one. This allows for a stretch and prepares them for the transition.

## Considerations

1. Moving furniture: If you need the students to help you move the furniture into another configuration before your next class or for the teacher who shares a space with you, walk to the *Visual Posting* with the furniture configurations. "Thank you for helping me arrange the furniture." Point to the configuration and say the name of it. Ask students to quietly move the furniture. Let them know how much you appreciate their support. If you are a teacher who moves furniture a lot, be sure to MTPA this procedure.
2. Have students create an ending mantra for cleaning up. If they generate the mantra, they are likely to be accountable to it.
3. Some students will need more time to clean up because they have difficulties with transitions, or they have more items to pack up. Consider providing them with a signal or engage in a quick check-in to remind them to begin to clean-up a couple of minutes before the last five minutes of class.

**Strategy:** *Getting Attention*

Adolescents like to talk, and they thrive on the energy of engaging with their peers over interesting learning opportunities. Teachers often speak of their frustration with students talking over them. This may result in falling into the habit of talking over students. Establishing an easily recognizable attention signal is essential for setting the stage for cooperation, engagement, and order. Nonverbals account for 80 to 90% of what is being communicated.[18] Because activities of the classroom take many forms, we recommend that the signal for getting attention have two forms. A visual signal paired with a verbal or auditory cue that will result in students settling into the procedure for *Getting Attention* with increased ease and skill. Waiting for silence takes practice and a belief that students will step into the procedure if we Model, Teach, Practice, and Assess it.

---

**What It Looks Like:** *Visual and Verbal Cue*

**Raised Hands Protocol** – Students will see you before they hear you.
- Raise your hand.
- Make eye contact with a couple of students who will also begin to raise their hands, and smile and nod as a gesture of thanks.
- As others see the raised hands, they too will join.
- Verbal cue as hands are being raised: "Please pause" or "Eyes up here" or "Attention please."
- Keep your hand raised until all students stop talking.
- "Thank you, everyone."

**Helpful Tips:**
- A reminder that the goal is securing the students' attention, not to have everyone raise their hand.
- It is critical that you keep your hand in the air, provide the verbal cue once, and not speak again until there is silence.
- Create a practice session where students can learn the signal for attention and time them. "With your partner share your favorite music, book, movies, TV show or food. Begin talking. When you see the signal, please stop. I will time you." It is critical to not begin speaking until all students come to *Silence*.

---

**What It Looks Like:** *Visual and Auditory Cue*

- See the directions above, steps 1-3.
- Auditory cue as hands are being raised: Use a chime, bell, rain stick, thunder tube to secure students' attention.
- Keep your hand raised until all students stop talking and you might repeat the sound.
- "Thank you, everyone."

**Helpful Tip:**
- Create a practice session where students can learn the auditory signal for *Silence*. Get them into cooperative groups. Provide them with a prompt. "When I need your attention, you will see me raise my hand first and then hear the sound of (the rain stick, the bell). As soon as you hear the signal, please stop what you are doing, look at me, and listen for next steps." "With your group, please discuss… Begin talking, and when you hear the sound, please stop. I will time you." Again, it is critical not to speak until all students come to *Silence*. Trust the process.

> **What It Looks Like:** *Stand in the Same Place*
>
> - Identify a place in the room where you will stand every day to get the students' attention
> - Let students know that when you stand there, you will signal for their attention.
> - When they see you moving to that place, many students will begin to prepare themselves to come to *Silence*.

## Considerations

1. Hold a *Circle* (p. 55) and have the students brainstorm the motivation behind the attention signal, and what role they have to implement it successfully. There are always a number of students who will say, "so we can listen to instructions/directions, so you can check in with us, and so you can make an announcement." Asking them to think about the reasons behind the attention signal will ensure their commitment to support you and the classroom procedure.

2. As you are shaping classroom behavior, it is important to provide *Value-Added Feedback* about what is going well. Check in with the students to see how they think they are doing with coming to *Silence*. "What are a couple of things we are doing well? What's one thing we might work on?"

3. Help students begin to make the transition to *Silence* by letting them know that the end time is near. "Take two more minutes to finish up." Or, "Let the last person in your group finish up their sentence. Thank you!"

### Strategy: *Maintaining Silence*

The role of *Maintaining Silence* in the classroom is powerful. It is an ally to introspection, reflection, thinking, and acting in meaningful ways. Our schools should teach children the skills to work with others—cooperative learning can be effective when practiced well and in moderation—but it is also vital to recognize that many people, especially introverts, need extra quiet and privacy in order to do their best work.[19] When strategically used in a classroom, *Silence* can reduce stress and tension as students enter a complex task knowing that you will move about and coach and support. *Silence* can refuel a student in the moment and allow them to tap into their inner resources, memories, and creative ideas related to the topic. Sometimes *Silence* can feel very uncomfortable for many adolescents, and they quickly want to fill the void with talk, music, podcasts, YouTube, and T.V. We have a responsibility to systematically incorporate authentic learning experiences that require students to become increasingly more comfortable with *Maintaining Silence* and its role in their learning lives, and to honor those students who truly need *Silence* in order to achieve academically. Integrating silent opportunities into our daily lesson will yield a classroom community that sees *Silence* as critical to their growth and development as learners. Building students' stamina for *Silence* and their comfort level with it is our opportunity and challenge.

| **What It Looks Like:** *Building student commitment for Maintaining Silence* |
|---|
| • Facilitate a *Circle* and take an inquiry stance with students on the role of silence in the classroom. Follow the protocol for *Circle* (see Appendix 4.8 – Problem-solving Circle Protocol) and ask a version of the following question: What are some of the reasons *Silence* is important in a classroom environment?<br>• Chart students' responses and add thoughts of your own if needed. Often students are keenly aware, if given an opportunity to voice their thinking, of why *Silence* is essential to their learning.<br>• This Anchor Chart needs to be prominently displayed in the classroom as you build the "silence muscle" in your students. |

| **What It Looks Like:** *Practicing Silence* and *Maintaining Silence* |
|---|
| • Serve up silent learning in very small chunks and build up to longer periods of sustained *Silence*.<br>• The timer is a neutral character in the cast. Let students know you will time the activity. In some class contexts, a student can be a timekeeper, and you can rotate this responsibility.<br>• Mid-way through a silent learning task, use your visual/verbal or visual/auditory signal for Getting Attention, and let students know: "Excuse me for interrupting. You are 5 minutes into your 10-minute task. You have 5 minutes left. Thank you for your *Silence*." |

## Considerations

1. *Silence* Interrupters

    - For students who have difficulty *Maintaining Silence*, you must act quickly and calmly. Try a version of the following:
    - Move toward the student and establish eye contact—most times this will help the student engage or re-engage in silence.
    - For some students, you can tap them on the shoulder, and the physical prompt along with Silence will redirect them. (You need to know that the student can handle physical touch.)
    - Provide an effective reminder and directive: "Deidre, this is silent time, and you have 6 more minutes to go. Thank you for settling in…"
    - If the student persists: "Deidre please stop talking so you can complete the task and be good to go. If you keep talking, you will work with me to complete the task. This is your choice."

2. *Circle:* If the class is struggling, hold a Problem-solving *Circle* (see Appendix 4.8– Problem-solving Circle Protocol) to share some data and generate ideas with the students about how to maintain *Silence* when it is required.

### Strategy: *Clear Instructions*

We have a tremendous responsibility and opportunity to help students lean into a task with confidence and direction based on how we formulate instructions. Giving *Clear Instructions*, related to the learning outcome and activity that are understandable, is a classroom procedure that sounds easy to do but in a real-time situation can be very challenging for many teachers. If we expect students to understand and take action, we need to become very intentional about providing *Clear Instructions* that are precise and succinct. We suggest providing *Clear Instructions* in two to three ways for students to ensure their understanding. Provide verbal and auditory instructions, and sometimes follow up with having a student summarize the instructions for the entire class when they are complex. *Clear Instructions* will ensure that each and every student has an opportunity to navigate the task in front of them.

#### What It Looks Like: *Presenting Verbal and Written Instructions*

- Secure the students' Attention and *Silence*, insert a brief pause, and prepare yourself to provide the instructions.
- Stand in a consistent place when giving *Instructions*. When you give Instructions from the same location every day, your students will associate that place with attention, silence, listening, reading, understanding, and applying what you tell them.
- Provide students with verbal *Instructions* and project/point to written instructions simultaneously. This provides students with a double dose of what is expected of them.
- Chunk your directions and pause after each chunk so students can process. First, you will… Second, you will… etc.
- Scan the room when giving *Instructions* and make eye contact with students. Make sure your facial expression is invitational.
- Encourage students to co-construct what it is they think they are supposed to do. This gives the students time to consider how the activity fits with the learning outcome and activity. Have a student summarize the instructions for the class when appropriate.

#### What It Looks Like: *Clarifying Instructions*

- Get clarification: Sometimes you may offer a Q&A session after complex multi-step *Instructions*. What questions do you have? Ask students to write down their questions, and compare with a partner first to see if their question can be answered and then take four to five from the group. Ask students whose questions were not answered to leave them on the desk and you will collect them to see the patterns and answer them when the time is right.
- Try Three Before Me: Refer students to the *Visual Posting* to indicate what they can do to help themselves. (1) Reread the instructions and ask yourself: What am I supposed to do? Underline key words that finish the prompt: I am supposed to…; (2) Write down your question on a sticky note and share it with a learning partner; (3) Have paper tents with the word "Help" on them that students store in their Interactive Notebook or binder. They pull these out and place on their desk when they are really stuck and need your help.

### Considerations

1. If you know you struggle with giving *Clear Instructions* that are sequenced, rehearse them prior to saying them to students. Find a mantra that you will use several times a day "You are going to…" Or, "In a moment you will…" as some students will picture themselves doing what you are asking. This ensures that the students will lean in and focus on the Instructions before jumping into the activity.

2. Be clear and precise about the what, who, and how, and the allotted time for the learning task: You will identify two solutions to the problem; you will work with your *Turn and Talk* partner; you will use your Interactive Notebook and readings from the text set; you will have 30 minutes. Brevity is key. Move about the room and check progress and provide feedback in the moment to clear up any confusions.
3. Act out/model the *Instructions* when possible to provide a moving picture of what you want students to do and use graphics/pictures when appropriate.

### Strategy: *Grouping Formats*

There are a multitude of ways that a teacher can arrange students for group work to align with learning outcomes. Incorporating flexible *Grouping Formats* throughout a unit provides students with multiple opportunities to work with and learn from their peers. When students engage with others in varied *Grouping Formats*, they learn to work cooperatively with a range of personalities. They have frequent opportunities to verbalize their ideas, listen to one another, share in authentic discussion, and partner to successfully meet the expectations of the task in front of them. When crafting lessons, we benefit from considering how the *Grouping Format* aligns with the learning outcome, learning task, and the duration of the activity. Determine the ways in which the students can be grouped (i.e., dyads, trios, quads, home groups, whole class). Consider if randomizing the groups is the goal or if intentional grouping is necessary. There are several ways for teachers to make the *Grouping* look like it is random, but students will catch on if the grouping is not flexible and does not take different forms for students to practice their skills. For example, we would not want to group all English language learners together all of the time. There are many benefits to grouping them with their peers including providing linguistic models, a sense of belonging, and a reason to use the target language. The *Grouping Format* you land on will influence the arrangement of the furniture. Flexible *Grouping* is a strategy that is developed over time. To ensure successful *Grouping Formats* to promote maximum learning, it is essential that the students assess how things are going.

---

**What It Looks Like:** *Randomized Group Formats*

Randomized groups are relatively easy and quick to administer, as there is little preparation needed. These groups enable students to work with peers they ordinarily would not. They seem fair to students and create a context for students to step up to the plate and take important risks as they get to know each other.

**Methods for Randomizing Partners**

Creating random groups in your classroom can be a quick and easy process, as a lot of these ideas can be prepared in advance, are ready at any time, and can be used over time.

- Scrabble Letters: Find your matching letter (pairs, trios, quads).
- Postcard Puzzles: Find images that match your area of focus and cut them into puzzle pieces (quads).
- Playing Cards: Find your matching suit (pairs, trios, quads).
- Count Off: Count off by numbers.
- Color Cards: Create a class set of index cards with different color sticker dots, for example, the red group, blue group.

**Storing**

- Consider an expandable file with labeled pockets. Put your grouping types in zip-sealed bags labeled with the number of cards and groups that can be made with them and keep them in the Resource Center.

> **What It Looks Like:** *Intentional Group Formats*
>
> Assigning students to groups strategically can set a tone for engagement and success. Heterogeneous groups (based on balanced criteria) and homogenous groups (based on shared criteria) have their place in the classroom. Start by identifying the outcome for the group, then divide students accordingly. Intentional groups rely on student data collected and analyzed by the teacher. Keep a record of how students are grouped so that students do not wind up with similar work partners.
>
> - **Interest Grouping:** Students are grouped together because they share a common interest.
> - **Roles Grouping:** Assign groups comprised of students with key roles that align with their strengths (facilitator, materials manager, recorder, designer, timekeeper).
> - **Task Grouping:** Students have an affinity for a particular type of task, such as drawing, or acting. Alternatively, students with a liking for different task-types can be grouped together to ensure everyone has a role they enjoy and excel in.
> - **Knowledge Grouping:** Students have similar knowledge on the subject. Alternatively, students with different knowledge and perspectives, especially if learned through a jigsaw task, can be grouped together in order to ensure that everyone in the group has something to contribute.

> **What It Looks Like:** *Home Groups*
>
> Home groups are usually composed of four students who work together over the course of a semester or year. They provide a structure and safe place for students to develop relationships and come to know each other and trust one another, which results in student support and increased accountability. Wait three to four weeks into the school year before forming home groups. This enables you to balance the groups with different talents, skill sets, and personalities.

### Considerations

1. Many teachers have reported that they worry most about transitioning students into groups. Identify a procedure for getting into and out of groups. Enlist the ideas from your class about how to successfully make these transitions, or come up with three to four ideas and discuss them in Problem-solving *Circle* (see Appendix 4.8 – Problem-solving Circle Protocol) with your students and have them weigh in on what might work best. Once identified, Model, Teach, Practice and Assess the procedure.

2. Determine what the *Furniture Arrangement* will look like for the various *Grouping Formats* you might use. For example, quads might require four desks pushed together to form a table. Teach the students what each configuration is called and have a Visual Posting that indicates the configuration.

Positive interdependence develops when the group's success is dependent upon the participation of all members so that students of varying achievement work together and help each other reach educational goals. See *Cooperative Learning* (p. 101). Students with different ability levels benefit from working with each other but not to the point where some students are carrying the load for the group, and others feel intimidated to participate which interferes with all students' growth and learning.

## Closing

We have a charge to engage in a vigorous and ongoing conversation about how to design classrooms to receive our students so they may settle, lean in, and engage with the content, their peers, and us. The essential challenge in front of us is to transform the physical space we have been given, no matter what cards we have been dealt with regard to room size, furniture, wall space, and lighting. It is an opportunity to tap into our imaginations and consider myriad ways to be creative so students feel connected, cared for, and inspired to learn. The procedures we bring into the class culture in the context of a well-designed space offer a promise for order, safety, tranquility, and productivity. One key to creating or transforming a classroom culture, then, is to believe and recognize the power of our decisions, no matter how small or large, with regard to the learning environment and instructional organization of our classroom.

> What strategies from this chapter align with your classroom context?

> What are the ways these support the 6 Conditions for Engagement?
>
> Attention, Goodwill, Effort, Interest, Participation, Commitment

---

[1] Evertson, C. M. (n.d.).State University. *Classroom management - Creating a learning environment, setting expectations, motivational climate, maintaining a learning environment, when problems occur.* Retrieved from http://education.stateuniversity.com/pages/1834/Classroom-Management.html

[2] Lieber, C., Tissiere, M., and Frazier, N. (2015). *Shifting gears: Recalibrating schoolwide discipline and student support – A restorative and accountable approach for middle and high schools.* Cambridge, MA: Engaging Schools.

[3] Johnson, D.D., Rice, M.P., Edgington, W.D. &Williams, P. (2005). For the uninitiated: How to succeed in classroom Management. *Kappa Delta Pi Record* 42 (1), 28-32.

[4] Zimmerman, A. (2014). *"Procedural Memory: Definitions and Examples."* Live Science. Retrieved from https://www.livescience.com/43595-procedural-memory.html

[5] Mastin, L. (2010). *The Human Memory*. Retrieved from: https://www.scribd.com/document/311171723/The-Human-Memory-Luke-Mastin-2010

[6] Catalano, R.F. & Hawkins, J.D. (1996). The social development model: A theory of antisocial behavior. Chapter 4 In Hawkins J.D. *Delinquency and Crime: Current Theories.* Cambridge: Cambridge University Press. (pp 149-197).

[7] Goldstein, A.P. (1981). *Psychological skill training.* New York, NY: Pergamon.

[8] Goldstein, A.P. (1988). *Prepare the curriculum: teaching prosocial competencies.* Champaign, IL: Research Press.

[9] Sayeski, K. L., & Brown, M. R. (2014). Developing a classroom management plan using a tiered approach. *Teaching Exceptional Children,* 47(2), 119-127.

[10] Yohe, R. (2006). *Rethinking the classroom: Spaces designed for active and engaged learning and teaching.* Telephone interview.

[11] Hannah, R. (2013). "The Effect of Classroom Environment on Student Learning." Honors Thesis paper 2375.

[12] Cheryan, S., Ziegler, S. A., Plaut, V. C., & Meltzoff, A. N. (2014). *Designing Classrooms to Maximize Student Achievement. Policy Insights from the Behavioral and Brain Sciences,* 1(1), 4–12. https://doi.org/10.1177/2372732214548677

[13] McClune, B., & Jarman, R. (2011). "From aspiration to action: A learning intentions model to promote critical engagement with science in the print-based media." *Research in Science Education,* 41(5), 691-710.

[14] Ibid: Yohe, R. (2006).

[15] Ibid.

[16] Lieber, C. (2009). *Making learning REAL: Reaching and engaging all learners in secondary classrooms.* Cambridge, MA: Engaging Schools.

[17] Slater, T. F. (2006). The First Three Minutes... of Class. *The Physics Teacher,* 44, 477-478.

[18] http://www.michaelgrinder.com/

[19] Cain, S. (2012). *Quiet: The power of introverts in a world that can't stop talking.* New York, NY: Broadway Books.

[20] Zimmerman, K. A. (2014, February 22). Procedural memory: Definitions and examples. *Live Science.* Retrieved from https://www.livescience.com/43595-procedural-memory.html

[21] Ibid.

# CHAPTER 6

## Content Design, Learning Tasks, and Protocols

**Chapter Outline**
- Introduction
- The Big Ideas That Inform Content Design, Learning Tasks, and Protocols
- Practice #5: Rigorous, Meaningful Learning Tasks
- Practice #6: Learning Protocols
- Closing

**Essential Question**
How do I ramp up engagement and rigor in order to increase academic achievement?

## Introduction

From our own lived experiences, as well as what research tells us, we understand that how students learn is as important as what they learn. When we think back on our own education, we can usually recall a class that was particularly engaging. Maybe this was because we had a personal interest in the content; we enjoyed science or had a flair for writing. Or perhaps it was a subject that we did not necessarily have an affinity for, but how learning happened in that classroom made all the difference. It might have been the hands-on tasks we were assigned, the content that felt relevant to our lives and rooted in real-world problems, or the chances we had to collaborate with peers that helped us engage in these classes. The tasks in these classrooms mirrored the messy, dynamic, and social process of learning outside traditional classroom walls. We were required to think rather than just recall information. We were also willing to step into this untidy process because it held value for us, we were challenged intellectually, and were given the tools we needed to succeed. These were rigorous and meaningful learning experiences that were strategically designed to support our success.

> Think of a meaningful and rigorous learning experience from your 6–12 education.
> - What made it rigorous?
> - What made it meaningful?
> - What were you learning?
> - How were you learning?
> - How did the teacher structure the learning to support your success?

What we ask students to do and how we structure these learning experiences matter. This chapter invites us to reflect on, discuss with colleagues, and consider two key practices that enable teachers to create academic environments in which learning occurs at high levels and students have the tools they need to be self-directed learners:

**Practice #5 – Rigorous, Meaningful Learning Tasks:** Academically challenging and personally relevant learning tasks that foster effort and ignite student interest.

**Practice #6 – Learning Protocols:** Structured processes that break tasks into their multiple parts, focusing student attention on the discrete skills and cognitive demands of each part of the task.

---

### The Big Ideas That Inform Content Design, Learning Tasks, and Protocols

- Critical, reflective, and creative thinking are at the heart of rigorous and meaningful tasks.
- Meaningful learning tasks foster a sense of agency.
- Tasks that balance meaning and rigor harness positive emotional states that drive learning.
- Learning protocols and rigorous, meaningful learning tasks are multisensory and incorporate movement.

---

### Critical, reflective, and creative thinking are at the heart of rigorous and meaningful tasks

We differentiate knowing from thinking. Knowing means retrieving foundational knowledge (key terms, facts, concepts, or procedures) from long-term memory by identifying, recalling, or defining. Teachers support students in acquiring foundational knowledge through strategies like mini-lessons, mini-lectures, videos, or demonstrations. Knowing is necessary but not sufficient to support rigorous, meaningful learning. Thinking is the process of engaging dynamically with foundational knowledge in order to make meaning. Thinking can be classified broadly in three ways: critical, reflective, and creative thinking:

- **Critical Thinking:** The capacity to skillfully conceptualize, question, apply, analyze, and evaluate foundational knowledge to arrive at an informed conclusion or successfully solve a problem.[2]

- **Reflective Thinking:** The ability to step back and think about our own thinking in order to plan, monitor actions, and evaluate outcomes.

- **Creative Thinking:** The capacity to perceive, represent, or generate novel ideas, connections, or solutions.[3,4]

These classifications align with the more challenging and complex thinking moves described in Bloom's cognitive taxonomy: understand, apply, analyze, evaluate, and create.[5] A **rigorous task** is complex enough to demand one or more of these types of thinking. And while we recognize that some academic skills require automaticity in order for students to engage in critical, reflective, or creative thinking when learning tasks require only memorization and recall, there is a missed opportunity for students to make meaning of their newly acquired knowledge. Moreover, knowing in and of itself does not equip students for the cognitively complex challenges of 21st century life that require them to interpret vast amounts of information, draw sound conclusions, plan effectively, and develop novel solutions to problems.

### Meaningful, rigorous tasks foster a sense of agency

Self-esteem "is a student's overall evaluation of him- or herself, including feelings of general happiness and satisfaction… Self-esteem is not developed by asking students to write down ten things they like about themselves. Perceptions and evaluation of personal competency and worthiness are not a cause of high achievement, but appear to be a consequence of high achievement."[6]

Teachers can nurture students' healthy self-esteem by incorporating these four elements into the classroom experience: (1) experiences of mastery in rigorous tasks that students value; (2) strong positive attachments to adults and peers; (3) opportunities for control, power, and choice in what and how students are learning; and (4) positive identity development that recognizes and supports students' racial, ethnic, and cultural diversity. Students who experience success and satisfaction in school and everyday life want to experience it again. They will keep doing the things that generate self-esteem and continued success.

A sense of agency can be defined as: "taking an active and intentional role in making choices and shaping and managing the course of one's life rather than being at the mercy of external forces." Agency requires students to (1) cultivate a belief that they can influence their environment and (2) develop the key competencies that make this belief possible.[7] When teachers plan meaningful learning tasks and support students in growing their Learning and Life Competencies, students strengthen their self-efficacy and capacity to impact reality with each new academic success. Ongoing engagement with meaningful learning tasks across the curriculum and over time fosters a sense of agency that each and every student needs to obtain positive academic outcomes, lead a fulfilling life, and participate in a democratic society.

### Tasks that balance meaning and rigor harness positive emotional states that drive learning

The emotional nature of learning cannot be underestimated. Cognitive psychology and educational neuroscience demonstrate that when students have positive associations with learning, they retain it longer.[8,9] This is particularly important for young adolescents, whose limbic system, the emotional part of the brain, is especially active.[10] It is the balance of rigor and meaning that supports positive associations with learning; too much rigor without meaning leads to frustration; all meaning with no rigor leads to low levels of student learning.

These positive learning associations can be fostered in a variety of ways. Learning tasks that require collaboration in order to make meaning build a sense of trust and belonging. When teachers problematize learning, they arouse curiosity and "generate anticipation of knowing a solution to what is causing the puzzlement/mental discontinuity," which results in a student who is "more wonderfully mentally aroused and engaged."[11]

> Problematizing a learning task means structuring a task as a problem that requires students to engage in critical, reflective or creative thinking in order to identify a solution(s). Intentionally designing a learning task in this way generates a heightened positive emotional state, builds students' sense of agency, motivation, and capacity for self-expression, and supports each and every student to reach targeted learning outcomes.

Choice is also a key strategy for channeling positive associations with learning. When students exercise choice, they can predict success, and the brain gets a boost of dopamine, the chemical released when we are motivated and in a state of anticipation.[12] Designing tasks that are culturally relevant and developmentally informed also provides the emotional "glue" that helps students hold learning in long-term memory. As young people link learning to personal interests or see their cultures represented in an assignment, they form positive associations that anchor foundational knowledge firmly in place.

### Learning protocols and rigorous, meaningful learning tasks are multisensory and incorporate movement

Neuroscience confirms what we have long known as classroom teachers—students are more apt to remember and use what they have learned when they engage in "full-body" classroom experiences. In *Research-Based Strategies to Ignite Student Learning*, Dr. Judy Willis explains that when our senses are stimulated, information is retained in the brain's different storage units.[13] Because the brain forges neural connections between the storage units, students have multiple access points to retrieve the information later on. And while it might be challenging to design lessons that consistently tickle students' taste buds, tapping senses beyond the auditory is critical and pays off. Integrating manipulatives or eye-catching visuals into protocols and/or tasks are two key strategies many teachers use to support students in interacting with foundational knowledge to make meaning. Learning tasks that incorporate purposeful movement ramp up rigor as well. As students get out of their seats, oxygen starts flowing through the blood and produces an energy boost the brain needs for high performance.[14] It also just feels good. When students engage in a learning task or protocol that involves movement, hormones are released that increase well-being and reduce stress.[15]

In this chapter, we will explore promotion and prevention practices and strategies that ramp up engagement and rigor by challenging students intellectually, igniting their interest and providing structured processes that support young people in being successful. See Figure 6.1 Content Design, Learning Tasks, and Protocols.

**FIGURE 6.1** Content Design, Learning Tasks, and Protocols

| Promotion and Prevention ||
|---|---|
| **Practice 5:** Rigorous, Meaningful Learning Tasks | **Practice 2:** Learning Protocols |
| Strategy:<br>• Representing to Learn<br>• Problematizing a Learning Task<br>• Student Voice and Choice<br>• End-of-Unit Assessments<br>• Developmentally Informed Content<br>• Culturally Relevant Content | Strategy:<br>• Text Protocols<br>• Activators<br>• Turn and Talk<br>• Cooperative Learning<br>• Whole Group Discussion |

| The following adult mindsets support the implementation of these practices with integrity and fidelity: |
|---|
| • I believe that how students learn is as important to student success as what students learn.<br>• I believe all students are capable of accomplishing rigorous tasks given the right supports.<br>• I believe students have a right to exercise Voice and Choice in learning tasks.<br>• I believe developmentally informed and culturally responsive learning tasks are critical to student engagement. |

# PRACTICE #5: Rigorous, Meaningful Learning Tasks

How do we develop academically challenging tasks that are relevant for young people? Tasks that require adolescents to think, problem-solve, and transfer learning to other contexts are rigorous; tasks that connect to students' interests and identities, encourage collaboration and curiosity, provide opportunities to demonstrate students' assets and apply learning, and that involve adolescents' physical and intellectual selves are meaningful. While every rigorous task may not hold equal value for every student, balancing rigor with meaning as much as possible fosters increased academic engagement for all types of learners. And, at the end of the day, this learning environment is more engaging for us as teachers as we see students wrestle with tasks, push the edges of their thinking, and discover new learnings about the content and themselves.

**Benefits of Rigorous, Meaningful Tasks**

- Stimulate thinking that increases effort, action, and investment in learning.
- Support students in retaining and retrieving information from long-term memory.
- Increase personal agency by inviting students to exert influence.

**Learning and Life Competencies Supported by Rigorous, Meaningful Tasks**

- Self-Awareness: I know myself, and I am aware of skills, behaviors, and attitudes that help me.
- Self-Management: I demonstrate perseverance and resiliency.
- Social Efficacy: I communicate and problem-solve effectively, I cooperate and participate, and I demonstrate empathy and respect.
- Academic Efficacy: I invest in quality work.

**FIGURE 6.2** Criteria of Rigorous and Meaningful Learning Tasks

| Rigorous Learning Tasks | Meaningful Tasks |
| --- | --- |
| We use the term rigor to describe instruction, schoolwork, learning tasks, and educational expectations that are academically challenging.<br><br>**Rigorous Tasks involve:**<br>- Critical thinking<br>- Reflective thinking<br>- Creative thinking<br>- Transference of learning to other contexts<br>- Problem analysis and problem-solving | We use meaningful to describe the value the student personally places on the task, process, and/or content.<br><br>**Meaningful tasks involve:**<br>- Connections to students' identities<br>- Connections to students' interests<br>- Opportunities to leverage personal assets<br>- Opportunities for collaboration<br>- Multiple senses<br>- Sparking student curiosity<br>- Purposeful application |
| *Rigorous, meaningful tasks might involve some or all of the above criteria.* ||

**Strategy:** *Representing to Learn*

As teachers, we have to introduce new content to students. Providing students the opportunity to act upon this new content and express their thinking through what Harvey Daniels calls *Representing to Learn*[16] is critical for supporting students in understanding and retaining new content in long-term memory. Consider the difference between simply copying notes from the board, or taking and then interpreting notes through responding, questioning, and/or sketching the student's understanding. This small shift is seismic in terms of asking students to think critically, reflectively, and creatively about new information and providing teachers with an insider's view regarding student comprehension. The strategy of *Representing to Learn* supports students in demonstrating their current understanding of new information and their growing understanding over time and through practice.

There are two predominant ways in which students represent their learning: linguistically through writing and speaking and non-linguistically through constructing mental images of incoming information by using, for example, graphic organizers or making sketches. The depth of a student's cognition is impacted by the interplay between linguistic and non-linguistic learning representations,[17] since adding another way of processing information creates "a seamless integration of semantic, visual and motor aspects of a memory trace" that helps the brain remember information.[18] As a result, students who have the opportunity to represent their thinking both ways experience significant achievement gains.[19]

---

**What It Looks Like:** *Two-Column Notes*

Two-Column Notes can be used to take notes from a mini-lecture, text, or video. Below we offer three common formats. The "Plus" in each format name indicates the step of synthesizing information.

---

| **What It Looks Like:** *Landmark Method Plus*[20] | **What It Looks Like:** *Cornell Notes Plus:*[21] | **What It Looks Like:** *Double-Entry Journal Plus:*[22] |
|---|---|---|
| Students divide a notebook page into two columns and write main ideas in the left-hand column and supporting details/subtopics in the right-hand column. On the back or on an opposite page or sticky note, students synthesize their thinking by connecting the notes to the lesson's learning outcome or Essential Question through writing and/or sketching. | Students divide a notebook page into two columns: a note-taking column on the right-hand side, which is twice the size of the left-hand column, where students jot down questions that help them understand and study the notes. On the bottom of the page, students record a summary. On the back or on an opposite page or sticky note, students synthesize their thinking by connecting the notes to the lesson's learning outcome or Essential Question through writing and/or sketching. | Students divide a notebook page into two columns and jot down main ideas, summaries or key quotes in the left-hand column; in the right-hand column students record responses, questions, or sketches to make meaning of the information in the left-hand column. On the back or on an opposite page or sticky note, students synthesize their thinking by connecting the notes to the lesson's learning outcome or Essential Question through writing and/or sketching. |

### What It Looks Like: *Interactive Notebook*

A blank notebook used by students to organize course and content information in which one page of the notebook is reserved for incoming information from the teacher and the other side is used for student processing of the incoming information and synthesizing thinking.[23]

See Appendix 6.1 - Interactive Notebooks.

### What It Looks Like: *Note-Catcher*

An organizing document provided by the teacher with strategic, rigorous questions and prompts that support student analysis and synthesis of thinking.

### What It Looks Like: *Graphic Organizers*

Visual representations of how ideas are related to each other to support students' thinking, for example, Venn diagrams, flow charts, webs, concept maps, timelines, cause and effect map, and problem-solving maps. Graphic organizers can be teacher-designed or created by students.

### What it Looks Like: *Sketches*

Students sketch simple pictures or diagrams to visualize what they are learning while taking notes and/or to synthesize their thinking afterward.

### What It Looks Like: *Storyboards*

Students insert sketches, symbols, and words into a series of boxes arranged in a logical sequence. Storyboards can be used to demonstrate an understanding of a text, event, process or complex word problem while taking notes and/or synthesizing thinking.

## Considerations

1. Model, Teach, Practice, and Assess (MTPA) the use of these representational systems (Interactive Notebook, note-catcher, graphic organizers, or two-column notes) to support academic efficacy, including sentence starters for writing about texts in Two-Column Notebooks. See Appendix 6.2 – Text Protocol Sentence Starters.

2. Keep your own version of these representational systems to support students who are absent or who struggle to organize, or photocopy a student's work who excels in this area to have on hand for students who are absent.

3. Identify the classroom folder systems to support students in keeping track of the representational systems they are using so they are not lost (see classroom folders on p. 67).

**Strategy:** *Problematizing a Learning Task*

Intentionally structuring a learning task as a problem that needs to be solved is a key strategy for deepening understanding. This is because, at its heart, a well-constructed problem is about thinking (engaging dynamically with foundational knowledge to make meaning), versus knowing (retrieving foundational knowledge). It also feels good to solve a problem, since endorphins are released that generate a heightened emotional state and help learning stick. As a result, *Problematizing a Learning Task* offers a big pay-off in fostering interest and effort, building students' sense of agency and capacity for self-expression, and supporting each and every student to reach targeted learning outcomes. In contrast to Problem Based Learning (PBL), in which a problem is introduced at the beginning of a unit and drives all subsequent learning, *Problematizing a Learning Task* can occur in small, bite-size chunks at any point in a unit after students have acquired some foundational knowledge in order to practice critical, reflective and/or creative thinking.

> **Consider the difference between these two tasks:**
>
> **Task A:** Find the perimeter of a rectangle that is 24 inches long and 18 inches wide
>
> **Task B:** You've just bought 125 feet of fencing for a dog run in your yard. What's the longest possible dog run you can design for an average sized dog?
>
> *While Task A requires students to know the formula for perimeter, Task B challenges students to think by inviting them to select from a variety of methods for applying their knowledge to solve the problem. The design of Task "B" is an example of what we describe as Problematizing a Learning Task in order to increase engagement by fostering motivation, providing opportunities for complex thinking and promoting students' sense of agency.*

Problematized learning tasks can vary in complexity, from individual or partner tasks that happen in five minutes to fifteen minutes to more complex group tasks that occur over one or more lessons. *Problematizing a Learning Task* provides opportunities for students to step into the roles of planner, problem-solver, and self-directed learner. At the same time, teachers shift into the roles of facilitator and coach, standing off to the side observing, asking questions, and offering feedback at key moments to put the student at the center of applying their learning.

| What It Looks Like: *Problematizing a Learning Task in Math* |||
|---|---|---|
| **Problem Type: Find the Error** |||
| Find mistakes and correct them, review common errors and misunderstandings, assess the accuracy of comprehension or practice skills. |||
| **Independent** | **Pairs** | **Groups** |
| *Can be completed independently in 5–15 minutes.* | *Can be completed in pairs in 5–15 minutes.* | *Can be solved in groups (of 3-4) in one lesson or more.* |
| Find the error in the proof that nullifies its argument. | Card Sort: Sort the mathematical statements into valid and invalid statements. | Look at your hypothesis, examine your data, and study the conclusions. Search for the errors in thinking that prompted incorrect causational conclusions instead of correct correlational conclusions and explain your reasoning. |

## What It Looks Like: *Problematizing a Learning Task* in World Languages/ELL

**Problem Type: Gaming-Up Content**

Demonstrate understanding of a set of facts, concepts, or skills in a task with specific rules, materials, and constraints.

| Independent | Pairs | Groups |
|---|---|---|
| *Can be completed independently in 5–15 minutes.* | *Can be completed in pairs in 5–15 minutes.* | *Can be solved in groups (of 3–4) in one lesson or more.* |
| You have 5 minutes… Without writing your name, describe yourself using 4-5 unit vocabulary, so that a classmate who gets your paper can guess who you are. | Vocabulary "Taboo": Select a word in the target language from the container and try to describe it in the target language or English (depending upon the level) without saying the word, so that your partner guesses it. Earn points by the number of words your partner guesses correctly. | With your group, create a Jeopardy game (questions and categories) to quiz your classmates on the unit vocabulary. |

## What It Looks Like: *Problematizing a Learning Task in ELA*

**Problem Type: Think Like a Practitioner**

Become a working practitioner who utilizes content area knowledge and skills to identify, prioritize, or solve a problem.

| Independent | Pairs | Groups |
|---|---|---|
| *Can be completed independently in 5–15 minutes.* | Can be completed in pairs in 5–15 minutes. | *Can be solved in groups (of 3–4) in one lesson or more.* |
| Be a copy editor and proof your partner's peer interview for run-on sentences. | One of you is Toni Morrison, and one of you is Toni Morrison's biographer. Prepare five questions for a 5-minute interview and rehearse how Toni Morrison will respond to your questions. | Your production team is pitching a new film version of Hamlet to Warner Bros. Create a proposal that includes the suggested setting, script edits, and casting recommendations. |

## What It Looks Like: *Problematizing a Learning Task in Social Studies*

**Problem Type: Simulations or Role Plays**

Involve students in a role-playing experience within an authentic event; a set of real-world conditions; or a formal decision-making forum. Students research their roles and analyze critical information in order to play out the simulation with accuracy and integrity.

| Independent | Pairs | Groups |
|---|---|---|
| *Can be completed independently in 5–15 minutes.* | *Can be completed in pairs in 5–15 minutes.* | *Can be solved in groups (of 3–4) in one lesson or more.* |
| In your role as a Supreme Court Justice who must decide whether Principal Morse's actions were constitutional (Morse v. Frederick), generate one question for the petitioner that will help your deliberations. | Using a "Silent Conversation" format, take on the roles of President Truman and a cabinet member debating the use of atomic weapons on Japan to end WWII.<br><br>*Partners engage in a silent conversation by exchanging written responses on index cards.* | In preparation for the model United Nations session, work together to draft a resolution that is intended to benefit your nation. |

| What It Looks Like: *Problematizing a Learning Task in Science* |
|---|
| **Problem Type: Real World Problems**<br>Apply core skills or scientific, mathematical, economic, historical, or political knowledge, principles, or methodologies in the service of identifying, prioritizing, or solving an actual "real-time" problem within a local community, regional, national, or global context. |

| Independent | Pairs | Groups |
|---|---|---|
| Can be completed independently in 5–15 minutes.<br><br>Brainstorm as many strategies as you can think of in 3 minutes for the school to save energy. Put a star next to the top 3 recommendations. | Can be completed in pairs in 5–15 minutes.<br><br>Analyze the perspectives of fisher(wo)men, conservation scientists, and the local government of a coastal town. What might be the interests of each group? Brainstorm policies that might allow all of these interests to be met. | Can be solved in groups (of 3–4) in one lesson or more.<br><br>Develop an educational campaign about a disease that affects your community. Create a logo, billboard, public space posters, and public service announcement. |

## Considerations

1. Start small so students can be successful and acquire the skills and stamina to engage in more complex, extended problems that also require collaboration. Begin with 5-minute problems that can be completed independently to build student endurance and the teacher's capacity to problematize before having students work in pairs and eventually small groups.

2. Ensure that students have the requisite foundational knowledge, resources, and support in order to be successful with the problem.

3. Create a sequence of the tasks in a timeline for complex problems so students have a visual of where they are headed.

### Strategy: *Student Voice and Choice*

Differentiated learning is a powerful tool to increase academic engagement. One way to incorporate differentiated learning is with *Student Voice and Choice*, a strategy for meeting individual students' needs, interests, and learning profiles that infuses meaning into learning tasks for teenagers. A hallmark of adolescence is the growing need for autonomy.[24] From questioning rules to expressing strong preferences for music or clothing, it is the adolescent's job to exercise greater control over their environment in order to cross into adulthood successfully. As a result, capitalizing on young people's healthy need for increased independence by integrating *Student Voice and Choice* is a key strategy for increasing motivation and performance outcomes,[25, 26, 27, 28] providing opportunities in decision-making and preparing democratic citizens.

While some ways of incorporating *Student Voice and Choice* might mean more work up front, over time, teacher toolkits expand, especially those fortunate enough to teach the same course for several years.

**What It Looks Like:** *Choice in Text Protocols*

Students select a guided process for interacting with a text that supports them in constructing meaning. See *Text Protocols* on p. 96.

**What it Looks Like:** *Choice in Note-Taking Methods*

Students identify their preference for a note-taking method that increases feelings of confidence and competence. See *Representing to Learn* on p. 86.

**What it Looks Like:** *Choice in Group Roles*

Students select a role that leverages strengths and supports positive interdependence (the group's success is dependent upon the participation of all members) in a cooperative learning task.

See Appendix 6.3 – Cooperative Learning Group Roles.

**What it Looks Like:** *Choice in Topic/Content*

Students select the content/topic that resonates with them in order to practice a skill or demonstrate understanding. Examples: ELA - select 5-7 key events in a story to demonstrate your understanding of how conflict escalates; Math - select a word problem to solve that aligns with an interest; Science - choose a metaphor to explain the parts of a cell; Social Studies - select an aspect of the Ghana Empire (religion, trade, government, art, social structure) to learn about and teach your classmates.

**What it Looks Like:** *Choice in Text*

Choice in a text might range from selecting one article out of 3-4 the teacher provides to choosing a book for independent reading from a teacher-created list or classroom library.

**What It Looks Like:** *Choice in Learning Mode*

Students select a learning mode to deepen their understanding of a concept, for example, creating a storyboard, developing and performing a role-play or writing an interview with the author.

## Considerations

1. Model, Teach, Practice, and Assess all *Text Protocols*, note-taking methods, and group roles first to maximize students' capacity to make effective choices.

2. Consider steering some students toward certain choices, based upon readiness (for example, a struggling reader might benefit from the structure of a teacher-designed graphic organizer).

3. If integrating *Student Voice and Choice* is a new strategy for you, think about an upcoming unit and identify 1-2 starting places where you might begin to incorporate this strategy in order to ramp up student interest.

**Strategy:** *End-Of-Unit Assessments*

A really engaging unit of study with a variety of rigorous and meaningful learning tasks merits an *End-Of-Unit Assessment* that is up to the job of continuing to deepen learning even as it provides important feedback about what a student knows and is able to do. And while exams have their place in many school cultures, just taking a test at the end of a unit is a missed opportunity to keep engagement high and move learning to the next level. As a result, students benefit from assessment "tasks" that encourage critical, reflective, and creative thinking and that provide continued opportunities to practice key Learning and Life Competencies, like self-awareness and self-management. And when adolescents have an opportunity to exercise choice among options that assess the same key unit knowledge and skills, students can leverage their strengths and interests in order to be successful. They are also more apt to retain what they have learned in long-term memory once the assessment is complete since they have put their personal footprint on the assignment.

> **What it Looks Like:** *End-of-Unit Assessment: Choice in Topic/Content*
>
> Students choose topics/content within a particular format to demonstrate learning of key unit knowledge/skills. Example: Choose from three question prompts/topics for an essay. See Appendix 6.4 – End-of-Unit Assessment Choice.

> **What It Looks Like:** *End-of-Unit Assessment: Choice Within a Medium*
>
> Students demonstrate learning of key unit knowledge and skills by making a choice within a medium (writing, graphic depictions, dramatic presentations, three-dimensional products).

> **What It Looks Like:** *End-of-Unit Assessment: Choice Among Multiple Media*
>
> Students choose a learning mode to demonstrate learning of key unit knowledge and skills: **visual** (for example, PowerPoint, illustrated maps, graphs), **oral** (for example, speech, public service announcement, monologue) **written** (for example, dialogue between characters, (editorial, informational essay). **Note:** Given the emphasis on writing in most schools, it is suggested that some written component be incorporated into all *End-of-Unit Assessments* even as students select a mode that aligns best with their learning profiles. One way you might consider doing this is by requiring a written learning reflection from each student.

## Considerations

1. Facilitate small group mini-lessons on specific media or learning modes to support students in understanding the criteria for each medium/learning mode.

2. Provide streamlined rubrics that support students with self-assessment in each medium/learning mode. See Appendix 6.4 – End-of-Unit Assessment Choice.

**Strategy:** *Developmentally Informed Content*

Until the adolescent years, young people's identities are closely connected to that of their parents. When they enter adolescence, teens have a strong need to carve out an identity that is uniquely theirs. Individual likes and dislikes emerge during this time, and adolescents begin to identify closely with music, fashion, and celebrities from popular culture.

Making the content relevant begins with understanding the needs and interests of adolescents. In her book *The Right to Learn*, Linda Darling-Hammond suggests that knowledge of adolescent development is a critical competency for secondary teachers since teens' social and emotional needs are linked to their intellectual growth and academic performance.[29] When we tap into what really matters to adolescents, we have a better chance of improving student outcomes.

---

**What It Looks Like:** *Draw Connections to Personal Interests*

Finding ways to integrate students' personal interests into learning tasks is a creative challenge that fosters goodwill, participation, and interest, leading to sustained engagement and retention of course content. Draw connections to personal interests by:

- Incorporating student interests into a task (designing math word problems that focus on students' hobbies, bring historical figures in social studies to life through social media).
- Linking course content and popular culture (analyzing popular song lyrics in a poetry unit, using movie excerpts in a science class).

---

**What It Looks Like:** *Incorporate Authentic Assessments*

Think about sports, drama, chorus, band, the newspaper, tutoring, art shows – all of these involve a legitimate product or performance. Young people like to demonstrate what they know and can do. And when students create a product for a third party who will evaluate their work, the stakes are raised and investment increases. Authentic assessments provide an opportunity for students to impact their environment, and, in the process, strengthen their sense of agency. Authentic assessments can include:

- A product for a real audience.
- A product for a particular audience who evaluates their work.

See Appendix 6.5 – Developmentally Informed Content.

---

**What It Looks Like:** *Inject Controversy through the Use of Multiple Perspectives on Real-World Issues*

Young people gravitate towards controversy around real-world issues. Adolescent thinking is sufficiently sophisticated to simultaneously hold multiple perspectives and grapple with issues that have grey areas. This is also a time when young people begin to engage in moral decision-making in their own lives, and they are hungry to practice in the classroom. And because teens have a strong radar for what is fair and unfair,[30,31] authentic, ethical dilemmas engage their hearts and minds. Introduce controversy through small or whole group discussions on:

- A moral dilemma.
- Deeply divided opinions on a topic.
- Different perspectives on a school community issue or a larger political, social, or economic topic.

See Appendix 6.5 – Developmentally Informed Content.

> **What It Looks Like:** *Link Course Content to the Real World*
>
> Teens have a strong need for learning to be grounded in authentic experiences.[32] When young people understand how course content applies to the real world, they have a reason for digging into a topic and learning increases.[33] These types of tasks also provide opportunities for exploring postsecondary aspirations, which are important drivers of student learning. Not only is contextualizing learning in this way motivating for adolescents — it has the potential to increase intelligence, according to cognitive psychologists Lauren Resnick and Howard Gardner.[34,35]
>
> **Connect course content to the real world through:**
>
> - Simulations, real-world problems or opportunities to "Think Like a Practitioner" (see *Problematizing a Learning Task* on p. 88).
> - Student presentations on how course content connects to a personal hobby/future aspiration.
> - Student presentations on the impact of the unit topic on individuals and/or the local community.
> - Interviews/oral histories.

## Considerations

1. Ensure that students have the requisite foundational knowledge to complete the task or assessment successfully.

2. Model, Teach, Practice, and Assess Learning and Life Competencies that support students in participating in the task or completing the assessment. See Appendix 1.3 – LLC Mini-Lesson.

3. When designing developmentally informed curricula, incorporate a student survey to assess student interest and needs.

**Strategy:** *Culturally Relevant Content*

Developing *Culturally Relevant Content* means forging specific connections between academic content and students' cultures in ways that validate young people's multiple identities (race, ethnicity, religion, class, gender, gender identity, and sexual orientation) increase their investment in tasks, and promote academic achievement.[36,37,38,39,40,41,42,43,44] *Culturally Relevant* tasks benefit all students by creating classrooms that reflect real-world diversity. As a result, each and every student has the opportunity to exercise critical thinking by examining divergent perspectives and questioning assumptions, which equips them to participate effectively as citizens in a multicultural, democratic society. Well-designed, *Culturally Relevant* assignments are particularly important for students of color who have not seen themselves consistently reflected in the classroom culture.[45] This is especially true for young adolescents, who, research indicates, have a heightened awareness of racial and ethnic identity.[46]

---

**What It Looks Like:** *Integrating Students' Cultures into the Content*

- English Language Arts: Incorporate texts representative of students' cultural backgrounds.
- Social Studies: Bring in guest speakers to offer a culturally relevant perspective on a unit topic, for example, inviting family or community members for a panel discussion on the Civil Rights movement.
- Math: Reference diverse cultures in word problems. For example, determine the most economical location for a *quinceañera*, using linear equations.
- Science: Identify a disease that runs in your family/cultural group and research what is happening with the cell in this disease.

---

**What It Looks Like:** *Explore Cultural Perspectives within a Discipline*

- English Language Arts: Write a "dialogue between multicultural authors" of two anchor texts to explore a unit's Essential Question.
- Social Studies: Create diary entries regarding a key historical event from different cultural perspectives.
- Math: Evaluate the extent to which a sample might be considered biased toward different groups.
- Science: Hold a Socratic seminar on a scientific issue from the perspective of different social or cultural groups.

## Considerations

1. Refer to relevant *Expectations* (see p. 113) and/or identify a few discussion guidelines that support a safe and productive group dialogue.
2. When facilitating whole class discussions that support students in exploring diverse perspectives, be mindful of taking a neutral stance so as not to assert a particular point-of-view.
3. Be mindful of not asking individual students to represent an entire cultural group's perspective.

# PRACTICE #6: Learning Protocols

Learning protocols are "structured processes... that promote (rigorous), meaningful... learning by strategically shaping students' involvement in a task."[47] As students make sense of a challenging text, engage in *Cooperative Learning* or participate in a *Whole Group Discussion*, they are required to practice complex thinking as well as key Learning and Life Competencies. Learning protocols slow down the process and break a task into its multiple components so students can focus their attention on the discrete skills and cognitive demands of each part of the task. By "going slow" and having multiple opportunities to learn and practice a particular protocol, students can eventually "go fast" as the protocol is embedded in procedural memory, and students become more self-managed and academically efficacious. For this reason, Modeling, Teaching, Practicing, and Assessing a few key protocols that align with a unit's major tasks, can support student mastery over the course of the unit.

> **Procedural memory** is the "knowing how" part of our memory. Motor and cognitive skills are embedded in procedural memory through repeated, saturated practice until they become automatic.[48]

---

**Key Benefits of Learning Protocols**

- Provide an infrastructure that promotes engagement in a task.
- Allow students to optimize their thinking, both independently and with peers.
- Support use of academic language.

**Learning and Life Competencies Supported by Learning Protocols**

- Self-Awareness: I am aware of skills, behaviors, and attitudes that help me.
- Self-Management: I exhibit self-regulation.
- Social Efficacy: I communicate and problem-solve effectively, demonstrate empathy and respect, cooperate and participate, and I am assertive and I self-advocate.
- Academic Efficacy: I invest in quality work.

---

**Strategy:** *Text Protocols*

A *Text Protocol* is a guided process for reading and interacting with the text in order to construct meaning. *Text Protocols* encourage students to understand that reading is an interactive process between the text and the reader and promote increased self-direction and self-awareness. For readers who struggle, *Text Protocols* structure the reading experience in order to build competence and confidence in reading comprehension. In this day and age, when so much reading occurs online, *Text Protocols* help all students pay attention to and monitor their thinking about the written word. These protocols can be used before, during, and after reading.

---

**What It Looks Like:** *Before Reading: Brainstorming*

Individually, and then as a whole group, students brainstorm and chart up ideas/associations related to a key idea in the text. When used with topics or titles that provoke students' curiosity, brainstorming fosters attention and interest. This protocol also surfaces misconceptions that can inform teacher feedback.

**What It Looks Like:** *Before Reading: Anticipation Guide[49]*

Students respond to a set of statements or questions related to the reading. This strategy focuses students' attention on the big ideas they will encounter in the text and ignites interest and motivation for reading. An Anticipation Guide can also quickly uncover student misconceptions. Students can return to the Anticipation Guide after reading to reflect on how their response shifted or deepened as a result of reading.

**What It Looks Like:** *Before Reading: Previewing*

Students explore the title, sub-headings, and illustrations to make predictions about what they will read. Students engage in individual think time to jot down some notes before sharing ideas with peers.

**What It Looks Like:** *During Reading: Silent Reading, Then Say Something*

We process text by talking as well as writing, and readers who struggle might find this an easier entry point for constructing the meaning of a challenging text. Students are paired and read sections of the text independently. At the end of the section, cued by the teacher, each student shares his/her understanding of the passage. It can be helpful to provide students with sentence starters to guide them in their responses.

See Appendix 6.2 – Text Protocol Sentence Starters.

**What It Looks Like:** *During Reading: Coding*

Students insert codes or symbols in the margins of a text or on sticky notes that represent their responses to specific lines of text, for example, C = connection; N = new idea; ? = question. This strategy encourages students to actively engage with the text and make their thinking visible without doing a lot of writing, so it's relatively user-friendly as well as rigorous since it requires students to think critically and reflectively. When introducing the protocol, we suggest selecting codes that work with multiple texts within a unit, so students gain ongoing practice with a discrete set of thinking moves. Gradually, new codes can be integrated (for example: ! = important, * = interesting) and students can eventually develop their own codes.

**What It Looks Like:** *During Reading: Sticky Notes*

The process of placing a sticky note next to a passage helps students slow down, prioritize, and provides a visual reference to return to after reading, especially when students are not able to write in the margins of texts. When introducing this strategy, we suggest narrowing the type of responses (e.g., reactions, summary statement, or questions), so students gain confidence with each reading strategy before moving to "free-range" sticky notes (comments, questions, reactions, connections, summaries, confusions). We recognize that sticky notes may be in limited supply in some schools; if so, use *Representing to Learn* strategies (p. 86) to support students in interacting with texts.

| **What It Looks Like:** *After Reading: What It Looks Like – Brainstorm Add-On* |
|---|
| As a whole class, students add to the pre-reading brainstorm while the teacher charts responses in another color magic marker to show how thinking has deepened/shifted as a result of reading. |

| **What It Looks Like:** *After Reading: One Sentence, One Phrase, or One Word* |
|---|
| This protocol provides students with a challenge that can "game up" the post-reading process. Students select one sentence, one phrase, or one word from the reading that they feel captures a key takeaway that aligns with the learning outcome. Sharing can happen in a variety of ways to reinforce learning and support divergent perspectives:<br>• Students share a sentence, phrase, or word with a *Turn and Talk* partner and explain their reason for selection.<br>• The teacher uses "Cosmic Chance" to randomly select a student who shares their sentence, phrase, or word and the rationale for selecting it.<br>• Whole class shares their word using a Wave *Activator* and the class identifies patterns afterward. |

| **What It Looks Like:** *After Reading: Student-Developed Questions* |
|---|
| This protocol encourages students to develop their own questions about what they read in order to deepen comprehension and enhance their capacity to be self-directed learners. Students can generate several questions, identify one to discuss with a partner, and the pair can, in turn, recommend a question for the whole class to discuss. Categorizing the questions that students generate after reading can be a way for students to dig even deeper to make sense of what they read. Below are some suggested categories.[50]<br>**Questions:**<br>• Can be answered in the text.<br>• Can be answered using background knowledge.<br>• Can be answered by making inferences from the text.<br>• Can be answered by further discussion.<br>• Require further research to be answered.<br>• Signal confusion. |

## Considerations

1. Select protocols that make the best sense for the type of texts students encounter most often in your course (i.e., textbooks, handouts, graphic text) and roll these out over time. Model/Teach each *Text Protocol* and give students time to gain proficiency with it through guided practice.

2. Once students have been introduced to several *Text Protocols*, encourage them to choose a protocol that is a good fit for their learning preference to strengthen student agency and decision-making.

3. Following up a text protocol with a *Turn and Talk*, Popcorn or other *Activator* to continue to deepen student understanding of a text. See *Activators* and *Turn and Talk* on p. 100.

**Strategy:** *Activators*

Since knowledge is socially constructed,[51] rigorous and meaningful tasks require students to process learning through conversation with their peers. *Activators* are learning protocols that incorporate individual think time with purposeful social interaction to promote academic engagement and achievement. Providing time for students to think before speaking has been shown to result in significant benefits to student learning, including increased number, length, accuracy and use of evidence to support responses.[52,53,54] And the purposeful social interaction at the heart of every *Activator* supports students in using academic language in an authentic context and incorporates cooperative learning elements, which studies have shown results in average gains of seventeen percent in student achievement of targeted outcomes.[55] Ranging anywhere from two to twenty-five minutes, *Activators* come in a variety of formats and can be used for a range of purposes. In order to maximize the impact of an *Activator*, it is critical to design a compelling prompt that is aligned closely with the lesson's learning outcome. This sets a strong purpose for student participation and turns up the power on the *Activator's* capacity to help students retain learning in long-term memory. Facilitating a whole group reflection immediately after the *Activator* about the content and/or the process allows teachers to continue to assess and deepen student learning. It is important to identify a few *Activators* that are a good fit for your unit and to provide multiple opportunities for learners to become increasingly confident and competent with each format.

---

**What It Looks Like:** *Card Sort*

Even the most reluctant learners can't help themselves from diving into a Card Sort. The novelty and hands-on aspect of this *Activator* intrigues students and keeps small groups on task as they discuss and deliberate over the content. Physically moving the cards around has the added benefit of creating visual patterns that anchor concepts in students' memories. Cards can be sorted by matching, sequencing or categorizing.

**Sample Student Directions:**

1. Spread the cards out on the desk so that everyone in your group can see them.
2. Take 30 seconds to examine all the cards individually.
3. Take turns reading aloud a card and suggesting how to sort it, using the criteria in the prompt.
4. Come to an agreement as a team as to how to sort each card.

See Appendix 6.6 – Activator Examples.

---

**What It Looks Like:** *Post-It-Up*

By placing a sticky or making a mark next to one or more options/prompts, students create a data "visual" that serves as a springboard for a learning-focused dialogue.

**Sample Student Directions:**

1. Read and consider the posted options.
2. At the signal, "vote" for the option most aligned with your thinking by placing your sticky in the space next to your selection.
3. Return to your seat, begin to examine the data, and make notes about observations you have in preparation for a *Turn and Talk* and a whole class reflection.

See Appendix 6.6 – Activator Examples.

> **What It Looks Like:** *4 or More Corners*
>
> Choice and movement are at the heart of Four (or more) Corners. In response to a prompt, students select a "corner" that represents their response, move to the corner and talk with a partner about why they are standing there. Because Four (or more) Corners requires a modest amount of movement, it can be a good place to start for teachers who want to begin getting students up and moving in order to keep their brains alert.
>
> Sample Student Directions:
>
> 1. Do a Quick Jot listing two or three reasons for choosing the corner you will move to.
> 2. At the signal, take your Quick Jot and move to the "corner" that represents your choice.
> 3. At your corner, *Turn and Talk* to a partner about your choice.
>
> See Appendix 6.6 – Activator Examples.

## Considerations

1. Introduce additional *Activator* formats once students have demonstrated proficiency with the foundational *Turn and Talk*.
2. Use Cosmic Chance (randomly select a student's name by pulling an index card, for example) and ask a student to share a paraphrase of their partner's response or a key learning after an *Activator* in order to increase individual accountability for participation.
3. For more information and content area examples, see *Activators: Classroom Strategies for Engaging Middle and High School Students* from Engaging Schools.

### Strategy: *Turn and Talk*

The *Turn and Talk* also referred to as Think-Pair-Share,[56] is a foundational *Activator* that supports each and every student to process learning with a partner. An effectively facilitated *Turn and Talk* with an engaging prompt is an essential tool for constructing a well-paced lesson that gets each and every student's voice in the room quickly. Since each student is expected to think and participate, this learning protocol ramps up accountability as well as engagement. Once students become proficient with the *Turn and Talk* format, they can step into more complex *Activator* formats successfully.

> **What It Looks Like:** *Turn and Talk*
>
> **Sample Student Directions:**
>
> 1. Silently, do a Quick Jot in response to the prompt.
> 2. Share your response with a partner for two minutes.
> 3. Ask questions or make connections to your partner's response.
>
> **Teacher Facilitation Moves:**
>
> 1. Design an engaging prompt that is provocative or sparks curiosity and promotes critical, reflective, or creative thinking,
> 2. Ensure each student is partnered up.
> 3. Provide clear written and oral directions.
> 4. Use a timer and remind students of the time remaining.
> 5. Circulate, collect data on student participation and provide feedback.

## Considerations

1. Effective facilitation of a *Turn and Talk* requires Modeling, Teaching, Practicing, and Assessing the skills students need to participate successfully.
2. When introducing *Turn and Talk*, consider formalizing the role of speaker and listener while students are still developing these skills, for example, Partner A speaks for one minute while Partner B listens in engaged silence. Repeat with Partner B speaking.
3. Consider formalizing your student data collection tool so you can capture what students are doing and saying live, which will enable you to use the data when speaking with the whole group, cooperative groups or individual students.

### Strategy: *Cooperative Learning*

*Cooperative Learning* is the instructional use of small groups that allow students to work together to maximize their own and each other's learning.[57] Well-constructed cooperative tasks result in students feeling a greater sense of belonging and having an increased capacity to retain learning[58] Effectively designed cooperative tasks also result in average gains of 17% in student achievement of targeted outcomes.[59] The positive feelings towards peers and improved academic outcomes that result from high-quality cooperative group work are even greater for low-income students and students of color.[60]

Effective *Cooperative Learning* depends upon (1) positive interdependence and (2) individual accountability. Positive interdependence occurs when the group's success is dependent upon the participation of all members,[61] and can be promoted by, for example, each group member taking on a different role that is required for accomplishing the task or each teammate having a different set of data or information that the group needs to achieve its outcome. Individual accountability requires assessing what individuals learn through the cooperative task. Examples include individual quizzes, teacher observation, self-assessment or collecting notes; individuals can also be held accountable through a technique like Numbered Heads Together™ [62] (group members select a number from one to the maximum number in a group; teacher selects a number, and that student is the spokesperson for the group). Underlying the most well-constructed *Cooperative Learning* task is the need to Model, Teach, Practice, and Assess the LLC target behaviors needed for students to participate effectively. For this reason, we suggest introducing *Cooperative Learning* with a task unrelated to the specific unit content, so students can focus their attention on the self-management, social, and academic skills required to be successful, (see *Anchor Experiences*, p. 54).

---

**What It Looks Like:** *Jigsaw*

- The Jigsaw is a technique where each student brings information to the group that is necessary for full understanding and successful completion of the task.[63]
- We recommend students be divided into groups of three-four to increase individual accountability.
- Each group member is assigned a different informational piece of the Jigsaw (for example, a text, data set, visual, object, or equation) to foster positive interdependence.

> **What It Looks Like:** *A Problem for the Group to Solve with Roles*
>
> Groups of three to four students select roles that support them in solving a compelling problem (see *Problematizing a Learning Task*, p. 88). If the task does not include clearly defined roles, the teacher can identify, model and teach "process" roles that will help the group be successful: Facilitator, Timekeeper, Resource Ranger, Clarifier, Accuracy Checker.
>
> See Appendix 6.3 – Cooperative Learning Group Roles.

## Considerations

1. Model and Teach social efficacy target behaviors that are critical for cooperative learning by using T-Charts and eliciting from students what the behavior might look like (in the first column) and sound like (in the second column). See Appendix 1.3 – LLC Mini-Lesson.

2. Assigning students to mixed groups (ability, gender/ethnicity/race, learning styles) encourages the group to leverage the strengths of different students in order to complete the task. Set the expectation from the beginning of the year that students will be grouped in a variety of ways and will be partnered up with everyone in the class at one point or another.

3. Consider room-set up in designing *Cooperative Learning* tasks. Depending upon the formats you plan to implement and the classroom furniture you have, this might mean paired desks or table groups. If this requires room re-arrangement due to sharing a room with colleagues, invest time in the beginning of the year to teach students how to help set up the room into the *Cooperative Learning* formations

### Strategy: *Whole Group Discussion*

In professional, community, and civic contexts, we need to be able to bring our voice into a group in ways that encourage others to lean in and listen to us. A *Whole Group Discussion* format is a powerful way for students to come into their own voice. Having a large audience encourages students to choose what they say and how they say it more carefully, which is transferable to other classrooms, work, and life. Structuring these discussions is critical to support equitable participation, intellectual rigor, and civil dialogue. *Whole Group Discussion* protocols teach and provide practice with critical public communication skills, including offering information, asking questions, and making a case for a different point of view or solution, as well as listening to divergent perspectives. An important goal of *Whole Group Discussion* is for each and every student to feel safe trying out ideas even if they are not fully formed. Ensuring that communication norms are in place can help us achieve this goal. Draw students' attention to relevant *Expectations* (see p. 113) or consider identifying one or two discussion guidelines for this purpose.

> **What It Looks Like:** *Skill Focused Discussion*
>
> - A Skill Focused Discussion lasts just long enough (15 to 20 minutes) so that everyone has a chance to practice specific skills. These might include attending non-verbally and pausing in between speakers, paraphrasing before asking a question, extending the previous speaker's response or providing textual evidence to support thinking.
>
> - As students step into practice mode, this protocol invites teachers to assume the role of the coach by modeling/teaching the skills and providing real-time feedback to students about implementation.
>
> See Appendix 6.7 – Skill Focused Discussion Protocol.

### What It Looks Like: *Fishbowl*

- This protocol includes an inner and outer circle of students and offers a high-structure format for holding large group discussions, especially those around a topic in which there might be deeply divided opinions.[64]
- Since students rotate being contributors and observers, a Fishbowl increases individual participation and allows students to observe closely what an effective conversation looks and sounds like.
- Observers use a structured method for documenting their observations and are invited to learn from classmates by listening respectfully without interrupting.

### What It Looks Like: *Socratic Seminar*

- This is a *Whole Group Discussion* in which students work collectively to come to a shared understanding of a text.
- The emphasis is on thinking, listening and speaking in ways that move participants toward common ground rather than asserting opinions or engaging in debate.[65]
- Focusing the discussion on a shared text (or map, graph or another type of visual) encourages students to support ideas with evidence and fosters a democratic discussion since all participants have access to the same resource to anchor the conversation.
- Students are at the center of a Socratic Seminar, since they ask questions and build on each other's ideas; the teacher acts as a facilitator who selects a text, offers or elicits guidelines for the discussion, and steps in only as needed.

See Appendix 6.8 – Socratic Seminar Protocol.

## Considerations

1. Because *Whole Group Discussion* protocols are tightly structured and can feel unnatural for adolescents who might want a more free-wielding conversation, it is critical that the teacher elicits purpose from students beforehand; instead of, for example, what might be some reasons for practicing paraphrasing in this way—In what ways might it help the listener? Speaker?

2. Consider your criteria for assessing student talk, possibly pulling from the LLC target behaviors. Make these transparent to students and use a roster to track students on these criteria. In addition, have students complete a self-assessment on these criteria and set goals for improvement in an Exit Ticket (see p. 129).

3. These protocols foster a belief that meaning-making is a collaborative and valuable venture and that young people have the capacity to do this effectively. This mindset will need to be intentionally cultivated in students through ongoing practice and reflection and invites both teachers and students to be patient with the process.

## Closing

What we ask students to do and how we ask them to do it will ultimately predict their performance both in and beyond the class we teach. If we offer students opportunities to see themselves reflected in the content, to apply learning in authentic contexts and to express themselves and make positive choices in their learning, students will be able to transfer their knowledge to the broader school context, work, and life. When students walk away from our course better thinkers, readers, writers, problem-solvers, collaborators, and communicators, our work as teachers is deeply satisfying.

The same way we encourage choice for students, we encourage choice for teachers. As you reflect back on the array of strategies outlined in this chapter, what piques your interest? What strategies truly align with your student population and your content? What are a couple strategies that might be quick wins for you and your students and become your "go-to" strategies? Explore, innovate, and give it a try.

> What strategies from this chapter align with your classroom context?

> What are the ways these support the 6 Conditions for Engagement?
>
> Attention, Goodwill, Effort, Interest, Participation, Commitment

[1] City E. A., Elmore R. F., Fiarman S. E., & Teitel L. (2009). *Instructional rounds in education: A network approach to improving teaching and learning.* Cambridge, MA: Harvard Education Press.

[2] Costa, Arthur. (2014). Thinking critically about critical thinking. *P21 Partnership for 21st Century Learning.* May 6 2014, 1:4, No. 2.

[3] Costa, A., & Kallick, B. (eds.). (2008). *Learning and leading with habits of mind.* Alexandria, VA: ASCD.

[4] Kallick, B., & Zmuda, A. (2017). *Students at the center: Personalizing learning with habits of mind.* Alexandria, VA: ASCD.

[5] Airasian, P.W., Cruikshank, K.A., Mayer, R.E., Pintrich, P.R., Raths, J., & Wittrock, M.C. (2001). *A taxonomy for learning, teaching, and assessing: A revision of Bloom's taxonomy of educational objectives.* Anderson, L.W., & Krathwohl, D.R. (Eds.). Boston, MA: Allyn & Bacon.

[6] Manning, M.L. (2007). Association for Childhood Education International. Olney, MD.

[7] Nagaoka, J., Farrington, C.A., Ehrlich, S.B., Heath, R.D., Johnson, D.W., Dickson, S., & Hayes, K. (2015). *Foundations for young adult success: A developmental framework.* Chicago, IL: The University of Chicago Consortium on Chicago School Research.

[8] Krashen, S. (1982). *Theory versus practice in language learning. In R.W. Blair. (Ed.), Innovative approaches to language teaching.* Rowley, MA: Newbury House.

[9] Willis, J. (2007). Cooperative learning is a brain turn-on. *Middle School Journal.* Retrieved from http://www.amle.org/portals/0/pdf/msj/Mar2007.pdf

[10] Armstrong, T. (2006). *The best schools: How human development research should inform educational practice.* Alexandria, VA: ASCD.

[11] Pritscher, C. P. (2011). *Brains inventing themselves.* Steinberg, S. R. (Ed.). Amsterdam, Netherlands: Sense Publishers. Retrieved from www.sensepublishers.com/media/121-brains-inventing-themselves.pdf

[12] Gregory, G., & Kaufeldt, M. (2015). *The motivated brain: Improving student attention, engagement and perseverance.* Alexandria, VA: ASCD.

[13] Willis, J. (2006). *Research-based strategies to ignite student learning: Insights from a neurologist and classroom teacher.* Alexandria, VA: ASCD.

[14] Jensen, E. (2005). *Teaching with the brain in mind, 2nd edition.* Alexandria, VA: ASCD.

[15] Ibid. Gregory & Kaufeldt. (2015).

[16] Daniels, H., & Bizar., M. (1998). *Methods that matter: Six structures for best practice classrooms.* Portsmouth, NH: Stenhouse Publishers.

[17] Paivio, A. (1990). *Mental representations: A dual coding approach.* New York, NY: Oxford University Press.

[18] Wammes, J.D., Meade, M.E., & Fernandes, M.A. (2016). The drawing effect: Evidence for reliable and robust memory benefits in free recall. *The Quarterly Journal of Experimental Psychology,* 69(9), 1752-1776. https://doi.org/10.1080/17470218.2015.1094494

[19] Haystead, M.W., & Marzano, R.J. (2009). *Meta-analytic synthesis of studies conducted at Marzano Research Laboratory on instructional strategies.* Englewood, CO: Marzano Research Laboratory.

[20] Landmark School Outreach Professional Development for Educators. Crossing, MA: https://www.landmarkoutreach.org/strategies/the-two-column-method-of-note-taking/

[21] Walter, P., & Owens, R.J.Q. (2010). *The Cornell system: Take effective notes. In How to study in college.* (10th ed., pp. 235-277). Boston, MA: Wadsworth.

[22] Daniels, H., & Zemelman, S. (2004). *Subjects matter: Every teacher's guide to content-area reading.* Portsmouth, NH: Heinemann.

[23] Young, J. (2003). Science interactive notebooks in the classroom. *Science Scope*, 26(4), 44-46.

[24] American Psychological Association. (2002). *Developing adolescents: A reference for professionals.* Washington, DC: American Psychological Association.

[25] Cordova, D. I., & Lepper, M. R. (1996). Intrinsic motivation and the process of learning: Beneficial effects of contextualization, personalization, and choice. *Journal of Educational Psychology*, 88(4), 715-730.

[26] Swann, W. B., & Pittman, T. S. (1977). Initiating play activity of children: The moderating influence of verbal cues on intrinsic motivation. *Child Development*, 48(3), 1128-1132.

[27] Zuckerman, M., Porac, J., Lathin, D., & Deci, E.L. (1978). On the importance of self-determination for intrinsically motivated behavior. *Personality and Social Psychology Bulletin*, 4(3), 443-446.

[28] Cooper, H., Robinson, J.C., & Patall, E.A. (2006). Does homework improve academic achievement? A synthesis of research, 1987–2003. *Review of Educational Research*, 76(1), 1–62. Patall, E.A., Cooper, H., & Wynn, S.R. (2010). The effectiveness and relative importance of choice in the classroom. *Journal of Educational Psychology*, 102(4), 896-915.

[29] Darling-Hammond, L. (2001). *The right to learn: A blueprint for creating schools that work.* San Francisco, CA: Jossey-Bass.

[30] Kellough, R.D., & Kellough, N.G. (2008). *Teaching young adolescents: a guide to methods and resources for middle school teaching*, 5th edition. New York, NY: Pearson.

[31] Scales, P. (1991). *A portrait of young adolescents in the 1990s: Implications for promoting healthy growth and development.* Carrboro, NC: Center for Early Adolescence, School of Medicine, the University of North Carolina at Chapel Hill.

[32] Ibid. Kellough & Kellough, (2008).

[33] Steinberg, A., Milley, J., & Liebowitz, M. (2003). Community Connected Learning. In DiMartino, J, Clarke, J., & Wolk, D. (eds.) *Personalized learning: Preparing high school students to create their futures.* Lanham, MD: Scarecrow Education.

[34] Allen, L., Hogan, C. J., & Steinberg, A. (1998). *Knowing and doing: Connecting learning & work.* Providence, RI: Northeast and Islands Regional Educational Laboratory at Brown University.

[35] Gardner, H. (2000). *Intelligence reframed.* New York, NY: Basic Books.

[36] Paris, D. (2012). Culturally sustaining pedagogy: A needed change in stance, terminology, and practice. *Educational Researcher*, 41(3), 93-97.

[37] Au, K.H., & Kawakami, A.J. (1994). Cultural congruence in instruction. In E. R. Hollins, J. E. King, & W. C. Hayman (Eds.), *Teaching diverse populations: Formulating a knowledge base.* (pp. 5–23). Albany, NY: State University of New York Press.

[38] Boykin, A.W., & Noguera, P. (2011). *Creating the opportunity to learn: Moving from research to practice to close the achievement gap.* Alexandria, VA: ASCD.

[39] Foster, M. (1995). African American teachers and culturally relevant pedagogy. In Banks, J.A. & Banks, C.A.M. (eds.), *Handbook of research on multicultural education* (pp. 570–581). New York, NY: MacMillan.

[40] Gay, G. (2000). *Culturally responsive teaching: Theory, research, and practice.* New York, NY: Teachers College Press.

[41] Gay, G. (2010). *Culturally responsive teaching (2nd ed.).* New York, NY: Teachers College Press.

[42] Ladson-Billings, G. (1994). *The dreamkeepers: successful teaching for African-American students.* San Francisco, CA: Jossey-Bass, pp. 17–18.

[43] Ladson-Billings, G. (1995). Toward a theory of culturally relevant pedagogy. *American Educational Research Journal,* 32(3), 465–491.

[44] Scherff, L., & Spector, K. (2011). *Culturally relevant pedagogy: clashes and confrontations.* Lanham, MD: Rowman & Littlefield Education.

[45] Sleeter, C.E. (2011). *The academic and social value of ethnic studies: A research review.* Washington, DC: The National Education Association.

[46] Scales, P.C. (2010). "Characteristics of young adolescents." *This we believe: keys to educating young adolescents* (p. 63-65). Westerville, OH: National Middle School Association.

[47] Matton, M. (2015). *What are protocols? Why use them?* Bloomington, IN: National School Reform Faculty Harmony Education Center. Retrieved from: http://www.nsrfharmony.org/system/files/protocols/WhatAreProtocols%2BWhyUse_0.pdf

[48] Mastin, L. (2010). *The Human Memory.* Retrieved from: https://www.scribd.com/document/311171723/The-Human-Memory-Luke-Mastin-2010

[49] Duffelmeyer, F. (1994). Effective Anticipation Guide statements for learning from expository prose. *Journal of Reading,* 37, 452-455.

[50] Harvey, S. & Goudvis. A. (2000). *Strategies that work.* New York, NY: Stenhouse Publishers.

[51] Vygotsky, L.S. (1986). *Thought and language.* Cambridge, MA: MIT Press.

[52] Rowe, M.B. (1987). "Wait time: Slowing down may be a way of speeding up." *American Educator,* 11(1), 38-43, 47.

[53] Stahl, R.J. (1990). *Using "think time" behaviors to promote students' information processing, learning and on-task participation: An instructional manual.* Tempe, AZ: Arizona State University.

[54] Tobin, K (1987). The role of wait time in higher cognitive level learning. *Review of Educational Research,* 57(1), 69-95.

[55] Dean, Ceri B., Hubbell, E.R., Pitler, H., & Stone, B.J. (2012). *Classroom instruction that works* (2nd ed.). Alexandria, VA: ASCD.

[56] Lyman, F. (1981). "The responsive classroom discussion: the inclusion of all students." *Mainstreaming Digest.* College Park, MD: University of Maryland College of Education.

[57] Johnson, D.W., Johnson, R.T., & Johnson-Holubec, E. (1994). *The new circles of learning.* Alexandria, VA: ASCD.

[58] Willis, J. (2007). *Brain-friendly strategies for the inclusion classroom.* Alexandria, VA: ASCD.

[59] Ibid. Dean, Hubbell, Pitler, & Stone (2012).

[60] Darling-Hammond, L., Barron, B., Pearson, D., Schoenfeld, A.H., Stage, E.H., Zimmerman, T.D. & Chen, M. (2008). *Powerful learning: What we know about teaching for understanding.* San Francisco, CA: Jossey-Bass.

[61] Ibid. Dean, Huggell, Pitler & Stone (2012).

[62] Kagan Publishing and Professional Development (2018). https://www.kaganonline.com/

[63] Aronson, E., Blaney, N., Sikes, J., Stephan, G., & Snapp, M. (1978). *The jigsaw classroom.* Beverly Hills, CA: Sage Publications.

[64] Facing History and Ourselves. (2016). *Fishbowl.* Retrieved from https://www.facinghistory.org/resource-library/teaching-strategies/fishbowl.

[65] Facing History and Ourselves. (2016). *Socratic Seminar.* Retrieved from: https://www.facinghistory.org/resource-library/teaching-strategies/socratic-seminar.

# CHAPTER 7

## Academic Support

**Chapter Outline**
- Introduction
- The Big Ideas that Inform Academic Support
- Practice #7: Academic Press
- Practice #8: Formative Assessment
- Practice #9: Academic Interventions
- Closing

**Essential Question**
How do I target my academic practices and strategies to meet the range of learners in my classroom?

## Introduction

Memories of firing up students to produce quality work, supporting learners to turn around failure, or pushing students to a new level of excellence generates lasting satisfaction for many of us. We remember these students because we know, in some way, we helped them change their academic trajectory and their perceptions of who they were as learners. We also learned about ourselves and our capacity to be nimble and flexible in our efforts to meet the diversity of learners in our care.

During the last 20 years, most secondary school improvement efforts have shared two common goals. They are: (1) supporting individual teachers and teacher teams to take responsibility for student learning, and (2) expecting, insisting, and supporting every student to meet standards of proficiency and complete quality work in every course. This orientation shifts the focus from "what I taught," to "what students learned." It differs from a more straightforward focus on the execution of a lesson because it places equal value on what teachers do before and after a lesson with what they do during a lesson to ensure that all students meet important learning outcomes, master curricular content, and strengthen social and emotional competencies.

> Academic support in the classroom refers to the instructional methods, learning supports, and interventions that teachers provide to enable all students to meet proficiency standards, to accelerate learning for students who struggle academically, and to push all students to achieve their personal best.

Nearly 100 years of educational research confirms the positive link between academic support and students' academic outcomes.[1] When teachers provide explicit support to individual learners, students' performance improves.[2] In secondary schools, this is a game-changer for students who struggle to achieve. High schools that show the most significant gains in graduation rates, course pass rates, and exit exam proficiency have one reform strategy in common. These schools are driven by a commitment to provide saturated academic support inside and outside the classroom to every student who is not learning.[3]

At the heart of academic support is the help we provide our students to complete quality work; it is also about the social and emotional support we offer that can push students' effort, boost their confidence, and encourage their persistence when the work feels hard. Positive personal relationships grow stronger every time teachers show their interest in students by engaging them in academic conversations about what and how they are learning. This chapter offers academic support practices and strategies that will significantly improve academic outcomes for all students, especially those who struggle to achieve:

**Practice #7 – Academic Press:** Teachers use multiple strategies to expect, insist on, and support each and every student to complete quality work.

**Practice #8 – Formative Assessment:** Teachers engage in real-time, reciprocal student-teacher feedback that enables them to assess students' skill acquisition and understanding and adjust next steps for instruction.

**Practice #9 – Academic Interventions:** Teachers facilitate intervention strategies to help students close serious learning gaps and turn-around their academic performance.

---

### The Big Ideas That Inform Academic Support

- Anticipate and prepare for a wide range in students' learning readiness.
- Academic support lives within a multi-tiered system that incorporates promotion, prevention, and required interventions when students are not learning.
- Many "high-impact" teaching strategies fall within the domain of academic support.
- Target behaviors aligned to Learning and Life Competencies are taught to all students and are incorporated into academic interventions.

---

### Anticipate and prepare for a wide range in students' learning readiness

Each student brings a unique learning profile to your course.[4] While some students walk into your classroom ready to tackle any task placed in front of them, others bring feelings of inadequacy, reluctance, or resistance that may make learning in your course a challenge from day one. You are also likely to encounter students who have rarely been pushed to improve their capacity to learn or achieve more than a passing grade. *"Teachers often think of learning readiness as dependent on the knowledge, understanding, and skills that an individual brings to a new learning situation. Readiness is also profoundly influenced by an individual's prior learning success or failure, self-esteem, sense of efficacy, cultural norms, social status within the class or group, life experience, dispositions and attitudes, and habits of mind."* [5]

Continual assessment of students' academic readiness and performance can help us diagnose what students know and can do, what they do not know or do not know how to do, and the degree of ease or difficulty students experience when completing a range of learning tasks. These data invite us to ask questions that can help us target the right academic support to different groups of learners:

- How might we incorporate learning tasks that enable students who struggle to experience some quick, but authentic academic wins?
- How might we provide a more explicit roadmap of foundational skills for students who are underperforming?
- For students who insist on doing things "their way," how might we use our creative flexibility and patient navigational pull to help them meet essential learning outcomes while offering alternative pathways to mastery?
- How might we increase the challenge level for students who are meeting proficiency levels and are ready for advanced work?

See Appendix 7.1 – Preparing for Five Kinds of Learners.

### Academic support lives within a multi-tiered system that incorporates promotion, prevention, and required interventions when students are not learning

Academic Press and Formative Assessment are Tier 1 universal practices that provide academic support to every learner. Academic Interventions are a Tier 2 practice that teachers facilitate when students are not learning. Interventions are used to improve students' academic efficacy, their performance, and their grade in a specific course. *"As the people who know the students best—and are most accountable for their success or failure—teachers are best suited to identify students at risk and assist them."*[6] Clearly stated thresholds (red flags) that indicate when students are not learning combined with follow-up intervention protocols help students understand what they are expected to do when they are not meeting academic expectations. Academic intervention strategies are customized to target a student's specific learning gap.

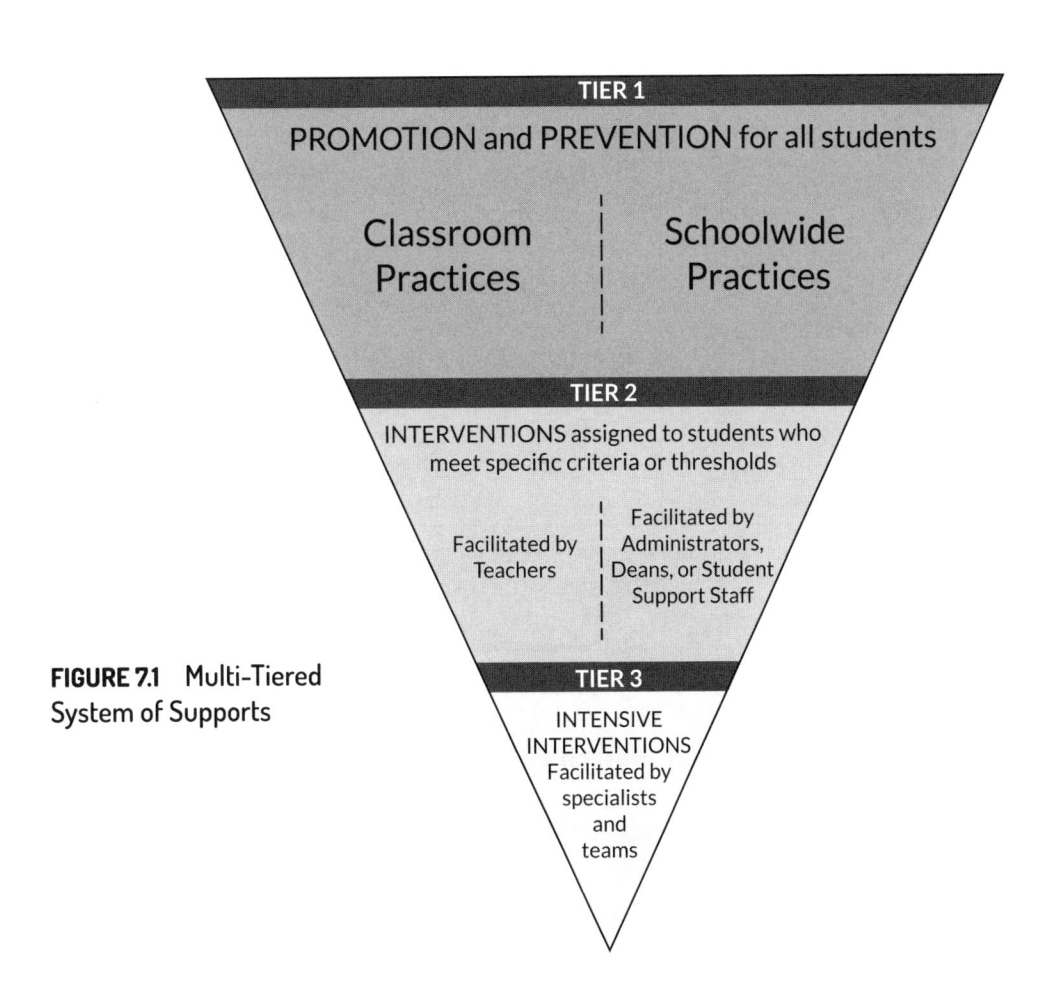

**FIGURE 7.1** Multi-Tiered System of Supports

**TIER 1**
PROMOTION and PREVENTION for all students
Classroom Practices | Schoolwide Practices

**TIER 2**
INTERVENTIONS assigned to students who meet specific criteria or thresholds
Facilitated by Teachers | Facilitated by Administrators, Deans, or Student Support Staff

**TIER 3**
INTENSIVE INTERVENTIONS Facilitated by specialists and teams

### Many "high-impact" teaching strategies fall within the domain of academic support

Strategies like setting universal expectations, systematic goal-setting, the use of study strategies in real time, formative assessment, and early academic intervention have a significant impact on achievement.[7] Incorporating these strategies into regular classroom routines and learning unit design strengthens students' academic efficacy, the "learning-to-learn" muscles that become increasingly important as students engage in more complex and more advanced coursework in high school.

### Target behaviors aligned to Learning and Life Competencies are taught to all students and are incorporated into academic interventions

Academic support is enhanced when teachers incorporate students' practice of Learning and Life Competencies (see Chapter 1) into daily lessons, so all students are able to recognize the link between improved performance and behaviors that increase self-awareness, self-management, and social and academic efficacy.[8] Integrating Learning and Life Competencies into interventions for students who experience severe skill gaps has the added benefit of fostering positive mindsets that increase a student's commitment to school and their motivation to succeed.

This chapter explores strategies that teachers use to expect, insist on, and support completion of quality work; to engage students in formative assessment, and to help learners who struggle close persistent learning gaps and improve their academic performance in the classroom. See Figure 7.2 – Academic Support.

**FIGURE 7.2** Academic Support

| Promotion and Prevention | | Intervention |
|---|---|---|
| **Practice 7:** Academic Press | **Practice 8:** Formative Assessment | **Practice 9:** Academic Interventions |
| Strategies:<br>• Setting and Monitoring Expectations<br>• Academic Reflection, Goal-Setting, and Progress Tracking<br>• Anticipating and Planning for Learning Gaps<br>• Study Strategies<br>• Revise, Edit/Proof, and Correct<br>• Guided Work Period | Strategies:<br>• Academic Check-ins<br>• Walk-around Look-fors<br>• Feedback for Self-correction<br>• Five-minute Assessment Tools | Strategies:<br>• Academic Problem-solving and Planning Conference<br>• Academic Turnaround Plan<br>• Progress Monitoring<br>• Academic Coaching |

**The following adult mindsets support the implementation of these practices with integrity and fidelity:**

- I believe that every student is capable of improving their academic performance with my support, guidance, and coaching.
- I believe it is my responsibility to expect, insist on, and support every student to complete quality work.
- I believe that academic interventions during and out of class time are the most direct means of supporting students who are not learning.

# PRACTICE #7: Academic Press

Academic press, a phrase coined by researchers Lee and Smith, involves high-impact strategies that teachers systematically use to ensure that all students meet universal learning outcomes and complete high-quality work. "*Academic press focuses on the extent that teachers and students experience a normative emphasis on school success and conformity to specific standards of achievement.*"[9] Multiple studies reveal that students experience significant gains in achievement when teachers expect, insist and support each and every student to complete quality work in ways that cultivate student ownership and academic efficacy.[10,11] Academic efficacy ("I can do this.") refers to an individual's conviction that they can successfully complete an academic task or attain a specific academic goal.[12,13,14]

Academic press strategies like Setting and Monitoring Expectations; Academic Reflection, Goal-Setting, and Progress Tracking; Study Strategies and Revise, Edit/Proof, and Correct cultivate a belief in the malleability of intelligence ("I can grow my brain and get smarter."). Integrating these strategies into every learning unit helps to close the gap between more successful students and those who struggle to succeed by providing explicit roadmaps and tools for ramping up academic engagement and performance.

> **Benefits of Academic Press**
> - Prepares teachers to close achievement gaps among different groups of students by providing clear pathways that students can follow to improve their grades and academic performance.
> - Increases effort-based learning, self-direction, and students' confidence and pride as learners.
> - Supports an early warning system of "red flags" to ensure that interventions occur before patterns of failure become persistent.
>
> **Learning and Life Competencies Aligned with the Practice**
> - Self-Awareness: I know myself, and I am aware of skills, behaviors, and attitudes that help me.
> - Self-Management: I demonstrate perseverance and resiliency.
> - Academic Efficacy: I invest in quality work, organize to learn and study, and I set goals and self-assess.

**Strategy:** *Setting and Monitoring Expectations*

Whether or not a teacher "believes in" a student and expects him to succeed has been shown to affect how well that student does in school, particularly among disadvantaged students."[15] *Expectations* publicly communicate the beliefs teachers hold about what students are capable of doing and achieving; they convey confidence in the students' capacity to succeed and thrive in school and life; they provide enduring guidelines for how we present and express ourselves and how we should behave.[16]

> **A sample set of classroom Expectations aligned with target behaviors identified in the Learning and Life Competencies**
>
> Thank you for:
> - Respecting the rights and dignity of each member of the class and their rights to be heard and valued, and to learn in a safe classroom.
> - Making our classroom a good place to learn by being friendly, contributing positively, and supporting your peers.
> - Holding a growth mindset by setting goals, monitoring your progress, working hard, and making your best effort.
> - Recognizing everyone makes mistakes or poor choices. When mistakes are made, I thank you for owning what you did and doing something to make it right. I am confident that you can recover and get back on track.
> - Remembering you have what it takes to succeed in this class.

Communicating clear *Expectations* is a high leverage strategy for closing the achievement gap; however, its power to improve student performance only works when the same expectations are applied universally to every student in the class. *Expectations* also help establish a well-managed classroom and support a learning environment that feels safe, orderly, and respectful. They help nurture two conditions of academic engagement in particular: participation and a commitment to self-identify as a learner and classroom community member.

*Expectations* come alive when a teacher's actual behaviors and interactions show that high standards of academic performance are expected of everyone. Robert Pianta, Dean of the Curry School of Education at UVA, calls these teacher behaviors "touch points," the words and actions that communicate a teacher's confidence in students' capacity to meet those expectations. Pianta found that when teachers had high expectations for their students, those students were given more specific feedback to improve, more smiles and approval, more interesting questions to answer, and more supportive reminders when they were off-task.[17] Countering our tendency to respond more positively to some students than others begins with deliberate efforts to provide more meaningful "touch points" to students who are struggling socially, emotionally, or academically. *"If teachers consciously work to change their biases but don't change their behavior toward those students from whom they have tended to expect less, their change of attitude will have little effect on student achievement."*[18]

---

**What It Looks Like:** *Setting and Monitoring Expectations*

**Crafting Expectations**
Craft no more than four to five *Expectations* that reflect target behaviors that are most essential for students to succeed in your class.

**Introducing Expectations**
Post your *Expectations* and take the first week of school to discuss the interests behind each one using these discussion questions:
- How might this *Expectation* help you learn and achieve?
- What are some things I can do to support you to meet these *Expectations*?
- What are some steps you can take to meet these *Expectations*?

*Explain to students…*
- Here is how I will support you when you do not meet important *Expectations*.
- Here is what you will need to do if you do not meet important *Expectations*.

During the first week of school, facilitate a *Circle* p. 55 or *Anchor Experience* p. 54 that invites students to unpack some important *Expectations*. This will build students' understanding of and commitment to these expectations and will serve as an important touchstone in the weeks and months ahead, as individuals and the group monitor how they are meeting *Expectations*.

**Monitoring Expectations**
- During the first few weeks, through individual written Reflections, Exit Tickets (see p. 129), and *Whole Group Discussions*, invite students to share specific things they have done, individually and as a group, that indicate the ways they are meeting *Expectations*.
- When the group experiences challenges around meeting a particular *Expectation*, stop and review what it takes to meet it and solicit suggestions that will help the group get back on track.
- When the group has shown significant improvements, post a congratulations sign that validates their efforts.
- For each grading period, you might ask students to log their progress toward meeting each expectation at the midpoint and end-of-term (What *Expectation* do you consistently live up to? What might be an *Expectation* you want to focus on more during the next month?).

## Considerations

1. Specialized learning environments may determine some *Expectations*: "Thank you for treating our science equipment with care and using it safely."

2. A skill set that is essential for mastering course content may also be expressed as an *Expectation*: "Thank you for your commitment to writing coherent, error-free paragraphs that incorporate convincing arguments and detailed explanations."

3. Some teachers craft explicit *Expectations* related to achievement benchmarks: "I am confident each of you will pass this course, achieving a grade of at least 70%."

4. Unpacking *Expectations* about respect can be helpful, so students have a clear picture of what respect toward teachers and peers sounds and looks like. "Thank you for demonstrating respect by addressing people by the name they want to be called and focusing your attention on a person when someone is speaking to you."

## Strategy: *Academic Reflection, Goal-Setting, and Progress Tracking*

*Academic Reflection, Goal-Setting, and Progress Tracking* is an interdependent strategy that supports students' ownership of their learning and strengthens their academic efficacy. Opportunities for written and verbal *Reflection* enable students to review knowledge, skills, and mindsets essential for passing the course and to reflect on their successes and challenges. Ritualized *Goal-Setting* directs students' attention toward improving their grades, mastering essential skills, and taking concrete action steps to achieve their goals.[19] *Goal-Setting* is for everyone, from those who are working on earning a respectable passing grade to more advanced students who are pushing beyond a personal best. *Progress Tracking*, the process of revisiting goals and assessing progress toward meeting them, has proven to be a powerful tool for boosting grades, increasing pass rates, and increasing the percentage of students "on-track" to graduate from high school in four years.[20] All three parts of this strategy help students strengthen their persistence and accurately assess their effort and the quality of their work.

We recommend using a group *Academic Conferencing* protocol at strategic times during the year to facilitate this strategy. Although the give-and-take of more extended 1:1 student-teacher conversations has its obvious merits, group academic conferencing makes this strategy viable given that teaching loads can be up to 35 or 40 students in each class. Students are invited to write and think solo, and then share their thinking with a peer or the whole group; teachers walk around from student to student engaging in targeted mini-chats during the session.

### What It Looks Like: *Planning and Set-up*

- Wait three or four weeks before students do their first *Academic Reflection and Goal-Setting* so they are very familiar with the knowledge and skills required to meet proficiency standards, and they have an approximate sense of their current grade in the class.

- Schedule sessions in advance so that they correspond to school progress report benchmarks (mid-marking period, close of marking period). In order for this to be a meaningful experience, students should know their current grade in the course every time you schedule an *Academic Reflection and Goal-Setting* Session.

- If possible, provide a folder for each student and collect *Reflections* at the end of each session. By having all reflection documents in one place, teachers and students can review *Reflections* at various points in a semester and note trendlines. Teachers can offer selected comments and encouragements, particularly for students who need the extra touch point to stay invested. This creates a visible record of a student's successes and challenges throughout the year and can be shared in family/adult ally conferences and/or at grade-level team meetings.

- If possible, configure tables or desks in a circle or modified square, so it is easy for you to engage in "walk-around" conferencing, and easy for students to share their thinking with a partner or the whole group.

> **What It Looks Like:** *First Academic Reflection and Goal-Setting Conference*
>
> Students record successes and challenges so far, set learning goals for the first making period, and create action steps to meet their goals.
> See Appendix 7.2 – Academic Reflection, Goal-Setting, and Progress Tracking.
> See Appendix 7.3 – Sample Obstacles, Learning Goals, and Action Steps Foldable.

> **What It Looks Like:** *Reflection at Mid-Point of Each Marking Period*
>
> Students track their progress and adjust their learning goals and action steps if appropriate.

> **What It Looks Like:** *Reflections at Close of Each Marking Period*
>
> Students respond to questions that help them assess their overall progress for the marking period and review and adjust their learning goals and action steps if appropriate.

## Considerations

Consider scheduling an induction group conference during the 2nd or 3rd week of school to set the stage for *Reflection and Goal-Setting* early in the course. Students can prepare for the conference ahead of time by writing their responses to selected questions so that the entire session can be used to share responses in pairs, fours, or the whole group.

**Sample Induction Questions:**

- What are your hopes for this class?
- What are your hesitations?
- What are some things you might want to learn more about in this course?
- If this is a course subject that you don't think you might like very much, what will it take to make this class okay for you?
- What might be some things that are fairly easy for you to do well in class?
- What might feel like a challenge for you in this class?
- What kinds of help would you like when something is difficult to learn?
- What kinds of activities make the classroom a good place for you to learn?

### Strategy: *Anticipating and Planning for Learning Gaps*

A learning gap is a difference between what a student has learned—i.e., the academic progress he or she has made—and what the student was expected to learn within a given learning task or at a certain point in a learning unit, course, or grade level. It refers to the relative performance of individual learners.[21] This strategy enables teachers to anticipate when learning gaps are most likely to occur and which students are most likely to experience persistent learning gaps.

*Anticipating and Planning for Learning Gaps* empowers teachers to meet the needs of diverse learners in their class. When teachers anticipate areas of difficulty, normalize the variance in time for achieving learning outcomes, and provide support for all students to develop skills and competencies to master important content, they are more likely to meet students' academic challenges with a clear approach, proactive strategies, and patience. Learning gaps are attributable to several different sources:

- **Content:** Teachers may notice common confusions and misconceptions that surface year after year in the same learning unit. Observant teachers are also aware of specific course concepts or skills within the curriculum that are hard for most students to grasp and require deliberate, scaffolded instruction, and time to master.[22]
- **Instruction Gone Awry:** As teachers, most of us have had at least one uncomfortable experience of giving a unit test that a majority of students failed—and then asking ourselves, "Where and how might my instruction have been off the mark in ways that interfered with student mastery?"

**Persistent Academic Difficulties:** Some students may enter your classroom already detached from learning and may not yet see school as relevant to their personal lives.[23] Other students have not yet acquired the skills related to self-awareness, self-management, and academic efficacy to sustain the focus necessary to complete quality work consistently. Still others may experience difficulties linked to prior poor academic performance, identified learning disabilities, limited English proficiency, or ongoing emotional crisis or trauma.[24] Above all, many learners who struggle have not developed sufficient literacy skills to meet the reading, research, and writing demands associated with rigorous coursework.

Teachers' day-to-day observations and interactions can help pinpoint whether students' learning gaps might be more attributable to students not meeting grade level/developmental expectations for reading and writing skills, note-taking and organizing skills, and study and retention skills; difficulties in grasping abstract concepts, self-regulation, attention, and time-management skills; a lack of persistence to complete assignments, or an absence of prior knowledge relevant to the course content.

---

**What It Looks Like:** *Anticipating and Planning for Learning Gaps*

- Identify three or four learning gaps that are most likely to interfere with students' mastery of unit learning outcomes (knowledge, concepts, processes, or skills that prompt confusion and misunderstandings or prove to be very difficult for some students to grasp).
    - Within the unit, preview confusing and hard-to-grasp content.
    - Clearly explain what makes these concepts hard to understand.
    - Provide frequent checks for understanding as you move through this content.
    - Provide practice sessions in which students demonstrate their skill or understanding.
    - Provide additional time for the entire class or a cohort in the class to re-teach key knowledge and skills.
- Assess students' prior knowledge to support understanding new material through a quick five-item "What do you know?" formative assessment, a thumbs-up/thumbs-down group check-in to assess familiarity of with key terms and understandings, an index card on which students jot down five things they think they know about _____. If prior knowledge is absent for some, be prepared with a couple of electronic or printed resources that can provide students with a quick catch-up.
- Address typical issues of learners who struggle before patterns of failure become pronounced.[25] See Appendix 7.1 – Preparing for Five Kinds of Learners.
- Use graphic organizers in advance of a unit to show key concepts, big ideas, vocabulary, and skills students will encounter. See p. 87 for more information on Graphic Organizers.

> **What It Looks Like:** *Red Flags that Prompt Required Interventions*
>
> *Red Flags* (or early warning signs) are easy-to-recognize indicators that alert students when they have not met proficiency requirements in the course or when they show a downward slide in performance. *Red Flags* work best when they are tied to specific thresholds like:
>
> - Course grade average is below 70%.
> - Two or more major assignments are missing, incomplete, or uncorrected.
> - Test / summative assessment average is below 70%.
>
> When *Red Flags* are clearly communicated, students are more self-aware when their performance has triggered concern and more accepting of a teacher's help when an academic intervention is required.
>
> A standardized set of interventions is explored in Practice #9 Academic Interventions.

## Considerations

1. Meet with your course-alike cohort, interdisciplinary team, or department to think together and brainstorm the areas of a unit that might be confusing or misunderstood. Identify the strategies that all of you will incorporate to support student success.

2. Provide extended time for students to read, process, and represent what they are learning when using texts with a high degree of difficulty and complexity. Help students learn how to chunk text, and offer alternative texts when literacy gaps are profound.

3. As students get older, reading and vocabulary difficulties present the greatest barrier to improved performance. We have noticed that fewer and fewer middle and high schools have the resources to hire reading specialists or provide sophisticated resources for readers who are not meeting grade-level literacy expectations. One possible intervention for English language learners and students with significant literacy gaps is to establish a Reader's Club that meets once a week to unpack, discuss, and write about texts prior to students encountering the text in class. Teachers slow down the pace of tackling a text so that students can practice comprehension monitoring strategies, asking and answering questions, and summarizing passages to build reading competence and confidence.[26] This kind of session might be offered by a media or reading specialist during the school day, or by the teacher after school.

### Strategy: *Study Strategies*

Study skill strategies support students' academic success.[27] College readiness expert David Conley defines study skills as deliberate "strategies used to comprehend reading material and complete academic tasks; prepare for and take examinations; take class notes; organize, manage, and prioritize time and tasks; use information and resources efficiently; and utilize study groups, teachers, and advisors for maximum academic success."[28] One common feature of effective *Study Strategies* is the act of recapturing information using a different sensory mode (from writing to speaking) or different format (from written notes to a concept map or sketch). This process helps students to rethink, reorganize, synthesize, and remember information.[29] *"It's the retrieval from memory...that deepens learning and makes it stick."*[30] To clarify, memory retention increases when you study, a process that involves actively doing something with the material you are learning. In contrast, when you review, you are simply re-reading or scanning what you have already read, written, or created.

Carol Dweck's push for effort-based learning also stresses the importance of developing *Study Strategies* to improve academic performance.[31] The question for every teacher is how to embed *Study Strategies* into real-time instruction and preparation for important tests and performance tasks. Consider building a study culture from the beginning of your course by extending the length of time devoted to the very first learning unit. Provide time for students to create study tools that help them prepare for the end-of-unit test or performance assessment. Ask students to buddy up with a partner to practice using their tools. After the test is returned and reviewed, invite students to rate the effectiveness of their study tools and share ways that the pre-test study session helped them improve their performance. Try making the use of *Study Strategies* a routine practice within every learning unit. Taking the time to front-load "how to study for this course" sends students the message that studying is critical to mastering the course content and earning good grades.

### What It Looks Like: *Study Strategies*

Five types of proven-effective *Study Strategies* emphasize *comprehension, organization, rehearsal, practice, and elaboration*.[32] Prioritize the study strategies you offer, choosing the ones most relevant to mastering the content in your course.

### Comprehension Strategies

**Comprehension:** Deepening understanding of what is read, heard, viewed, or demonstrated.

1. Teach students how to take meaningful and substantive notes. This will help students retrieve, organize, and cull the right information. (*Representing to Learn* p. x for more on note-taking)
2. Teach students to highlight, edit, and mark up their notes with the goals of evaluating: a) what they know and what they have questions about; b) what concepts and ideas are fully annotated and which ones need more specifics; c) what discipline-specific vocabulary words are clearly defined and which ones need more detail or examples; and d) what sample problems, graphs, formulae, or processes need more explanation.
3. For essay questions that students can prepare for in advance, re-read supporting information from notes and/or related readings and create a set of bullet points that address the question.

### Organization Strategies

**Organization:** Sorting, chunking, prioritizing, and synthesizing key information from notes and other resources.[33]

1. Create a unit map that helps answer the essential question for the learning unit and forces you to sort and select only what is essential: for example, 3 key understandings; 7 key terms; 4 steps that explain; 3 reasons why; 5 properties or characteristics of …
2. Create a graphic organizer to chart a cycle or sequence of events; explain causal relationships; show connections among important concepts.
3. Make an "evidence of study" card a requirement that students submit before they:
4. Take a test.
5. Participate in a discussion or text seminar.
6. Deliver a presentation, performance, or demonstration.

### Rehearsal Strategies

**Rehearsal:** Using oral strategies to strengthen recall of precise information and complicated explanations that are difficult to remember.

1. Say the topic and then repeat the precise information at least three times out loud; pause and work on something else; then repeat the same process.
2. Rehearse complicated explanations out loud as if you were teaching it to someone. Even better, find someone to teach it to, and invite that person to ask questions that probe for deeper understanding.
3. Using flash cards, read the question out loud, and then say the answer out loud. Return to same questions and answers at least two more times within a day or two.

### Practice Strategies

**Practice:** Deliberate repetition of a process to demonstrate mastery of a specific skill.

1. Complete multiple samples of a model problem that are error-free.
2. Create your own set of practice problems that meet specific criteria.
3. Find and correct spelling and grammar errors using multiple sample paragraphs.
4. Use the same graphic organizer to capture key information every time you are preparing for a written unit test.

### Elaboration

**Elaboration:** Providing details and examples to explain key understandings, principles, or processes; making meaningful connections between new and more familiar information.

1. Generate examples of a key term or concept that are relevant to your own life experiences.
2. Create a five letter acronym in which each letter identifies an important detail or example.
3. On a large index card use the front side to summarize an important idea and use the back side to write down examples, details, relationships, and questions that expand on your understanding.
4. Imagine a walk-through of your house, touching objects as you go that represent specific facts related to a topic or parts of a cycle, formula, principle, or category of things.

## Considerations

1. Meet with your course-alike cohort, interdisciplinary team, or department to identify note-taking and *Study Strategies* that can be reinforced from course to course.
2. Invite students to use "Quizlet: Learning Tools and Flashcards for Free https://quizlet.com/.
3. Some teachers allow students to use their "evidence of study" cards during the test. This encourages students to make this a habit. The content that students can organize and cluster on a 4 x 6 index card can be quite impressive.

**Strategy:** *Revise, Edit/Proof, and Correct*

Providing opportunities for students to *Revise, Edit/Proof, and Correct* their work is a highly effective strategy for improving both quality and accuracy.[34] Students' written submissions, whether a unit test, a series of math problems, a science lab, or an essay, remain the primary means of assessment in high school and college. Improving a final product involves several steps:

**Revise:** Re-think and make changes that push for clarity of organization, coherence, sequence, content, vision, and purpose of a piece of writing, a visual product, a project, performance, or presentation. This includes improving the quality and depth of specific sections, arguments, explanations, or descriptions.

**Edit/Proof:** Improve the overall quality of writing by checking for clarity and sophistication of language and word choice and eliminating errors in spelling, punctuation, and grammar, and ensuring the use of more formal language conventions.[35]

**Correct:** After an assessment, project, or assignment has been returned to a student, they fix errors or complete the product, so that the final version meets a designated level of quality (a specific grade, corrected solution, or content that is error free).

In a study focused on college writing, instructors stressed that writing is a developmental process. *"Students don't understand that writing is a craft that you improve and you're constantly improving and that it's not as if you can write or you can't."*[36]

In a culture that values speed and immediate results, the idea of revisiting the same task after a first effort feels like a counter-intuitive process. Written work demands deliberate efforts to slow down one's thinking rather than speed it up. Students need to know that the habit of *Revising, Editing/Proofing, and Correcting* one's work is a prized asset in the workplace and in college courses. This academic press strategy supports every student to meet a higher level of quality, from developing writers to those who are more advanced.

See Appendix 7.4 – Student Checklist for Revising, Editing/Proofing for Expository Writing.

| **What It Looks Like:** *Revise, Edit/Proof, Correct* |
|---|
| *Revision* Tasks in Any Course: |
| <ul><li>Set aside independent time for individuals or pairs to revise using a Student Checklist for *Revise, Edit/Proof, Correct* to improve content quality and ensure that necessary elements of the product are present.</li><li>Use student work samples to review: "What is working? What is missing? What is unclear? What is extraneous/off- point? What is lacking in evidence or detail?"</li><li>Ask students to complete a 3-2-1 Exit Ticket when they turn in their product drafts:<ul><li>3 strengths / pluses</li><li>2 things I am unsure about</li><li>1 thing I can improve</li></ul></li><li>Present students with a high-challenge "Problem of the Week" that you know will require some re-thinking and re-working in order to arrive at a correct solution. Check in with the group at mid-week and present solutions on Friday.</li><li>For paper and pencil tests, take the last five minutes to ask students to circle three written responses that they commit to re-reading and correcting or improving before they turn in the test.</li></ul> |

| |
|---|
| *Edit/Proof* Tasks |
| **English/Language Arts, Social Studies, Science, Foreign Language:**<br>• Use student work samples to practice (1) making effective edits that improve word choice and (2) finding and correcting errors in spelling, grammar, and language conventions.<br>• Set aside a specific amount of time for independent or peer *Editing/Proofing* before turning in the final product.<br>**Math:**<br>• Before students turn in multi-step performance tasks or problems, engage in peer *Editing/Proofing* looking for accuracy of solutions. |

| |
|---|
| *Correction* Tasks in Any Course: |
| • "Excellence Portfolio Entry" – every quarter students choose one major performance task, paper, or project to correct and complete to an A level quality of work.<br>• "*Correction* Central" – cull student responses on test items (short answers, brief paragraphs, math problems, etc.) that contain multiple errors. Ask students to work individually or in pairs to identify and correct all errors.<br>• "No Grade Until" – a final grade on a test is not submitted until the student has completed minimal corrections to attain 75% proficiency. |

## Considerations

1. One of the best tools for improving writing is requiring students to write a one paragraph precis every week that summarizes a specific argument, opinion, explanation, or narrative from a challenging text or brief article. Students continue to *Revise, Edit/Proof, and Correct* based upon teacher and/or peer feedback until it is clear and error free. This task works equally well for explicating a math problem or scientific principle, explaining a government law, or capturing the theme of a literary work.

2. Collaborate with a grade level team, course-alike cohort, or department members to establish a set of editing symbols to support all students across a grade or all students taking courses in the same department.

**Strategy:** *Guided Work Period*

*Guided Work Period (GWP)* is a strategy to support academic efficacy in our students. It is an environment that offers students high structure and high support to prioritize and manage their time and tasks, and experiment with a range of *Study Strategies* such as *Revise, Edit/Proof, and Correct* in order to complete quality work and receive additional support, as needed. *GWP* can be incorporated regularly into a course and can also serve as a foundational structure for an Intervention Period. *GWP* is distinct from a traditional study hall as the teacher plays a pivotal role in helping students acquire the skills and target behaviors to become more self-directed learners. A *Guided Work Period* offers students:

- An intentional "work culture" where the expectations are to engage with a learning task and bring it to completion with effort and quality;
- Individual 1:1 check-ins with the teacher to confer about their goals, the learning task they are working on, or to make a plan for the period; and
- Tier 2 Academic Interventions in 1:1 or small group formats (see Practice #9: Academic Interventions) for students who need additional and targeted support.

For students who struggle with school, *GWP* is an opportunity for them to practice basic work habits, complete a task, and experience a measure of success. High-achieving students also benefit from this structure which helps them fine-tune time management and prioritization skills and supports conversations with the teacher about managing stress or taking intellectual risks. Ultimately, *GWP* supports all students to practice the academic efficacy skill set in real-time.

> **What It Looks Like:** *Guided Work Period*
>
> 1. Teachers *Meet and Greet* students at the door to make sure they have the necessary materials for *Guided Work Period*.
> 2. Students enter the classroom, retrieve their student data folder, and take their seats. This folder, kept in a designated place in your classroom, can be used to store students' *Guided Work Period* tracker, *Academic Reflection, Goal Setting and Progress Tracking* sheets and student data.
> 3. As a group, students generate a list of possible "to-dos" for *GWP* and the teacher lists these on the board. If the *GWP* occurs in a class, course projects, upcoming tests and homework assignments might be identified as well as steps for accomplishing particular tasks and study strategies in preparation for an exam. If conducted in an Intervention Period, students might lift up assignments from a variety of classes. This provides all students with the landscape of the work ahead and will help many prioritize their choice.
> 4. The teacher draws attention to a posted list of students they will be conducting check-ins or working with during the *GWP* session and directs students to a poster or other visual aid that outlines *GWP* guidelines and relevant *Expectations*.
> 5. Students fill out their *GWP* tracker with the task they will work on, their reasons for prioritizing this task and a prediction for how long it will take them to complete it, and place it on their desks.
> 6. The teacher circulates to determine who might need some support before engaging in check-ins or working with the identified individuals or groups.
> 7. The teacher ends the session by (1) reminding students to indicate on their tracker what they accomplished (2) asking students to organize their materials and store their folders and (3) reminding students to follow the Exit Procedure (see *Ending Class*, p. 71).

## Considerations

1. When launching *GWP*, Model and Teach guidelines and purpose to build student commitment to the strategy ("What are some ways *Guided Work Period* might support you as a learner?" "What are some things we might hear/see everyone doing when *Guided Work Period* is really humming along?") and draw connections to relevant *Expectations* or LLC target behaviors ("What might it look like to respect the rights of each member of class to learn in a safe classroom during *Guided Work Period*?" "What are some things you might consider when prioritizing a task?").

2. Incorporate *GWP* often enough to support students in understanding and being self-directed with the guidelines. Hold off on conducting 1:1 check-ins or integrating Tier 2 interventions until *GWP* is firmly in place.

3. Be prepared to think flexibly about students who arrive to *Guided Work Periods* without necessary resources (for example, invite them to talk to a student who has the same class, encourage them to practice *Study Strategies* (see p. 118), conduct a check-in with the student to review *GWP* guidelines or facilitate a *Coaching* session on a relevant skill).

# PRACTICE #8: Formative Assessment

Formative assessment is one of the most robust levers for increasing student achievement and can be particularly helpful for students who are struggling academically.[37] We define formative assessment as real-time, reciprocal student-teacher feedback that enables teachers to: (1) assess students' skill acquisition and understanding; (2) provide feedback that supports students to close learning gaps and correct errors and misunderstandings in order to successfully meet learning outcomes; and (3) adjust next steps for instruction.[38]

Formative assessment is non-threatening because it is not about a grade.[39] Instead, it focuses a student's attention on improving the level and quality of understanding or performance. *"Formative assessment supports the expectation that all students can meet important proficiency standards and counteracts the cycle in which students attribute poor performance to lack of ability and therefore become permanently discouraged or unwilling to invest in further learning."*[40] Formative assessment communicates to students that they can improve as a result of thoughtful effort when they have the right learning strategies to use.

The formative assessment strategies presented in this section meet three important criteria. They are proven to have a high impact on student learning; they foster academic engagement; and they can be embedded in any lesson relatively easily.[41]

---

**Benefits of Formative Assessment**

- Supports students to become more comfortable speaking about and assessing their own learning.
- Supports students' deepened understanding of key knowledge and skills.
- Helps teachers to accurately assess content mastery, diagnose learning gaps, target academic support to individual students, and adjust lessons to meet the needs of different learners.
- Normalizes errors, misconceptions, and confusions, which are part of the learning process.

**Learning and Life Competencies Aligned with the Practice**

- Self-Management: I demonstrate perseverance and resiliency.
- Social Efficacy: I communicate and problem-solve effectively.
- Academic Efficacy: I invest in quality work, and I set goals and self-assess.

---

### Strategy: *Academic Check-ins*

*Academic Check-ins* enable teachers to assess in "real time" what a student is learning, doing, or thinking at a particular point in the lesson or unit.[42] When teachers show an interest and are prepared to lean in and listen, even the most reluctant learners eventually become comfortable with the idea of sharing their work out loud. By helping students verbalize their thinking in the moment, *Academic Check-ins* boost confidence in a student's academic efficacy to share what they like or are excited about, talk through problems and pinpoint their misconceptions or confusions more precisely.

Incorporating 2-3 minute *Academic Check-ins* as a ritualized weekly practice ensures that every student engages with the teacher several times a month. Some teachers schedule at least two opportunities for *Academic Check-ins* every week. Choosing the right learning tasks and assignments, and collecting relevant data will generate rich thinking and conversations.

> **What It Looks Like:** *Academic Check-in Protocol*
>
> 1. Inform the class that you will move around and check in with students to hear their smart thinking and questions, which will help you support their learning.
> 2. To build rapport, approach the student for a one-to-one check-in by moving to their side, positioning yourself at the same level as the student, and greeting the student by name.
> 3. Use a simple three-question sequence to help students think about where they are in the learning process or completion of a task.
>
>    **a. What are you working on?**
>    - Example: "Hi, Renee. Where are you in the lab?"
>    - Example: "Hey Lilah. Show me where you are right now with your timeline."
>
>    **b. How is it going?**
>    - Example: "What are your thoughts and feelings about your essay so far?"
>    - Example: "How are is your geometric proof coming along?"
>
>    **c. What are you going to do next?**
>    - Example: "Describe for me what you are going to work on next?"
>    - Example: "Now that you figured that out, what might you do next?"

## Considerations

1. When clearing up errors, confusions, or misconceptions, point to any written cues, procedures, or directions that might help students to make improvements or corrections on their own.
2. For students who have a tendency to do just enough to get by, add this question: "What can you do to make it even more clear / descriptive / evidence-based / expressive?
3. Think about the frequency of *Check-ins* needed to reach optimal improvement and mastery. Some teachers schedule at least two opportunities for *Academic Check-ins* every week.

### Strategy: *Walk-around Look-fors*

While students work independently or in small groups, the teacher walks around collecting data on what students understand and can do and what students do not yet understand or cannot yet do related to the learning outcome. For the teacher, this data clarifies the skills or understandings students are demonstrating. Based on the patterns observed, the teacher determines next steps for instruction (i.e., students need additional teaching, the whole class is ready for the next step, a few students need some additional feedback and supports).

Each week craft your *"Look-fors"* ahead of time for two reasons: (1) they will be much more thoughtful and precise; and (2) You can take the telescopic view of your week and choose to embed *Look-fors* into the activities that will yield critical information to support student learning and guide your instruction.

> **What It Looks Like:** *Walk-around Look-fors*
>
> *"As you start working on the homework, I am going to walk around to see how everyone's doing with simplifying the exponential expression."* The teacher walks around and documents how many students are able to simplify the expression and any trends in mistakes that are being made.
>
> *"I'm going to be looking for the research question you've formulated and the list of possible topics relevant to your question."* The teacher walks around and checks that topics are relevant to the research question, documenting trends.
>
> *"I'm going to be looking for how you provide text evidence for each of the three questions in your two column notes. Be sure you document the page and location of evidence."* The teacher moves from student to student to assess the quality and quantity of evidence students are citing.
>
> *"As you're working in your groups, I'm going to be listening for ways you're working cooperatively and doing your fair share of work."* The teacher walks around documenting participation levels by all group members.

### Considerations:

Identify a tracking system to collect, organize, and update data on individual students and the group at large, using a viable structure that aligns with your style. Some teachers hole-punch a set of index cards enclosed with a metal ring, assigning one student to each index card. Others create an easy-to-use spreadsheet or use a bound notebook to keep a running record, assigning a page to each student. Some teachers use a technology format to collect data on their students. This will serve you well when planning the next lesson/unit, arranging student conferences or family meetings, and collaborating with grade-level team members when you are troubleshooting around individuals who have fallen behind or repeatedly struggle and are in need of additional supports and interventions.

### Strategy: *Feedback for Self-correction*

When students' understanding of an idea or execution of a task is incorrect, the number one temptation is to simply supply the answer ourselves, correct the error for the student, or provide a precise "how-to" for fixing it in the spirit of helpfulness and efficiency. *Feedback for Self-correction* is a more nuanced strategy for addressing learning gaps, which requires the student to wrestle with their thinking and take responsibility for their learning. *Feedback for Self-correction* communicates what a teacher has observed, heard, seen, read, and/or noticed that indicates errors, confusion, or misunderstandings. Also, *Feedback for Self-correction* provides students with clues, concrete suggestions, or a mini re-teach that supports them to play a more proactive role in identifying the cause of the error or confusion and then correcting it themselves, which enhances their engagement and academic efficacy.

*Feedback for Self-correction* can be as simple as a brief written, visual or oral prompt or be incorporated into an *Academic Check-in* that supports smart problem-solving. As well, *Feedback for Self-correction* can be provided to an individual student, a small cooperative group, or to the whole group based upon trends the teacher is noticing. Finally, this strategy can be done in the moment or the next day, after reviewing Exit Tickets, for example. When it is done effectively, the process pushes students to do the kind of thinking that results in deep learning and ownership.

> **What It Looks Like:** *Feedback for Self-correction*
>
> **Examples:**
> - The teacher puts a dot (•) at the end of any line that includes a run-on or sentence fragment.
> - "I'm noticing some missing steps in your proofs. Look again at the suggested steps and identify the step you're on."
> - "Go back and highlight evidence in your middle paragraphs that shows you have met the rubric criteria."
> - "Circle all relevant variables connected to your research problem."
> - "I'm not seeing evidence of groups working productively yet. Look at the T-charts we created. Commit to two behaviors you're going to demonstrate in the next 5 minutes."
> - "In reviewing yesterday's Exit Tickets, I noticed that there was some confusion about the differences between _____ and _____. Let's turn to our notes and look for the definition of each term."
> - "About half of you solved the problem correctly, and about half of you are showing some confusions. For those of you who didn't arrive at a correct solution, take a moment to circle the step where you think you got off track. Now pair up with someone who got it right and talk through where the error occurred and then finish solving the problem correctly."

## Considerations

It takes time and practice to provide high-quality, *Feedback for Self-correction* in the moment. So, begin practicing this strategy by crafting *Feedback for Self-correction* prompts ahead of time in situations when:

- You are absolutely sure that a sizable number of students are going to experience some kind of difficulty with the task;
- You have reviewed student work and you are providing *Feedback for Self-correction* the following day; and
- You have asked students to identify their "confusions" on an Exit Ticket, and you will close the confusion loop the next day.

### Strategy: *Five-minute Assessment Tools*

"In-the-moment" *Five-minute Assessment Tools* provide snapshots of student understanding and skills at specific points in a lesson. The teacher asks all students to demonstrate their current understanding of the content, skill, or process by responding to a universal prompt that all students are required to complete. This formative assessment strategy offers teachers immediate insights into student learning and an immediate opportunity to clarify student thinking.
The teacher and students, depending on the tool, look for patterns to leverage strengths, or identify areas of confusion to support re-teaching and clarification. Consistent and systematic implementation of these *Five-minute Assessment Tools* builds students' commitment and accountability to persevere through challenging learning tasks and complete them with pride and satisfaction. They also support students' investment, effort, participation, and goodwill.

### What It Looks Like: *Most Important Point (MIP)*

- A MIP is a quick way to check for broad understanding after a text reading, video, demonstration, or mini-lecture.
- Pass out an index card or sticky note to each student.
- Ask students to jot down their MIP that captures the main idea.
- Share out responses with the group or post responses and cluster them to lift up responses that are on-target and unpack responses that are off the mark.

### What It Looks Like: *Mini-Whiteboards*

Mini whiteboards serve to engage individuals or pairs in making a response visible to their group or the entire class so they can self-check their understanding of knowledge or skills. They can be used with a variety of learning tasks. For example when students have to:

- Re-read a key passage and craft a summary sentence.
- Generate questions to deepen understanding of the current topic.
- Capture a key idea in one statement or headline.
- Hone estimation and quick reasoning skills using multiple choice test questions. Ask students to post the answer they think is most reasonable on the left and post the least reasonable response on the right and then invite students to share the reasoning behind their choices.
- "One Word, One Headline, One Sentence," described above, can be used in conjunction with mini-whiteboards.

Procedure:

1. Provide the prompt and how much time students will have.
2. Circulate, monitor, and support students to focus on the learning task.
3. Ask students to hold up their whiteboards. Move about and take a few minutes to read responses around the room.
4. Have several pairs or individuals share their responses, and ask the group: What are some trends you noticed? What are some things you might have learned from others' responses on the whiteboards? What responses might you have questions about?
5. After the students have reflected on what they heard and saw, comment on the accuracy of responses to "one answer" questions, the range of responses to questions with many possible answers or solutions, any patterns you noticed in the responses, or share any questions or wonderings that emerge from observations and comments.

**Tip:** Instead of purchasing whiteboards, try using white card stock placed in clear plastic protective covers and dry-erase markers.

> **What It Looks Like:** *Exit Tickets*
>
> Students are given a "ticket" before the lesson ends and turn in their tickets as they leave the classroom. Teachers scan the responses and share what they learned from students' responses in the next class (themes and patterns, misconceptions, incomplete understanding) and adjust the lesson if some re-teaching is required.
>
> Exits Tickets are used to:
> - Check for understanding of a key concept presented in the day's lesson.
> - Check for proficiency of a key skill presented in the day's lesson.
> - Provide feedback on the day's lesson.
> - Reflect on Learning and Life Competencies used in class today.
> - Solicit questions that emerged from the day's lesson.
> - Make connections between lesson content and students' thoughts and experiences.
> - Link lesson content to real-world application.

**Considerations:**

1. We encourage teachers to identify a handful of *Five-minute Assessment Tools* that align with their course content and class culture that they will use time and again. This enables the teacher to become practiced in the implementation of the strategy, which will ensure that they systematically embed it into the unit/lesson. Just as importantly, students will come to value the tool, as they know that the teacher cares about their success, wants to hear their voice, and will support them when confusions arise.

2. When you want to incorporate collaborative thinking into formative assessment tasks, ask students to work in pairs when using *Five-minute Assessment Tools*.

## PRACTICE #9: Academic Interventions

Academic Interventions are the logical follow-through step when a student experiences repeated difficulty after a variety of Tier 1 strategies have been implemented. Academic interventions involve an assessment of a student's academic, social, or emotional challenges and the creation of a plan for addressing the learning gap or other problems that have presented barriers to learning. Establishing thresholds or red flags that prompt required interventions keeps your readiness to intervene front and center and lets students know in advance what will be required of them when you notice a slippage (see *Anticipating and Planning for Learning Gaps* on p. 116). Academic interventions, whether they focus on skill development, academic efficacy, or social behaviors, need to be delivered within the context of caring conversations, emotional support, and confidence-building that inspire students to place value on academic success and activate their desire to succeed through sustained effort.

Tier 2 teacher-facilitated interventions need to have a specific endpoint that both supports academic success and builds students' capacity to think and work independently.[43] Academic interventions usually involve four steps.

1. The first step is conducting an *Academic Problem-solving and Planning Conference* to discuss specific learning or behavior gaps and develop a plan for addressing the gap.
2. The second step is determining the combination of remediation, *Coaching*, or guided practice that will help students meet their goals.
3. The third step is *Progress Monitoring*: a systemized process for assessing the student's growth in relation to an academic skill goal or target behavior, their rate of improvement, and their responsiveness to the intervention developed. This is an essential step for any intervention plan.
4. The final step is contacting a parent or guardian to briefly discuss the academic learning gap, share the plan for improvement, and get feedback from the family (see Chapter 11, The Value of Teacher-Family Partnerships).

> **Benefits of Academic Interventions**
> - Closes learning gaps, supports students to meet learning outcomes, and turns around a downward academic trajectory.
> - Fosters positive student-teacher relationships.
> - Promotes student accountability and conscious use of desired behaviors.
> - Helps students develop an accurate assessment of performance and makes progress visible.
>
> **Learning and Life Competencies Aligned with the Practice**
> - Self-Management: I identify, express, and manage my emotions, exhibit self-regulation, and I demonstrate perseverance and resiliency.
> - Social Efficacy: I communicate and problem-solve effectively.
> - Academic Efficacy: I invest in quality work, organize to learn and study, and I set goals and self-assess.

### Strategy: *Academic Problem-solving and Planning Conference*

When learning gaps impede academic success and high functioning in the classroom, a private *Academic Problem-solving and Planning Conference* is a platform for changing a student's academic trajectory. The focus in this *Conference* is sharing a discrete academic skill or target behavior related to academic efficacy that the student needs to focus on. Our role is not to fix the problem and tell the student exactly what to do; rather, our role is to listen with empathy, pause, and paraphrase and invite and empower students to explore actions steps that will help them strengthen their academic skill and or target behavior to improve their performance. See Appendix 7.5 – Responsive Listening. The tone of these *Conferences* is hopeful because students walk away with a plan. The conference itself presents authentic opportunities for students to practice LLC target behaviors that include verbalizing one's needs, expressing emotions skillfully, solving problems, and setting goals.

*Conferences* can last between 15-20 minutes, and will most likely take place outside of class, during scheduled team time, a planning period, lunch, or after school. Consider setting aside one hour per week for individual *Conferencing* with students outside of the classroom. Use student data from *Academic Reflection, Goal-Setting, and Progress Tracking* group *Conferences* to identify and prioritize students who would benefit the most from a 1:1 *Academic Problem-solving and Planning Conference*.

See Appendix 7.6 – Academic Problem-Solving and Planning Conference Protocol.
See Appendix 7.7 – Academic Problem-Solving and Planning Conference Template.
See Appendix 7.8 – Academic Card Sort: Sample Action Steps.

Academic Support

**Strategy:** *Progress Monitoring*

*Progress Monitoring* is an essential element of all effective intervention plans.[44] It involves the systematic assessment of a student's regular use of target behaviors or academic skills that support improved academic performance. Unless teachers monitor progress and students receive feedback about the target behavior or skill they are working on, there is no way to accurately assess their growth and rate of improvement or determine whether the intervention and your support have actually produced the desired outcome.

The student self-assesses daily and the teacher provides a weekly rating; ideally, at the end of the week. The student and teacher do a quick review to assess whether the trendline indicates improvement, slippage, or no change, and they make any needed adjustments to action steps that support the desired end behavior. If a student's self-awareness is low, the teacher can step in to highlight areas of growth and areas that continue to need attention and care.

*Progress Monitoring* has other benefits as well when students are actively involved in the process. It fosters positive student-teacher relationships, promotes student accountability and agency, increases a student's awareness and conscious use of target behaviors, and strengthens a student's confidence and efficacy by making progress visible.

Effective *Progress Monitoring* tools share the following features:[45]

- The target behavior or academic skill and action steps are described as concretely as possible. See Appendix 7.8 - Academic Card Sort: Sample Action Steps.
- The rating scale for evaluating the regular use of the behavior is simple and standardized.
- The rating is recorded immediately at the end of the class period by the student, and the teacher provides a weekly rating to discuss with the student at the end of the week. Some teachers may select to provide a daily rating.
- *Progress Monitoring* continues for at least three weeks to track sustainable improvement. During this time it is important to check in with parents about the student's progress.
- The *Progress Monitoring* tool is easy to use and requires just seconds to record.

**FIGURE 7.3** Target Behavior or Skills and Action Steps

| Target Behavior or Skill | Action Step |
|---|---|
| I complete assigned tasks regularly. | • I complete the "Reflect and Connect" within 5 minutes every day.<br>• I use a checklist to mark off tasks completed for the week and show it to Ms._____.<br>• I share my work with a study partner to check for completion. |
| I solve algebraic word problems correctly. | • I re-read directions and write them in my own words before I begin so I know what to do.<br>• I use my word problem checklist to unpack word problems and solve them.<br>• I put out my "help sign" when I'm stuck and need support to do the next step. |
| I take turns, listen to and encourage others, and do my fair share. | • I ask to hear other points-of-view. "What do you think, Pilar?"<br>• I paraphrase what someone has said at least once a class period to show that I am listening.<br>• I say or do at least two things every day that show I am contributing to a group discussion, helping to complete a group product, or achieve the goal of a learning activity. |

See Appendix 7.9 – Sample Progress Monitoring Tool.

**Strategy:** *Academic Turnaround Plan*

Earning a D or F at mid-marking period or end of marking period is a red flag that should prompt an intervention with students within one or two weeks. An *Academic Turnaround Plan* is intended to interrupt a persistent pattern of academic slippage and help students identify target behaviors or academic skills that will help them improve their grade by the end of the marking period.

We recommend supporting students to create their *Academic Turnaround Plans* by facilitating a group *Conference* during class, while other students are engaged in independent learning tasks. Setting aside time to have a conversation with students about their academic challenges is the most direct way to communicate your belief that all of your students are capable of meeting the academic expectations you set for your course. Messaging to your class that you will meet with groups of students for different reasons throughout the year enables you to implement *Academic Turnaround Conferences* in your classroom with success.

---

**What It Looks Like:** *Academic Turnaround Plan*

Below is a preview of the questions students will respond to, to develop their Academic Turnaround Plan.

- Identify obstacles: *"What are one or two obstacles that got in my way of passing the class or earning better than a D grade?"*
- Identify learning goal: *"What is a learning goal (target behavior or academic skill)I want to work on?"*
- Identify action steps: *"What are two to three specific action steps I want to take to meet my learning goal and improve my grade?"*
- Identify desired grade: *"What grade do I plan to earn for the next marking period?"*
- Identify supports: *"What can my teacher do to help me achieve my learning goal and my target grade?"*
- Acknowledge emotions: *"So, what are some of your thoughts and feelings about this plan?"*

---

**What it Looks Like:** *Group Academic Turnaround Conference*

1. *Circle* students up for the conference.
2. Welcome students by appreciating their commitment to take steps to turnaround their grades.
3. Hand out the *Academic Turnaround Plan* and Foldable (see Appendix 7.10 – Academic Turnaround Plan, and Appendix 7.3 – Sample Obstacles, Learning Goals, and Action Steps Foldable).
4. Give students a few minutes to complete their *Academic Turnaround Plans* and answer any questions that arise.
5. Spend most of the session walking around from student to student to:
   - Review the plans that students have developed so far: *"So, let's take a look at your plan to see if you are good to go, and if you have any remaining questions or thoughts."*
   - Make additional suggestions: *"Here are one or two more things I would like you to consider doing to meet your learning goal and improve your grade."*
   - Communicate your support: *"I have confidence that you can do this. I will check in with you every week to discuss how your plan is working. Thanks for making this commitment."*
6. Invite students to share their learning goals and action steps out loud with a partner or the group. Sharing fosters student accountability, builds commitment and confidence, and encourages peer support. Encourage students to support one another in and outside of class.
7. Hand out the *Progress Monitoring* tool: *Let's take a look at your progress monitoring tool. This helps you track your progress, and it helps me support you.* Have students fill in their *Progress Monitoring* tool and collect them. See Appendix 7.9 – Sample Progress Monitoring Tool.
8. Make an appreciative comment to close the conference: *"Thank you again for your focus today. I am here to support you, and I know that you will take the steps you need to, to meet your learning goal and get the grade you want. You reach out to me with any questions you might have."*

### Post-Conference

- Copy each student's *Progress Monitoring* tool (see Appendix 7.9 – Sample Progress Monitoring Tool) and make a packet with enough copies for the remainder of the marking period for each student. Place them in a folder where the students can pick them up at the start of a class.
- Check in with parent or guardian to share the plan using a version of this suggested script:
    1. "Good evening, my name is _____ and I teach your son/daughter in _____."
    2. Say something positive or interesting that you have noticed about the student. *"He has told me about his interest in _____."*
    3. "I am calling because _____ earned a/an _____ in the course this marking period and I want to support him to improve his grade next marking period."
    4. "_____ and I have discussed his grade and _____ has made a plan to earn at least a _____. _____ has agreed to _____."
    5. "Do you have any questions or ideas for how I might support _____ to do his best?"
    6. "I will be checking in every week to monitor _____ progress. I will contact you to let you know how it is going. Is a phone call, email, or text message the best way to reach you?"
    7. "Is there anything else that is on your mind?"
    8. "Thank you so much for listening. I really appreciate your support, and I am confident that _____ will be more successful next marking period."
- Check in with the students weekly for the remainder of the marking period to assess progress. Each week the teacher provides three items of feedback: (1) the grade for the week; (2) one thing the student has done well; and (3) one thing the student can improve. You might meet with students individually, you might have a time in your week where you meet with them in a group, or you might hand out their *Progress Monitoring* tools and have them read them independently. It will be important to sort out your communication plan with families to keep them in the loop to support their child.

### Strategy: *Academic Coaching*

*Academic Coaching* sessions provide time for individuals or small groups to engage in saturated practice of a specific target behavior or skill; to engage in guided study time to prepare for tests; to complete, revise, or correct important work; or to re-learn or begin to learn a skill required to complete current learning tasks.

The most viable time slot for facilitating *Academic Coaching* sessions is during regular class time. Many teachers ritualize this time by scheduling at least two independent work times of twenty minutes or more during class every week when they can offer additional instruction and coaching to individuals and small groups. Scheduling *Academic Coaching* sessions outside of the regular class period will depend on the school schedule, teacher availability, and student availability. Some schools provide an intervention period during the school day or offer an end-of-day tutorial period several times a week that is written into teacher contracts. Still, other schools establish an expected professional norm that teachers set aside one hour a week before or after school, or during lunch to work with students.

## What It Looks Like: *Academic Coaching*

**1:1** *Academic Coaching Session*

1:1 *Academic Coaching* sessions provide time for students to work on their action steps related to the behaviors or skills they want to improve as a result of an *Academic Problem-solving and Planning Conference* or *Academic Turnaround Plan*. This kind of personalized coaching session can also be assigned to students whose performance has raised a red flag that prompts a required intervention session. (For example, non-completion of two or more major assignments equals a *Coaching* session to suss out the challenges and make progress toward completing the assignments).

**Small Group Work Session or Test Preparation**

Small group guided study sessions involve students who are tackling the same challenge: they need extra time and guidance to complete, revise, or correct the same assignment, or they need extra time and guidance to prepare for the same test or performance task. The teacher lays out the goal and directions for the guided study session, clarifies any confusions and questions, and engages in *Academic Check-ins* with students throughout the session.

**Small Group Skill Clinics**

Small group *Academic Coaching* sessions bring students together who need a more saturated dose of re-teaching and guided practice related to a very specific skill set. For example:

- **Math:** strengthening math fact automaticity and estimation skills or solving linear equations and explaining solutions
- **Science:** re-writing chemistry labs to meet proficiency requirements or re-teaching fundamentals of electric circuits
- **English-Language Arts:** working on paragraph construction or practicing pre-reading strategies to increase comprehension
- **Social Studies:** making meaning of specialized vocabulary related to the Constitution or improving written responses to document-based questions (DBQs)

Small group *Academic Coaching* sessions enable teachers to reach more students who need additional assistance. These sessions also invite students to help and encourage each other.

## Considerations

1. One way to lighten the load for individual teachers is to collaborate with other course-alike teachers to offer a variety of *Academic Coaching* sessions after school or during an intervention period; each teacher becomes an expert facilitator for specific topics, and students can be assigned to the coaching session that best addresses their current learning gap.

2. Consider scheduling an "end of unit catch-up day" near the close of a learning unit when all students can update the status of their course work and prepare final "to-do's" before the unit ends.

## Closing

Providing more saturated academic support to all learners, especially to adolescents who struggle, can have a greater impact on students' grades and academic performance than any other intentional change you choose to make in your teaching practice. Ensuring that academic support is incorporated into your unit planning, weekly routines, and everyday practice makes the role of effort much more transparent to students, and it builds greater confidence in their capacity to persevere and tackle challenging tasks until they achieve some measure of proficiency. Every time you press for improved quality through the use of goal-setting, study and revision strategies, formative assessments, and academic interventions, your academic expectations become grounded in authentic actions that communicate, *"You can count on my support to help each and every one of you succeed in our classroom."*

> What strategies from this chapter align with your classroom context?

> What are the ways these support the 6 Conditions for Engagement?
>
> Attention, Goodwill, Effort, Interest, Participation, Commitment

[1] Flexner, A., & Bachman, F.P. (1918). *The Gary schools: A general account.* New York, NY: General Education Board.

[2] Lee, V., Smith, J., Perry, T., & Smylie, M. (1999). *Social support, academic press, and student achievement: A view from the middle grades in Chicago.* Chicago, IL: University of Chicago Consortium on School Research.

[3] Billig, S.H., Jaime, I.I., Abrams, A., Fitzpatrick, M., & Kendrick, E. (2005). *Closing the achievement gap: Lessons from successful schools.* U.S. Department of Education Office of Vocational and Adult Education.

[4] Lewis, M.A. (2014). *Learning styles, motivations, and resource needs of students enrolled in a massive open online class* (Master's thesis). Retrieved from https://cdr.lib.unc.edu/indexablecontent/uuid:6caa790d-8235-4dd6-bd24-54ddf9bbf33e

[5] Powell, W., & Kusuma-Powell, O. (2011). *How to teach now: Five keys to personalized learning in the global classroom.* Alexandria, VA: ASCD.

[6] Ballantine, R., & Pell, A. (2010, October). Interventions that work. *Educational Leadership*, 68(2), Alexandria, VA: ASCD.

[7] Winne, P.H, Jamieson-Noel, D.L., & Muis, K.R. (2002). Methodological issues and advances in researching tactics, strategies, and self-regulated learning. In P. R. Pintrich & M. L. Maehr (Eds.), *Advances in motivation and achievement: New directions in measures and methods.* (Vol. 12, pp. 121-155). Greenwich, CT: JAI Press.

[8] Allensworth, E., Farrington, C., Gordon, M., Johnson, D., Klein, K., McDaniel, B., & Nagaoka, J. (2018). *Supporting social, emotional, & academic development: Research implications for educators.* Chicago, IL: University of Chicago Consortium on School Research.

[9] Lee, V., Smith, J., Perry, T., & Smylie, M. (1999). *Social support, academic press, and student achievement: A view from the middle grades in Chicago.* Chicago, IL: University of Chicago Consortium on School Research.

[10] Mazzeo, C., Fleischman, S., Heppen, J., & Jahangir, T. (2016). Improving high school success: Searching for evidence of promise. *Teachers College Record*, 118(13), 1–32.

[11] Cannata, M.A., Smith, T.M., & Haynes, K.T. (2017). Integrating academic press and support by increasing student ownership and responsibility. *AERA Open*, 3(3), 1-13. https://doi.org/10.1177/2332858417713181

[12] Bandura, A. (1997). *Self-efficacy: The exercise of control.* New York, NY: Freeman and Company.

[13] Eccles, J.S., & Wigfield, A. (2002). Motivational beliefs, values and goals. *Annual Review of Psychology*, 53, 109–132.

[14] Linnenbrink, E.A., & Pintrich, P.R. (2002). Motivation as an enabler for academic success. *School Psychology Review*, 31(3), 313-327.

[15] Gershenson, S., Holt, S.B., & Papageorge, N. (2016). Who believes in me? The effect of student-teacher demographic match on teacher expectations. *Economics of Education Review*, 52, 209-224.

[16] Good, T.L. (1987). Two decades of research on teacher expectations: Findings and future directions. *Journal of Teacher Education*, 38(4), 32-47. https://doi.org/10.1177/002248718703800406

[17] "Spiegel, A. (2012, September 17). *Teachers' expectations can influence how students perform.* National Public Radio Morning Edition Podcast. Podcast retrieved from https://www.npr.org/sections/health-shots/2012/09/18/161159263/teachers-expectations-can-influence-how-students-perform.

[18] Ibid.

[19] Farrington, C.A., Roderick, M., Allensworth, E., Nagaoka, J., Keyes, T.S., Johnson, D.W., & Beechum, N.O. (2012). *Teaching adolescents to become learners: The role of noncognitive factors in shaping school performance: A critical literature review.* The University of Chicago Consortium on Chicago School Research.

[20] Allensworth, E. (2013). The use of ninth-grade early warning indicators to improve Chicago Schools. *Journal of Education for Students Placed At Risk*, 18(1), 68–83. https://doi.org/10.1080/10824669.2013.745181

[21] Glossary of Educational Reform, retrieved from edglossary.org.

[22] ASCD Education Update August 2012 | Volume 54 Number 8 Pages 3-5.

[23] Kohl, H.R. (1995). *"I won't learn from you": And other thoughts on creative maladjustment.* New York, NY: The New Press.

[24] Ibid. (ASCD Education Update.)

[25] DuFour, R., DuFour, R., Eaker, R., & Karhanek, G. (2010). *Raising the bar and closing the gap.* Bloomington, IN: Solution Tree Press.

[26] Boardman, A.G., Roberts, G., Vaughn, S., Wexler, J., Murray, C.S., & Kosanovich, M. (2008). *Effective instruction for adolescent struggling readers: A practice brief.* Portsmouth, NH: RMC Research Corporation, Center on Instruction.

[27] Farrington, C.A., Roderick, M., Allensworth, E., Nagaoka, J., Keyes, T.S., Johnson, D.W., & Beechum, N.O. (2012). *Teaching adolescents to become learners: The role of noncognitive factors in shaping school performance: A critical literature review.* The University of Chicago Consortium on Chicago School Research.

[28] Conley, D.T. (2007). *Redefining college readiness.* Eugene, OR: Educational Policy Improvement Center.

[29] Pashler, H., Bain, P.M., Bottge, B.A., Graesser, A., Koedinger, K., McDaniel, M., & Metcalfe, J. (2007). *Organizing instruction and study to improve student learning: A practice guide.* Washington, DC: National Center for Educational Research, U.S. Department of Education. Retrieved from https://ies.ed.gov/ncee/wwc/Docs/PracticeGuide/20072004.pdf.

[30] Brown, P.C., Roediger, H.L., & McDaniel, M.A. (2014). *Make it stick: The science of successful learning.* Cambridge, MA: Harvard University Press.

[31] Dweck, C.S. (2007). *Mindset: The new psychology of success.* New York, NY: Ballantine Books.

[32] McGuire, S.Y., & McGuire, S. (2015). *Teach students how to learn: Strategies you can incorporate in any course to improve student metacognition, study skills, and motivation.* Sterling, VA: Stylus Publishing, LLC.

[33] Pashler, H., Bain, P.M., Bottge, B.A., Graesser, A., Koedinger, K., McDaniel, M., & Metcalfe, J. (2007). *Organizing instruction and study to improve student learning: A practice guide.* Washington, DC: National Center for Educational Research, U.S. Department of Education. Retrieved from https://ies.ed.gov/ncee/wwc/Docs/PracticeGuide/20072004.pdf.

[34] Witte, S. (2013). Preaching what we practice: A study of revision. *Journal of Curriculum and Instruction*, 6(2), 33-59.

[35] Melzer, D. (2014). *Assignments across the curriculum: A national study of college writing.* Boulder, CO: University Press of Colorado.

[36] Brockman, E., Taylor, M., Kreth, M., & Crawford, M.K. (2011). What do professors really say about college writing? *English Journal*, 100(3), 75–81.

[37] Black, P.J., & Wiliam, D. (2009). Developing the theory of formative assessment. Educational Assessment, *Evaluation and Accountability*, 21(1), 5-31. https://doi.org/10.1007/s11092-008-9068-5.

[38] Lieber, C. (2009). *Making learning REAL: Reaching and engaging all learners in secondary classrooms.* Cambridge, MA: Engaging Schools.

[39] Black, P., & Wiliam, D. (1998). Inside the black box: Raising standards through classroom assessment. *Phi Delta Kappan*, 80(2), 139-144.

[40] Boston, C. (2002). The concept of formative assessment. *ERIC Digest.* College Park, MD: ERIC The Educational Resources Information Center.

[41] Hattie, J. (2015). *195 Influences and effect sizes related to student achievement.* Retrieved from https://visible-learning.org/hattie-ranking-influences-effect-sizes-learning-achievement/

[42] Zemelman, S., Daniels, H., & Hyde, A. (2012). *Best practice: Bringing standards to life in America's classrooms.* (4th ed.). Portsmouth, NH: Heinemann Press.

[43] Ibid. (ASCD Education Update.)

[44] American Institutes of Research, National Center for Intensive Intervention, Washington, DC.

[45] Chafouleas, S. M., Riley-Tillman, T. C., & Sugai, G. M. (2007). *School-based behavioral assessment: Informing intervention and instruction.* New York, NY: Guilford Press.

# CHAPTER 8

## Restorative and Accountable Discipline and Behavior Support

**Chapter Outline**
- Introduction
- The Big Ideas That Inform Restorative and Accountable Discipline and Behavior Support
- Practice #10: Planning for Behavior Concerns
- Practice #11: Defusing Charged Situations
- Practice #12: Behavioral Interventions
- Closing

**Essential Question**
How do I plan for, respond to, and manage behavior concerns and intervene in high-impact situations?

## Introduction

Many of us are of two minds when we hear the words *discipline* and *adolescents* in the same sentence. On the one hand, helping young people find their way to greater self-regulation, good habits, and the determination to practice until they get it right is something we appreciate and navigate daily. On the other hand, helping a wide range of students seek out and stay on the road to self-discipline can feel loaded with caution signs and challenge. We invite you to use this chapter as your personal GPS to reach the destination of student discipline and behavior support that feels accountable, restorative, viable, fair, and respectful.

Developing positive personal relationships (Chapter 4), organizing the learning environment (Chapter 5), planning content design, learning tasks, and implementing learning protocols (Chapter 6), and providing comprehensive academic support (Chapter 7) enable teachers to create a high-performing and well-managed classroom that supports academic success for every student. They are not substitutes, however, for a set of practices and strategies that allow teachers to respond effectively when typical adolescent behavioral concerns and disciplinary incidents arise in real time.

**Classroom management** is about how we organize and manage our classrooms for student success. Teachers identify and implement the routines, procedures, protocols, and rituals that help create and establish safe, orderly, and respectful classrooms and support students to develop target behaviors.

**Classroom discipline** is about restoring order, and/or safety when students engage in unskillful, inappropriate, and unacceptable behaviors. When students exhibit these behaviors, teachers engage in interventions to support the student to learn more skillful behaviors. They also create opportunities to help students restore themselves and relationships with others where appropriate.

In this chapter, we explore three practices that enable teachers to establish and maintain a restorative and accountable approach to discipline, consider ways to respond to a range of student behavior concerns and incidents; and provide supportive interventions when students experience chronic or serious behavioral challenges. These practices and related strategies support students' development of Learning and Life Competencies (LLCs) that will help them become more self-aware, self-managed, and socially and academically efficacious. The practices include:

> **Practice #10 – Planning for Behavior Concerns:** Teachers map out a classroom behavior plan to help students develop and strengthen target behaviors. Teachers also use prevention strategies to respond to behavior concerns before they become major incidents.
>
> **Practice #11 – Defusing Charged Situations:** Teachers use depersonalization and defusing strategies to respond effectively to emotionally upset students and inappropriate, unskillful, and unacceptable behaviors in ways that reduce confrontations, ensure student safety, and help students cool down and regain their equilibrium.
>
> **Practice #12 – Behavioral Interventions:** Teachers engage in restorative conversations, behavioral problem-solving and planning conferences, progress monitoring, and coaching sessions to address challenging or chronic behavior concerns with the aim of helping students right themselves, repair the harm, mend relationships, and restore their good standing.

---

**The Big Ideas That Inform Restorative and Accountable Discipline and Behavior Support**

- Respect and caring are at the center of every student-teacher interaction.
- A restorative and accountable approach to discipline transforms teacher-student interactions.
- Classroom discipline and student support are situated within a multi-tiered system that fosters promotion, prevention, and teacher-facilitated interventions.
- Improving student behavior is in support of improving students' academic performance.
- Being mindful of one's biases and zones of discomfort increases teacher effectiveness with students who exhibit challenging behaviors.

---

### Respect and caring are at the center of every student-teacher interaction

In her book, *Culturally Responsive Teaching: Theory, Research, and Practice*, Geneva Gay calls on teachers to hold *"unequivocal faith in the human dignity and intellectual capabilities of every student."*[1] When we affirm each person's identity, value, and voice, our interactions with students will communicate our unwavering respect. Adolescents overwhelmingly corroborate that they feel respected when they are listened to and taken seriously. Students who demonstrate chronic unskillful behaviors or who challenge us the most especially need to understand that we want to support them. Through the responsiveness of being "cared for," students learn how to "care about" the conditions and treatment of others. A caring classroom community provides the conditions that make it possible and compelling for students to respond in supportive and kind ways to others. Consequently, we see respectful adult-to-student communication as the cornerstone for all disciplinary practices. Communicating our care for students emphasizes a relational view of the classroom community. Nel Noddings, who has written extensively on the ethics of care, posits, *"To care and be cared for are fundamental human needs. All human beings need to be understood, received, respected, and recognized."*[2]

## A restorative and accountable approach to discipline transforms teacher-student interactions

A restorative and accountable approach to discipline is associated with improved school climate, improved student-teacher relationships, and significant reductions in referrals and suspensions.[3] This approach focuses on restoring relationships, the community, and self.[4] It is based on the belief that students are resilient, capable of turning around adverse situations, and can restore themselves and their relationships with the understanding and guidance of caring adults.[5] When students experience behavioral challenges, interventions enable them to regain their equilibrium, strengthen resilience, and develop mindsets and Learning and Life Competencies that support self-awareness, self-management, and social and academic efficacy.

> **A consequence** is a disciplinary response that is a direct result of a student's unskillful, inappropriate, or unacceptable behavior. It signals to the student that they are accountable for their actions.
>
> **An intervention** engages the student in some action or learning process that enables them to repair relationships and the harm they have done to others, to restore their good standing in the community, and to learn skills and competencies to improve their personal social and academic efficacy.

Educators and parents alike seek for each and every student to grow in their capacity to be self-disciplined, responsible, and accountable. When students have engaged in behaviors that prompt a referral, they receive a consequence with an aligned intervention. Being accountable involves an obligation or willingness to account for one's words and actions to others, accept consequences with goodwill, and fully participate in interventions designed to address specific behaviors and disciplinary incidents. Figure 8.1 Three Approaches to Discipline shows that a restorative and accountable orientation to discipline is an approach in which students are actually accountable to engage in some action to correct behavior, resolve the problem, and make things right.

Fair process is another key element of a restorative and accountable approach to discipline and student support. People are more cooperative, responsive, and more likely to make positive changes in behavior when adults use fair processes[6] that (1) involve individuals in decisions that affect them; (2) provide clear explanations of the reasoning behind decisions; and (3) ensure that all participants know exactly what is expected of them in the future.

**FIGURE 8.1** Summary of Three Approaches to Classroom Discipline

| Punishment | Do-Nothing | Restorative and Accountable Discipline |
|---|---|---|
| **Punishment** is an end in itself. The intention is to inflict sufficient discomfort, unpleasantness, or an undesired consequence in order to stop the unskillful behavior. | **Do Nothing** is about avoidance and a teacher's reluctance to engage students—out of fear of confrontation or of being disliked; uneasiness about one's authority; disinterest in helping students change behavior; belief that nothing will work; or concerns that a strategic response will take too much time and energy. | **Restorative and Accountable Discipline** is a learning opportunity in which the student accounts for her behavior and takes some action to problem-solve, self-correct, right oneself, repair the harm done, learn more skillful behaviors, and develop greater personal efficacy. |

| Punishment | Do-Nothing | Restorative and Accountable Discipline |
|---|---|---|
| **Immediate Goal:** Actions are done to the student (exclusion or belittlement often accompanied by blame and fault-finding). | **Immediate Goal:** Teacher ignores unskillful behavior and attends to the needs of the rest of the class. | **Immediate Goal:** Actions are done by the student with the support of a caring adult to help student cooperate, self-correct, regain control, refocus, and get back on track. |
| **Focus:** Primary focus on the past. (What did you do?) | **Focus:** Focus on the present, but attention is directed toward others, not the student engaged in unskillful behavior. | **Focus:** Focus on the present (What is the impact of your behavior?) and the future (What do you want to do to make it right?) |
| **Accountability:** Involves a consequence of "doing time" through the assignment of punishment or penalty. | **Accountability:** There is none. | **Accountability:** Involves a consequence of "owing time" to account for one's actions, take personal responsibility, reflect on one's behavior, and engage in some action to make it right. |
| **Longer-term Goals:** Hope that the student is sufficiently repentant so they avoid the unskillful behavior in the future. | **Longer-term Goals:** Hope that student will figure out behavioral norms and right themselves on their own. | **Longer-term Goals:** Explore root causes and learn and practice target behaviors to become more skillful and responsible. |
| **Effects on Student:** Likely to encourage lying, blame, defensiveness; intensify feelings of anger, resentment, hostility, or alienation, resulting in low motivation to change. | **Effects on Student:** Likely to encourage detachment and passivity or an inflated sense of power to act out, test limits, and challenge authority. | **Effects on Student:** Likely to encourage feelings of respect, trust, personal agency and competence, and being cared for, resulting in greater motivation to change. |
| **Effects on Relationship:** Relationship between student and teacher is likely to worsen and is perceived as adversarial and win-lose. | **Effects on Relationship:** The teacher and student remain unattached and unaccountable to each other. | **Effects on Relationship:** The relationship between student and teacher is maintained and is perceived as supportive and win-win |

### Classroom discipline and student support are situated within a multi-tiered system that fosters promotion, prevention, and teacher-facilitated interventions

An accountable and restorative approach to discipline supports teachers to strategically integrate Tier 1 disciplinary practices to help prevent, reduce, and correct behavior concerns with the aim of re-engaging students immediately when they are off-task. Tier 2 teacher-facilitated interventions provide strategic support to students with chronic or more challenging behavioral gaps. These interventions help students become more skillful and develop more positive mindsets that increase self-awareness and self-direction resulting in responsible behaviors. See Chapter 1 for detailed information on Multi-Tiered System of Supports.

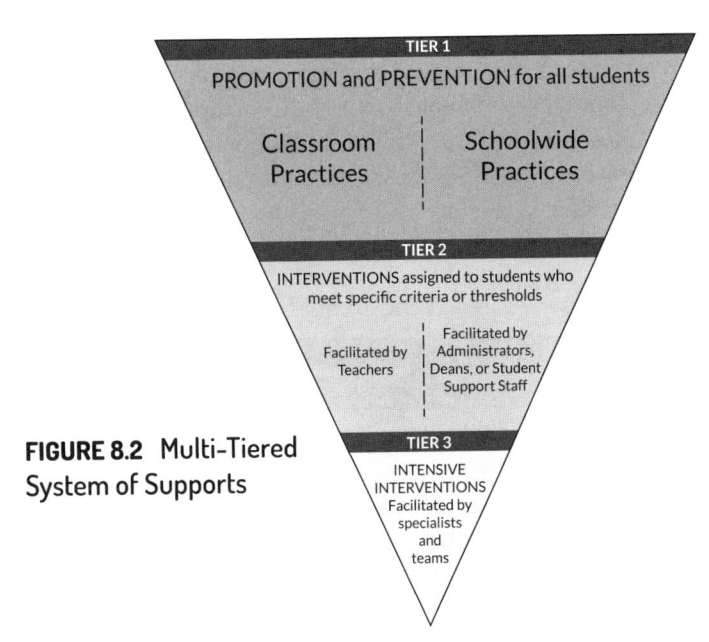

**FIGURE 8.2** Multi-Tiered System of Supports

**TIER 1**
PROMOTION and PREVENTION for all students
Classroom Practices | Schoolwide Practices

**TIER 2**
INTERVENTIONS assigned to students who meet specific criteria or thresholds
Facilitated by Teachers | Facilitated by Administrators, Deans, or Student Support Staff

**TIER 3**
INTENSIVE INTERVENTIONS Facilitated by specialists and teams

### Improving student behavior is in support of improving academic performance

Addressing discipline problems in isolation can easily lead to a narrow goal of simply wanting the unskillful behavior to stop. However, when we recognize the interdependent relationship between students' academic and behavioral challenges and their overall success, we uncover root causes that create barriers to learning, use strategies that help students re-engage in academic learning tasks immediately, and support students' practice of target behaviors that will result in improved academic efficacy and performance. From a student's perspective, "helping me do better academically" (rather than "fixing me, or punishing me because of my bad behavior") feels authentically respectful and supportive. This message of support communicates a commitment to and confidence in the student's capacity to improve and succeed in school.

### Being mindful of one's biases and zones of discomfort increases teacher effectiveness with students who exhibit challenging behaviors

Responding effectively to students who exhibit challenging behaviors can be one of the hardest things to do well. Behaviors that we perceive as disrespectful, aggressive, or oppositional tend to intensify our own emotions by triggering disapproval, disappointment, fear, or frustration. Our heightened emotional state can produce a flight, fight, or freeze response—and none of these options are effective in charged situations.[7] Complicating matters, our emotional discomfort may trigger social, behavioral, and cognitive biases that contribute to the ineffective and prejudicial treatment of students.

Social, behavioral, and cognitive biases are real—and they never really go away. Understanding how our own ethnicity, family background, and experiences influence our values and beliefs about students, learning, and discipline helps us red flag biases that might prompt prejudicial or preferential treatment of different students. Biases often begin with unconscious perceptions and feelings about specific characteristics or attributes that we associate with a specific group. Biases also emerge when a fixation on a single behavior overrides a holistic view of an individual. The brain transforms these mental shortcuts into stereotypes that, in turn, influence how we interact with different groups of students, advantaging some and disadvantaging others.[8] Stereotypes like "aggressive students have no capacity to cooperate" or "Black boys are hostile to authority" are likely to prompt "one size fits all" responses, regardless of the individual characteristics of a student or the context of the situation. A combination of biases has the potential to influence our first thoughts about students and how we respond to them. Therefore, understanding students culturally and developmentally, and increasing our understanding of specific strategies to respond to challenging behaviors with skill and confidence, is one path forward for confronting and countering our biases to improve our teaching practice and move our classrooms toward greater equity. See Appendix 1.1 – Adolescent Development Essentials. Consequently, these strategic efforts galvanize our commitment to know each individual student personally and support each and every student with care and respect. Figure 8.3 illustrates cultural and developmental biases that can influence how we teach and treat students.

**FIGURE 8.3** Biases that Can Influence How We Teach and Treat Students

| Biases | How Biases Influence How We Teach and Treat Students |
|---|---|
| Gender Biases | There is a tendency in schools to punish or disparage many typical adolescent boy behaviors (difficulty sitting still, impulsive and more boisterous expression, less perseverance, and a greater desire for competition, movement, and active learning) and reward and reinforce compliant and self-management behaviors attributed more typically to girls.[9,10,11] |
| Biases Related to Students' Developmental Delays and Disabilities | A lack of knowledge and understanding of students with developmental delays and disabilities may lead to assumptions that students with Individual Educational Plans (IEPs) are unable to learn within a regular curriculum and will automatically exhibit behavior problems.[12] |
| Learning Biases | Unless some kind of transformative experience in early adulthood counters our own personal history of schooling, we tend to teach how we were taught, we tend to prefer students who "learn like us," and we tend to see those who learn differently as lacking desirable student qualities.[13] Learning biases can be particularly problematic for teachers who moved through high school within an honors/AP track, isolated from students who presented a full range of learning profiles. |
| Racial / Cultural Biases | People tend to have a far greater affinity with those who look, sound, behave, and grow up similarly and share the same values. When we perceive others as distinctly different from ourselves, feelings of mistrust, anxiety, and fear can trigger negative stereotyping that leads to physical and emotional distancing and diminished human regard for the "other" as less worthy of our kindness, generosity, optimism, and support. For example, when racial biases toward Black boys trigger associations of dangerous behavior, aggressiveness, or irresponsibility, we might assign Black boys harsher punishments, hold lower academic expectations for them, and provide less encouragement, praise, or helpful feedback.[14] If we believe that poor students lack motivation and a strong work ethic, we may rob these students of our best efforts to push for quality and excellence.[15] |

| | |
|---|---|
| **Negativity Bias** | People tend to have far greater recall of negative memories than positive ones, reinforcing a tendency to target students who engage in repeated behaviors that we experience as negative. The more we fixate on the negative behavior, the harder it becomes to truly "see" the whole student and the less likely we are to encourage and recognize positive behaviors. Psychology researcher Daniel Kahneman invites us to consider applying the 5:1 positivity ratio in our interactions with students: since it takes five positive actions to counter every negative experience.[16] For every time you notice a student getting off-track, consider the 5:1 positivity ratio to ensure you are on the lookout for students doing the right thing five times and acknowledge them. |
| **Aggression/ Conflict Aversion Bias** | Research suggests that when teachers reflect on the entire continuum of student behaviors, they are least comfortable responding to behaviors labeled as aggressive and identify aggressive behaviors as the most problematic and negative of all student behaviors.[17,18] Aggressive acts are often associated with conflict and confrontation. Most people experience modest to severe discomfort with conflict which can translate into reluctance or incapacity to engage constructively with students who are perceived as aggressive. |

This chapter invites the reader to consider the mindsets, practices, and strategies that are essential for establishing Restorative and Accountable Discipline and Behavior Support in the classroom. See Figure 8.4 Restorative and Accountable Discipline and Behavior Support.

**FIGURE 8.4** Restorative and Accountable Discipline and Behavior Support

| Promotion and Prevention | Intervention ||
|---|---|---|
| **Practice #10:** Planning for Behavior Concerns | **Practice #11:** Defusing Charged Situations | **Practice #12:** Behavioral Interventions |
| **Strategies:**<br>• Classroom Behavior Plan<br>• First Response to Behavior Concerns<br>• Behavior Check-ins | **Strategies:**<br>• Depersonalization<br>• Responding to Disrespectful Behavior<br>• Defusing Upset Students<br>• Defusing Power Struggles<br>• Re-set Protocols<br>• Interrupting Physical Altercations<br>• Responding to Oppositional Behavior | **Strategies:**<br>• Restorative Conversations<br>• Behavioral Problem-solving and Planning Conferences<br>• Progress Monitoring<br>• Behavioral Coaching |

**The following adult mindsets support the implementation of these practices with integrity and fidelity:**

- I believe that every student is capable of changing their behavior with guidance, instruction, support, and coaching.
- I believe that building and maintaining trusting relationships make disciplinary interactions with students more respectful and collaborative and less aggressive and adversarial.
- I believe that restorative interventions help build students' capacity to be accountable for their words and actions, and strengthens their capacity to self-reflect, problem-solve, and learn new strategies that increase self-awareness, self-management, and social efficacy.

# PRACTICE #10: Planning for Behavior Concerns

A goal that we know teachers collectively hold is to grow their students' capacity to manage themselves and participate fully in a high-functioning classroom community. Teachers report that most classroom misbehaviors do not start out as highly-charged confrontations or serious acts of aggression that jeopardize safety or put learning at a standstill. There is also an interest from many teachers to become more effective at preventing behavior concerns from becoming serious high-impact situations. In working with secondary teachers throughout the country, they have expressed, universally, that when they strategically plan for behavior concerns, they can respond to students with care, attention, and focused redirection. Discipline researchers also concur that when teachers respond to behavior concerns immediately in ways that are brief, respectful, and invitational, students are more likely to self-correct and re-engage without a fuss or a lot of drama.[19]

> **Benefits of Planning for Disciplinary Concerns**
>
> - Supports, strengthens, and sustains healthy and trusting student-teacher relationships.
> - Prevents most behavior concerns from becoming major disciplinary incidents.
> - Increases students' accountability of their behaviors and builds personal agency through problem-solving.
>
> **Learning and Life Competencies Aligned with the Practice**
>
> - Self-Awareness: I am aware of the skills, behaviors, and attitudes that help me.
> - Self-Management: I identify, express, and manage emotions, exhibit self-regulation, and I demonstrate perseverance and resilience.
> - Social Efficacy: I communicate and problem-solve effectively, and I demonstrate civic responsibility.

Two important promotion strategies linked to Practice #10 are described in:

Chapter 7: *Setting and Monitoring Expectations*

Chapter 1: Learning and Life Competencies

**Strategy:** *Classroom Behavior Plan*

A *Classroom Behavior Plan* empowers teachers to handle most behavior concerns skillfully with care and dignity. It helps teachers prioritize unskillful and inappropriate behaviors they want to prevent, if possible, and respond to immediately before they become more serious. Low-impact behavior concerns like sidebar talking, the inability to be silent, making distracting noises, or interrupting others, should not prompt a student's removal from the classroom unless the behavior intensifies and seriously disrupts learning or jeopardizes the safety of others (see Figure 8.5 – Categories of Behavior Concerns). Sending students out of class for low-impact behaviors poses the risk of relinquishing a teacher's management of the classroom. Of equal importance, it creates a loss of trust and authority in the eyes of students. A *Classroom Behavior Plan* supports proactive steps to prepare for unskillful and inappropriate adolescent behaviors and maintain a safe, welcoming, and engaging classroom environment.

> **What it Looks Like:** *Creating a Classroom Behavior Plan*
>
> **Step 1:** Brainstorm behavior concerns common to your experience or that you anticipate. Take the time to carefully consider the behavioral issues that are common to adolescents and your experience. Make a list.
>
> **Step 2:** Cluster behavior concerns, so they are easy to identify.
> Look at the clusters of behaviors in Figure 8.5 – Categories of Behavior Concerns. Look at your list and identify the categories these behaviors align with. Prioritize and highlight three to four behaviors you want to prepare for. Accurately describing a behavior sets the stage for choosing the most appropriate goal and the most effective and immediate response to a behavior concern.
>
> **Step 3:** Identify the target behaviors you want students to learn.
> Look at the LLC target behaviors and identify which ones you want to Model, Teach, Practice, and Assess to mitigate the behavior concerns you have highlighted.
>
> **Step 4:** Identify the procedures that might support students in these target behaviors.
> For some behavioral issues, a procedure can ensure that most students will re-engage or be easily redirected. Study your behavior concerns; not, which ones might benefit from a classroom procedure?
>
> **Step 5:** Prepare the responses you want to incorporate into a *Classroom Behavior Plan*(s). When the behavioral issue occurs, identify the strategies you will use to respond in-the-moment. We offer two effective strategies to support you with your behavioral plan: *First Response to Behavior Concerns* (p. 151) and the *Behavior Check-in* (p. 125).
>
> **Step 6:** Communicate with the class that if a behavior persists, they will participate in a conference to figure out how to stop the unskillful behavior. See *Behavioral Problem-solving and Planning Conference* (p. 167).
>
> See Figure 8.6 Sample Classroom Behavior Plan.
> See Appendix 8.1 – Classroom Behavior Plan Template.

## Considerations

1. Spend time with students discussing and practicing the target behaviors that will mitigate and prevent many unskillful behaviors.

2. Collaborate with colleagues/team members to identify common behavioral concerns and the process for teaching target behaviors. Identify responses to these behaviors when they arise that will assist students in getting back on track. A collaborative approach builds the efficacy and competencies of your colleagues to navigate behavioral issues. Also, students become aware of their teachers working together to support them strategically, which builds goodwill and commitment to change behavior.

3. For planning and responding to more challenging behaviors, see Practice #12, Behavioral Interventions.

**FIGURE 8.5** Categories of Behavior Concerns

Most behavior concerns in 1, 2, and 3 are considered low-impact. These can be addressed by using the following strategies: *First Response to Behavior Concerns*; *Behavior Check-ins*; or the strategies for *Defusing Charged Situations*. When these behaviors become chronic, the response is likely to include a behavioral intervention. Most behaviors in 4 and 5 are considered high-impact behaviors that are likely to violate schoolwide rules and prompt a behavior referral, an immediate consequence implemented by a dean or administrator, and an intervention. The behaviors below the dotted line warrant a teacher sending a student out of the class.

### 1. Procedural Infractions

1. Does not bring necessary materials to class.
2. Does not manage classroom materials.
3. Does not complete assigned work.

### 2. Non-cooperation and Non-participation

4. Non-participation in learning activities and experiences.
5. Initiating or joining in "sidebar" conversations.
6. Playing around or goofing off with others.
7. Difficulty working cooperatively with others.

### 3. Impulse Control, Self-Management, and Personal Distress

8. Distracting or disruptive movement or noise.
9. Interrupting others or blurting out inappropriate or off-point comments.
10. Needing to have the last word.
11. Persistent complaining or badgering.
12. Inability to work silently without bothering others.
13. Inability to manage confusion, frustration, or anger or deal with personal discomfort and effectively.
14. Easily triggered, annoyed, or upset by others.
15. Engages in persistent attention seeking behaviors.

-------------------------------------------------------------------------------

**Immediate Classroom Send-Out**

16. Deliberate use of negative speech that sabotages the group.
17. Out of control emotions and self-destructive behaviors.

### 4. Student to Student Aggression

The context will determine whether the teacher manages the behavior in the moment and perhaps conferences with the student later, or sends the student out of the classroom immediately. This depends on the severity of the behavior and the impact on the student(s) being targeted and the class.

18. Hostile, rude, or provocative verbal responses, gestures, and posturing directed at an student.
19. Deliberately annoying, provoking, or bothering peers.
20. Cursing, yelling, or excessive use of criticism, blame, sarcasm, and accusations directed at a student.
21. Teasing, taunting, put-downs, and name calling.

------

**Immediate Classroom Send-Out**

22. Uninvited contact with another student: pushing, shoving, hitting, punching, kicking.
23. Verbal intimidations and threats.
24. Physical intimidation.
25. Harassment (abusive, obscene, or offensive language, gestures, propositions, or behaviors intended to target or harm an individual or a group based on race, color, origins, gender, sexual identity, age, religion, class, or disability).
26. Bullying.
27. Assault with intent to harm.

### 5. Student to Teacher Aggression

The context will determine whether the teacher manages the behavior in the moment and perhaps conferences with the student later, or sends the student out of the classroom immediately. This depends on the severity of the behavior and the impact on the adult being targeted and the class.

28. Hostile, rude, or provocative verbal responses, gestures, and posturing directed at an adult.
29. Persistent demands, argumentative and adversarial speech.
30. Walking away when an adult is speaking.

------

**Immediate Classroom Send-Out**

31. Refusal to make a choice or follow a directive after repeated requests to accept and carry out consequences.
32. Acts of spite and revenge directed at an adult.
33. Cursing that is specifically directed at an adult.
34. Verbal threats, hostile and aggressive confrontations, or physical intimidation directed at an adult.
35. Assault with intent to harm.

*Please see your district policies and school rules for guidance about electronics, dress code, and attendance violations.*

**FIGURE 8.6** Sample Classroom Behavior Plan

| | | | |
|---|---|---|---|
| | | **My Classroom Behavior Plan** | |
| **Promotion / Prevention** | Step 1 | Identify Typical Behavior to Be Ready For | Sidebar Conversations |
| | Step 2 | Identify Learning and Life Competency, Skill, and Target Behaviors | **Competency:** Self-management<br>**Skill:** I exhibit self-regulation.<br>**Target Behavior:** I work silently without bothering others. |
| | Step 3 | When the behavior occurs use *First Response* ... | First *Depersonalize:*<br>Choose one or more from the options below:<br>☐ Use proximity and physical prompts.<br>☐ Use a visual prompt or cue.<br>☐ Use an effective directive.<br>☐ Provide encouragement.<br>☐ Invite choice-making.<br>☐ Invite problem-solving.<br>☐ Postpone and re-visit.<br>☐ Other. |
| | Step 4 | When the behavior persists... | Facilitate a brief *Behavior Check-in* |
| **Intervention** | Step 5 | When the behavior becomes chronic and seriously interferes with learning... | Consider the following:<br>*Behavioral Problem-Solving and Planning Conference* (see p. 167).<br>Consult with grade level team, or student support specialist, or another colleague.<br>*Behavioral Coaching* (see p. 167). |
| | | What response(s) do I want to be mindful of avoiding when this behavior occurs? Raising my voice. | |

1. If there is a sizable group of students who engage in the same unskillful behavior, consider conducting a Problem-solving *Circle*.

2. If it is a few students, consider a brief *Behavioral Coaching* session in which students unpack the issue and next steps.

3. In some cases, the unskillful behavior may require a classroom procedure to support all students to meet the target behavior. In the example above, a procedure for *Getting Attention* and *Maintaining Silence* could mitigate sidebar talking if it is a class problem.

### Strategy: *First Response to Behavior Concerns*

This strategy enables teachers to engage in a strategic set of actions/steps to re-engage students at the first signs of behaving unskillfully or inappropriately. *First Responses* communicate a teacher's strong and caring presence and their investment in helping students. And, *First Responses* are immediate, low-key, respectful, and invitational. Skillful implementation of *First Responses* maintains the relationship with the student and their dignity. Teachers practiced in the *First Response to Behavior Concerns* expect that on any given day, students will demonstrate a range of behaviors, and they feel empowered and responsible for helping students re-set in the moment, all the while maintaining order in their classroom.

---

**What it Looks Like:** *First Response to Behavior Concerns*

1. **Get ready:** De-couple the behavior from anything to do with you (*Depersonalize* see p. 155). Use a self-talk mantra that helps you shift to a more neutral stance (i.e., "This is not about me." OR "I'm the skillful one here." OR "What's going on for this student?").
2. **Name what you are seeing to yourself:** This enables you to focus clearly on the behavior you are observing and match the appropriate response to the behavior you see.
3. **What's my goal here?** Re-engaging the student.
4. **Implement one or more of the "in the moment" responses:** The following are several responses to consider. Identify what aligns with your style and make any necessary revisions.

   - **Use proximity and physical prompts:** Move closer; assume a relaxed stance; make eye contact and put on a neutral, "flat face" (showing no emotion); freeze for a few seconds in silence to get attention. This sequence signals to a student (s) to consider what they are doing and self-correct.
   - **Use visual prompts and cues:** While engaged in instruction, walk toward your *Visual Postings*: Expectations, procedures, directions or agenda and place your hand on a specific point to redirect the student(s).
   - **Use effective directives:** Provide a brief statement in an unemotional tone of voice that explains the expected behavior: "Take a look at the steps posted on the board and figure out what you should be doing now." "Okay, group, what do we need to finish today before you leave class?" "Let's remind each other—what should we see and hear when we work in small groups?" "Love that hat. Thank you for putting it in your backpack." "Eyes front, please." "Thank you."
   - **Provide encouragement:** "This must feel frustrating right now. And I know you can do it." "If you make the effort, I am confident you will pass." "You've been successful before. You can use those strengths and qualities to be successful again."
   - **Invite choice-making or problem-solving:** "You have a choice here. You're welcome to sit at this table or the round table. Take 30 seconds to think about it, and you decide." Or "It looks like you two are having difficulty getting started. Take 30 seconds and decide on the next step."
   - **Postpone and revisit:** "You seem really upset which is interfering with you getting started. Am I reading this correctly?" "Okay, take a minute to regroup, and I'll check back in with you in a moment."

---

### Considerations

1. Students will often hear our tone before they process what we're saying. To support adolescent learners to self-correct, speak in a calm and credible voice at low volume.
2. When a student or group self-corrects or re-engages, provide positive reinforcement—a thank you, words of encouragement, or specific positive feedback.
3. If the student appears to be emotionally charged or the behavior fits within the category of high-impact incidents, the strategies described in Practice #11 and Practice #12 in this chapter will be more effective.

**Strategy:** *Behavior Check-ins*

A *Behavior Check-in* gently guides students to self-assess in the moment and redirect their behavior. Check-ins message to the student "I am interested and curious about how you are doing right now." They communicate care, respect, and high expectations to be responsible, self-directed learners. *Behavior Check-ins* suss out the source of the problem, helping the student identify a strategy that will support her to get back on track.

---

**What it Looks Like:** *Behavior Check-In: Getting Ready*

1. Observe the student's behavior quietly and discreetly.
2. Approach the student with a curious mindset: "What are the reasons he/she might be engaging in the end behaviors that I see?"
3. Move to the student's side for a one-to-one conversation: position yourself at the same level as the student to establish rapport, and greet the student by name. (Assign the rest of the class a quick task: *Turn and Talk* with your partner and…).

---

**When the misbehavior looks like a temporary distraction from the task at hand**

1. Ask an open-ended question that will enable the student to do something immediately to re-engage and get back on task.
2. Paraphrase the student's suggestion.
3. Thank the student for self-correcting and re-focusing.

**Sample Situations and Questions:**

- When a student is goofing off with another student: "Hey, Jackson and Arturo. What can you do right now to get back on track and stay focused on this assignment?"
- When a student is not following a classroom procedure: "Pilar. What do you think the procedure is for _____?"
- When the student is engaging in sidebar conversations during silent independent work time: "Moe. What are the reasons it's important to work by yourself during independent work time?"

| **When the source of the misbehavior is not clear** |
|---|
| 1. Share what you are observing and ask an open-ended question to suss out the problem.<br>2. Paraphrase what the student said and follow up with another question if the source of the problem remains unclear.<br>3. Assess and summarize what is impeding student learning: A learning task mismatch; confusion about what to do; skill gap; and negative feelings (dislike) about a particular task.<br>4. Ask a student a question that aligns with your assessment.<br>5. Ask the student to identify one thing she can do right now to re-engage.<br>6. Thank the student for problem-solving and making a good choice for what to do.<br><br>**Sample Situations and Questions:**<br>- When a student appears confused: "So tell me what you think the task is right now."<br>- When a student is unable to name a next step: "Here are a couple of options to choose from." Provide options and say, "Which one might work for you?<br>- When a student appears anxious or frustrated: "You look___. What's going on for you?" OR "Are you okay?"<br>- When a student is stuck: "What can I do to help?"<br>- When a student is glazed over and doing nothing: "So what are some things getting in the way of completing this learning task?"<br>- When a student is not positively contributing in a small group task: "What might be something you can do to reconnect with your group?" |

See Appendix 7.5 – Responsive Listening to support the successful implementation of *Behavior Check-ins*.

## Considerations

At the beginning of the school year, discuss with the class what *Behavior Check-ins* sound like and explain how you will be checking in with students when they go off-task, feel stuck, or are confused. "This happens to everyone sometimes, and it's my job to help you help yourself to get back on track."

1. Designing well-paced student lessons where students regularly engage in independent and small group work allows the teacher greater flexibility to engage in *Behavior Check-ins*, as needed.

2. When a behavior concern persists and becomes chronic, document what the student is saying and doing exactly so you can discuss it later in a *Behavioral Problem-solving and Planning Conference*. (See p. 167.)

3. For some typical behaviors that become chronic you might consider using logical consequences:
   - For repeated sidebar talking → change seats.
   - For making a mess or marking on furniture → clean it up.
   - For inappropriate use of materials and equipment → do it over to get it right.

# PRACTICE #11: Defusing Charged Situations

For many adolescents, intense and sudden expressions of charged emotions are a normal part of their development. They can emotionally escalate very quickly, so a teacher's capacity to strategically defuse charged situations enables them to intervene effectively and with immediacy when students are upset, engage in power struggles, or present disrespectful, aggressive, or oppositional behaviors. Having access to effective strategies also ensures that the teacher models effective expression and management of emotions to students, maintaining healthy relationships with them.

> Disrespect involves comments or actions directed personally at an individual and violate one's dignity and identity. Disrespectful actions often happen between people in close proximity.

Understanding and managing the cycle of emotional escalation is key to defusing students. As illustrated in Figure 8.7, when students are triggered, teachers have a brief window to respond before adrenaline accelerates emotional escalation. As students escalate to the peak of emotional discharge (the release of anger and agitation expressed in words and actions), they lose their capacity to think and reason. When agitation accompanies challenging behaviors, students need teachers' reassurance that they are worthy of a caring response to help them calm themselves and regain focus. A return to emotional equilibrium requires both time and space. This requires teachers to have a set of strategies they can use real time to maintain their relationships with students and to support them to re-set.

**FIGURE 8.7** Emotional Escalation

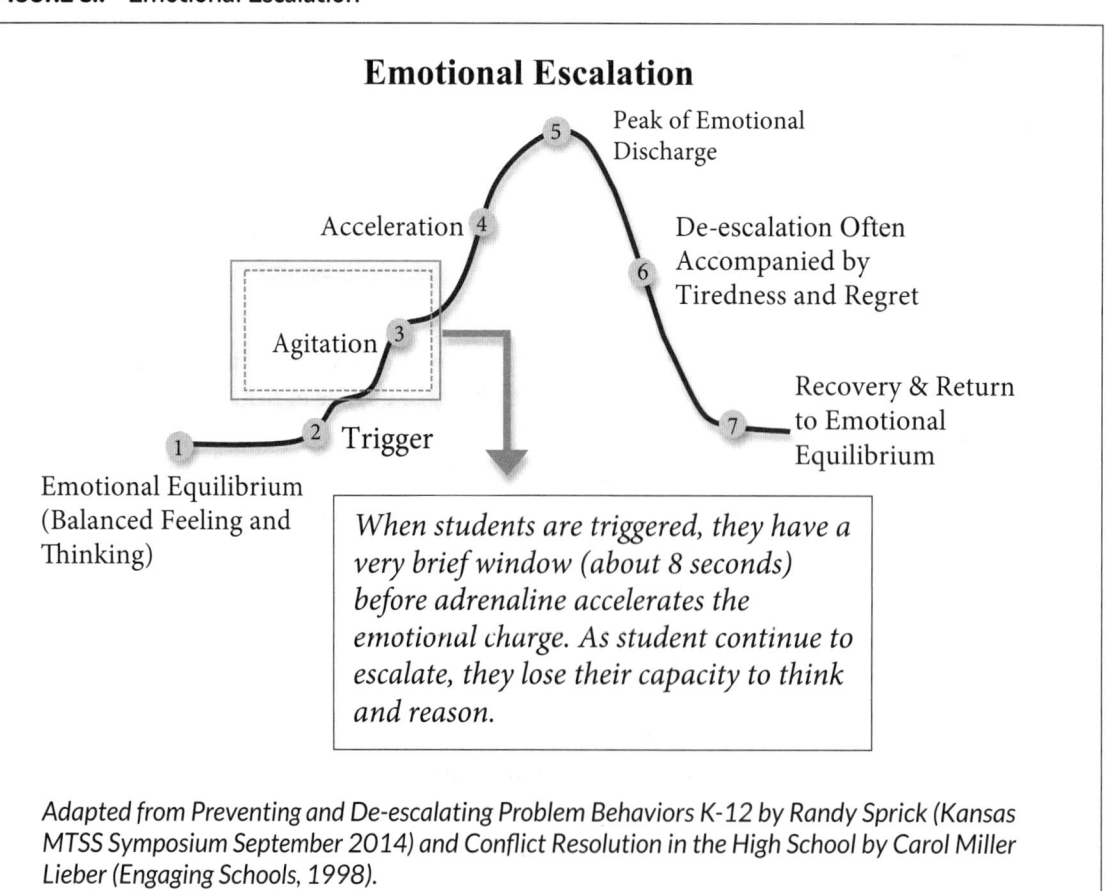

**Emotional Escalation**

1. Emotional Equilibrium (Balanced Feeling and Thinking)
2. Trigger
3. Agitation
4. Acceleration
5. Peak of Emotional Discharge
6. De-escalation Often Accompanied by Tiredness and Regret
7. Recovery & Return to Emotional Equilibrium

*When students are triggered, they have a very brief window (about 8 seconds) before adrenaline accelerates the emotional charge. As student continue to escalate, they lose their capacity to think and reason.*

*Adapted from Preventing and De-escalating Problem Behaviors K-12 by Randy Sprick (Kansas MTSS Symposium September 2014) and Conflict Resolution in the High School by Carol Miller Lieber (Engaging Schools, 1998).*

> **Benefits of Defusing Charged Situations**
> - Affirms for the students that "feelings are real." It is how we handle them that results in positive or negative outcomes.
> - Reduces student agitation, defensiveness, and resistance.
>
> **Learning and Life Competencies Aligned with the Practice**
> - Self-Awareness: I am aware of the skills, behaviors, and attitudes that help me.
> - Self-Management: I identify, express, and manage emotions, and I exhibit self-regulation.
> - Social Efficacy: I communicate and problem-solve effectively.

**Strategy:** *Depersonalization*

Teaching is, in many ways, the most personal of professions and something of a paradox. On the one hand, our personal relationships and emotional connections to students are the very things that increase our commitment to students and increase their attachment to school and learning. On the other hand, we can get emotionally triggered and feel personally offended by student behaviors that appear rude, provocative, and disrespectful.

Effectively responding to these behaviors requires a mindset that enables us to *Depersonalize* what adolescents say and/or do. When we truly understand that adolescents between the ages of 12-16 are far more likely than younger children to challenge authority, question rules, and policies and engage in unskillful, inappropriate, and impulsive behaviors, we can more easily *Depersonalize* and not take students' words, actions or body language personally. For these reasons, students need to count on us to be emotionally balanced and neutral. *Depersonalizing* conflictual situations in a manner that displays our understanding of adolescents, earns students' respect while also presenting them a model for how to express and manage emotions appropriately. Also, *Depersonalizing* student behaviors supports teachers to maintain a calm stance and classroom order, decreasing their stress levels, enabling them to sustain their energy for all of their students and the day ahead.

> **What it Looks Like:** *Depersonalization*
>
> 1. **Use your self-talk mantra:** (i.e., "This is not about me." "What's going on for this student?" Or, "I'm the skillful one here."
> 2. **Remind yourself of the goal:** (To help the student re-engage.)
> 3. **Shift your physical stance:** Take in a full breath; find your relaxed posture; slowly pivot toward the student(s) and move closer; stand straight; make eye contact and put on a neutral, "flat face" (relaxed but showing no emotion); freeze and focus for attention for a few seconds in silence. This sequence alone may defuse the student and enable them to self-correct.
> 4. **Identify your next moves:** Point to a Visual Posting; move toward the student while still teaching; engage in a brief behavioral check-in; OR, assign the class an independent task and ask the student to walk with you to a more private place to talk.

**Strategy:** *Responding to Disrespectful Behaviors*

Naming an action as disrespectful can be a landmine because it often triggers a heightened emotional state and a swift judgment of disapproval. Distinguishing between acts of disrespect and other behaviors that might "feel" disrespectful is a critical clarification. See Figure 8.8 that explores the difference between Disrespectful Behaviors vs. Unskillful, Inappropriate, or Immature Behaviors. Mild forms of disrespectful behavior call for us to respond swiftly, skillfully and with care to help students correct their speech or perform an action again using a more respectful, civil, or courteous manner. Egregious forms of disrespect require a prompt referral and the student's removal from the class, followed later by a more intensive intervention.

**FIGURE 8.8** What Disrespect Is and Is Not...

| Disrespectful Behaviors | Unskillful, Inappropriate, Immature Behaviors |
|---|---|
| • Disrespect involves comments or actions directed personally at an individual that violates one's dignity and identity.<br>• Disrespectful actions occur between people within close proximity of each other most of the time.<br>Examples of disrespect: abusive insults and name-calling, cursing, or offensive language and gestures directed at teachers or peers, walking away when someone is speaking to you directly. | • Non-compliance: e.g. not following rules and procedures.<br>• Non-cooperation: e.g. sidebar talking to a peer.<br>• Non-participation: e.g. student resting her head-on desk.<br>• Non-completion: e.g. not attempting the assignment.<br>These behaviors are not a personal attack directed at an individual, and there are myriad reasons why students might not be fully engaged and on task at a particular point in time. |

**What it Looks Like:** *Responding to Disrespectful Behaviors*

1. Shift your physical stance (See *Depersonalizing* p. 155).
2. Remind yourself of the goal (to help the student re-engage)
3. Offer a neutral *Response to Disrespectful Behavior* and an invitation to self-correct:
   If you need to speak, be brief, and use a voice that is steady, low-key, and matter of fact.

**Examples:**

- "Please say that again?" OR "Let's try that again."
- "Whoa! Let's rewind the tape and try that again."
- "I want to help you. Tell me what you need politely."
- "Check your language please and try asking again."
- "I heard that. Clean up the language please."
- And then say a quick "Thank you with their name," when the student has self-corrected.

## Considerations

1. The best antidote for preventing disrespectful behavior is to "teach by walking around." When you make daily efforts to engage individual students in quick, friendly banter, and supportive conversations about the work they are doing, students are less likely to turn their personal confusion and anxiety, moodiness, feelings of inadequacy, or issues with authority into snarky comments to their peers or to you.

2. Sometimes both the student and you need time to process what happened and consider next steps. Note the incident, explain that you will address this later in the day, and move on. "I heard that, and it felt extremely disrespectful. We will work this through. We will discuss this later today and decide what you can do to make it right."

3. For students who make snarky/impertinent facial expressions and physical gesturing, avoid calling them out when you see it. Wait until you have noticed a pattern of this behavior and speak to them privately, engaging them in a quick *Behavior Check-In*. Example: "Lately I've noticed that you've been rolling your eyes and making faces at least three or four times in a class. I want to help. What is going on for you? What were you thinking or feeling at the time? What do you think the impact might be on other students and me? So the next time you are feeling_____, what can you do instead of rolling your eyes and making faces? Okay, you've got a plan. I'm confident that you can do this. Thank you."

**Strategy:** *Defusing Students Who Are Upset*

When a student is emotionally escalating, our immediate goal is to help her maintain her dignity and respond with care and support her to cool down, regain equilibrium, and re-engage. *Defusing Students who are Upset* at the early stages of emotional escalation requires teachers to use a steady and assertive non-verbal and verbal stance to support students to regain a sense of control so they can access the reasoning, problem-solving, and the cognitive part of their brain. A predictable "defusing stance" helps the teacher be centered, fair, and firm, enabling the student to de-escalate and calm down. A question that teachers ask themselves to cultivate this empowered stance is: In what ways is my facial expression, body language, and tone of voice supporting the student to find their balance/equilibrium?

---

**What It Looks Like:** *Defusing Students Who Are Upset*

1. **Depersonalize:** Scan to assess the situation and depersonalize to get ready (see *Depersonalization* p. 155).
   - If you are at the front of the classroom and engaged in whole-group instruction, give the class an independent task so you can speak more privately with the student.
2. **Physical proximity and privacy:** Approach the student for a one-to-one conversation by moving to their side; position yourself at the same level as the student to get in rapport.
3. **Acknowledge emotions:** Call the student by name and reflect/acknowledge the emotion you think you see or hear and ask the student what is going on. "Hey, Amelio. You look pretty upset. What's going on for you?" Or simply ask, "Amelio, how are you doing?"
4. **Communicate with care:** Paraphrase, pause, and question to discover the cause(s) of the elevated emotional state. "What's not working for you right now?" "Is there anything else bothering you?" "What else might help me understand?" See Appendix 7.5 – Responsive Listening.
5. **Student voice:** Ask the student what they need to get themselves into a better space or offer a suggestion or options for what a student can do. "What might help you cool down right now?" "Take a moment to settle yourself." "Take the restroom pass and go get a drink." OR, "Take a walk to the back of the room and then come back and settle in." Or, "Just sit back and take a mental break, and I will come back to you to get you started. Breathe."
6. **Appreciation:** Thank the student for getting it together. "Thanks for stepping up to manage yourself. I hope your day gets better. Let me know if you need anything."

> **When a student is physically and/or verbally escalating**
>
> 1. **Depersonalize:** Scan to assess the situation and depersonalize to get ready (see *Depersonalization* p. 155).
> 2. **Physical proximity:** Do not directly confront. Approach the student for a one-to-one conversation by moving to their side. Give the student space.
> 3. **Communicate with care:**
>    - Acknowledge the unsafe situation in a calm, credible, and assertive voice. "Russ, this is not safe, and I want you to be safe. Walk with me out into the hallway for a minute."
>    - Tell the rest of the class to remain in their seats. "Class - I need you to stay in your seats for a moment. I want to speak with Russ, and I will be right here at the door. Thank you."
> 4. **Acknowledge emotions and student's effort to cool down:** At the doorway, thank the student for making a good choice, acknowledge their emotional state, and communicate care again. "Thanks, Russ, for stepping out of the class with me. You seem very angry right now, and I want you to be okay, and I want to help."

## Considerations

1. If a student is not responsive to your efforts, or if the student is seriously out-of-control, a brief and direct response is required. "This is not safe Robbie. We can talk about what is going on later, so I can support you. Right now I am going to contact X to come pick you up."

2. Many schools have re-entry protocols after a student has been removed from the classroom for a major incident. It is well worth your time to meet with the student, express your care and interest to have the student back in the classroom, and consider the ways in which you can support them to be self-managed. Consider a *Behavioral Problem-solving and Planning Conference* on p. 167.

3. If a student is having chronic/extreme behavioral difficulties across classes, consider finding a natural time when your colleagues meet or seek out your colleagues to sort out the consistent and strategic ways you might support this student collectively.

### Strategy: *Defusing Power Struggles*

A power struggle is a move for control. Students often engage in power struggles when they are feeling vulnerable, misunderstood, uncared for, anxious, confused, or frustrated. Their end behavior can sound argumentative, hostile, or confrontational. Student confrontations are often played out in front of the class. Thus, a power struggle involving a student and teacher is critical to avoid. These types of situations require teachers to skillfully navigate the action and behaviors of the student, as "all eyes are on you." Our immediate goal is to *Defuse the Power Struggle* in the moment, maintain the student's dignity and the teachers too, and move on. This will ensure safety, order, and care for all class members. *Defusing Power Struggles* requires clear headedness, a focus on the goal, and in the moment actions to maintain your relationship with the student and the class. We recognize that this takes time, practice, and often support from colleagues. Researchers, administrators, psychologists, and teachers agree that a version of the protocol below is the most effective way to avoid or *Defuse* Student-Teacher *Power Struggles*.[20]

> **What It Looks Like:** *Defusing Power Struggles*
>
> 1. **Depersonalize:** Scan to assess the situation and depersonalize to get ready (See *Depersonalization* p. 155).
> 2. **Stay neutral:** Avoid confronting the student. When a student is already agitated, a confrontation is likely to increase their emotional intensity and argumentative and hostile behaviors. Do not pick up the student's metaphorical "rope" by getting into a verbal tug-of-war and arguing with the student, explaining yourself or answering questions. The longer you sustain the interaction, the more likely you will get upset, lose focus, and escalate the situation.
> 3. **Acknowledge emotions and move on:** Reflect/acknowledge the emotion you think you see or hear and make one brief statement that respectfully communicates that you will not argue with the student. This validates the student's emotional state while signaling that you will not pick up the rope.
>    - **Example:** "You seem frustrated right now. Settle in, and I will talk with you in a moment." OR "You seem angry about something. Take a moment, and I will be back to check in with you."
> 4. **Step away:** Physically move away from the student allowing them time and space to cool down and regain equilibrium. This also allows you to think of your next move.

## Considerations

1. A student could be having a bad day when they try to get into a power struggle with you, or, it could be a persistent behavioral style that you observe. If the latter, set up a time to have a *Behavioral Problem-solving and Planning Conference* (p. 167) to discuss what things trigger the student, what actions the student might take to change this behavioral pattern, and what you can do to support the student in their efforts.

2. If a team is wrapped around this student, and power struggles are showing up in several classes, identify the teacher who has the best relationship with the student and engage in a *Behavioral Problem-solving and Planning Conference*. Following the conference, the teachers can meet with the team to look at the collective effort all teachers can take to support the student.

## Strategy: *Re-set Protocols*

Adolescents need time and space to cool down, recover, and regain their equilibrium when emotionally upset. Many students come to us not knowing how to self-soothe or calm down on their own. Encouraging students to consider what they might do to "*Re-set*," to start anew, fosters student agency, and puts the student in charge ("I can regain control of myself."). Through guided support, reflection, and practice, the student is empowered to strengthen their self-management competencies by identifying, expressing, and managing their emotions, exhibiting self-regulation, and demonstrating perseverance and resilience. Supporting students to build their vocabulary around the variety of emotions they are experiencing is critical to their success in *Re-setting* in the moment. The following are some healthy options to expose students to that can promote self-management and prevent emotional meltdowns.

> **What It Looks Like:** *Re-set Protocols*
>
> **Options:**
> 1. Encourage the student to take a quiet moment to regain a sense of calm and control.
>    - "Take a few breaths, or silently count to ten to help you feel more relaxed. Give me a signal when you are ready to rejoin us."
> 2. Offer a five-minute *Re-set*:
>    - A student can *Re-Set* at the desk using a designated object to communicate a *Re-set* (for example a stress ball) or move to a designated space in the classroom that is public knowledge to all as a "*Re-set Zone*."
> 3. Encourage students to use self-talk to help them settle and refocus:
>    - Example: "I know I'm angry right now, but I don't want to blow it. Let me take some deep breaths, and get back to the task. I can deal with this later."
> 4. Encourage students to get in the habit of asking themselves a question:
>    - "One to ten, how mad or frustrated do I feel right now? What can I do for myself to calm down?"
> 5. Encourage a student to jot down what they are feeling, what triggered the feeling, and what they might do to address those feelings.
> 6. When a student needs to calm down, ask students to picture an image of a favorite place that helps them feel relaxed and calm.
>    - "When you feel upset, think of this image as your "anchor" to relax and breathe for a minute."

## Considerations

1. Facilitate a Problem-solving *Circle* (see Appendix 4.8 – Problem-Solving Circle Protocol) with the topic being calming/self-soothing strategies: What are some actions we can take to calm down, in the moment, when we are upset? Encourage students to brainstorm the number of strategies they have to calm down and offer others to add to their list. Create a laminated menu that sits in a "*Re-set*" area/zone in the classroom. Modeling and teaching the tools that are available in this area at the beginning of the year, and during anticipated stressful periods throughout the year, is a proactive step you can take to support students in self-regulation, significantly reducing instructional interruptions.

2. Provide *Re-set* passes when students need more support. When students feel genuinely hijacked by strong emotions, they may need additional support to recover. Many schools are making a *Re-set* pass available for situations when the most appropriate option is for a student to leave the classroom briefly (no more than 15 minutes) to check in with a counselor or student support team member and then return ready to re-engage in class. We are aware that a school context will drive whether this is a true option and if so, students need to be escorted to the appropriate place. Also, the *Re-set* pass would need to be a designated color throughout the school, to ensure that the student is going to the appropriate destination.

**Strategy:** *Interrupting Physical Altercations*

Managing students who engage in physical acts of aggression is stressful. The altercation might involve two students fighting or one student physically attacking another student without provocation. *Interrupting Physical Altercations* until safety staff or an administrator arrives requires an immediate and skillful set of predictable verbal and non-verbal moves from the teacher. A teacher's adrenaline is often heightened in these situations. We encourage teachers to think about "What is my goal here?" The goal is to not get into the middle of the fight but to interrupt the escalating trajectory of violence as quickly as possible and ratchet down the students' emotional volatility. Using a non-confrontational "limit setting strategy" helps to stop the behavior, giving the student(s) time and space to work their way to a calmer emotional state. Knowing the school policy and having an established response protocol enables teachers to act swiftly to ensure the safety of everyone involved. In many schools, teachers are expected to call safety personnel, a Dean, or an AP immediately to handle the situation.

---

**What It Looks Like:** *Interrupting Physical Altercations*

1. Be aware of the physical space the students need and stay several feet from them. Position yourself accordingly by moving to their side as this feels less confrontational.
2. Use a credible voice (firm, strong, and low-pitch) and be brief.
   - "Separate."
   - "This is not safe."
   - "Separate now."
   - "I am calling to get some additional support for you. I want to help."
3. Follow the district/school protocol for physical altercations.

---

## Considerations

1. It is critical to become very familiar with the school policy when it comes to student removal from the classroom related to physical altercations.

2. Share with your students at the start of the year, in the context of *Circle* (see p. 55), and under the umbrella of "we will make mistakes" that there might be a fight in the classroom this year. If so, share the protocol, and your interest to keep the students involved in the altercation safe and the classroom too. Have students read the school policy and answer any questions they might have. You might also inquire about what might help students who engage in a physical altercation and see how viable the students' ideas might be.

3. Many schools have re-entry protocols after a student has been removed from the classroom for physical altercations. It is well worth your time to meet with the students, express your care and interest to have them back in the classroom, and consider the ways in which you can support them to be self-managed. Consider using the *Behavioral Problem-solving and Planning Conference* on p. 167 if appropriate.

**Strategy:** *Responding to Oppositional Behavior*

Oppositional behaviors are characterized by persistent and regular defiance, anger, vindictiveness, irritability, limited patience, and being quickly and easily annoyed by others. Students who exhibit these end behaviors can move from a calm, rational state to out of control in a matter of seconds. Often these students have extreme difficulty taking responsibility for their actions, and instead, have reasons why their behavior is someone else's fault. Many students who exhibit oppositional behaviors have a long history of negative experiences in school. They often feel disliked by teachers and peers, and they often lack the skills, confidence, and motivation to take on the identity of a learner and a cooperative classmate. Moreover, recent research on students who have experienced trauma suggests that many acting out behaviors that appear to be hostile or oppositional "may serve as coping mechanisms in an effort to feel safe and in control." While only a small number of students are diagnosed with Oppositional Defiant Disorder (ODD) (estimated 2% to 10% of children), we are likely to encounter students who at some time or another engage in one or more behaviors associated with defiance.[21] To be clear, occasional non-compliance, uncooperativeness, questioning of authority, argumentative confrontations, or angry outbursts are part of the normal adolescent experience and do not equate with oppositional defiance.

Many of us find these students confusing and the end behaviors of these students very hard to manage. Interacting and supporting students who present oppositional behaviors can feel intimidating and exhausting. So much so, that sometimes, we are reluctant to get to know these students. Not knowing what makes a student tick, however, deprives us of valuable information that can help us reach and teach them. When a student engages in one or more oppositional behaviors repeatedly, two initial steps will help us support these students effectively and compassionately: (1) being prepared to use a set of strategies to help these young people forge a more positive path at school; and (2) collaborating with student support team members and parents who can provide helpful insights on these students.

---

**What It Looks Like:** *Responding to Oppositional Behavior*

1. **Depersonalize:** Scan to assess the situation and depersonalize to get ready (see *Depersonalization* p. 155).

2. **Stay neutral and redirect:** Avoid confronting the student.
   - When a student is demonstrating oppositional behaviors, a confrontation is likely to increase a student's emotional intensity and argumentative and hostile behaviors. Do not pick up the student's metaphorical "rope" by getting into a verbal tug-of-war and arguing with the student, explaining yourself, or answering questions. The longer you sustain the interaction, the more likely you will get upset, lose focus, and escalate the situation.

3. **Acknowledge the resistance:** This can disarm a student and reduce further confrontation.
   - Examples: "You're right. I can't make you do this." "I know that _____ is not your favorite thing." "So you're telling me you don't want to do this."

4. **Acknowledge a student's power in the moment:** Provide an alternative choice from acceptable options to get the student to say "yes" to something constructive. Name very specific options. See examples in Figure 8.9.

5. **Provide specific support and positive attention:** This maintains a connection with the students and helps the student attempt to lean into the learning task. See examples in Figure 8.9.

**FIGURE 8.9** Choice and Attention

| Providing Choice | Providing Support and Positive Attention |
|---|---|
| • **Minor modifications to the process of completing a task:** "So choose whether you want to do this in your notebook or on index cards."<br><br>• **Options for completing an alternative task that meets the same learning outcome:** Some students with defiant behaviors turn into non-completers if there is only one task and only one way to do it. "It's important for you to meet this learning goal, so let's figure out a way to get it done that works for you. Instead of _____, you can do _____ or _____."<br><br>• **Options for a plan for students who resist completing any work:** "We need to figure out a strategy for completing some tasks. "There are three learning tasks…You pick one to start and complete it." | • **Provide a preview:** Give the student a personal "heads up" on a learning task. "I want to let you know in advance that we are _____. Thank you for getting ready.<br><br>• **Prepare the student for positive feedback:** "I'd like to tell you something good that you did. Do you want to hear it?" If the student says "No," respect the response and try again another time.<br><br>• **Scan the class frequently:** Notice when the student is doing the right thing. In private or in a note, tell the student you noticed the specific positive behavior and you appreciate their cooperation, hard work, sustained focus, etc. Remember the 5:1 positivity ratio, p. 143.<br><br>• **Offer assistance:** When students are engaged in independent work or guided practice. Ask students, "Do you want some help?" Or "Would you like some help?" rather than "Do you need some help?" "Want" and "like" create a positive sense of agency in students while "need" can prompt feelings of inadequacy. |

## Considerations

1. With students whom you find particularly challenging, see Appendix 4.4 – One Student / Five Actions / Five Days.

2. Avoid escalating commands that intensify confrontations. They can sound like: "Do your work now." "I told you to put that away and do your work." "You are not listening – stop procrastinating." "How many times have I asked you to do this?" "Don't talk to me like that." The end result? The teacher experiences exhaustion and frustration while the student remains oppositional.[22]

# PRACTICE #12: Behavioral Interventions

Intensive behavioral interventions are needed when student behaviors have an adverse impact on the student and the classroom community. For a subset of our students, behavioral interventions are implemented when behaviors become chronic and repeatedly occur over a period of days or a week or two without observable change. Behaviors also become chronic when they jeopardize students' feelings of safety, violate students' dignity and well-being, seriously disrupt the learning environment, silence the group, or involve acts of aggression toward adults and peers (see Figure 8.5 – Categories of Behavior Concerns). Establishing predictable consequences and interventions prepares students for "What will happen when_____?" They become part of a natural learning cycle in the classroom, and students enter the process with much less resistance and more goodwill.

> **A consequence** is a disciplinary response that is a direct result of a student's unskillful, inappropriate, or unacceptable behavior. It signals to the student that they are accountable for their actions.
>
> **An intervention** engages the student in some action or learning process that enables them to repair relationships and the harm they have done to others, to restore their good standing in the community, and to learn skills and competencies to improve their personal social and academic efficacy.

Chronic behavior concerns often stem from academic learning gaps, disengagement, avoidance, or social isolation. Exploring the root cause behind the behavior concern helps determine the changes in behavior that will support a student to get back on track. Strategic behavioral interventions will support students to (1) take responsibility for their words and actions; and, (2) learn and practice target behaviors and strategies that will improve their behavior and academic performance in the classroom.

For the majority of students who need Tier 2 behavioral interventions, it is important for teachers to facilitate them. Teachers know their students best, and when they engage in solving the problem with the student, they are messaging care and concern for them, "I want to help you help yourself." This maintains trust with the student, which is so essential to the relationship and the student believing that the teacher has her best interest at heart. Lastly, the teacher often has the capacity to implement the behavioral intervention in a timely fashion, ensuring that it will achieve its desired result.

---

### Benefits of Behavioral Interventions

- Help build personal agency through problem-solving.
- Targets very specific behavioral skill gaps and pinpoints specific target behaviors so students can experience some immediate successes.
- Encourages personal accountability for one's behavior.

### Learning and Life Competencies Aligned with Behavioral Interventions

- Self-Awareness: I know myself, and I am aware of skills, behaviors, and attitudes that help me.
- Self-Management: I identify, express, and manage emotions, demonstrate perseverance and resiliency, and exhibit self-regulation.
- Social Efficacy: I communicate and problem-solve effectively, demonstrate empathy and respect, I am assertive and self-advocate, and I communicate and problem-solve effectively.

**Strategy:** *Restorative Conversations*

*Restorative Conversations* are about restoring relationships. They are an effective intervention when one student behaves in a way that directly harms an individual or the group, or when two or more students are involved in an interpersonal conflict. *Restorative Conversations* ideally occur as soon as possible after an incident has occurred (depending upon the student's emotional state) and involve a combination of strategic questions. The situation and the amount of time you set aside for a *Restorative Conversation* will determine whether you ask all seven questions in the protocol or just a few. A student's degree of self-awareness will also influence how many questions you use in the process. Some students have the capacity to stay focused in a conversation involving all seven questions and others do not. Selecting questions that maximize the growth opportunity for the individuals involved, with a fairly immediate resolution, are at the heart of this conversation. More serious incidents merit the time and attention to move through the entire sequence of questions. *Restorative Conversations* help students take responsibility for what happened, reflect on the impact of the incident on others, and arrive at a solution that mends relationships and helps to leave the past behind and move ahead.

**What it Looks Like:** *Restorative Questions*

1. What happened? What was your role in what happened?

    *(This question encourages students to take responsibility and own their behavior.)*

2. What were you thinking and feeling at the time?

    *(This question supports students to identify thoughts and feelings that may have triggered their behavior.)*

3. Who else was affected by this? How?

    *(This question supports flexible thinking and helps students take the perspective of the other and reflect on the impact of their behavior.)*

4. What are you thinking/feeling now?

    *(This question encourages students to reflect on the incident after the emotional charge has dissipated, and the student is in a calmer emotional state that enables him to think.)*

5. What do you want to do to make things right?

    *(This question encourages the student to take action that shows or expresses regret or remorse or decide on a solution that meets important needs of everyone involved.)*

6. What can I (others) do to support you?

    *(This question reassures the student that you and others want to support a successful resolution to the problem.)*

7. When a situation like this comes up again, what actions might you take next time?

    *(This question encourages students to take what they have learned and apply it to similar situations in the future.)*

See examples of *Restorative Conversations* in Figure 8.10.

**FIGURE 8.10** Restorative Conversations Examples

**Example A:** One student has clearly done or said something that has harmed, embarrassed, or hurt the feelings of another student.

| Individual conversation with the targeted person: | Individual conversation with the aggressor: |
|---|---|
| • "What happened?" <br> • "How did this affect you?" <br> • "What can _____ do to make it right?" | • "What happened? <br> • "What were you thinking/feeling at the time?" <br> • "How do you think this affected _____?" <br> • "What can you do to make it right?" |

*After you have met with both students, bring them together to respond to "What can each of you do to make it right between you and move on?"*

**Example B:** Two students have had a verbal disagreement that turns into a shouting match.

Joint conversation:
- "What happened? What was your role in this?"
- "What are you thinking/feeling about this now?"
- "What can each of you to do make it right between you and move on?"

**Example C:** One student has sucked the energy out of the room by going "off" on the teacher, railing about how boring the class is, and how dumb the classmates are.

- In this situation, unpacking the incident merits the use of all seven **Restorative Questions**.

## Considerations

1. Students' emotional states will influence whether you conference immediately after the incident has occurred or later in the day.
2. The history and quality of the relationship between conflicting students will determine your choice to conference with students individually or together.
3. Sometimes additional steps need to be taken to repair the harm, mend relationships, or restore one's good standing. Consider the following:
4. A sincere verbal or written apology that expresses regret or remorse and expresses a commitment to change how the student will treat the other person or group in the future.
    - An apology of action that is a gesture of kindness and goodwill intended to put the past behind and repair the relationship. This can be any action from offering to do something nice for the other person, to an action that helps a teacher or makes the classroom a better place.
    - Restitution or replacement when something has been damaged.
    - A reading and/or video and written response that highlights how students have experienced a similar incident to foster empathy and perspective taking.

**Strategy:** *Behavioral Problem-solving and Planning Conference*

A *Behavioral Problem-solving and Planning Conference* focuses on a single discrete behavior that needs to be replaced to support the student academically, socially, and emotionally. While students may engage in more than one behavior in need of replacement, it is important to make the shift in behavior feel manageable and begin with one. Often students who benefit from this intervention have low self-awareness about what behaviors derail them and interfere with their learning. They also have difficulty identifying exactly which target behaviors and action steps will help them focus and right themselves to re-engage with a learning task. A *Behavioral Problem-solving and Planning Conference* is a powerful way to communicate concern and care, and also strengthen the student's capacity to self-reflect and problem-solve. This conference demonstrates a teacher's commitment to listen and help the student think through a plan that will extinguish the unskillful behavior and learn a target behavior. See Appendices 8.2 and 8.3 – *Behavioral Problem-solving and Planning Conference Protocol* and Template. Consider using cards with action steps the student could take to tackle the behavior getting in the way of their learning. See Appendix 8.4 – Behavior Card Sort: Sample Action Steps.

**Strategy:** *Progress Monitoring*

When a teacher has engaged in a *Behavioral Problem-solving and Planning Conference* with a student to discuss the discrete behavior that is interfering with learning, and the actions the student will take to replace the behavior, the teacher also works with the student to talk about how progress will be monitored and tracked. A consistent, clear, and easily measured rating tool will be used; a weekly or daily check-in will be scheduled depending on the teacher's schedule; and the number of days or weeks the *Progress Monitoring* tool will be used. The teacher and student will monitor the student's use of explicit target behaviors, and the action steps agreed upon to meet the target behaviors. Behavior replacement and *Progress Monitoring* are thoroughly researched interventions proven to produce significant improvements in behaviors. (See Appendix 7.9 – Sample Progress Monitoring Tool.)

**Strategy:** *Behavioral Coaching*

For students to learn and practice a specific procedure, skill, or target behavior, a *Behavioral Coaching* session involves time outside of the regular classroom schedule. This kind of session incorporates side-by-side modeling, instruction, rehearsal, and feedback. We know this is an up-front investment for the teacher. Our own experiences and those of hundreds of teachers we have met confirm that the time is well worth the results of actually witnessing significant improvements in student behavior. *Coaching* a student to mediate their thinking, so they own the process and the action steps to meet target behaviors, requires the teacher to feel and be efficacious with responsive listening skills such asking opened ended questions, paraphrasing, and pausing to understand. See Appendix 7.5 – Responsive Listening. *Behavioral Coaching* sessions are very rewarding, as we witness students build their capacity to replace unproductive behaviors with new behaviors that will serve them in school and in their lives. *Coaching* a student to learn and use a target behavior involves four steps which are outlined in Figure 8.10. Consider using Appendix 8.4 – Behavior Card Sort: Sample Action Steps to identify action steps that students can rehearse to demonstrate the target behavior.

| |
|---|
| **What it Looks Like:** *Behavioral Coaching* |
| **Behavior Concern: Constant sidebar talking during whole group learning.** |
| **Step 1:** Identify the target behavior using the LLC chart on p. 12–13.<br>• I sustain my focus and pay attention throughout an activity or task. |
| **Step 2:** Elicit the benefits of using the target behavior.<br>• I won't get a referral.<br>• I will understand the instructions better.<br>• I'll feel good about participating and contributing something to make this a good class.<br>• I'll learn more and get a better grade. |
| **Step 3:** Teacher and the student brainstorm action steps to meet the target behavior.<br>• Ask questions about instructions.<br>• Jot notes to myself that help me stay focused on the task or topic<br>• Contribute a relevant comment or question to a discussion. |
| **Step 4:** Teacher models action steps agreed upon and student practices specific action steps using different classroom scenarios. Teacher provides positive and corrective feedback. |

| |
|---|
| **What it Looks Like:** *Behavioral Coaching* |
| **Behavior Concern: Student's constant frustration results in emotional outbursts and cursing.** |
| **Step 1:** Identify the target behavior using the LLC chart on p. 12–13.<br>• I express emotions skillfully, even when I feel angry, frustrated, or disrespected. |
| **Step 2:** Elicit the benefits of using the target behavior.<br>• I want to be in control.<br>• I won't have to leave the room because I disrupted the class.<br>• I show that I can manage my emotions.<br>• I can re-focus and get back to work. |
| **Step 3:** Teacher and the student brainstorm action steps to meet the target behavior.<br>• On a sticky note, jot down the feelings – what is causing me to feel this way?<br>• Ask yourself, how can I appropriately express what I'm feeling to get my needs taken care of?<br>• Practice replacing unacceptable language with neutral school-appropriate language. |
| **Step 4:** Teacher models action steps agreed upon and student practices specific action steps using different classroom scenarios. Teacher provides positive and corrective feedback. |

## Closing

When embracing a restorative and accountable approach to classroom discipline and behavior support, teachers believe in their own efficacy to establish well-managed classrooms and to skillfully and confidently navigate a wide range of student behaviors with care and respect. They respond in ways that respect the cultural and developmental needs and differences of each student. Teachers also recognize that adolescents will engage in unskillful and inappropriate behaviors that lead to mistakes, and they believe that every student has the capacity to learn from their mistakes, correct their behavior, recover from adverse situations, and develop the competencies to fully participate and cooperate in the classroom. When predictable expectations, protocols, and interventions become part of the classroom culture, students enter the process of growing their Learning and Life Competencies with effort, focus, commitment, and goodwill. You will have noticed that throughout this chapter, many of the protocols overlap. It is our intention to support you in your skill development to ensure that your responses to student behaviors become intuitive and an integral part of your identity as a teacher.

> What strategies from this chapter align with your classroom context?

> What are the ways these support the 6 Conditions for Engagement?
>
> Attention, Goodwill, Effort, Interest, Participation, Commitment

---

[1] Gay, G. (2010). *Culturally responsive teaching: Theory, research, and practice* (2nd ed.). J. A. Banks (Ed.). New York, NY: Teachers College Press.

[2] Noddings, N. (2013). *Caring: A relational approach to ethics and moral education* (2nd ed.). Los Angeles, CA: University of California Press.

[3] Fronius, T., Persson, H., Guckenburg, S., Hurley, N., & Petrosino, A. (2016). *Restorative justice in U.S. schools: A research review*. San Francisco, CA: WestEd.

[4] *Restorative Practices* (n.d.). In International Institute of Restorative Practices. Retrieved from http://www.iirp.edu/.

[5] Amstutz, L.S., & Mullet, J.H. (2015). *The little book of restorative discipline for schools: Teaching responsibility; creating caring climates*. Intercourse, PA: Good Books.

[6] Kim, W.C., & Mauborgne, R. (2004, July-August). 1997 Value innovation: The strategic logic of high growth. *Harvard Business Review*, 103-112.

[7] Chang, L. (2003). Variable effects of children's aggression, social withdrawal, and prosocial leadership as functions of teacher beliefs and behaviors. *Child Development*, 74(2), 535-548.

[8] Rudd, T. (2014, February). *Racial disproportionality in school discipline: Implicit bias is heavily implicated: Kirwan Institute issue brief.* Retrieved from http://kirwaninstitute.osu.edu/wp-content/uploads/2014/02/racial-disproportionality-schools-02.pdf.

[9] Tobin, J. (2000). *"Good guys don't wear hats": Children's talk about the media.* New York, NY: Teachers University Press.

[10] Cornwell, C., Mustard, D. B., & Van Parys, J. (2013). Non-cognitive skills and the gender disparities in test scores and teacher assessments: Evidence from primary school. *The Journal of Human Resources*, 48(1), 236-264. https://doi.org/10.3368/jhr.48.1.236.

[11] Kindlon, D., & Thompson, M. (2000) *Raising Cain: Protecting the emotional life of boys.* New York, NY: Ballantine Books.

[12] Macfarlane, K. & Woolfson, L.M. (2013). Teacher attitudes and behavior toward the inclusion of children with social, emotional, and behavioral difficulties in mainstream schools: An application of the theory of planned behavior. *Teaching and Teacher Education*, 29, 46-52. https://doi.org/10.1016/j.tate.2012.08.006.

[13] Lortie, D.C. (2002). *Schoolteacher: A sociological study* (2nd ed.). Chicago, IL: University of Chicago Press.

[14] Gregory, A., Skiba, R.J., & Noguera, P. (2010). The achievement gap and the discipline gap: Two sides of the same coin? *Educational Researcher*, 39 (1), 59-68. https://doi.org/10.3102/0013189X09357621.

[15] Gorski, P. (2008, April). The myth of the culture of poverty. *Educational Leadership*, 65(7), 32-36.

[16] Gilovich, T., Griffin, D.W., & Kahneman, D. (Eds.). (2002). *Heuristics and biases: The psychology of intuitive judgment.* Cambridge, United Kingdom: Cambridge University Press.

[17] Coleman, M. C., & Gilliam, J. E. (1983). Disturbing behaviors in the classroom: A survey of teacher attitudes. *Journal of Special Education*, 17(2), 121-129. https://doi.org/10.1177/002246698301700203.

[18] Lewin, P., Nelson, R.E., & Tollefson, N. (1983). Teacher attitudes toward disruptive children. *Elementary School Guidance & Counseling*, 17(3), 188-193.

[19] Woolfolk Hoy, A., & Weinstein, C. (2006). Student-teacher perspectives on classroom management. In Evertson, C.M. & Weinstein, C. S. (eds.), *Handbook of classroom management: Research, practice, and contemporary issue.* New York, NY: Routledge Press.

[20] Sequieira-Belvel, P. (2010). *Rethinking classroom management: Strategies for prevention, intervention, and Problem-Solving.* Thousand Oaks, CA: Corwin Press.

[21] American Academy of Child and Adolescent Psychiatry. (2013). *Oppositional defiant disorder No. 72.* Retrieved from https://www.aacap.org/aacap/families_and_youth/facts_for_families/fff-guide/Children-With-Oppositional-Defiant-Disorder-072.aspx.

[22] Walker, H.M., Ramsey, E., & Gresham, F. (2016). *How disruptive students escalate hostility and disorder—and how teachers can avoid it.* American Federation of Teachers. Retrieved from https://www.aft.org/periodical/american-educator/winter-2003-2004/how-disruptive-students-escalate-hostility.

# Section III

# Pulling it Together

# CHAPTER 9

## Planning Engaging Units and Purposeful, Well-Paced Lessons

**Chapter Outline**
- Introduction
- Unit Planning for Engagement, Inclusion, and Mastery
- Planning the First Learning Unit
- A Purposeful, Well-Paced Lesson
- Ritualizing the Day, the Week, and the Marking Period
- Closing

**Essential Question**
How do I plan learning units and lessons to support each and every learner to meet essential learning outcomes?

## Introduction

Planning for student learning is one of the most important responsibilities of teachers. We deepen student understanding by identifying, clarifying, and planning for the knowledge and skills students must master to be successful in school, work, and life. Through unit planning, we ensure that students are spending their time learning what is most essential. Unit plans provide a vision for an integrated and flexible lesson sequence. This chapter is designed to support teachers to thoughtfully plan a unit with the academic success of each and every student in mind. Our intention is to show the myriad ways teachers can get into a rhythm and—through practice over time—make unit planning not just viable, but indispensable to their work and partnership with students.

Thus far, we have explored the practices and strategies that support the development of Six Conditions for Academic Engagement and to strengthen students' Learning and Life Competencies. Perhaps you find yourself energized and ready to integrate critical practices that align with your context. Maybe you feel a little overwhelmed and unsure of where to start. As with any new learning, it is the application and synthesis of skills that really supports the deepening of knowledge. In this chapter, we offer a framework that supports you as a practitioner in applying and synthesizing your learning by:

- Deepening understanding of the elements of an effective unit plan and refining or developing a unit plan of your own;
- Considering ways to ritualize the day, the week, the unit, and the marking period and how this can support deeper learning and connection with students and make planning easier for teachers; and
- Examining how effective unit plans inform Purposeful, Well-Paced Lessons.

> **Why Effective Planning for Student Learning & Connection Matters**
>
> - "Teaching, on its own, never causes learning. Only successful attempts by a learner to learn causes learning."[1] Advance planning of engaging, rigorous, and meaningful learning tasks increases the likelihood that students will learn the content, skills, competencies, and target behaviors we are responsible for teaching them.
>
> - We gain insight into student understanding through observation of student application of knowledge in authentic contexts. Planning in advance what we are looking for in students' performance on any given task enables us to make critical observations about the group and individuals' level of knowledge and skill.
>
> - We deepen student understanding by making adjustments to our teaching based on our formative observations of and reflection on student knowledge application in authentic contexts. By intentional planning for the inevitable bumps in the road to student mastery, we can be more flexible, agile, and responsive to a diversity of student needs through opportunities for re-teaching, academic conferencing, and small group interventions.

## Unit Planning for Engagement, Inclusion, and Mastery

Grant Wiggins and Jay McTighe have long been considered the forerunners of unit planning. In this section, many of their ideas can be easily recognized in the suggestions we make and criteria we offer for effective unit plans. Also sitting on our shoulders are other experts—the many teachers with whom we have worked over the past four decades. We are aware that unit planning can feel overwhelming when trying to fit one's ideas into a prescribed unit-planning template. In this section, we offer methods that are responsive to multiple working and thinking styles, while holding true to the intended outcomes for student learning that are the basis of Wiggins and McTighe's framework.

Unit planning is a complex process with many elements to consider: student learning outcomes, student learning gaps, a diversity of student needs and interests, and infinite instructional pathways that may or may not lead to student mastery. In his *Checklist Manifesto*, Atul Gwande explains the power of the checklist to support complex tasks by breaking them down into the essential steps needed to arrive at an effective outcome. *"Checklists seem to provide protection against [the] failures [of faulty memory or skipping critical tasks]. They remind us of the minimum necessary steps and make them explicit. They not only offer the possibility of verification but also instill a kind of discipline of higher performance."*[2] In this spirit, we offer a series of checklists for unit design to support teachers in balancing the need to see the broader goals of the unit as well as the critical details. While the checklists outline the necessary steps, they also create a sense of discipline and increase the standards for unit plans that will best support every learner. These checklists also support building automaticity in unit planning as the process becomes increasingly embedded in one's memory.

We have seen a diversity in the methods teachers use to plan their units, from traditional planning notebooks, to electronic tools, to wall calendars with moveable sticky notes. The following checklists allow teachers to use their preferred method of planning and still focus on the elements of effective unit plans throughout the process. As you begin to synthesize your learning from the previous chapters into a coherent unit plan with academic engagement in mind, we offer three checklists, one for each stage of effective unit planning: (1) Identifying Desired Results and Organizing Content, (2) Determining Acceptable Evidence, and (3) Anticipating and Planning for Learning Gaps. While there will be familiarity with some steps in the process, we have also referenced portions of this book that will be useful in planning your unit that may not have been in the forefront of your mind in your past planning experience. Each of the unit planning checklists in this chapter can also be found in Appendix 9.1 – Unit Planning Checklists.

### Stage 1: *Identifying Desired Results and Organizing Content*

Setting the learning outcomes in advance is a critical first step in creating equitable classrooms where all students have access to high-level content. In this stage, you will identify the unit's: (1) key knowledge and skills, (2) key understandings, (3) essential questions, (4) key state learning standards, (5) Learning and Life Competency target behaviors for success in the unit (LLCs), (6) developmentally informed content, and (7) culturally relevant content.

In his paper, *Redefining College Readiness*[3], Dr. David Conley introduces aspects of comprehensive college readiness that create a more intentional alignment between what students should learn and understand before they leave high school and what students are expected to do in college. He states that when it comes to academic knowledge and skill, it is critical that all teachers across academic disciplines help students develop and strengthen three overarching academic skills that are gateways to college success:

- **Expository, descriptive, and persuasive writing tasks** that require students to make a claim or express a point of view; provide evidence to support a claim or point of view; and offer an explanation for their reasoning. Students need to know how to pre-write, and how to rewrite and edit a piece that is largely free of grammatical, spelling, and usage errors before submitting a final draft.

- **Research skills** that include developing search strategies that generate and answer questions; access different types of information; determine relevant information; distinguish between credible and non-credible source material; develop a coherent and defensible claim; and cluster, organize, and synthesize material into a paper or report.

- **Comprehension and discussion of challenging texts across the disciplines** that includes "close reading" for the big ideas and the details; ease with academic vocabulary; strategies for comprehending dense and difficult texts; and the capacity to discuss and connect texts to other topics and other texts.

When planning the desired results for a unit, it is important to incorporate some or all of these college readiness skills.

| **Checklist 1: Identifying Desired Results and Organizing Content** |
|---|
| **Key Knowledge & Skills** <br> ☐ Is this the most critical knowledge for students to walk away with from this unit? <br> ☐ Are these the most critical skills for students to walk away with from this unit? <br> ☐ Which college readiness skills might be most important for students to work on in this unit? |

| **Key Understandings** | **Essential Questions** |
|---|---|
| ☐ Are these key understandings at the "heart" of the discipline and in need of uncovering? <br> ☐ Will the synthesis of this unit's key knowledge and skills support students in reaching these key understandings? | ☐ Are my essential questions open-ended, thought-provoking and intellectually engaging? Will they spark discussion and debate? <br> ☐ Do the essential questions support students in exploring the key understandings? |

| **Key State Learning Standards** |
|---|
| ☐ Are these the essential, priority learning standards for students to demonstrate mastery in this unit? <br> ☐ Have I chunked together similar standards into priority or "power" standards that support my own planning and student understanding? |

| **Learning and Life Competency Target Behaviors (Chapter 1)** |
|---|
| ☐ Are these the five to six target behaviors that will most support student success in meeting the desired results for this unit? See Appendix 1.3 – LLC Sample Mini-Lesson. |

| **Developmentally Informed Content (Chapter 6)** <br> Will my content: | **Culturally Relevant Content (Chapter 6)** <br> Will my content: |
|---|---|
| ☐ Draw connections to personal interests? <br> ☐ Inject controversy through the use of multiple perspectives on real-world issues? <br> ☐ Link course content to the real world? | ☐ Explore the students' identities? <br> ☐ Integrate students' cultures? <br> ☐ Solicit cultural perspectives? |

**Stage 2:** *Determining Acceptable Evidence*

In this stage, you will determine the acceptable evidence to collect that supports your understanding of each student's learning throughout the unit. This includes identifying the key formative assessments you will use daily to ensure students are on track (*Walk-around Look-fors, Corrective Feedback, Five-minute Assessment Tools*), interim assessments to check where students are in their mastery prior to a unit's end (mid-unit assessments, written assessments, college readiness tasks), and summative assessments that will demonstrate student mastery (performance tasks, projects, end-of-unit assessments).

| Checklist 2: Determining Acceptable Evidence |
| --- |
| **Formative Assessments (Chapter 7)**<br>☐ Have I embedded formative assessments that will provide me with direct evidence of student knowledge, skills, or target behaviors corresponding to my desired results?<br>☐ Have I planned ways to collect, track, and use this information once I have it to inform instruction, strategy selection, and interventions? |
| **Interim Assessments and Interventions (Chapter 7)**<br>☐ Have I planned interim assessments that will provide me with enough evidence of student understanding to predict performance on the *End-of-Unit Assessment*?<br>☐ Have I identified the levels of understanding that would prompt additional levels of intervention?<br>☐ Have I identified what these interventions should be and built in time and systems into my unit plan to support students in need of additional interventions? |
| **End-of-Unit Assessments of Learning (Chapter 6)**<br>☐ Have I identified *End-of-Unit Assessments* that will provide me with enough evidence of student mastery of the desired content?<br>☐ Will these assessments support students' continued growth and progress toward mastery?<br>☐ Have I incorporated *Student Voice and Choice* to increase commitment to and success with these assessments (Chapter 6)?<br>☐ Are these assessments authentic (Chapter 6)?<br>☐ Have I designed ways for students who still haven't demonstrated mastery to continue to be supported toward mastery (ex. *Revise, Edit/Proof, and Correct*, Chapter 7)? |

## Stage 3: *Anticipating and Planning for Learning Gaps*

In this stage, you will *Anticipate and Plan for Learning Gaps* and identify strategies to ensure the deep learning of every student. This includes relying on your learning of Academic Supports from Chapter 7 to consider in advance what you might do to promote students to overcome learning gaps, prevent students from getting stuck, and intervene when students are not learning the intended content or skills. "One of the more consequential features of learning gaps is their tendency, if left unaddressed, to compound over time and become more severe and pronounced, which can increase the chances that a student will struggle academically and socially or drop out of school."[4]

> A learning gap is the difference between what a student has learned—i.e., the academic progress he or she has made—and what the student was expected to learn within a given learning task or at a certain point in a learning unit, a course, or a grade level. It refers to the relative performance of individual learners.

| Checklist 3: Anticipating and Planning for Learning Gaps (Chapter 7) |
|---|
| **Anticipating Learning Gaps** |
| ☐ Have I identified the learning gaps in content that I have run into the most in my prior classroom experience (or if new to the profession: Are these the learning gaps my colleagues have encountered most often)? |
| ☐ Have I planned to assess students' prior knowledge and skills that would support them in meeting the desired results for the unit? |
| **Planning Strategies & Interventions** |
| ☐ Have I identified the Tier 1 strategies that will promote most students' success in acquiring this unit's key knowledge, skills, target behaviors and avoid the learning gaps I have identified? |
| ☐ Have I identified the Tier 2 interventions that will support some students to overcome learning gaps in this unit's key knowledge, skills, and target behaviors? |

## Planning the First Learning Unit

When planning the first learning unit, it is important to embrace the mantra, "Go slow to go fast." The first unit needs to be packaged differently. It is critical to grow relationships with and among students as well as norm the group around the expectations for their success in the course. While you may not cover as much content in the first weeks of school, investment in "getting started" activities will result in fewer students giving up and acting out, more students remaining engaged and motivated, and, most notably, less frustration and greater satisfaction for you and the students you're teaching. Taking additional time in the first unit ensures that you are able to:

1. Get to Know Students (See Chapter 4 – Practice #1);
2. Build Group Cohesion and positive peer relationships (See Chapter 4 – Practice #2);
3. Orient students to the learning environment (See Chapter 5 – Practice #3);
4. Model, Teach, Practice, and Assess critical Procedures, rituals, routines, and Learning Protocols (See Chapter 5 – Practice #4);
5. *Set, Discuss, and Monitor Expectations* (See Chapter 7 – Practice #7);
6. Build a study culture by introducing *Study Strategies* (See Chapter 7 – Practice #7); and
7. Incorporate Rigorous and Meaningful Learning Tasks (See Chapter 6 – Practice #5) within the critical practices and strategies outlined.

We do not recommend forgoing instruction in the first days of your course in order to focus exclusively on course explanations, procedure practice, or induction activities; but rather, incorporating orientation activities and course work into every period from day one. You only get one start with each new group of students to set the tone and support students in understanding, "this is how we do things here." By considering how you will create community among students in the first unit, you will actually accelerate their learning in future units when they are better able to perform as a high functioning group of learners.

### A Purposeful, Well-Paced Lesson

A Purposeful, Well-Paced Lesson increases academic engagement and strengthens students' Learning and Life Competencies over time, supporting students to become more self-aware, self-managing, socially efficacious, and academically efficacious. A Purposeful, Well-Paced Lesson incorporates the following components: (1) the lesson purpose, (2) time chunks, (3) grouping formats, and (4) voice levels. See Figure 9.1.

**FIGURE 9.1** A Purposeful, Well-Paced Lesson

# A Purposeful, Well-Paced Lesson

**Lesson Purpose**
Clarifying the purpose of a lesson is a crucial first step to ensure that the lesson has a clear learning outcome that drives your choice of key strategies to support academic engagement. Below are several lesson purposes for you to consider in your lesson design:

- ☐ Introduction of new key knowledge or skills
- ☐ Deepened learning of key knowledge or skills
- ☐ Application of key knowledge or skills
- ☐ Direct experience of key knowledge or skill
- ☐ Independent practice

- ☐ Community Building
- ☐ Academic conferencing and coaching
- ☐ Academic discourse
- ☐ Research
- ☐ Reading and Writing Workshop
- ☐ Student performances and presentations

- ☐ Planning, creating, vetting, and finalizing major projects
- ☐ End of unit catch-up
- ☐ Preparation for assessments
- ☐ Interim and summative assessments
- ☐ Other

| Time Chunks | Grouping Formats | Voice Levels |
|---|---|---|
| 3 minutes | Whole Group | Silence |
| 7 minutes | Independent | One Voice |
| 10 minutes | Pairs | Low Partner Chat |
| 15 minutes | Trios | Medium: Multi-Group Conversations |
| 20 minutes | Quads | High Energy: Multi-Group Conversations |
| 30 minutes | | |

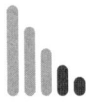

**Lesson Purpose:** What is the purpose of the lesson? What learning outcome(s) align with this purpose? Clarifying the purpose(s) of a lesson is a crucial first step to ensure that the lesson has a clear learning outcome that drives your choice of key strategies to support academic engagement. By beginning with the purpose, we decrease the emphasis on what we as teachers will be doing, and we increase student accountability to the learning we intend them to experience. These lesson purposes can live in a diversity of "containers" with which many of us are familiar, i.e., workshop, inquiry-based learning, and project-based learning.

**Strategies:** What strategies most align with your lesson purpose? Recall the Domains of the Engaged Classroom (Chapter 3). We acknowledge that this is not a complete list of strategies and you may have more to add; however, this is a good reference when considering strategies that align with the purpose for a specific lesson and support students in reaching the lesson outcome(s). To support you and your colleagues in planning your lessons, we refer you to Appendix 9.2 – A Purposeful, Well-Paced Lesson and Appendix 9.3 – Domains of the Engaged Classroom (Practices and Strategies).

**Time:** What are the ideal amounts of time for each learning strategy to maximize engagement and learning? Offering just the right amount of time to engage students and maintain their focus is an art, that over time, and through observation, teachers master. In a diverse group of learners, some students will always need less time and others more. The key is to make a note of this through observation and offer creative opportunities to those who need less time to stay engaged and provide additional practice time and support for those who need more time.

**Grouping Formats:** What are the ideal *Grouping Formats* for each learning strategy to maximize student engagement and learning throughout the lesson? By offering students opportunities to work independently or in groups, you create more time to monitor and assess what students are actually learning; you reduce the incidents of students going off-task during whole group instruction; you get more time to do *Personal Check-ins* and *Academic Check-ins* with individual students; and students are better able to process their thinking with peers through purposeful social interaction. Supporting students to work effectively in groups requires initial time to Model, Teach, Practice and Assess their performance, but the pay off in being able to observe student learning in action is well worth it.

**Volume Level:** What are the ideal volume levels for each learning strategy to support the learning environment? The brain likes change. Think about how a silent pause in the middle of a beautiful piece of music can be arresting. In a similar way, varying the volume levels in a classroom keeps it engaging for students. It also supports the different learners in the room and serves the variety of learning experiences in a lesson by providing Silence that fosters reflection, as well as partner talk or group chat that cultivates socially-constructed learning. When teachers are clear up front with students about what the volume level should be and in what ways this supports the learning of individuals and the group, students begin to shape their behavior to the context and transfer their volume level to similar situations. Offering a *Visual Posting* to the group about the volume level supports the quick redirection of students.

At this point in your unit planning, you have defined your desired results, defined acceptable evidence, *Anticipated and Planned for Learning Gaps*, and determined your daily, weekly, and marking period rituals and routines. As your plan becomes more detailed, it is critical to develop a level of flexibility that allows your plan to remain student-centered rather than content-centered, expressly for the benefit of each and every student mastering the unit content and skills. Your intentional unit planning has set the stage for planning lessons and lesson sequences. We recommend using a metaphorical (or real) pencil to now sketch your Purposeful, Well-Paced Lessons. The more you "ink" this in, the less malleable and responsive your lessons will be to meet your students' needs. While it is important to consider your processes for *Starting* and *Ending Class* each day, we do not see lessons necessarily as daily; a lesson with an overarching learning outcome may span an entire week.

# Ritualizing the Day, the Week, the Unit, and the Marking Period

Rituals hold meaning. They are strategies that are repeated at regular intervals in order to increase academic engagement and support Learning and Life Competencies (e.g., *Academic Reflection, Goal Setting, and Progress Tracking* and *Meet and Greet*). Rituals can occur with varied frequency from daily, to weekly, to once a unit, to once per marking period. Rituals support students in understanding, "This is how we do things here in our classroom. This is how we work and learn together." Rituals support teacher planning and can reduce the need to start from a blank slate for each lesson offering us comfort, predictability, and security in what we are asking our students to engage in. By creating daily and weekly rituals teachers are better able to plan for and deeply attend to students' social, emotional, and academic learning needs.

| Ritualizing the Day, the Week, and the Marking Period ||
|---|---|
| **Daily Rituals** ||
| We recommend integrating the following rituals daily to increase engagement, strengthen students' LLCs and meet learning outcomes:<br><br>☐ *Meet and Greet* (Chapter 4)  ☐ *Starting Class* Procedure (Chapter 5)<br>☐ *Value-added Feedback* (Chapter 4)  ☐ *Ending Class* Procedure (Chapter 5)<br>☐ *Reflect and Connect* (Chapter 5)  ☐ *Formative Assessment* (Chapter 7)<br>☐ *Turn and Talk* (Chapter 6) | We invite you to identify daily rituals that have been successful for you |
| **Weekly Rituals** ||
| We recommend integrating the following rituals at least once per week to increase engagement, strengthen students' LLCs and meet learning outcomes:<br><br>☐ *Preview the Week*  ☐ *Whole Group Discussions* (Chapter 6)<br>☐ *Closing the Week* (Chapter 4)  ☐ *Guided Work Period* (Chapter 7)<br>☐ *Gatherings* (Chapter 4)  ☐ *Study Strategies* (Chapter 7)<br>☐ *Circle* (Chapter 4)  ☐ *Informational Updates* (Chapter 11)<br>☐ *Student Feedback* (Chapter 5)  ☐ Good News Communications (Chapter 11)<br>☐ *Personal Check-ins* (Chapter 4)  ☐ Independent Work Time (Chapters 6 & 7)<br>☐ *Academic Check-ins* (Chapter 7)<br>☐ *Text Protocols* (Chapter 6) | We invite you to identify weekly rituals that have been successful for you |
| **Marking Period Rituals** ||
| We recommend integrating the following rituals each marking period, depending upon the time of year and your context, to increase engagement, strengthen students' LLCs and meet learning outcomes:<br><br>☐ *Student Names* (Chapter 4)  ☐ *Academic Reflection, Goal Setting, and Progress Tracking* (Chapter 7)<br>☐ *Student Profile Data* (Chapter 4)  ☐ *Classroom Behavior Plan* (Chapter 8)<br>☐ Foundational Procedures (Chapter 5)  ☐ Course and Personal Introductions (Chapter 11)<br>☐ Setting and Monitoring Expectations (Chapter 7)  ☐ Student Led Conferences (Chapter 11) | We invite you to identify marking period rituals that have been successful for you |

## Closing

We hope this chapter has offered a strategic journey that, at its end, has resulted in a unit plan that prepares you to meet your students where they are and move them to where they need to be. There is no doubt that detailed unit planning takes intentional time up front, and as a result of your efforts, your students will engage with you, their peers, and the rigorous, meaningful tasks and content you have designed. As a teacher, the rewards are immense. Intentional unit planning supports your lesson design so you can observe student learning in action, work side-by-side with students to develop shared knowledge of the content, skills, competencies, and target behaviors, and accelerate your own learning unit plan by unit plan. This can be beneficial to your practice all on its own; however, working in collaboration with colleagues to plan, review data, discuss student work, problem-solve, and set goals can further accelerate the skill sets of individuals in such teams. The next chapter offers many entry points into a collaborative model.

---

[1] Wiggins, G., & McTighe, J. (2005). *Understanding by design* (2nd ed.). Alexandria, VA: Association for Supervision and Curriculum Development.

[2] Gawande, A. (2011). *The checklist manifesto: How to get things right* [Kindle version]. Retrieved from Amazon.com.

[3] Conley, D. T. (2007). *Redefining college readiness.* Eugene, OR: Educational Policy Improvement Center.

[4] Glossary of Education Reform. Learning Gap. Retrieved from https://www.edglossary.org/learning-gap/ 11/06/2018.

# CHAPTER 10

# Collaborative Teaming for Ramping Up Academic Engagement and Student Achievement

**Chapter Outline**
- Introduction
- The Problem of Practice
- The Professional Learning Cycle
- Examples of Successful Team Collaboration
- Building Collaborative Efficacy
- Closing

**Essential Question**
In what ways might collaboration with my colleagues around a problem of practice, deepen my expertise as a teacher in service of ramping up academic engagement and achievement for each and every student?

## Introduction

In our work across urban districts we have met hundreds of school leaders and hundreds of thousands of teachers working in schools from Alaska to Massachusetts, and one thing we can say with certainty—no one school or group of teachers faces the exact same set of challenges as another. However, in supporting educators in these diverse settings, our approach remains steadfast: the work of ramping up academic engagement, deepening student learning, increasing equity, and supporting systemic change in classroom practice happens through the *collaboration* with and between the teachers and instructional leaders (i.e., assistant principals, instructional coaches, teacher leaders, or department heads) actually doing the work in schools. We define collaboration as a process through which a group of people constructively explores ideas in search of solutions that extend beyond one's own personal experience and lens. Collaboration is the marriage of two Latin roots, *com-* meaning with, together, or jointly, and *laborare* meaning to labor. Collaborative teams "labor together" to innovate, inspire, lead, hold a vision, and motivate one another in the face of challenges that confronted individually, would feel, and likely be, insurmountable.

Knowing the critical role collaboration plays in school improvement, more schools are organizing in ways that support collaborative dialogue in teams. Collaboration expands the body of knowledge at our disposal exponentially because it is not just the collective and shared teaching experience of the group; there is also the potential knowledge that can be co-created within teams. If you work in such a school, you know that developing the structures for teaming and collaboration is just a first step. Just like any new practice, fundamental learning about how to work effectively in teams must occur to truly realize the potential that teams bring to improving and refining their practice. This chapter offers tools and supports to assist teams in making the most of this precious time.

# The Problem of Practice

> "Changing where it counts the most—in the daily interactions of teachers and students—is the hardest to achieve and the most important."
> — David Tyack & Larry Cuban, *Tinkering Toward Utopia: A Century of School Reform.*[1]

Changing where it counts the most is possible when teacher teams collaborate around a clearly defined *"Problem of Practice"*: a collective, context-dependent problem that requires the collaborative learning of a group to solve it, whether this is a single grade-level team, course-alike cohort, department, and/or the whole school. The Problem of Practice is *an unresolved problem of student learning* derived from the collaborative examination of school-based evidence such as student data (qualitative and quantitative), survey responses, and observations. We frame the Problem of Practice around student learning intentionally, in order to build teacher and school leader commitment to examining substantive changes in instructional practices that would have a direct impact on student outcomes.

> **Deciding Who Decides:** It is critical for leaders, when identifying a Problem of Practice, to set the boundaries in advance for the decision-making process. In urgent urban environments, when there are specific required problems to work on, schools may not have extended time to come to a consensus on the Problem of Practice before getting to work. Leaders will need to find a balance between efficiency and voice which will always be context dependent. What is most critical is the transparency and sharing of interests behind the decision-making process to ensure faculty trust and commitment.

When schools identify the Problem of Practice as a first step, it offers a North Star that gives the work of school improvement collective meaning, purpose, and direction. Identifying the Problem of Practice collaboratively offers an entry point for faculty to engage in real-time authentic collaboration through the meaningful consideration of their current practices, the experience of students, and current student data to strategically plan for student improvement.

Identifying a powerful Problem of Practice requires school leaders to:

- Review a triangulated set of data (i.e., student outcomes, teacher/student/family surveys, classroom practice observations) to make a compelling case for the Problem of Practice.
- Prioritize an area of focus and draft a Problem of Practice.
- Verify it with the appropriate teacher cohort.
- Discuss the root causes with the teacher cohort.
- Research and identify target strategies that will begin to address the Problem of Practice.
- Identify formative student data to assess progress and make adjustments to instruction as needed.
- Identify long term indicators of success to assess impact of the strategies on the Problem of Practice.

> **Formative Student Data:** Together with instructional leaders, teachers identify academic skills and/or target behaviors and a set of aligned assessments to monitor ongoing progress on the Problem of Practice and adjust instruction accordingly. For example, if the identified academic skill is using vocabulary building strategies, the formative student data set might be: quizzes, a vocabulary unit test, use of vocabulary in academic discourse, or in written assignments, academic check-ins, labs, etc.

**Long Term Indicators of Success:**

When setting long-term indicators: (1) identify the data that will be used to measure success, and (2) identify the improvement in these data that will indicate success. When identifying a Problem of Practice, teachers together with instructional leaders will standardize data sets to measure student outcomes/success over time, for example, grades, benchmark data, and state test scores. When studying impact data, it is critical to systematize this and evaluate progress at the end of a marking period and/or semester. The schedule for this type of ongoing data analysis is dependent on the Problem of Practice.

Once your school, department, course-alike cohort, and/or grade-level teams have moved through this process, then you will be ready to develop a coherent professional learning plan in service of the Problem of Practice.

## The Professional Learning Cycle

Just as other professions require ongoing training and specialized skills, so too does teaching. Research indicates that ongoing professional learning over six-to-twelve months is correlated to gains of 21 percentile points on achievement tests.[2] We know that "one-shot" professional learning sessions do not result in deepening teacher practices and, in fact, most teachers report that 90% of the professional learning they receive is not valuable to them.[3] We also know that as academic standards have become more demanding for all students, effective teachers rely on a deep bench of knowledge and skills to support learning disabilities, language learning needs, and experiences of trauma.[4] Managing these increased demands requires us to deepen our collective professional practice. To do this, we need the support of our school leaders to help us learn and grow. In his 2006 report, *Bridging the Gap Between Standards and Achievement*, Richard Elmore discusses the Principle of Reciprocity:

> Accountability must be a reciprocal process. For every increment of performance, I (the school leader) demand from you (the teacher), I have an equal responsibility to provide you with the capacity to meet that expectation. Likewise, for every investment you (the school leader) make in my skill and knowledge, I (the teacher) have a reciprocal responsibility to demonstrate some new increment in performance.[5]

The Professional Learning Cycle supports mutual accountability by providing sustained professional learning focused on specific, targeted strategies that equip teacher teams and instructional leaders to address the collectively held Problem of Practice over time. Tackling a Problem of Practice can take several Professional Learning Cycles, and in many cases an entire year. One Professional Learning Cycle can range from four-to-eight weeks and is contingent on many factors, for example, teachers wanting more time to work on a strategy, the need to collect more formative student data, or to adjust the strategy when students are not making measurable progress. When teams experience success as a result of moving through Professional Learning Cycles and identifying solutions to the Problem of Practice, they begin to believe their work together can produce desired effects. When these types of mastery experiences are repeated over time, a peer culture begins to emerge among teachers in which the norm becomes, *"We do what it takes to excel, and we persist in the face of uncertainty and challenges."* While peer accountability increases, individual teachers begin to feel calmer in the face of challenges, knowing the group will support the development of effective solutions to the very real challenges facing the school.[6]

**FIGURE 10.1** The Professional Learning Cycle

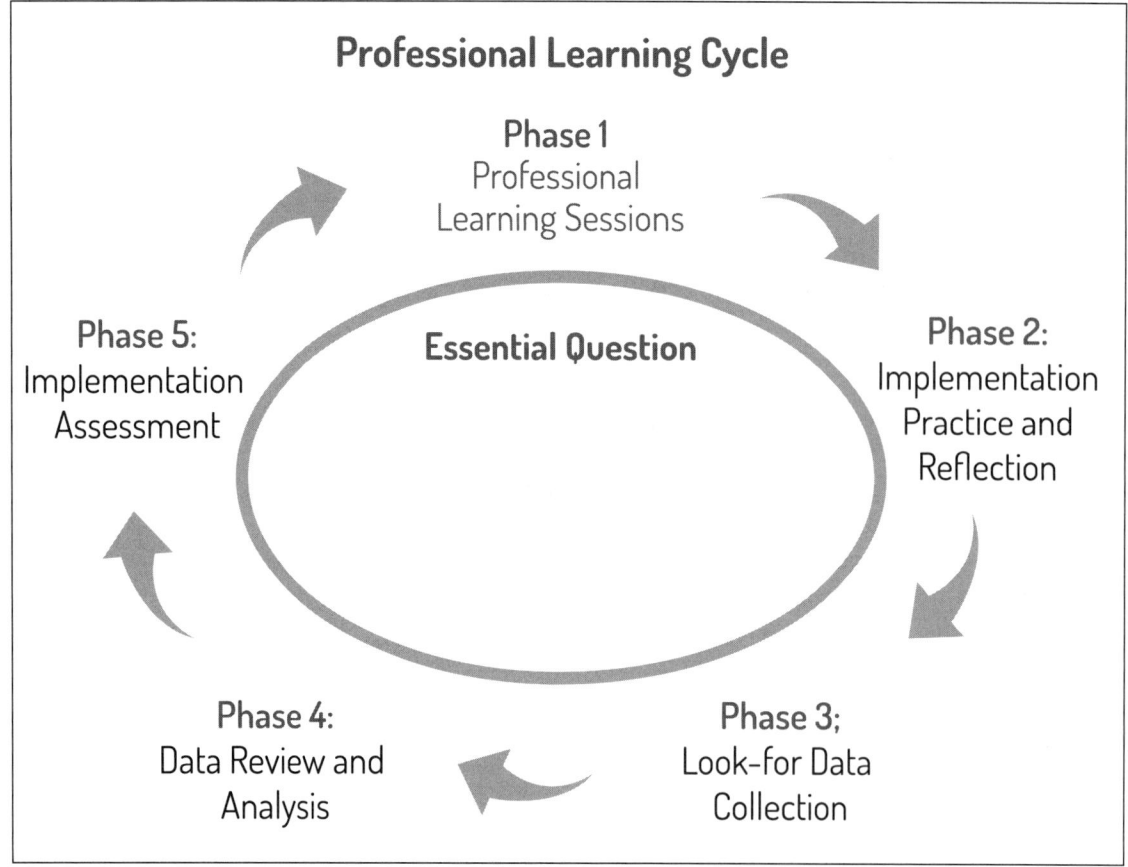

## Professional Learning Cycle

**Phase 1** Professional Learning Sessions

**Phase 2:** Implementation Practice and Reflection

**Phase 3:** Look-for Data Collection

**Phase 4:** Data Review and Analysis

**Phase 5:** Implementation Assessment

Essential Question

**Phase 1: Professional Learning Sessions**

> "Probably nothing within a school has more impact on children, in terms of skill development, self-confidence, or classroom behavior, than the personal and professional growth of the teachers...when teachers individually and collectively examine, question and reflect on their ideals and develop new practices that lead toward those ideals, the school, and its inhabitants are alive. When teachers stop growing, so do their students."
> — Roland Barth, *Run School Run.*[7]

The Professional Learning Sessions phase of the cycle supports faculty to deepen or learn strategies aligned to the Problem of Practice and to plan with their peers for implementation of them. Teachers reflect on and share how they are currently implementing the strategy successfully in their courses, engage in research, reading, and dialogue to identify new or refined ways of integrating the strategy, observe and discuss real-time modeling or video, and plan for application and assessment in their courses. The Problem of Practice drives learning in this phase as the faculty collectively grapples with the question, *"What is it that we do not yet know how to do effectively and how are we going to learn it?"* in order to discover and plan for solutions that improve student outcomes.

## Phase 2: Implementation Practice and Reflection

> "Being effective at what we value resonates with something beyond feeling competent. At some level, competence connects with our dreams, with the part of us that yearns for unity with something greater than ourselves. We want to matter."
> — Raymond Wlodkowski, *Enhancing Adult Motivation to Learn*[8]

The Implementation Practice and Reflection phase supports building the efficacy of each individual member of the team as well as the collective efficacy of the team itself. Teachers experiment with the strategy then return to the team to share their experience and evidence of student learning associated with the strategy. Individuals bring successes and implementation obstacles to the group and the team considers the conditions that led to success, and troubleshoots possible solutions and ways forward with regard to obstacles. A critical thought: making one's practice "public" requires setting up an intentional culture that acknowledges the vulnerability it takes to share successes and challenges with each other, the need for norms, and the importance of skillfully facilitated dialogue.

During Implementation Practice and Reflection, teachers and instructional leaders are also engaged in a conversation of what the "Look-for" data are for the specific strategy when it is implemented with fidelity and integrity. The conversations about Look-for data sharpen teachers' focus on implementation, create greater consistency with the strategy from class to class, and allow teachers to communicate and assess student actions in relation to the strategy. The Look-for data generated by the teachers, in collaboration with instructional leaders, inform the Look-for tool. Because of this collaboration, teachers view the Look-for tool as an authentic assessment of their implementation of the strategies. See Appendix 10.1 – Protocol for Identifying Implementation Look-fors.

## Phase 3: Look-for Data Collection

Once teachers have had time to practice implementing the strategy, a team of instructional leaders, learning specialists, and/or teachers begin to collect data on implementation using the Look-for tool. (See Appendix 10.1 – Protocol for Identifying Implementation Look-fors). The purpose is to collect objective data on what teachers are doing and what students are experiencing across classrooms. Collecting data on a team versus individual teachers promotes a peer culture that holds itself accountable for implementation and encourages risk-taking with a new strategy.

In order for a school to learn from data collection on implementation:

1. Teachers understand and believe that data collected is formative rather than evaluative.
2. Data collectors are clear about what they are looking for: teachers' implementation of the strategy, and how students are engaging with the strategy.
3. The data are compiled and presented to support teachers in making meaning of the classroom strategy across the grade-level, course-alike cohort, department, or school (not by the individual teacher).

See Appendix 10.2 – Look-for Data Collection and Analysis.

## Phase 4: Data Review and Analysis

> "It is a capital mistake to theorize before one has data. Insensibly one begins to twist facts to suit theories, instead of theories to suit facts."
>
> — Sherlock Holmes in Sir Arthur Conan Doyle's *Scandal in Bohemia*

The Data Review and Analysis phase supports teachers to understand how their collective practice is impacting student learning and engagement, and how shifts in strategies are addressing the Problem of Practice. Teams have a structured opportunity to make meaning of the Look-for data, and to set it alongside formative student data (see the sidebar on p. 184 titled Formative Student Data), in order to draw conclusions about the impact of the strategy on academic engagement and learning (See Appendix 10.2 – Look-for Data Collection and Analysis).

**Note to the reader:** Schools embarking on complex school improvement initiatives are often pressured to see quick changes in long-term indicators of success (grades, standardized tests, graduation rates, and four-year on track rates). While we are embarking on this work to increase academic engagement to, in turn, increase pass rates and higher levels of mastery, individual Professional Learning Cycles *will not* bring with them substantive changes in student outcomes. It is the collective iteration of the Professional Learning Cycle over time that yields the improvements in teacher efficacy that then impact student learning. To this end, a yearlong professional learning experience includes careful examination and monitoring of formative data as well as student grades and GPAs. The main drivers of student grades and GPAs are student attendance and effort—much more so than test scores, demographic factors, or which classes students take.[14] Looking at student grades across the team enables teachers to assess if their collective changes in practice over time are supporting increased academic engagement and effort.

## Phase 5: Implementation Assessment

> "Professional communities are born and nurtured in webs of conversation. What we talk about in our schools and how we talk about those things says much about who we are, who we think we are, and who we wish to be both in the moment and in the collective future that we are creating for ourselves as colleagues and for the students we serve."
>
> — Robert Garmston & Bruce Wellman, *The Adaptive School: A Sourcebook for Developing Collaborative Groups.*[9]

The Implementation Assessment phase is critical to supporting teachers to identify key understandings and reflect on the progress made towards tackling the Problem of Practice. As a result of this reflection and dialogue, teachers and instructional leaders will decide whether to move on to learning about another related strategy, or to continue strengthening expertise with the current strategy.

As teams move through the Professional Learning Cycle and build their collaborative efficacy they become more adept at making their practice public, increasing their data literacy, and engaging in problem-solving resulting in a sense of optimism, a deepened commitment to enhancing practice, and a school community that develops a shared vision, language, and purpose over time. This is something we have directly witnessed in our partnerships with schools, and schools that are most successful understand the importance that building *collaborative efficacy* plays in improving student outcomes.

We know that the Professional Learning Cycle requires multiple resources: time, people, and funding. We do not underestimate the impact of budget and scheduling restrictions, and limited staffing resources, among other factors, on a school's capacity to bring staff together to grow their practice. What we do know and understand is that finding time for staff to collaborate takes intentional consideration. It requires staff who are talented in creative scheduling design, clever uses of funding, and re-imagining time and resources with the support of assertive, adaptive and relational leadership.

We work with many schools with limited professional development time, and they often elect to spend six months to a year developing the readiness conditions for the implementation of Professional Learning Cycles that are sustainable:

- Leadership holds a belief that collaboration is a long-term school improvement strategy and is prepared to champion the effort.
- The right instructional leaders are in the right seats to systematically and consistently implement the Professional Learning Cycle.
- A professional learning schedule is ritualized, allowing for meaningful and ongoing collaboration.
- The Problem of Practice has been identified.
- Outside professional learning supports for teacher knowledge and skill gaps have been identified and aligned with the Problem of Practice.

## Examples of Successful Team Collaboration

In our work in schools, we have seen instructional leaders and teachers come together in a variety of collaborative structures to solve a wide range of Problems of Practice (see Appendix 10.3 – Teaming Structures: Purposes & Benefits). In the following section, we offer ways schools can leverage the power of collaboration to grow their collective efficacy in service of supporting students' academic, social, and emotional growth.

### Example #1: Grade-Level Collaboration—9th and 10th Grade

**Data Set Highlighting Concerns:**
- High rates of office referrals and suspensions
- High chronic absenteeism
- Low four-year graduation rate

### Identifying the Problem of Practice

1. **The Context:** In a large comprehensive high school, there are many student data points causing concern for the state, the district, and the school: (1) an in-school suspension rate of 80.7% and an out-of-school suspension rate of 29.9%, (2) a chronic absenteeism rate of 24.1%, and (3) a four-year cohort graduation rate of 75.5%. The school serves 75.3% of students eligible for free or reduced lunch, 15.4% of students learning English as a second language, and 17.7% of students with Individualized Education Programs (IEPs).

2. **The Problem of Practice is:** A substantial subset of 9th and 10th grade students are not earning requisite credits to be on track for graduation.

3. **Potential Root Causes:** With the volume of students in need of additional support (entering high school below grade-level), the current model does not effectively support early intervention. Deans, assistant principals, case managers, and social workers are working very hard but cannot support the high numbers of referrals and student needs.

4. **Essential Question:** What are the appropriate and targeted interventions that are needed for students to earn requisite credits to be on track for graduation in four years?

5. **Measurable Long-Term Indicators of Success:** Increase the percentage* of 9th and 10th grade students on track to graduate with their four-year cohorts.

    *Each school will determine what percentage increase feels realistic and viable based on the context.

    > **Note to Reader:** To meet long-term indicators, it is critical for teachers and instructional leaders to identify formative student data that will be assessed systematically to measure progress on the skills and/or target behaviors that help remediate the Problem of Practice.

6. **Collaborating to Solve the Problem:** The school restructures the schedule to support 9th and 10th grade students to belong to smaller cohorts of approximately 110 students, each with four dedicated content teachers—Math, Science, Social Studies, and English—to oversee and support student progress. Through the restructuring of the schedule, 9th and 10th grade teachers are given an additional six hours per week of common planning time. The grade-level teacher teams divide their cohort into four equal groups with each teacher assuming responsibility for communication and support of their subset of students. Teachers receive training on the roles and responsibilities of serving as a mentor for their cohort.

## Example #1 Summary: Grade-Level Collaboration

| | Developing a Plan of Action via the Professional Learning Cycle |
|---|---|
| Team Composition | Grade-level teacher teams support a specific subset of students. |
| Strategies | Teachers will study the following strategies over time in the context of individual Professional Learning Cycles (PLC):<br>• PLC #1 – *Academic Turnaround Plan* for single failures.<br>• PLC #2 – *Academic Problem-solving and Planning Conferences* for students with multiple failures.<br>• PLC #3 – *Progress Monitoring*. |
| Student Outcomes | Students will be able to proactively improve their academic performance over time through conferencing and progress monitoring by:<br>1. Persisting in their effort and finishing tasks.<br>2. Pursuing and sustaining efforts to complete long-term tasks and achieve long-term goals.<br>3. Using a range of study strategies to remember and apply key knowledge, skills, and understandings.<br>4. Engaging in critical, reflective, and creative thinking. |
| Professional Learning Cycle #1* | 1. Professional Learning Session<br>   a. *Academic Turnaround Plan*.<br>2. Implementation Practice & Reflection<br>   a. Identify *Academic Turnaround Plan* Look-for data.<br>   b. Experiment with the strategy.<br>   c. Share implementation stories.<br>   d. Share evidence of student work.<br>3. Look-for Data Collection<br>   a. Observe for implementation of *Academic Turnaround Plan* Look-for data.<br>4. Data Review and Analysis<br>   a. Reflect on *Academic Turnaround Plan* Look-for data.<br>   b. Analyze formative student data on academic skills and/or target behaviors that indicate progress on the Problem of Practice.<br>5. Implementation Assessment<br>   a. Team identifies key understandings.<br>   b. Team self-assesses progress on Problem of Practice.<br>   c. Team sets goal for the next learning cycle.<br>*There are multiple Professional Learning Cycles to tackle this Problem of Practice. The length of time devoted for each phase in the PLC (1-5 above) will vary.* |

### Example #2: Interdepartmental Team Collaboration—English and Social Studies

**Data Set Highlighting Concerns:**
- Low pass rate for the required state graduation exam for English and Social Studies
- Quantitative data indicates low college readiness
- Low four-year graduation rate

### Identifying the Problem of Practice

1. **The Context:** In a large comprehensive high school, the four-year graduation rate is 66%; 44% of students pass the required state graduation exam with enough proficiency to receive the highest academic diploma.

2. **Problem of Practice:** A substantial number of students are struggling to meet proficiency levels in English/Language Arts and Social Studies courses, and on state standardized tests.

3. **Potential Root Causes:** Uneven academic expectations across Social Studies and English/Language Arts that create confusion for students; no standardized strategies for close reading of dense text; no clear standards for written work across all English/Language Arts and Social Studies courses; no clear criteria for rigorous assessments; lack of communication among teachers who teach the same students.

4. **Essential Question:** What are the high-leverage strategies and interventions to increase pass rates in English/Language Arts and Social Studies to ensure success on required state graduation tests?

5. **Measurable Long-Term Indicators of Success:** Increase the percentage* of students on track to graduate, by increasing pass rates for English/Language Arts and Social Studies courses. Increase the percentage of students passing the required state graduation exam.

    *Each school will determine what percentage increase feels realistic and viable based on the context.

    > **Note to Reader:** To meet long-term indicators, it is critical for teachers and instructional leaders to identify formative student data that will be assessed systematically to measure progress on the skills and/or target behaviors that help remediate the Problem of Practice.

6. **Collaborating to Solve the Problem:** In an effort to better support students, the school creates humanities teams composed of one Social Studies and one English/Language Arts teacher who share the same classroom cohort of students for the year. All teachers involved meet weekly, by grade level, to establish common instructional and grading practices that meet Social Studies and English/Language Arts learning standards, and college and career readiness standards.

## Example #2 Summary: Interdepartmental Team Collaboration

| | Developing a Plan of Action via the Professional Learning Cycle |
|---|---|
| **Team Composition** | Interdepartmental humanities teams (paired English/Language Arts and Social Studies teachers by grade level). |
| **Strategies** | Teachers will study the following strategies over time in the context of individual Professional Learning Cycles (PLC):<br>• PLC #1 - Support students in using *Text Protocols*.<br>• PLC #2 - Support students to *Represent Their Learning*.<br>• PLC #3 - Support students to *Revise, Edit/Proof, and Correct* their work.<br>• PLC #4 - Incorporate choice and standardized criteria and processes for rigorous end-of-unit humanities projects. |
| **Student Outcomes** | Students will be able to:<br>1. Comprehend complex text using various *Text Protocols*.<br>2. *Represent Their Learning*.<br>3. *Revise, Edit/Proof and Correct* their work.<br>4. Complete a rigorous end-of-unit project of their choice. |
| **Professional Learning Cycle #1\*** | 1. Professional Learning Session<br>   a. *Text Protocols*.<br>2. Implementation Practice and Reflection<br>   a. Identify *Text Protocol* Look-for data.<br>   b. Experiment with the strategy.<br>   c. Share implementation stories.<br>   d. Share evidence of student work.<br>3. Look-for Data Collection<br>   a. Observe for implementation of *Text Protocol* Look-for data.<br>4. Data Review and Analysis<br>   a. Reflect on *Text Protocol* Look-for data.<br>   b. Analyze formative student data on academic skills and/or target behaviors that indicate progress on the Problem of Practice.<br>5. Implementation Assessment<br>   a. Team identifies key understandings.<br>   b. Team self-assesses progress on Problem of Practice.<br>   c. Team sets goal for the next learning cycle.<br>*\*There are multiple Professional Learning Cycles to tackle this Problem of Practice. The length of time devoted for each phase in the PLC (1-5 above) will vary.* |
| **Considerations** | We want to acknowledge that within secondary school populations there are a significant number of students who have great challenges decoding and encoding text. These students require targeted interventions to address the gaps. |

## Example #3: Course-Alike Cohort Collaboration—Biology

> **Data Set Highlighting Concerns:**
> - Disproportionately high numbers of 9th grade students failing Biology.

### Identifying the Problem of Practice

1. **The Context:** In a large comprehensive high school, a department head notices in the schoolwide data that the course in which the most 9th grade students are failing is Biology. After the first six weeks of school, 21.4% of students are not passing.

2. **Problem of Practice:** Students taking Biology are failing at a rate far higher than other 9th grade courses.

3. **Potential Root Causes:**
   - Examination of behavior, attendance, and grade data finds that absenteeism and behavior explain only a very small fraction of the student failures.
   - In conducting *Academic Check-ins* with some of their students who are failing, teachers find that students have two significant obstacles to success:
     - New and unfamiliar vocabulary that has to be understood and memorized to make meaning of the text/course.
     - Most of the learning is accomplished through lecture or reading.
     - A review of common assessments indicated that students were having extreme difficulty processing the language of the text as evident in their written responses.

4. **Essential Question:** What strategies and interventions will increase reading comprehension, academic efficacy, and pass rates in Biology?

5. **Measurable Long-term Indicators of Success:** Decrease the percentage* of students failing Biology.

   *The teacher cohort will determine what percentage decrease feels realistic and viable based on the context.

   > **Note to Reader:** To meet long-term indicators, it is critical for teachers and instructional leaders to identify formative student data that will be assessed systematically to measure progress on the skills and/or target behaviors that help remediate the Problem of Practice.

6. **Collaborating to Solve the Problem:** In an effort to better support students, all 9th grade Biology teachers begin to work together during their department time as a course-alike cohort to strategically think together about strategies that will support each and every student to navigate the content and cognitive load of the course. The teachers will consult with the grade-level reading specialist to deepen their understanding of strategic reading processes and practices.

## Example #3 Summary: Course-Alike Cohort Collaboration

| | Developing a Plan of Action via the Professional Learning Cycle |
|---|---|
| Team Composition | **Course-alike cohort:** 9th grade Biology |
| Strategies | Teachers will study the following strategies over time in the context of individual Professional Learning Cycles (PLC):<br>• PLC #1 - Support students to use effective vocabulary building strategies.<br>• PLC #2 - Support students in using *Text Protocols*.<br>• PLC #3 - Support students to *Represent Their Learning*.<br>• PLC #4 - Support students to use academic language in context with their peers through the *Turn and Talk*. |
| Student Outcomes | Students will be able to:<br>1. Learn course specific vocabulary and concepts using targeted strategies.<br>2. Comprehend complex text using strategic reading processes and various *Text Protocols*.<br>3. *Represent Their Learning* through note-taking, graphic organizers, etc.<br>4. Use academic language accurately in conversations with peers using a *Turn and Talk*. |
| Professional Learning Cycle #1* | 1. Professional Learning Session<br>   a. Strategies that build content specific vocabulary mastery (using contextual cues, creating graphic explorations of words, developing flash cards).<br>2. Implementation Practice and Reflection<br>   a. Identify the vocabulary strategies Look-for data.<br>   b. Experiment with the strategies.<br>   c. Share implementation stories.<br>   d. Share evidence of student work.<br>3. Look-for Data Collection<br>   a. Observe for implementation of the vocabulary strategies.<br>4. Data Review and Analysis<br>   a. Reflect on the vocabulary strategies Look-for data.<br>   b. Analyze formative student data on academic skills and/or target behaviors that indicate progress on the problem of practice.<br>5. Implementation Assessment<br>   a. Team identifies key understandings.<br>   b. Team self-assesses progress on Problem of Practice.<br>   c. Team sets goal for the next learning cycle.<br>*There are multiple Professional Learning Cycles to tackle this Problem of Practice. The length of time devoted for each phase in the PLC (1-5 above) will vary. |

## Example #4: Schoolwide Collaboration—Middle School Department Teams

> **Data Set Highlighting Concerns**
> - Low state reading scores
> - District benchmark data and reading screenings indicate low percentages of students reading at grade-level in the 6th, 7th, and 8th grades

### Identifying the Problem of Practice

1. **The Context:** In a mid-sized middle school, schoolwide data indicates that only 56% of 6th graders, 62.3% of 7th graders, and 63% of 8th graders are reading at grade level.

2. **Problem of Practice:** A significant number of students in grades 6-8 are assessed at reading at least two years below grade level.

3. **Potential Root Causes:** Lack of appropriate reading strategies intended to focus specifically on encoding/reading comprehension. Lack of content-specific reading strategies being used consistently within departments. Lack of culturally relevant reading materials to build reading comprehension.

4. **Essential Question:**

    a. What culturally relevant materials can we select to ensure that students engage in strategic reading practices?

    b. What high-leverage reading strategies will we all use within our departments? In what ways will we scaffold and differentiate these reading strategies to align with developmental needs in 6th through 8th grade?

    > Researching and identifying the right culturally relevant materials requires a dedicated curriculum review team representative of all departments. We recognize that this takes intentionality and time to ensure that culturally relevant materials are seamlessly integrated into all courses.

5. **Measurable Long-Term Indicators of Success:** Increase the percentage* of students reading at grade level as measured on the district benchmarks.

    *Each department will determine what percentage increase feels realistic and viable based on the context.

    > **Note to Reader:** To meet long-term indicators, it is critical for teachers and instructional leaders to identify formative student data that will be assessed systematically to measure progress on the skills and/or target behaviors that help remediate the Problem of Practice.

6. **Collaborating to Solve the Problem:** Middle school teachers across disciplines use existing departmental time to think systematically together about reading instruction and practice and how to grow strategic readers. The departments will consult with the middle school reading specialist/instructional coach to deepen their understanding of strategic reading processes and practices.

    > It is critical that representatives from each department meet systematically in order to lift up strategies that are universal across departments so that teachers create a cohesive experience for students by using the same language to Model, Teach, Practice and Assess the strategies.

Example #4 Summary: Schoolwide Collaboration—Middle School Department Teams

| | Developing a Plan of Action via the Professional Learning Cycle |
|---|---|
| **Team Composition** | All Departmental teams. |
| **Strategies** | Teachers will study the following strategies over time in the context of individual Professional Learning Cycles (PLC):<br>• PLC #1 - Support students in using *Text Protocols* using culturally relevant materials.<br>• PLC #2 - Support students to use effective vocabulary building strategies.<br>• PLC #3 - Support students to use academic language in context with their peers through the *Turn and Talk*.<br>• PLC #4 - Support students to *Represent Their Learning*.<br>• PLC #5 - Support students to improve their reading skills through *Academic Coaching* sessions. |
| **Student Outcomes** | Students will be able to:<br>1. Comprehend culturally relevant text using strategic reading processes and various *Text Protocols*.<br>2. Learn course-specific vocabulary using targeted strategies.<br>3. Use academic language accurately in conversations with peers using the *Turn and Talk*.<br>4. *Represent Their Learning* through note-taking, graphic organizers, etc.<br>5. Improve reading skills through *Academic Coaching* sessions. |
| **Professional Learning Cycle #1\*** | 1. Professional Learning Session<br>   a. *Text Protocols* emphasizing comprehension.<br>2. Implementation Practice and Reflection<br>   a. Identify *Text Protocol* Look-for data.<br>   b. Experiment with the strategy.<br>   c. Share implementation stories.<br>   d. Share evidence of student work.<br>3. Look-for Data Collection<br>   a. Observe for implementation of *Text Protocol* Look-for data.<br>4. Data Review and Analysis<br>   a. Reflect on *Text Protocol* Look-for data.<br>   b. Analyze formative student data on academic skills and/or target behaviors that indicate progress on the Problem of Practice.<br>5. Implementation Assessment<br>   a. Team identifies key understandings.<br>   b. Team self-assesses progress on Problem of Practice.<br>   c. Team sets goal for the next learning cycle.<br>*There are multiple Professional Learning Cycles to tackle this Problem of Practice. The length of time devoted for each phase in the PLC (1-5 above) will vary. |
| **Considerations** | • A team would need to be identified to engage in planning for this type of comprehensive intervention that impacts all faculty members.<br>• With this Problem of Practice, there is a percentage of students who are reading three years below grade level and require a reading remediation program. This also requires a sub-group of faculty to investigate and recommend the remediation intervention. |

## Building Collaborative Efficacy

> "In collaborative cultures, failure and uncertainty are not protected and defended, but instead are shared and discussed with a view to gaining help and support. Collaborative cultures require broad agreement on values, but they also tolerate and to some extent actively encourage disagreement within these limits. Schools characterized by collaborative cultures are also places of hard work and dedication, collective responsibility, and pride in the school. Collaborative cultures…acknowledge that teachers have purposes and commitments of their own."
>
> — Andy Hargreaves & Michael Fullan, *Professional Capital: Transforming Teaching in Every School*[10]

Collaboration is the cornerstone of the Professional Learning Cycle and critical to tackling Problems of Practice; yet, not all individuals come to the work of collaboration with the necessary competencies, skills or mindsets to effectively partner. Almost everyone has a story about working in teams that represents the antithesis of collaboration: conversations were focused on the negative, no decisions were made, and no new learning occurred. *"Schools where teachers' conversations dwell on the insurmountable difficulties of educating their students are likely to undermine teachers' sense of efficacy. Schools where teachers work together to find ways to address the learning, motivation and behavior problems of their students are likely to enhance teachers' feelings of efficacy."*[11] Schools and teams that grow their effectiveness over time grow to understand and embrace the following:

1. **Effective teams move through developmental stages:** Just like any other entity, teams develop over time and thus, demonstrate developmental stages. In 1965 Bruce Tuckman explored the development of small groups and identified four developmental stages[12]:

    a. **Forming:** Group members are orienting themselves to the group by testing the interpersonal boundaries and task behaviors that will be accepted. Group members are largely dependent on external factors such as leaders or pre-existing standards in their work as a team.

    b. **Storming:** Individual group members may find themselves in conflict around interpersonal issues or task requirements. This behavior supports individuals in resisting the influence of the group, a protective response in the absence of trust.

    c. **Norming:** A sense of group cohesion forms and thus, resistance is overcome, replaced by increased standards for the work and increased interpersonal trust. Teams become more independent in their work.

    d. **Performing:** Interpersonal relationships become the foundation for task activities. Group members are flexible in their roles, as the group's tasks become the principle focus. These teams are independent with an internal sense of accountability and responsibility.

2. **Effective teams use norms:** Effective teams share their thinking through dialogue, which develops shared understanding through collective meaning-making. Effective dialogue supports team members' sense of connection, belonging, and safety. Garmsten and Wellman observed hundreds of teams and studied their overall effectiveness and the norms they used when in conversation with one another. From this study, they developed the Seven Norms of Collaboration which can be found at this site: http://www.thinkingcollaborative.com/inventories-norms-collaboration-effective-meetings/.

3. **Effective teams grapple with differing perspectives:** Effective teams make an effort to grapple with multiple, differing perspectives and, in doing so, they create a level of trust that

leads to greater participation among group members. When there is a high level of group cohesion and trust, the group is equipped to use differing perspectives to its advantage and develop creative solutions to the Problem of Practice.

4. **Effective teams manage conflict productively:** Conflict is part of the developmental trajectory of teams as they move through the storming phase. It is how this conflict is managed that helps teams move forward to the norming and performing phases of group development. Effective teams confront and address difficult behaviors in order to maintain relationships while still keeping the group focused on the goal. Effective teams are able to develop win-win solutions in which everyone's needs are met, but these solutions can only be developed when individual group members are equipped to interrupt non-collaborative behaviors.

5. **Effective teams support the deepening of self-awareness and group awareness and monitor their progress and set goals:** Teams that seek feedback, discuss obstacles, reflect, and experiment have demonstrated significant performance gains over teams that do not engage in these learning behaviors. These teams continuously reflect on the following questions:

    a. What was my most important learning as an individual during this Professional Learning Cycle in relation to the Problem of Practice?

    b. In what ways is this team better able to support students after this Professional Learning Cycle in relation to the Problem of Practice?

    c. In what ways has our team grown in relation to the phases of group development? In what ways can we continue to improve?

    d. What do we need to tackle next in relation to the Problem of Practice?

Principals and instructional leaders hold the mantle for shaping the culture of teacher collaboration in the service of student learning and achievement. When the expectations for effective teaming are clearly defined and collectively shared by a faculty, teachers are energized and enthusiastic about their work and are willing to try new things. They learn how to dialogue and reflect, consider how their mindsets inform their current teaching practices, broaden perspective based on new learnings, contribute expertise, accept feedback, and authentically support one another. The individuals who benefit the most from healthy and effective collaboration are our students. Thus, an intentional focus on teaming opens communication, decreases isolation, encourages pedagogical innovation, and creates interdependence all in the service of student success and achievement.

## Closing

While we have offered research-based practices throughout this book to support teachers in engaging adolescent learners, if after reading it, individual educators retreat to their classrooms to use this as a manual to improve practice independently, then we will have missed a critical opportunity. The great hope of this chapter is that individual educators look past their own agency, their own students, and their own curriculum to focus on the collective agency of the group, the students, and the school. It is the collegial connections and positive relationships within a school that lead to the increased learning of the individuals and the school at large. "Schools and teachers that have better quality collaboration across instructional domains also have higher achievement gains, and usually at statistically significant and meaningful levels."[13]

We hope that the tools provided in this chapter support your school in moving toward or deepening a commitment to the relationships, structures, systems, and protocols that will foster a collaborative culture in service of students' overall success.

## Literature and Research

**In a review of current research, there is empirical evidence that:**

- Academic optimism makes a significant contribution to student achievement after controlling for demographic variables and previous achievement. Academic optimism is achieved through the culminating effects of three conditions:
  - **Academic Emphasis:** Schools set high but achievable goals for students; there is an orderly and serious learning environment; students work hard and value academic achievement (Chapters 6 and 7).
  - **Faculty Trust in Parents and Students:** Cooperation and trust among teachers, students, and parents has direct correlations to attendance, persistent learning, and faculty experimentation with new practices and strategies (Chapters 4 and 11), and
  - **Collective Efficacy:** This is the perceived judgment of teachers that the faculty, as a whole, can employ their collective agency to have a positive effect on student outcomes schoolwide.[15]
- Teachers' beliefs about their *individual efficacy* are strongly linked to the implementation of effective practices in the classroom and increases in student achievement.[16,17,18,19,20]
- In schools where the *collective efficacy* of the faculty as a whole is high, teachers' sense of *individual efficacy* is higher. Teachers' beliefs about their *collective efficacy* are strongly linked to student achievement.[21,22,23]
- Increased *social capital* has been highly correlated with increased student achievement test scores in reading and math and with the quality of instruction that is in turn correlated significantly to gains in student achievement.[24,25]
- Schools with distributed leadership and participative decision-making outperformed schools in which teachers worked autonomously in isolation.[26]
- Students in schools with a teaming structure performed better on state achievement tests than students in schools without teaming structures. Schools with job-embedded common planning time had the greatest two-year gains in student achievement scores and schools that had been collaborating through common planning time for five or more years had the highest achievement scores.[27]
- Schools with collaborative structures had fewer office disciplinary referrals and suspensions than similar schools without teaming.[28,29]

These increases in student achievement have been attributed to teachers developing a sense of shared responsibility for their students' success. Working together increases teacher focus on students' academic and behavioral outcomes.[30]

Collaboration supports the deepening of teacher capacity to solve Problems of Practice by increasing the organization's *social capital*, the resources embedded in the relationships among the people within an organization. When schools get three things right, they are better able to realize the potential of social capital to increase student learning: [31]

- **They are Organized for Collaboration:** Schools with structures that support collaboration are better able to absorb and assimilate new knowledge in the knowledge-intensive setting of schools.
- **There is a High Degree of Organizational Trust:** When faculty believe peers are acting in the best interest of the organization, they are more likely to share sensitive and important information with one another.
- **There is a Shared Language and Codes that Provide the Foundation for Communication:** they are better able to combine knowledge to develop the organization's intellectual capital.[32]

[1] Tyack, D. & Cuban, L. (1997). *Tinkering Toward Utopia: A Century of School Reform.* Cambridge, MA: Harvard University Press.

[2] Darling-Hammond, L., Chung Wei, R. & Andree, A. (2010). How High-Achieving Countries Develop Great Teachers. *Stanford Center for Opportunity Policy in Education, Research Brief*, August 2010. https://edpolicy.stanford.edu/sites/default/files/publications/how-high-achieving-countries-develop-great-teachers.pdf.

[3] Gulamhussein, A. (2013). *Teaching the Teachers; Effective professional development in an era of high stakes accountability.* National School Boards Association Center for Public Education.

[4] Darling-Hammond, L. (2006). *Powerful teacher education: Lessons from exemplary programs.* San Francisco, CA: Jossey-Bass.

[5] Elmore, R. (2002). *Bridging the gap between standards and achievement: The imperative for professional development in education.* Washington, DC: Albert Shanker Institute.

[6] Goddard, R., Hoy, W. & Hoy, A. (2004). Collective Efficacy Beliefs: Theoretical developments, empirical evidence, and Future Directions. *Educational Researcher*, Vol. 33, No. 3, pp. 3-13.

[7] Barth, R. (1980). *Run School Run.* Cambridge, MA: Harvard University Press.

[8] Wlodkowski, R.J. (2008). *Enhancing adult motivation to learn: A comprehensive guide for teaching all adults.* Third Edition. San Francisco, CA: Jossey Bass.

[9] Garmston, R. & Wellman, B. (2016). *The Adaptive School: A sourcebook for developing collaborative groups,* 3rd edition. New York, NY: Rowman & Littlefield.

[10] Hargreaves, A. & Fullan M. (2012). *Professional capital: Transforming teaching in every school.* New York, NY and London, UK: Teachers College Press.

[11] Tschannen-Moran, M., Woolfolk Hoy, A. & Hoy, W. (1998). Teacher Efficacy: Its meaning and measure. *Review of Educational Research.* Vol. 69, No. 2, pp. 202 – 248.

[12] Tuckman, B. W. (1965). Developmental Sequence in Small Groups. *Psychological Bulletin* 63.

[13] Ronfeldt, M., Owens Farmer, A., McQueen, K. & Grissom, J. (2015). Teacher Collaboration in Instructional Teams and Student Achievement. *American Educational Research Journal.* June 2015, Vol. 52, No. 3, pp. 475–514. DOI: 10.3102/0002831215585562.

[14] Allensworth, E., Farrington, C., Gordon, M., Johnson, D., Klein, K., McDaniel, B., & Nagaoka, J. (2018*). Supporting social, emotional, & academic development: Research implications for educators.* Chicago, IL: University of Chicago Consortium on School Research.

[15] Hoy, W., Tarter, J., & Hoy, A. (2006). Academic Optimism of Schools: A force for student achievement. *American Educational Research Journal*, Vol. 43, N. 3, pp.425 – 446.

[16] Armor, D., Conroy-Oseguera, P., Cox, M., King, N., McDonnell, L., Pascall, A., Pauly, E. & Zellman, G. (1976). Analysis of the School Preferred Reading Programs in Los Angeles Minority Schools, RAND Corporation, Santa Monica, CA, *Report No. R-2007-LAUSD*, ERIC Document Reproduction Service No. 130 243.

[17] Anderson, R., Greene, M., & Loewen, P. (1988). Relationships among teachers' and students' thinking skills, sense of efficacy, and student achievement. *The Alberta Journal of Educational Research*, 34, 148-165.

[18] Webb, R. & Ashton, P. (1987). Teachers' motivation and the conditions of teaching: A call for ecological reform. In S. Walker, S. and L. Barton, *Changing policies, changing teachers: New directions for schooling* (pp. 22-40). Philadelphia, PA: Open University Press.

[19] Midgley, C., Feldlaufer, H., & Eccles, J. (1989). Change in teacher efficacy and student self and task-related beliefs in mathematics during the transition to junior high school. *Journal of Educational Psychology*, 81, 247-258.

[20] Bandura, A. (1997). *Self-efficacy: The exercise of control.* New York: W.H. Freeman and Company.

[21] Tschannen, M., Woolfolk H., Hoy, A., Hoy, W. (1998). Teacher Efficacy: Its meaning and measure. *Review of Educational Research*. Vol. 69, No. 2, pp. 202 – 248.

[22] Goddard, R., Hoy, W. & Hoy, A. (2004). Collective Efficacy Beliefs: Theoretical developments, empirical evidence, and future directions. *Educational Researcher*, Vol. 33, No. 3, pp. 3-13.

[23] Hoy, W., Sweetland, S., & Smith, P. (2002). Toward an organizational model of achievement in high schools: The significance of collective efficacy. *Educational Administration Quarterly*, 38(1), 77-93.

[24] Leana, C. & Pil, F. (2006). Social Capital and Organizational Performance: Evidence from Urban Public Schools. *Organization Science, INFORMS*, vol. 17(3), pages 353-366, June.

[25] Goddard, Y., Goddard, R. & Tschannen-Moran, M. (2007). A Theoretical and Empirical Investigation of Teacher Collaboration for School Improvement and Student Achievement in Public Elementary Schools. *Teachers College Record*, V. 109, N. 4, pp. 877-896.

[26] Smylie, M., Lazarus, V., & Brownlee-Conyers, J. (1996). Instructional outcomes of school-based participative decision making. *Educational Evaluation and Policy Analysis*, 18, 181–198.

[27] Flowers, N., Mertens, S., & Mullhall, P. (2015). The impact of teaming: Five research-based outcomes. *Middle School Journal*, 31:2, 57-60.

[28] Crow, G., & Pounder, D. (1997, April). Faculty teams: Work group enhancement as a teacher involvement strategy. Paper presented at the meeting of the *American Educational Research Association*, Chicago, IL.

[29] Pounder, D. (1998). Teacher teams: Redesigning teachers' work for collaboration. In D.G. Pounder (Ed.), *Restructuring schools for collaboration: Promises and pitfalls* (pp. 65–88). Albany, NY: State University of New York Press.

[30] Erb, T. (1995). Teamwork in middle school education. In H. G. Garner (Ed.), *Teamwork models and experience in education* (pp. 175–198). Boston, MA: Allyn & Bacon.

[31] Bryk, A. & Schneider, B. (2004). *Trust in schools: A core resource for improvement.* New York: Russell Sage Foundation.

[32] Nahapiet, J. & Ghoshal, S. (1998). Social capital, intellectual capital, and the organizational advantage. *Acad. Management Rev.* 23 242–266.

# CHAPTER 11

## The Value of Teacher-Family Partnerships

**Chapter Outline**
- Introduction
- The Big Ideas That Inform Teacher-Family Partnerships
- Connecting with All Families
- Involving Families in Student Interventions
- Enhancing Family Engagement through Teaming
- Closing

**Essential Question**
What are my priority strategies for meaningful family engagement that will support each and every student's success at school?

## Introduction

We can never overestimate the importance of a parent's enduring love, sustained presence, and real-world guidance. Adolescents rightly turn to a parent or adult ally when they need an extra push in school, when they need to sort out their day-to-day hopes and worries, or when they need a dose of wisdom and encouragement to navigate tough situations that life presents.

Teachers, parents, and researchers agree that family engagement in their children's education leads to improved student performance at school.[1] A study that examined multiple measures of academic achievement in urban secondary schools—including grades, standardized tests, teacher rating scales, and indices of academic attitudes and behaviors—found that home-school involvement of parents across all racial backgrounds positively affects academic achievement.[2] Teacher-family partnerships have the potential to build a shared vision about education, healthy development, and student success that boosts students' resilience to navigate life opportunities regardless of setbacks or adverse circumstances.[3]

> In this chapter, we use the terms families and parents interchangeably for any adult who has legal guardianship of the student (e.g. aunts/uncles, grandparents, foster parents, adoptive) and who supports him/her on a consistent basis, serves as primary caregivers, and advocates for our students.

The value of family engagement is uncontested. Yet, the teachers' commitment to forge school-home connections is countered by genuine concerns that include: (1) the viability of developing relationships with all families when teachers are likely to be assigned 100 or more students at any given time in the school year; and (2) lingering doubts about what impact communication with parents of teenagers has on student outcomes. This chapter makes a case for strong teacher-parent partnerships and offers practical strategies that make family engagement a viable undertaking for classroom teachers.

> **The Big Ideas That Inform Teacher-Family Partnerships**
>
> - School-home partnerships begin with understanding and valuing all kinds of families.
> - Parents and guardians have a great influence on adolescents' future aspirations.
> - The most impactful school-home connections involve teachers.

### School-home partnerships begin with understanding and valuing all kinds of families

It is critical for educators and administrators to find language that reflects the broad diversity of families they serve. Addressing letters or notes home to "Parents and guardians," instead of "Parents" can make all the difference to many caregivers.[4] One of our core beliefs is that families hold vital knowledge and insights that we can tap into as educators who support their children. We approach parents and guardians with an asset-based lens, considering all of the opportunities open to us when we embrace families as partners in the learning process. Purposefully welcoming all kinds of families communicates the belief that parents and guardians are integral to their children's success and development. We recognize that due to myriad reasons, some families are not able to partner in the ways we would like at certain times in the course of their child's schooling. These situations warrant our empathy and understanding, enabling us to keep the door open when families are ready to partner.

### Parents and guardians have a great influence on adolescents' future aspirations

Parents of adolescents continue to have a significant influence on their children's academic achievement and their future aspirations regardless of race, socio-economic status, and family structure.[5] Academic, attendance, and behavior outcomes all improve when (1) parents place a high value on education in general, and their children's education in particular; (2) parents hold high expectations for their children to achieve academically throughout their K–12 schooling; and (3) parents believe their children will complete some type of postsecondary education. Parents' aspirations for their children tend to solidify their children's commitment to continue their education. Moreover, meaningful conversations between parents and school staff about their children's progress contribute to *"raising parental expectations, strengthening parents' beliefs in the value of schooling, and building parents' knowledge of the language of schooling and college and career planning that support high aspirations."*[6]

Research focused on family involvement in the middle and high school years shows that low parent participation in school activities is not a reflection of parents' lack of interest in their child's education or their desire to be informed about their child's progress.[7] Rather, parents may value more varied approaches to supporting their child's education as he or she grows older—from ensuring that children attend school every day and arrive safely, to providing study time, to encouraging their children to take greater responsibility for their success at school.[8] Inviting parents to share their hopes about their children and the ways that they support their children's success provides a platform for validating a parent's role and showing respect for their parenting perspective. Every encounter with a parent is an opportunity to recognize and embrace the multiple ways in which families care about education; support their children's healthy development, academic progress, and future aspirations; and involve themselves in their children's schooling.

### The most impactful school-home connections involve teachers

What do parents want from their children's schools? In 2011, the National School Public Relations Association conducted an extensive survey of parents from 50 urban, suburban, and rural districts to explore the kind of communication parents wanted with their children's schools.[9] The four highest priorities, identified by secondary parents, were:

1. Communication with teachers about their children's progress and how their child might improve;
2. Timely notification when their child's performance was slipping;
3. Information about what their child is expected to learn in their course work; and
4. Teachers' grading and homework policies.

The classroom teacher is at the center of all four priorities. Although school-family engagement strategies often involve parents in evening events, volunteer activities, school decision making, or community collaborations, meaningful and timely communication with a child's teachers appears to be a more robust strategy that has a direct impact on student achievement.[10]

A recent study from Harvard and Brown Universities shows how teachers can serve as the cornerstone of successful school-home communication.[11] For half of 435 underperforming students who were involved in the study, teachers communicated weekly with parents through very brief text messages or phone calls that centered around one actionable step students could take to improve their grades. At the completion of their course work, these students were 41% less likely to fail than the control group whose parents received no weekly communication from teachers. Researchers speculate that the consistent and predictable communication from teachers served as a catalyst for parents to engage in more frequent and specific conversations with their children about their progress in the course and their efforts to improve their grades.

Other studies have also found that teachers' direct engagement with families had more impact on parental involvement and student success than school-level communication and events.[12] To this point, we encourage middle and high school leadership teams to rethink their focus on family engagement and channel more attention to supporting teachers to engage directly with parents.[13]

The following high-leverage practices provide an array of strategies for incorporating family engagement into your professional practice. While we recognize the need to involve families when serious concerns arise about a student, we hope teachers will recognize the value in connecting with the families of all students in their care. Given the limitations of time that teachers can realistically devote to family engagement activities, the recommended strategies meet two important conditions: (1) they have proven to significantly impact the academic performance of adolescent learners; and (2) they are viable for individual teachers or teams to implement. See Figure 11.1 – Creating Teacher-Family Partnerships.

**FIGURE 11.1** Creating Teacher-Family Partnerships

| Promotion and Prevention | Intervention |
| --- | --- |
| **Connecting with All Families:** Teachers embed strategic opportunities to connect with all families throughout the year to generate goodwill and communicate the value they place in partnering with families. | **Involving Families in Student Interventions:** Teachers involve families in intervention strategies when students are struggling in their classes. |
| Strategies:<br>• Course and Personal Introductions<br>• Information Updates<br>• Good News Communications<br>• Student-led Conferences | Strategies:<br>• Tell Me More Interviews<br>• Family Conference<br>• Progress Monitoring After a Family Conference<br>• Parent Requests a Call or Conference |

**The following adult mindsets support the implementation of these practices with integrity and fidelity:**

- I believe that parents are valued partners who are committed to supporting their children's academic, social, and emotional development.
- I believe that parents place greater value on education and their children's future aspirations when they know more about their children's school experience and discuss what students are learning with their children.
- I believe in the power of listening to understand parents' cultural backgrounds, their child's school history, and their thinking and feelings with the aim of finding common goals that support their children.

**Benefits of Family Engagement:**

- Communicates to parents and students that family involvement in their children's education is important.
- Provides information for parents that can encourage parent-child conversations about school and their academic progress.
- Expands our own understanding of students and offers entry-points for developing stronger relationships with them.
- Inspires parental pride and investment in their child's accomplishments and inspires student pride in what they are learning.
- We believe that healthy relationships with families support and enhance parents' and students' development of Learning and Life Competencies.

### A note about making time for family engagement:

Establishing a plan for family engagement efforts eliminates the guesswork involved in figuring out how to incorporate these practices into your professional schedule. Consider setting aside at least one hour every week to intentionally connect with parents. Teachers with whom we have partnered consider the following options for time allocation: (1) before or after school, (2) during part of a lunch period, (3) a preparation period, or (4) team planning time for parent communications, note-writing, texts, calls, and conferences. Devoting one hour per week to connect directly with 10 families will result in about 400 personal connections with families by the end of the year. Imagine the impact. For teachers, families, and their children, this can be truly transformative.

## Connecting with All Families

This is a Tier 1 promotion and prevention practice that offers ways to touch base with all families of your students, sending a welcoming message to parents from day one. Early communication with families sets a hopeful and friendly tone that invites parents to be interested in what their children are learning and doing in your class. The fact that you choose to be the first to initiate contact with families can also help diminish the alienation or discomfort that some parents might feel about their encounters with schools and school staff. Most of these strategies enable you to reach all parents of students you teach at the same time using print or electronic media. Preparation for many of these parent-friendly communications can be done before the school year begins.

**Strategy:** *Course and Personal Introductions*

What do we want families to know about us, our course, and our hopes and expectations? What might parents specifically do to help their children be successful in our class? How might we communicate that our classroom is a welcoming space that values their perspective, expertise, and involvement in their children's education? Engaging in strategic ways to introduce ourselves and our course is the first step to building rapport with parents and cultivating their interest in what students are learning. These little "communication bites" can prompt words of encouragement and on-going parent-child conversations about students' progress in your course.

---

**What It Looks Like:** *Introductory Letter*

Write a short letter that introduces your course and offers a snapshot of you as a person and a teacher.

- Keep the communication to one page.
- Prior to the start of the school year, have the letter translated into multiple languages based on what you know about your student population.
- Give two copies to each student—one to keep at home, and one that parents sign and return to you. You may want to invite families to write in three things on the signed letter that they return to you: (1) the preferred way that they would like to be contacted whether by phone, text, or email; (2) the best time of day for a phone call; and (3) one special thing they would like you to know about their child.

See Appendix 11.1 – Sample Introductory Letter.

---

**What It Looks Like:** *Introductory Video*

Film a short video that gives a sense of you and of your course. It might feature your classroom so that families immediately feel part of the space. It might feel like a personal conversation, or it might be humorous, scholarly, or formal—whatever fits with your personality and style. If you consider using a commercial video platform, you need to check on the district policy about posting on social media platforms.

### Considerations

1. Invite students to update their Personal Contact Card (see Appendix 4.2 – Personal Contact Card) at the beginning of every marking period to ensure that communications are reaching all families.

2. When making decisions on how to communicate, be mindful of using technology that is accessible to most of your families and that aligns with district policies.

3. Reaching out to families who speak a home language other than English:
   - Connecting with newcomer families, or those whose home language is not English, can be particularly challenging, yet well worth the effort.[14] Solicit help from any of the following people to translate your welcome letter into other languages: designated adult and student translators in your school; a parent who is fluent in English and a home language; or a member of a community organization who supports newcomer families and is fluent in English and a home language.[15]

### Strategy: *Informational Updates*

How might you communicate what students are learning and how students are progressing throughout the year? This strategy keeps all families in the loop about the content of your class, expected outcomes, and important assessments. It is particularly beneficial to students and families who have come to expect that only "bad news" is sent home. Although this type of communication is mostly one-directional, it is an important initial step to inviting family voices to be part of two-way conversations. It also supports a conversation between the parent and their child about what is happening at school.

Good news from research about family preferences regarding school-home communications makes this strategy more viable: electronic tools have emerged as the preferred method of families for sharing school-home information.[16] School Websites, parent portals, email, and text messages make sending general information and updates easier and more accessible for all involved.

> **What It Looks Like:** *Quarterly Memo*
>
> A newsy quarterly memo (emailed if you have access to family email addresses, or printed to send home) keeps families informed about what students have accomplished in the class so far; what they will be learning in the next quarter; and what projects, exams, and milestones are on the horizon. Keeping this to one template that you populate is more viable for you and most likely will be read by the parent.
>
> See Appendix 11.2 – Informational Update Formats.

### What It Looks Like: *Special News Blast*

Compose a brief, but succinct email or printed memo to all families when a group of students has met a particularly difficult academic challenge; when everyone in the class has completed an important assessment with proficiency; when the array of ways students have completed a product, project, or presentation is truly worth a shout-out. Design a template that you can populate. This increases the likelihood of sending out an occasional News Blast.

See Appendix 11.2 – Informational Update Formats.

### What It Looks Like: *Reminders*

A Reminder, like a "Special News Blast" is a very brief printed memo or email that alerts the family about major assessments or assignments, often accompanied by deadlines. Reminders give parents a reason to check in with their children about the status of their work and provide opportunities to offer timely doses of encouragement as students are nearing completion of an important piece of work or preparing and rehearsing for an important test or presentation.

See Appendix 11.2 – Informational Update Formats.

### What It Looks Like: *Student Reflections*

Students create a written assessment of their progress thus far to bring home and discuss with their families. The assessment can include a description of what they have learned, their strengths and accomplishments, and their goals for improvement. If students are engaged in *Academic Reflection, Goal Setting, and Progress Tracking*, they will have access to information to share with their families. *Reflections* can be used at any time, but are particularly effective at the end of a marking period.

## Considerations

1. Consider creating an e-newsletter using a free online template.

2. Involve students in designing a *Student Reflections* template as part of an in-class project or as a way to review the last quarter's learning. Print multiple copies so that students can complete them at any time. Add a section for family comments on the back page of the *Reflections* sheet and ask students to return it to you as a way to build in two-way communication and family feedback. This will support students' commitment to engage with their family about the course.

3. If you have parents who want ways to be more involved in the class, consider enlisting their help in sending out memos or translating them.

**Strategy:** *Good News Communications*

Building relational trust with our students through one to one personal check-ins and even quick casual conversations shows our interest in a student's well-being. Similarly, families benefit when we touch base with them to share good news about their children. This quick and easy strategy goes a long way to countering all-too-frequent situations where families only hear from teachers when their child is experiencing academic or behavioral challenges.

> **What It Looks Like:** *Good News Communications*
>
> - Send a text or written note with a quick acknowledgment of a student's success in the form of *Value-Added Feedback* (see pg. 51).
> - Make a phone call just to tell a parent about something important that their child has accomplished; a learning experience that was made special by their presence and personal expression, or a social or academic behavior they have worked on that has made them a more effective learner and/or community member.
> - If you want to be even more creative, keep a set of postcards on hand and write personal notes on them. Send them home with students or mail them, since there is something particularly special about an old-fashioned post, provided there is funding for stamps and accurate mailing addresses.

## Consideration

1. Create a tracking sheet so that you are systematically communicating with families about students who are in most need of these *Good News Communications*.

**Strategy:** *Student-led Conferences*

> *"What may seem like a small change—parent conferences run by students instead of teachers—can change the entire culture of a school in powerful ways. When students must report to their families what they're learning—what skills and understandings they have, what areas still challenge them, and where they hope to get to—they must understand their own learning and progress. They take pride in what they can do and take responsibility for what they need to work on. Education stops being something done to them and begins being something that they are leading."*[17]

*Student-led Conferences* in which students share their academic progress at the middle of a marking period or end of a marking period, or present their work on a special project invites families to gain a deeper understanding of and appreciation for what students are actually learning and experiencing at school. Grade report conferences give students an opportunity to assess their progress across courses, highlight accomplishments and challenges, and share their plans for improving or extending their learning. Project conferences enable students to present a significant piece of work from one course or a combination of courses that reflects a sophisticated application of the knowledge and skills they have acquired over a marking period, semester, or whole year. *Student-led Conferences* have the potential to draw very large numbers of parents to a school-sponsored event. At one urban high school we partnered with, *Student-led Conferences* were organized for 300 9th graders. Prior to this event, typical parent turn-out for traditional grade report pick-up was fewer than fifty families. In this case, more than 200 9th grade families participated in *Student-led Conferences*.

> **What It Looks Like:** *Preparing for Student-led Grade Report and Project Conferences*
>
> Students and teachers work together to plan the structure for *Student-Led Conferences*. The type of *Student-led Conference* is identified, and students organize and rehearse what they are going to share and the process for sharing. Conferences typically include an agenda and guidelines for students' and parents' roles in the conference.
>
> See Appendix 11.3 – Student-Led Conference Check Lists.

## Considerations

1. Setting aside adequate time for preparation and rehearsal is essential for a successful outcome.

2. For students whose families choose not to attend the event, schedule a special time during lunch or after school when students can share their work with a group of teachers, administrators, and student support staff who want to validate their efforts.

3. When schools choose to introduce *Student-led Conferences*, a pilot initiative involving one grade, one grade-level team, or one department may be a good first step. This enables the grade or team to work out the bugs in the process and share the highlights with staff at large.

## Involving Families in Student Interventions

Tier 2 teacher-facilitated interventions when students are struggling academically and/or behaviorally are at the heart of supporting students to improve their performance. Conferring with parents, whether it a quick two-minute check-in or an extended family conference is the most direct way to garner both goodwill and a shared vision of common goals and support strategies.

The vast majority of parents want to be contacted immediately when a concern arises, offering us an opportunity to practice sharing our concerns, conveying our belief in their children's potential to get on track, and affirming our desire to partner and join efforts. Many teachers at the secondary level frequently experience feelings of anxiety, fear, or inadequacy when they consider contacting families.[18] These feelings may intensify when teachers work in communities different from their own. They may experience cultural disconnects that can prompt worries about competence in collaborating with families.

Parents, too, may have their own negative memories of school that keep them from feeling confident in reaching out to teachers directly. In addition, many parents have already experienced a series of adversarial or unpleasant interactions with school personnel by the time their children reach middle and high school.[19] These experiences can quickly reinforce feelings of distrust and discomfort for parents and students in their relationships with teachers.[20] Keeping these realities in mind, we believe that every teacher has the capacity to reverse a cycle of negative encounters and make teacher-parent conferencing a productive and emotionally satisfying experience for families and you. We offer four guidelines that reduce the hesitations we might feel and support a healthy and productive partnership with families.

1. **Hold a "family-driven, youth-guided" vision of family engagement:** When students are experiencing academic and behavioral challenges, it is important to be mindful of the concept of "family-driven, youth-guided care," an approach that respects and encourages the decision making roles of parents and adolescents within the intervention process.[21] This approach encourages parents and adolescents to be active participants in the *Problem-solving and Planning Conferences* that are the cornerstone of this practice.

2. **When we don't know, ask:** When you feel stuck trying to "figure out" an issue that is prompting your concerns about a student, invite the parent to share their insights, their family background, and their child's history. Ask parents to define their view of their child's strengths and challenges. When you are unsure about how to approach a particular parent, seek out someone on the staff for information and advice who might know the student and their family better than you do. When you worry about responding to a parent in a way that is culturally respectful, be open to consulting with colleagues about responsive ways to approach parents. Lastly, rehearse in writing how you want to open the door to the conversation, as this will set the tone for the remainder of the check-in with the parent.

3. **Hold a positive presupposition about all parents:** Parents want the best for their children. When we communicate our confidence in parents to support their children, and we share how much we appreciate their involvement, parents' own sense of self-efficacy grows, and their belief in their capacity to exert a positive influence on their children's educational outcomes is strengthened.[22]

4. **Bring your optimism and empathy with you:** Believe in the power of resilience and compassion. As human beings, we all have the capacity within us to right ourselves, overcome challenges, make a better choice, and begin a different journey. Every new day brings hope with it and entering a conference with a family with intentional listening, non-judgment, and general curiosity will benefit the student, parent, and you.

**Strategy:** *Tell Me More Interviews*

These are quick phone conversations targeted to families of students about whom you know very little. Parents tend to be thrilled when you call to say "I would like to know _____ a little better. What should I know about _____ that will help me support your child to be successful in this class?" *Tell Me More Interviews* communicate a heightened level of care and investment since you have chosen to take the time to speak with parents directly.

---

**What It Looks Like:** *Tell Me More Interviews*

We offer the following script as a jumping off point and know you will incorporate your own style to connect with students' families.

- Draft a list of families to call based on what you know about your students already. Prioritize students you are having a difficult time connecting with or supporting in ways that feel effective.
- Here is a suggested script for making your calls. When we are intentional about what we say in our opening, middle, and closing to the call, we become practiced and at ease about our efforts to reach out to families.

**Opening:**

"Hello, this is (your name), your child's (name of your course) teacher."

"I'd like to spend a couple of minutes learning a bit more about _____. Is this a good time to talk?"

**Middle**

"Thank you for your time. I'm sure that you can share things about your son/daughter that will help me support him/her to be successful in this class. What are some things I should know about _____ that will help me know him/her a bit better?"

"Is there anything about his/her history in school that would be helpful to know?"

"What is one thing you would like me to do to support his/her success?"

**Closing:**

"Thank you so much for sharing your insights. I look forward to supporting _____ the best way I can, and I am confident that he will have a successful year in this class."

"Please don't hesitate to call me if you would like to connect in the future. I would be happy to connect with you. Here is my phone number and email."

---

## Considerations

1. If the parent indicates that this is not a good time to talk, invite the parent to name a more convenient time that works for him/her, and reschedule the call.

2. Try combining a *Tell Me More Interview* with the strategy in Appendix 4.4 – 1 Student / 5 Actions / 5 Days. This can forge a stronger relationship with students whom you want to know better.

### Strategy: *Family Conferences*

When in-class strategies to address academic slippage or persistent behavior concerns have not led to improved student outcomes, a *Family Conference* is a critical strategy to consider. To ensure that the voices of both the student and the parent are part of the conferencing process, we suggest a three-part protocol:

1. Engage in an academic or behavioral *Problem-solving and Planning Conference* with the student beforehand, so that you and the student have already agreed on target behaviors, skills and action steps that will improve the student's performance in class. (See Chapters 7 and 8 for *Problem-solving and Planning Conferences* for academic and behavioral concerns.)

2. Arrange for a *Family Conference*. This conference generally involves a phone call between the teacher and a parent. Depending on the situation, however, it could be an in-person conference at school that might also include the student. The purpose of the conference is to share the issue that prompted a conference with the student, discuss the plan the student and you have created, and invite the parent to share their ideas for supporting their child. Because you are calling with a spirit of optimism about moving forward, this turns what could feel like a "bad news" encounter into a "good news" opportunity. (See Appendix 11.4 – Family Conference Protocol and Appendix 7.5 – Responsive Listening.)

3. Decide on the number of weeks to monitor a student's progress and check in weekly with the student's parent. (See Strategy: *Progress Monitoring* on pg. 131.)

---

**What It Looks Like:** *Preparation for a Family Conference*

- Set aside a time to meet with the student for an academic or behavioral *Problem-solving and Planning Conference*.
- Reach out to the parent via email, text message, or phone call to arrange a call or in-person conference.
- Schedule a time to engage in calls with parents when you feel somewhat relaxed and optimistic.
- Create a brief agenda that can be shared with the parent visually or orally and jot down notes to move through the conference protocol with clarity and efficiency.
- Use a scripted protocol like the one in Appendix 11.4 – Family Conference Protocol so that you cover the bases in a timely manner.

---

### Considerations

1. When arranging calls and conferences with parents ahead of time, give parents options that reflect your professional boundaries around time.

2. When a parent's home language is not English, check whether an interpreter is available for a *Family Conference*.

### Strategy: *Progress Monitoring After a Family Conference*

Researchers agree that follow-up parent communication to share a student's progress related to their plan for improving their behavior and/or academic performance boosts the effectiveness of behavioral and academic interventions. This strategy involves a weekly two-minute phone call, email, or text message to parents for a designated period of weeks. Sharing brief, but specific weekly reflections with families reinforces common goals and reassures students and families of your continued interest in supporting the student's success in your class.

> **What It Looks Like:** *Progress Monitoring Update*
>
> 1. Decide on a ritualized format for your communication that is viable and efficient to implement with the parent.
> 2. Decide on a couple of things that you would like to share with the parent that would support them in encouraging their child to continue to improve, for example:
>    - Student's grade.
>    - Student's use of a specific target behavior or academic skill.
>    - One thing the student can do to improve their grade.
>    - One thing the student has also done well.

## Considerations

1. Discuss *Progress Monitoring* with the student first and invite the student to help decide exactly what academic skills and/or target behaviors and action steps to monitor.
2. Before you speak to the parent each week, check in with the student to get his take on the week's progress and share your take on the week's progress.
3. You might invite the student to make the call home and take the lead in updating their progress.

### Strategy: *Parent Requests a Call or Conference*

At times, parents will request a call or conference to share their concerns about a child's grade, a child's treatment in class, or a particular incident that occurred. Try to respond to these requests within 24 hours to schedule a time to speak with a parent or meet with them in person. When parents make an effort to initiate a conversation with you, their concerns are often infused with a sense of urgency and some distress or frustration. Your capacity to listen calmly and responsively will support you to reflect back their concern clearly and talk through ways to resolve the situation. Taking notes during the call or conference will help you stay focused and organize your thoughts. (See Appendix 7.5 – Responsive Listening and Appendix 11.5 – Calls and Conferences at the Request of a Parent.)

> #### A Note on Home Visits
>
> We wanted to share a few words about home visits because of their power to make a bridge with families. Home visits are a highly effective strategy for developing relationships with families, especially those families who may not, yet, feel connected to your school or classroom community. Two high school teachers share their home visit experience this way: *"Home visits make us better teachers. These visits are the most direct way to get the parents' support. We're able to gain their trust. It makes the connection instant and so much deeper."*[23] Every teacher we've met who engages in-home visits walks away with a greater compassion for families in general, and more appreciation for all the ways parents love and care for their children.

Schools who are successful with home visits have a unified vision for integrating them into a larger schoolwide strategy. And, school leadership has deep clarity about the interests and outcomes for embedding home visits into a school culture. If you and your colleagues are interested in finding out more about home visits and their impact, we suggest browsing the Website PTHVT.org. The Parent-Teacher Home Visits Project is a highly respected training organization and network of home visit advocates.

## Enhancing Family Engagement through Teaming

If you are fortunate enough to be a member of a grade-level team, making regular contact with parents a priority becomes even more viable. For teachers who share the same group of 110 to 125 students, divide students among all team members, so teachers are assigned approximately twenty students for whom they serve as the primary contact with students' families. There are many benefits to establishing this structure. For families and students, it creates the opportunity to develop a stable relationship with one teacher who will share information and updates with the family throughout the year and whom parents can contact in situations when "need to know" information from the family can support the student at school. Knowing that there is one person at school whose role is to take special care to know their child puts many families at ease, especially when they have concerns about how their child is navigating school, peers, or academic responsibilities.

Benefits for the team include the opportunity to distribute coordination and development of teacher-parent communications and activities. Twenty students per teacher makes it possible for every parent to receive a welcome call at the beginning of the school year in which teachers explain their role as a point person and advocate for their child and bring important information about the student and family back to the team. The primary contact teacher can also be the person who (1) facilitates a team consultation when concerns about a student arise; (2) engages in *Problem-solving and Planning Conferences* with the student and parent; and (3) collects feedback from team members to share with the student and parent when *Progress Monitoring* is part of a plan for improvement.

## Closing

We hope this chapter has provided new information and strategies that reaffirm the value of engaging families as your partners. Our teaching careers span across a continuum – from those of us just starting out, to those of us who are master teachers with years of experience. Similarly, we are each on a spectrum of how confident and active we are in building family partnerships.

One of the best things we can do that sets the stage for successful family engagement is to be intentional in our approach. Ask yourself, "What is the larger purpose behind communicating with parents?" Being purposeful requires us to be aware of when, why, and how we are engaging families. It requires us to know our school and know our students: to be cognizant of the school's philosophy, approach, and requirements when it comes to parent partnerships; and to be aware of the particular expectations, interests, and prior experiences of the families our schools serve.

Parents come to us with hopes and hesitations about their own parenting and their interactions with school staff members. Parents need to know that they are perceived as honored partners whose role in supporting their children's education and aspirations is irreplaceable. Listening to parents with deep regard and open hearts is the cornerstone of family engagement. When we extend the respect and compassion we have for our students to their families, we strengthen the circle of care and support to ensure that every child fulfills their promise.

[1] Henderson, A. T., & Mapp, K. L. (2002). *A new wave of evidence: The impact of school, family and community connections on student achievement.* Annual synthesis, 2002. Austin, TX: Southwest Educational Development Laboratory (SEDL).

[2] Jeynes, W. H. (2007). The relationship between parental involvement and urban secondary school student academic achievement: A meta-analysis. *Urban Education*, 42(1), 82-110. doi:10.1177/0042085906293818

[3] Brendtro, L.K., Brokenleg, M., & Bockern, S.V. (1990). *Reclaiming youth at risk: Our hope for the future.* Bloomington, IN: National Education Service.

[4] Benson, F., & Martin, S. (2003). Organizing successful parental involvement in urban schools. *Child Study Journal*, 33(3), 187-193.

[5] Patrikakou, E. (2004). Adolescence: Are parents relevant to students' high school and post-secondary attainment? *Family Involvement Research Digests*, Harvard Family Research Projects.

[6] Hattie, J. (2009). *Visible learning: A synthesis of meta-analyses relating to achievement.* New York, NY: Routledge.

[7] Lightfoot, D. (2004). "Some parents just don't care": Decoding the meanings of parental involvement in urban schools. *Urban Education*, 39(1), 91-107. https://doi.org/10.1177/0042085903259290

[8] Watson, G.L., Sanders-Lawson, E.R., & McNeal, L. (2012). Understanding parental involvement in American public education. *International Journal of Humanities and Social Science*, 2(19).

[9] www.nspra.org/2011capsurvey

[10] Fan, W., & Williams, C.M. (2009). The effects of parental involvement on students' academic self-efficacy, engagement and intrinsic motivation. *Educational Psychology*, 30(1), 53- 74. https://doi.org/10.1080/01443410903353302

[11] Kraft, M.A., & Dougherty, S.M. (2013). The effect of teacher–family communication on student engagement: Evidence from a randomized field experiment. *Journal of Research on Educational Effectiveness*, 6(3), 199-222.

[12] Ibid Fan & Williams

[13] Lieber, C., Tissiere, M., & Frazier, N. (2015). *Shifting Gears: Recalibrating schoolwide discipline and student support.* Cambridge, MA: Engaging Schools.

[14] Reynolds, A.D., Crea, T.M., Medina, J.A., Degnan, E., & McRoy, R. (2014). A mixed-methods case study of parent involvement in an urban high school serving minority students. *Urban Education*, 50(6), 750-775. https://doi.org/10.1177/0042085914534272

[15] U.S. Department of Education, Office of English Language Acquisition. (2017). *Newcomer Tool Kit.* Retrieved from https://www2.ed.gov/about/offices/list/oela/newcomers-toolkit/ncomertoolkit.pdf

[16] www.nspra.org/2011capsurvey

[17] Berger, R. (2014, March). When students lead their learning. *Educational Leadership*, 71(6). Retrieved from http://www.ascd.org/publications/educational-leadership/mar14/vol71/num06/When-Students-Lead-Their-Learning.aspx

[18] Graham-Clay, S. (2005). Communicating with parents: Strategies for teachers. *School Community Journal*, 15(1), 117-129.

[19] Hill, K. B. (2018). *Trust, distrust and the relationships between parents and schools in New York City* (Unpublished doctoral dissertation). New York, NY: Columbia University Teachers College.

[20] Watson, G.L., Sanders-Lawson, E.R., & McNeal, L.(2012). Understanding Parent Involvement in American Public Education. *International Journal of Humanities and Social Science*, Vol.2, No 19, 2012.

[21] *System-Based practice: Family driven, youth guided care.* (2009). American Academy of Child and Adolescent Psychiatry. Retrieved from http://www.aacap.org/App_Themes/AACAP/docs/resources_for_primary_care/training_toolkit_for_systems_based_practice/Systems%20Based%20Practice%20Module%20-%20Family%20For%20Web%20September%202014.pdf

[22] Ibid. Watson, Sanders-Lawson, & Mc Neal.

[23] Sieff, K. (2011, October 9). Teachers increasingly use home visits to connect with students' families. *Washington Post*. Retrieved from https://www.washingtonpost.com/local/education/teachers-increasingly-use-home-visits-to-connect-with-students-families/2011/10/03/gIQAzwVKYL_story.html?noredirect=on&utm_term=.a31cd3ea8c82

# Section IV

**Appendices
Index
About the Authors
About Engaging Schools**

# APPENDIX 1.1

## Adolescent Development Essentials

Unless otherwise noted, the following is supported by Elkind, D. (1981). Children and Adolescents. New York, NY: Oxford University Press.

1. Timing and pacing of adolescent maturation are uneven and unpredictable. Although social, emotional, physical, intellectual, and identity aspects of development influence each other, they each have a different timetable within the same individual. Also, sudden changes or temporary shifts in students' personalities, behaviors, attitudes, and habits are normal.

2. The second most significant growth spurt in the brain (the first is between birth and age three) occurs during adolescence. The synapses in the brain can double in number in one year of adolescence. The overproduction of synapses can also make it difficult to keep track of multiple thoughts and retrieve information quickly. Patterns of behavior can become habitualized in adolescence unless there is a compelling, dramatic, transformative experience that motivates and inspires one to change an ingrained habit. The good news is that teens can re-pattern behavior, learn new skills and habits, and make significant changes in how they operate day-to-day. It is critical to know and understand that habits, preferences, and patterns of behavior get hardwired as students move through adolescence. Think of the teenage brain from a "use it or lose it" perspective. By age 18, the brain starts losing neurons that are not hardwired by experience, called "pruning," and it allows the brain to function more efficiently. The brain keeps what it uses and tosses away what it does not.[1]

3. The frontal cortex is one of the last parts of the brain to mature. It is the CEO of the brain, in charge of executive functions like planning, organizing, setting priorities, making sound and informed judgments, assessing risk, and managing intense and out of control emotions. The brain circuit board is not completely installed until the mid-twenties. There is a good reason why adolescents do not gain full adult status until they are 21. During adolescence, the cortex is asleep at the switch—some or even most of the time. Consequently, adolescents' judgment is highly erratic and they are capable of making both extraordinarily good judgments and really bad ones.[2]

4. Under the influence of enormous hormonal changes, teenagers rely more on the emotional center (amygdala) in the limbic system than on the reason center of the brain (cortex). During adolescence, the amygdala is revved up, in hyperdrive, and intense feelings like anger, fear, and elation are normal and frequent.[3] The amygdala gets activated when "your button gets pushed," and it captures and stores emotionally intense memories. This is one reason why trauma can impede and interrupt learning.[4]

5. Students learn best in the state of "relaxed alertness" or "unanxious anticipation." Emotional turmoil can hijack kids to the land of "not learn." Transitions to help students shift gears and get "brain ready" for learning are crucial.[5]

6. Knowledge is constructed socially, and mediated conversations with adults are essential to move learning beyond what one already knows and can do. There is a need to process information and check it out with others, so cooperative, experiential, and interactive learning supports a majority of students.[6]

7. Strong emotional connections with the teacher, the subject, or the task (whether positive or negative) generate learning with more "sticking power" related to memory, retention, comprehension, and appreciation.[7] The good news is that tapping into students' excitement, anticipation, laughter, surprise, and sense of well-being and competency increases learning. On the other hand, negative feelings about a teacher, a course subject, or specific type of learning task will stay with students way beyond the initial event and likely influence future experiences in a similar setting our context.

8. Less than half of our students are "book smart" linear/sequential learners who thrive in traditional text-heavy courses because they tend to process large amounts of information quickly.[8] Maximizing learning for the vast majority of adolescents demands a combination of passive and abstract learning tasks with more active experiences that involve rich materials, social interaction, inductive discovery, physical engagement, and concrete tasks and problems that place learning in a real-world context.

9. The corpus callosum, which is linked to self-awareness and intelligence, continues to develop until the mid-twenties.[9] The corpus callosum is also associated with performing complex cognitive tasks that involve encoding, retaining, retrieving, and generating verbal information.[10]

10. Greater emotional intensity as a result of hormonal changes actually reduces young adolescents' social skillfulness and interpersonal effectiveness before they become increasingly competent in navigating social settings, new kinds of relationships, and new social expectations. Modeling, teaching, practicing, and assessing social skills prevent 12-to 15-year-olds from losing ground during this stage of development.[11]

11. Adolescent biological clocks are different. Melatonin levels are elevated in the early part of the school day. The brain is saying, "it is nighttime." At the end of the day, teens are not chemically ready for sleep until around 11 pm. Yet teens require more sleep than adults (at least 8 to 9 hours) and hormones critical to growth and maturation are released during sleep. Sleep is brain food. Sleep deprivation reduces REM sleep and can result in memory and judgment impairment, irritability, and mild depression.[12]

12. Adolescent learning should merge the concrete and abstract (formal operational thinking) as much as possible. It is important to remember that most adults and adolescents spend very little time engaging in abstract thought that is divorced from living and working in the concrete world. Critical thinking and abstract ability should be taught in a concrete context as much as possible. We also need to remember that text is abstract until and unless the students make meaning of it by connecting it to what they know and what they have experienced.[13]

13. Students' learning preferences and performance gaps become even more hardened as they get older. Readers who struggle, for example, find it increasingly difficult to slog through text after text, day after day. Students who learn best by "doing" want more, not fewer, opportunities in which practical application is a valued component of learning.

14. For many students, adolescence includes a period of questioning and challenging authority. In particular, students who have seen or experienced negative interactions with people in authority or who have very different backgrounds than most of the authority figures around them may be more likely to distrust adult authority and the intentions of adults in general. Authoritarian (as opposed to authoritative) teachers who demand, command, and use power over students are more likely to trigger hostility and defiance rather than cooperation.

15. Adolescent "frequent fliers" (students who experience chronic academic and behavioral difficulties) are least likely to respond positively and productively to punishment. In fact, a punitive approach to discipline without opportunities for reflection, self-correction, instruction, support, and meaningful consequences and interventions usually escalates feelings of anger, hostility, alienation, and rejection in already troubled students.[14]

16. Overlapping factors that place students at-risk (i.e., violence, substance abuse, pregnancy) and diminish optimal life chances include:[15]
    - **Individual:** Early aggressive behavior; developmental delays associated with impulsiveness, poor judgment, and limited social skills;
    - **Families:** Lack of parental supervision, support, and stability; abuse, serial crises, addiction within the family;
    - **School:** Lack of attachment to school; poor grades; truancy; chronic suspension; hostile school environment in which students feel unsupported and disrespected;
    - **Peers:** Affiliation with negative peer groups; drug availability among peers; and
    - **Community:** High levels of neighborhood poverty, violence, instability, and drug availability.

17. Young people who behave aggressively over a long period of time often share four things in common:
    - They are unable to identify their own emotions, "read" the feelings of others, or empathize with the target of their aggression;
    - They have difficulty predicting the consequences of their actions;
    - Aggression, whether verbal, psychological, or physical, is the only tool in their conflict toolbox—they do not know alternative responses; and
    - They tend to attribute hostile or aggressive intentions to new people they encounter.

18. During adolescence, it is within the normal range of behavior to:
    - Argue for the sake of arguing because it is one way that adolescents test their reasoning abilities;
    - Jump to conclusions because logical thinking comes and goes;
    - Find fault with an adult's position and perspective because their newfound capacity to think critically ignites the fire to find discrepancies and contradictions;
    - Be overly dramatic because of the intensity and fluctuation of their hormones. In most cases, this is a style of presenting oneself rather than a forecast of extreme action.[16]

[1] Patia Spear, L. (2013). "Adolescent Neurodevelopment". *Journal of Adolescent Health*, Volume 52, Issue 2, Supplement 2, Pages S7–S13. DOI: 10.1016/j.jadohealth.2012.05.006

[2] Ibid.

[3] Ibid.

[4] De Bellis, M.D. & Zisk, A. (2014). "The Biological Effects of Childhood Trauma". *Child and Adolescent Psychiatric Clinics of North America*, 23(2), 185-222. https://doi.org/10.1016/j.chc.2014.01.002

[5] Sizer, N. & Sizer, T. (2000) *The Students are watching: Schools and the moral contract.* Boston, MA: Beacon Press.

[6] Wadsworth, B. J. (1996). *Piaget's theory of cognitive and affective development: Foundations of constructivism.* White Plains, NY: Longman Publishers USA. Vygotsky, L.S. (1978). *Mind in society: The development of higher psychological processes.* Cambridge: MA Harvard University Press. Darling-Hammond, L., Barron, B., Pearson, P. D., Schoenfeld, A. H., Stage, E. K., Zimmerman, T. D., & Tilson, J. L. (2008). *Powerful learning: What we know about teaching for understanding.* San Francisco, CA: Jossey-Bass.

[7] Krashen, S. (1982). Theory versus practice in language training. In R. W. Blair. (Ed.), *Innovative approaches to language teaching* (pp. 15–30). Rowley, MA: Newbury.

[8] McCarthy, B. (2002). *Reviews of literature on individual differences and hemispheric specialization and their influence on learning.* Wauconda, IL: About Learning, Incorporated.

[9] Keshavan, M.S. et al. (2002). Development of the corpus callosum in childhood, adolescence and early adulthood. *Life Science*, 70(16), 1909-22.

[10] Erickson, R., Paul, L., & Brown, W. (2014). Verbal learning and memory in agenesis of the corpus collosum. *Neuropsychologia*, 2014 Jul: 60 121-130.

[11] Sallquist, J., Eisenberg, N., & Spinrad, T. (2009). Positive and negative emotionality: Trajectories across six years and relations with social competence Emotion. *American Psychological Association*, Vol. 9, No. 1, 15–28 1528-3542/09/$12.00 DOI: 10.1037/a0013970

[12] Crowley S.J., et al. (2015). Increased sensitivity of the circadian system to light in early/mid-puberty. *Journal of Clinical Endocrinology and Metabolism*, 100(11), 4067-73.

[13] McCarthy, J. B. (2000). *Adolescent development and psychopathology.* Lanham, MD: University Press of America.

[14] Sugai, G., Horner, R.H, Dunlap, G., Hieneman, M., Lewis, T.J. Nelson, C.M., & Ruef, M. (2000). Applying positive behavior support and functional behavior assessment in schools. *Journal of Positive Behavior Interventions.* 2(3), 131-143.

[15] Catalano, R. & Hawkins, J. (1996). The social development model: a theory of antisocial behavior. In: Hawkins, J.D. Ed. *Delinquency and Crime: Current Theories.* New York, NY: Cambridge University Press; 1996: 149-197.

[16] Gentry, J. H. & Campbell, M. (2002). *Developing adolescents: A reference for professionals.* Washington, D.C. American Psychological Association.

# APPENDIX 1.2

## Learning and Life Competencies: Classroom Snapshot

So what does embedding Learning and Life Competencies into classroom practices look and sound like? The snapshot that follows highlights how a teacher can naturally integrate Learning and Life Competencies into an academic lesson in real time in a high school classroom.

The chart that follows identifies the **competency**, **skill**, and **target behavior** in the right column. The left column reveals what the teacher is doing and what students are doing to learn and strengthen Learning and Life Competencies.

| Actions / Activities | Competency | Skill |
|---|---|---|
| | *Target Behavior* | |
| **During the passing period**, Ms. Green is standing in her classroom doorway to meet and greet students as they arrive. She welcomes students by name and smiles warmly as students enter the classroom. *"Jake. Marcus. Janelle. Good morning. Hi, Ladonna."* Students respond with friendly hellos and smiles. Ms. Green also does a quick, personalized check-in with several students. *"Marisol, welcome back! Are you feeling better?"* and *"Gilberto! Tell me how the baseball team did last night."* | Social Efficacy | Healthy Relationships |
| | *I greet and talk to people in a friendly manner.* | |
| **Students walk into the classroom** and see that the "Reflect and Connect" instructions are posted on the board with a reminder to get started the moment the bell rings. Students immediately find their seats and start pulling out their notebooks and reading the directions. | Self-Management | Self-Regulation |
| | *I follow instructions, procedures, and rules.* | |
| **When the bell rings**, Ms. Green closes the door and says, *"Thank you for all arriving to class on time and getting started on the Reflect and Connect. I'm going to take attendance quickly and stamp your homework. We will start in three minutes."* She projects a visual timer that counts down from three minutes on the overhead. | Academic Efficacy | Organize to Learn and Study |
| | *I attend class every day and arrive to class on time.* *I prioritize and manage my time and tasks.* | |

| Actions / Activities | Competency | Skill |
|---|---|---|
| | Target Behavior | |
| **One student quietly asks** her neighbor to borrow a pencil. Another student realizes he forgot his notebook and asks to go to his locker. The teacher responds non-verbally by pointing to a sign on the wall that says *"Forgot your NB? Use a piece of lined paper today and tape it into your notebook tonight."* There is a stack of lined paper sitting in a basket below the sign. | Social Efficacy | Assertion and Self-Advocacy |
| | *I take the initiative to seek help.* | |
| | Academic Efficacy | Organize to Learn and Study |
| | *I organize myself and manage my materials.* | |
| **While students work on the Reflect and Connect**, the teacher walks around and quickly stamps the homework that students automatically placed on the corner of their desk. Ms. Green also takes attendance on her laptop, jotting down the names of two students who did not do their homework assignment so she can check in with them later. | Academic Efficacy | Quality Work |
| | *I complete assigned tasks regularly.* | |
| | Self-Management | Self-Regulation |
| | *I sustain my focus and pay attention throughout an activity or task.* *I work silently without bothering others.* | |
| **The timer goes off at 3 minutes**, and Ms. Green announces to the group, *"Ok, time's up, thank you for getting right to work today. The next step in our Reflect and Connect is to do a Turn and Talk with your Color Partners to share your thinking. If you need any help remembering the expectations for a Turn and Talk, where can you look?"* Several students gesture to the *Turn and Talk Tips* sign on the wall. *"Great, I'll be looking to see those in action. I'm going to set my timer for 90 seconds, please turn to your Color Partner and begin sharing how you responded to the Reflect and Connect question. Be prepared to summarize your partner's response if I call your name."* Students turn to face their partner and quickly decide who will begin sharing. | Social Efficacy | Cooperation and Participation |
| | *I work effectively with different students.* *I take turns, listen to and encourage others, and do my fair share.* | |
| | Social Efficacy | Communication and Problem Solving |
| | *I focus my attention on people who are speaking to me.* *I listen respectfully and paraphrase/summarize or question before speaking.* | |
| | Self-Management | Self-Regulation |
| | *I follow instructions, procedures, and rules.* | |
| **When the timer goes off**, Ms. Green moves to stand by the space on the whiteboard that features the Check-off Agenda and uses a hand signal to get the groups' attention and silence. She checks off the *Reflect and Connect* box and provides a quick verbal overview of the day's lesson, the learning outcomes, and what students will need to do to "show what they know and are able to do" by the end of class. | Self-Management | Self-Regulation |
| | *I follow instructions, procedures, and rules.* *I sustain my focus and pay attention throughout an activity or task.* | |
| | Academic Efficacy | Goal-Setting and Self-Assessment |
| | *I can identify the evidence that shows my effort to meet my goal.* | |

# Learning and Life Competencies: Classroom Snapshot

| Actions / Activities | Competency | Skill |
|---|---|---|
| | Target Behavior ||
| **Before starting the mini-lesson**, Ms. Green projects a sample page of student notes from the previous day. The model is well organized and includes a coding system that makes keywords stand out and highlights key points and summarizing statements. The teacher invites students to spend a minute silently comparing it to their own notes and reflecting on what they could do to make sure their notes are useful tools for learning and studying. The teacher then asks students to turn to their Number Partner and share one way they might improve the way they take notes, so they have a good resource when it comes time to study for the unit test. | Academic Efficacy | Quality Work |
| | *I revise, edit/proof, and correct for quality and accuracy.* ||
| | Academic Efficacy | Organizing to Learn and Study |
| | *I use a range of study strategies to remember and apply key knowledge, skills, and understandings.* ||
| | Social Efficacy | Cooperation and Participation |
| | *I work effectively with different students.* *I take turns, listen to and encourage others, and do my fair share.* ||
| **During her brief mini-lesson**, one student moves up to a desk at the front of the room. This is a pre-arranged plan the student and the teacher came up with to support the student with chronic blurting out and engaging in side conversations that disrupted the class. There is a fidget object at the table and a Post-it note on the corner of the desk that the student takes responsibility for marking every time he has the urge to blurt out but controls the impulse. The teacher also has a Post-it note discreetly placed on her clipboard that she is using to track every time the student blurts out. They will compare Post-it notes at the end of class so the student can reflect and monitor her/his progress with reducing behaviors that distract the group. | Self-Management | Self-Regulation |
| | *I sustain my focus and pay attention throughout an activity or task.* *I work silently without bothering others.* ||
| | Social Efficacy | Civic Responsibility |
| | *I take responsibility for my words and actions and acknowledge the impact of my behavior on the community.* ||
| **After the ten-minute mini-lesson**, students work in trios on a card sort to help them practice applying the concepts introduced in the mini-lesson. Students are taking turns reading the cards, analyzing the information, and sorting it into the appropriate category. | Social Efficacy | Cooperative and Participation |
| | *I work effectively with different students.* *I take turns, listen to and encourage others, and do my fair share.* ||
| | Academic Efficacy | Quality Work |
| | *I engage in critical, reflective, and creative thinking.* ||

| Actions / Activities | Competency | Skill |
|---|---|---|
| | \multicolumn{2}{c}{*Target Behavior*} |
| **Ms. Green walks around the room** and notices one group is using aggressive speech and even a little name-calling as they disagree about the placement of a card. She stops by, gives the group some feedback and asks an open-ended question to prompt the group to self-correct, *"The high energy at this table is really giving you a chance to engage with this task."* Some of these are tricky and intended to spark a debate. How can you rephrase your differences of opinion in a way that keeps the dialogue respectful?" One student says, *"My bad"* and then attempts to restate his claim using one of the accountable talk stems from a poster on the wall titled "Student Resources." *"I hear you saying… and I'd like to offer another perspective…"* Ms. Green listens in for a moment as the students continue their debate and then moves on to listen in on other groups. | Self-Management | Self-Regulation |
| | \multicolumn{2}{c}{*I accept help, feedback, correction, or consequences with goodwill.*} |
| | Social Efficacy | Communication and Problem Solving |
| | \multicolumn{2}{c}{*I resolve interpersonal conflicts constructively.*} |
| | Social Efficacy | Cooperation and Participation |
| | \multicolumn{2}{c}{*I work effectively with different students.*} |
| | Social Efficacy | Assertiveness and Self-Advocacy |
| | \multicolumn{2}{c}{*I use neutral, non-aggressive language to express myself.*} |
| **To wrap up the lesson**, Ms. Green brings the group back together and uses follow-up questions to clarify any misconceptions. Then she posts a *"Show me what you know"* question on the board and gives students five minutes to explain how they would respond based on what they learned that day. While students are writing, she is walking around the room looking for keywords and phrases in the students' responses. She makes a note if she notices a student's response is off-point so she can check in with the student the next day and provide additional instruction and support. | Academic Efficacy | Quality Work |
| | \multicolumn{2}{c}{*I attempt each part of the question, task, assignment, or test.*  *I engage in critical, reflective, and creative thinking.*} |
| **A few minutes before the bell rings**, Ms. Green reminds students that the end-of-unit test is scheduled for next week. She asks students to flip to the Unit Learning Outcomes Student Self-Assessment page in their notebook. As an exit ticket, students are asked to reflect and jot down on a Post-it note which learning outcome(s) they are still challenged by and to articulate one thing they don't understand or are struggling with. As students exit, they post their notes on the Ticket Out space by the door where the teacher is standing and saying goodbye to students as they exit. | Academic Efficacy | Goal-Setting and Self-Assessment |
| | \multicolumn{2}{c}{*I monitor my academic progress through written and oral self-reflection and conferencing.*} |

# Learning and Life Competencies: Classroom Snapshot

# APPENDIX 1.3

## LLC Sample Mini-Lesson

### Overview

For students to grow their competencies in the areas of self-awareness, self-management, and social and academic efficacy, they need to understand the ways in which the skills and target behaviors will support them in school, in their social relationships, and in their lives, and what it looks like to practice these effectively. We have outlined a fifteen-minute mini-lesson to raise the awareness and understanding of the skill and target behaviors and make transparent how you can intentionally integrate them into your lesson that day. As a starting place, we suggest facilitating an inquiry-based mini-lesson that could be used any time you introduce a new LLC.

### Prior to the Lesson:

Identify a <u>skill and target behavior</u> that students will need to practice in order to successfully engage in the learning task.

### Materials

- LLC Chart and the skill and target behavior you are going to teach
- A copy of an LLC Chart that students can put into their notebook to reference throughout the year
- Chart Paper: T-Chart

### Grouping Format

- Partners and Whole group

### Mini-Lesson Inquiry

1. **Introduction**:
   a. *In today's lesson, we will we will work in <u>cooperative groups</u>. What are some reasons we work in cooperative groups?* Take four to six responses from the group and chart them on the whiteboard.
   b. *Make a T-chart in your notebook. On one side write "See" and the other "Hear."*

2. **Introduce the competency and target behavior aligned with the learning task.**
   a. *Let's take a look at the skill and target behavior we will work on during your <u>cooperative group</u>.* Refer students to the LLC chart in their notebook. *We will practice: I take turns, listen to and encourage others, and do my fair share.*

3. **Turn and Talk**:
   a. *If you were successfully engaging in/doing this target behavior, what would you see and hear in your cooperative group?*
   b. *Talk with your partner and jot down your ideas in your T-chart.*

4. **Whole Group**:
   a. For a couple of minutes take ideas from the Turn and Talk partners and chart them on your full-size T-Chart.

5. **Transition**:
   a. Introduce the cooperative learning task to the students, and post the target behavior that they will practice in their groups. Let them know: *You will have time at the end of class to assess how you did, and I will be taking notes about what I see and hear* (i.e., science lab, literature group, writing group, math problem of the week group).

# APPENDIX 1.4

## LLC Self-Assessment and Reflection Tool

**Directions**

**Part 1:** Read each of the target behaviors below and circle the number that best matches how <u>easily</u> and <u>consistently</u> you demonstrate the target behavior.

> 4 = 100% of the time
> 3 = Most of the time
> 2 = Sometimes or occasionally
> 1 = Not yet able to do this

**Target Behavior:** Type in the target behavior.

4    3    2    1

**Target Behavior:** Type in the target behavior.

4    3    2    1

**Target Behavior:** Type in the target behavior.

4    3    2    1

**Target Behavior:** Type in the target behavior.

4    3    2    1

**Part 2:** Identify a strength and a target behavior to work on improving.

_____

Put a ✚ by the target behavior that you think is a strength for you.

Put a ✱ by the target behavior that you want to work on improving.

Explain your reason for selecting this behavior to work on:

_____
_____
_____
_____
_____

**Part 3:** Identify two to three specific action steps you plan to take (things you could say or do) to improve on the target behavior you identified above.

_____
_____
_____
_____
_____

# APPENDIX 3.1

## Adult Mindsets Aligned to the Domains of the Engaged Classroom

| Domain | Aligned Adult Mindsets |
|---|---|
| **Positive Personal Relationships** | • I believe that all students being known and valued strengthens their identity as a learner, validates a sense of belonging, and increases a student's motivation and effort to succeed in school.<br>• I believe that students connecting with each other will create a culture and climate of trust and engagement, where students feel attached to one another, rely on each other, and persevere through tasks to achieve individually and collaboratively. |
| **Organizing the Learning Environment** | • I believe that supporting academic engagement will require me to intentionally design the learning environment. It will also require me to identify, align, and teach critical procedures to align with my classroom context.<br>• I believe that when an adolescent enters our learning space, they will make an in-the-moment judgment about the class they are taking, the teacher, and the investment and effort they might be willing to put forth. |
| **Content Design, Learning Tasks, and Protocols** | • I believe that how students learn is as important to student success as what students learn.<br>• I believe all students are capable of accomplishing rigorous tasks given the right supports.<br>• I believe students have a right to exercise Voice and Choice in learning tasks.<br>• I believe developmentally informed, and culturally responsive learning tasks are critical to student engagement. |
| **Academic Support** | • I believe that every student is capable of improving their academic performance with my support, guidance, and coaching.<br>• I believe it is my responsibility to expect, insist on, and support every student to complete quality work.<br>• I believe that academic interventions during and out of class time are the most direct means of supporting students who are not learning. |
| **Restorative and Accountable Discipline and Behavior Support** | • I believe that every student is capable of changing their behavior with guidance, instruction, support, and coaching.<br>• I believe that building and maintaining trusting relationships makes disciplinary interactions with students more respectful and collaborative, and less aggressive and adversarial.<br>• I believe that restorative interventions help build students' capacity to be accountable for their words and actions, and strengthens their capacity to self-reflect, problem solve, and learn new strategies that increase self-awareness, self-management, and social efficacy. |

Copyright ©2019 Engaging Schools | www.engagingschools.org | 800-370-2515

# APPENDIX 4.1

## The Story of My Name

**The Story of My Name**

Welcome to this class. I am glad you are here and look forward to getting to know you. Names are important to me, and I want to make sure that your classmates and I call you by the name you prefer. I also want to make sure we pronounce your name correctly.

Thank you for taking the time to help your classmates and me learn your name!

**My full name is:** _____

**Please call me:** _____

What are some things you know about how you received your name? Or, what are some things you like about the name you prefer to be called?

_____
_____
_____
_____
_____

---

**The Story of My Name**

Welcome to this class. I am glad you are here and look forward to getting to know you. Names are important to me, and I want to make sure that your classmates and I call you by the name you prefer. I also want to make sure we pronounce your name correctly.

Thank you for taking the time to help your classmates and me learn your name!

**My full name is:** _____

**Please call me:** _____

What are some things you know about how you received your name? Or, what are some things you like about the name you prefer to be called?

_____
_____
_____
_____
_____

Copyright ©2019 Engaging Schools | www.engagingschools.org | 800-370-2515

## APPENDIX 4.2

# Personal Contact Card

*Welcome.* My role as your teacher is to support you as a learner and member of this classroom and school community. I am asking for the information below because there will be times this year when I want to acknowledge some things you have done well and share them with someone who cares about you. Also, I want to be sure to care for you when you might need help over the course of this year. Thank you for taking the time to fill this out. I am glad you are here and look forward to getting to know you.

My full name is: _____

Please call me by this name: _____

My birthday is: _____

My cell phone number is: _____

My home phone number is: _____

My email is: _____

My address is: _____

My parent or legal guardian's name: _____

You can reach them at this number: _____

Their relationship to me is: _____

- - - - - - - - - - - - - - - - - - - - - - - - - - - - - - - - - - - - - - - - - - - - - - - - - - - - - - - - - - - - - - - -

*Welcome.* My role as your teacher is to support you as a learner and member of this classroom and school community. I am asking for the information below because there will be times this year when I want to acknowledge some things you have done well and share them with someone who cares about you. Also, I want to be sure to care for you when you might need help over the course of this year. Thank you for taking the time to fill this out. I am glad you are here and look forward to getting to know you.

My full name is: _____

Please call me by this name: _____

My birthday is: _____

My cell phone number is: _____

My home phone number is: _____

My email is: _____

My address is: _____

My parent or legal guardian's name: _____

You can reach them at this number: _____

Their relationship to me is: _____

Copyright ©2019 Engaging Schools | www.engagingschools.org | 800-370-2515

# APPENDIX 4.3

## My Personal Story

**Personal story for** _____

I want to know who you are. I believe that if I know you as a person, I can help you more as a learner. I want to learn about where you come from and people who are important to you. I also want to understand some experiences you have had in your life that have made you who you are. When we share parts of our story, it can raise our awareness, stretch our hearts and minds, and help us connect. Sharing facts and experiences from your life can take emotional and mental energy. For some of you it may take courage too, so share what feels comfortable to you right now, and you will have other opportunities to add to your personal story throughout the year. I look forward to learning about you over time, and I thank you for giving it a try.

Where I started – family, neighborhood, state, country:
_____

A person or a couple of people in my life who have cared for me, supported me, influenced me:
_____

An important event(s) in my life that has mattered to me:
_____

An important life lesson that I learned:
_____

A couple of things I love to do that are healthy for me:
_____

A turning point in my life; I used to…, and now I…
_____

A proud moment in my life:
_____

A time when I really struggled:
_____

Something I did once to help another person:
_____

Something I'm really good at:
_____

Something that makes me unique/different:
_____

A hope or dream I have for the future:
_____

## APPENDIX 4.4

### 1 Student / 5 Actions / 5 Days

Think about **one student** who could really benefit from a saturated dose of encouragement and support. Consider the strategies and place a ✔ next to five actions you will take. Write in the day you plan to implement the action.

☐ _____ Take special notice of something about the student during *Meet and Greet*, independent work time, or *Ending Class*.

☐ _____ Engage in a *Personal Check-in* at the start of class or independent work time and let the student know how glad you are to see him/her today.

☐ _____ Ask a question that invites students to rate their day or share a high and low of the day so far during *Meet and Greet*, independent work time, or *Ending Class*.

☐ _____ Give the student a *Value-added Feedback* card or Post-it that offers a specific, concrete observation of what the student did and names the asset or personal quality that enabled the student to do it. Examples:

- ☐ **Social Efficacy:** "I noticed you wanted to hear everyone's opinion in your group before making a decision. You really demonstrated your capacity to work cooperatively in your small group."
- ☐ **Self-Management:** "I noticed how you completed your last three labs. You tackled every part of each lab. That showed real perseverance."
- ☐ **Academic Efficacy:** "Before you started on your project today, I noticed that you took the time to check the machinery and get all of your tools out before jumping in. That shows me you are organized and responsible. Thank you."
- ☐ **Self-awareness and Social Efficacy:** "I saw that you were frustrated today when we were graphing linear equations and you took a break and asked for help. This demonstrated real self-awareness and your ability to be your own advocate in order to learn something you find challenging."

☐ _____ Make a *Good News Call* to the student's parent/adult ally about something they have done well in class, a skill they have improved, or something they have done to contribute positively to the classroom community.

☐ _____ **Seek a student out at lunch** or before or after school with the aim of getting to know the student better, finding out about: their likes, dislikes, and interests, or their perceptions of the class.

☐ _____ Engage in an *Academic Check-in* with the aim of closing anticipated learning gaps or supporting the student to complete work one step at a time.

☐ _____ Arrange to meet the student before, during, or after school to engage in an *Academic Problem-solving and Planning Conference* to begin to close learning gaps and engage in behaviors that support academic improvement.

☐ _____ **Ask questions or comment about activities that the student is doing outside of your class:** sports, extra-curricular activities/specials, and other events and projects inside and outside of school.

☐ _____ Invite the student to **help you do something in the classroom.**

☐ _____ Use **specific affirmative statements** to acknowledge the student's contributions to class. ("I appreciate you asking that.")

☐ _____ Another idea: _____

# APPENDIX 4.5

## Lava River Anchor Experience

### Overview:
This *Anchor Experience* is a group challenge to support cooperation, communication, and perseverance. This dynamic activity, followed by the structured reflection protocol, can help: (1) establish your *Expectations* related to how we work together; (2) make connections to already existing *Expectations*; and (3) identify target behaviors for working together cooperatively. You can refer back to this *Anchor Experience* when students are expected to work in pairs, trios, or quads to reinforce *Expectations* and practice Learning and Life Competencies.

**Note:** If you have any students with physical disabilities or who might be uncomfortable with this activity, let them know the day before what the activity is, the different roles that people will play, and ask them what they would be comfortable doing (e.g., group leader, observer, timer, resource manager, direction giver).

### Materials and Prep:
- You will need: painter's tape or two ropes 12 feet in length each to establish the Lava River boundary in your space, and 12-20 pieces of large construction paper or 8½ by 11-inch copy paper for the charcoal rocks.
- Clear a large space in your room or use a hallway, cafeteria, gym, or outside area.
- Place the painter's tape or ropes on opposite sides of the space about 25 feet apart to establish the "banks" of the Lava River ensuring there is enough space for your students to stand on each side of the river bank.

### Grouping Format:
- Divide the class into two equal groups that will stand on opposite sides of the Lava River.

### Directions:
1. Explain to students that they are going to participate in a group challenge. Some students may feel uncomfortable not knowing the bigger purpose for this, so your frame is important. *"Lean into this experience with me, and I will support you to make connections to our work together in class at the end of the activity."*
2. Instruct the two groups to stand on opposite sides of the ropes/tape leaving the space between empty.
3. Distribute the large pieces of paper ("magic charcoal") to each side in this ratio: 40 students = 10 pieces of "charcoal" per side, 35 students = 9 pieces of charcoal rocks per side, 30 students = 8 pieces of charcoal per side, 25 students = 6 pieces of charcoal per side, 20 students = 5 pieces of charcoal per side.

4. Describe the challenge:
   - *The space between the ropes is the Lava River. The problem is that it's boiling hot, so that falling in it would be a disaster. Your goal here is to get everyone across the river, from one side to the other. The squares you have are big pieces of charcoal that will float on top of the Lava River, so if you use them to step on, you can get across safely. If you fall off the charcoal or touch the Lava River at any point, you have to go back and start over.*
   - *One more thing. I'm the Lava Lizard in the river and charcoal is my favorite snack. If I see charcoal in the river that no one is standing on, I will snatch it up.*
   - *You will have about five minutes to strategize with your group and play around with the charcoal pieces. Then you will have about 15 minutes for each side to cross to the other side of the Lava River.*
   - *There are four guidelines for this kind of physically active experience: (1) Work Hard; (2) Play Safe, (3) Be Kind; and (4) Play Fair. Ask the group for some suggestions for what this would look like and sound like and how they apply to this particular team challenge.*

5. Let students know that you'll answer three questions before they begin.

6. If anyone asks whether they can talk to the other group, you can say that each group can identify one person to negotiate with the other side.

7. Give the group about five to eight minutes to strategize and practice and then give them about 15 minutes to complete the challenge.

## Whole Group Reflection:

1. Select a few reflection questions from below and begin by having students silently journal their responses for 2-3 minutes.

2. Have students Turn and Talk with one of their group partners to discuss their responses.

3. Facilitate a whole group discussion of the initial reflection questions. Chart student responses on poster paper or project them digitally so you have an artifact/document to refer to later when you want to reinforce collaboration expectations.

4. Share some of the data you collected during your observation of the groups and follow-up with additional reflection questions to unpack the nuances of what gets in the way of and what supports effective collaboration.
   - What are some things you observed about how your group worked together? What did your teammates do or say that helped your team be successful?
   - What skills and attitudes helped the group to come up with a successful strategy to meet the goal?
   - What were some of our challenges/obstacles? How did we respond to challenges and frustrations?
   - What are some things that supported you in persevering and completing the task successfully?
   - What are some skills and understandings we take from this experience that will help us work together every day as a class community? (If there are connections to the *Expectations* you plan to introduce, make them transparent for the student.)
   - What are some ways the group lived up to our *Expectations* in this *Anchor Experience*? (This is a great question if you have already shared your *Expectations* with your students.)

## Closing Talking Point:

*Cooperation, communication, and perseverance are all important Learning and Life Competencies. We're not born knowing how to work together effectively in a group. We learn by watching other people and practicing these competencies ourselves.*

## Considerations and Tips:

- Students often assume this is a competition. It is not, and it requires both sides to work together to accomplish the goal and share the charcoal rocks.

- During the activity, if the groups are having a lot of difficulty listening to each other, or working cooperatively, stop, and ask everyone to freeze. Take three comments from the group, saying: "I'm open to hearing three observations from the group that help describe what's not working." Then say, "I'll take three suggestions from the group about strategies that you think will help you achieve the goal of getting everyone across the Lava River."

- After trial and error by the group, typically they accomplish the goal by each side moving single file in a line and meeting in the middle, so they can share the other sides' rocks. This usually requires them to work together and coordinate each person's steps so that they are sharing the rocks and ensuring someone's foot is always on each of the charcoal rocks.

# APPENDIX 4.6

## Tallest Tower Anchor Experience

### Overview

This small group challenge is an opportunity for students to practice cooperation, communication, and perseverance. This dynamic activity followed by the structured reflection protocol can help: (1) establish your *Expectations* to support how we work together; (2) make connections to already existing *Expectations*; and (3) identify target behaviors for working together cooperatively. Tallest Tower can serve as an *Anchor Experience* that can be referred to when students are expected to work in pairs, trios, or quads to reinforce *Expectations* and practice Learning and Life Competencies.

### Materials and Prep:
- You will need 3x5 cards (50 per group), rolls of tape (1 per group), and a measuring tape.
- Set room up in desk/table groups of 4.

### Grouping Format:
- Groups of 4.

### Directions:
1. Explain to students that they are going to participate in a group challenge. Some students may feel uncomfortable not knowing the bigger purpose for this, so your frame is important. *"Lean into this experience with me, and I will support you to make connections to our work together in class at the end of the activity."*
1. Describe the challenge: Each group will have 12 minutes to build the Tallest Tower using only the 3x5 cards and the tape. The tower needs to be 30 inches or higher and must be freestanding.
2. Give students 2 minutes to strategize and then distribute the 3x5 cards and tape, instruct the groups to begin, and start your timer.
3. Have students complete the task with no help from you. Closely observe the skills and behaviors they used during their collaboration and take notes so you have specific observations to share with the students.
4. Announce when time is up and have each group bring their tower up to the front of the room.
5. Measure each tower and test for sturdiness by seeing if it tips over when gently pushed.

### Whole Group Reflection:
1. Share that the reason you invested class time in this activity is because it provides an opportunity for everyone to reflect on what it takes to work together in small groups.
2. Select a few reflection questions from below and begin by having students silently journal their responses for 2-3 minutes.
3. Have students *Turn and Talk* with one of their group partners to discuss their responses.
4. Facilitate a whole group discussion of the initial reflection questions. Chart student responses on poster paper or project them digitally so you have an artifact/document to refer to later when you want to reinforce collaboration expectations.
5. Share some of the data you collected during your observation of the groups and follow-up with additional reflection questions to unpack the nuances of what gets in the way of and what supports effective collaboration.

## Reflection Questions

- In order to successfully meet the goal of this activity what skills and behaviors did you need to use?
- What are some ways you communicated with each other? In what ways might that communication style support your success or make it more challenging?
- What are some things that supported you in persevering and completing the task successfully?
- What roles did group members take on while working on the challenge?
- What helped everyone participate or kept some from participating?
- If you were to do this activity again, name two ways you might improve how you work together.
- What are some ways the other groups might have impacted your effort?
- What are some ways the group lived up to our Expectations in this Anchor Experience? (This is a great question if you have already shared your classroom expectations with your students.)

## Closing Talking Point:

*Cooperation, communication, and perseverance are all important Learning and Life Competencies. We will be working on growing these skills over the course of the class and you will have time to practice them and get better at them every time you work in small groups. Remember, we are not born with the skills to work together effectively in a group. We learn these skills by watching other people and practicing them ourselves.*

## Considerations and Tips:

- Sometimes students will want to focus solely on the tower itself during the whole group reflection. This can lead to interesting analogies about strong foundations, strong support structures and connections, need for flexibility, planning before acting, etc. However, the first priority is to make sure they reflect on their communication, collaboration, and listening skills.
- Also, this *Anchor Experience* offers an opportunity to explore effort, and how our effort combined with effective strategies enables us to get better at meeting and accomplishing tasks.
- If there was a wide variance between more success and less successful "builders," you might invite the group to do this a second time to see if they can best their prior effort. This generates big talking points related to effort, practice, and perseverance.

# APPENDIX 4.7

# Community Circle Protocol

Community *Circles* are meant to support group cohesion and a strong sense of connection among students, over time, by sharing feelings, news, and good moments in their lives, highs and lows, interests, celebrations, and more. This *Circle* reinforces that we all have value here, and dignifies each and every individual, their voice, and what they bring to the class community.

**Step One:** *Circle* Is About to Begin:
- Using an auditory cue (bell, chimes, rain stick) signal that *Circle* is about to begin. Students will follow the procedure for arranging themselves and/or the physical space for *Circle*.

**Step Two:** *Gathering*
- Welcome your students with a two-minute *Gathering* to support the transition to *Circle*. The Gathering ensures all voices are engaged from the start.
- Example: Using your hand, from 1-5, where is your energy right now (1 low – 5 high)?
- Example: On a scale of 1-10, 1 being low and 10 being high, rate your day so far.

**Step Three:** Agenda Check, *Expectations*/Guidelines, and *Circle* Topic
- Review the agenda.
- Review the topic
- Example: *What's something that you love to do that we might not know about you?* This question enables students to learn about one another, discover possible connections, and spark conversations because students have an interest in getting to know each other more.
- Review relevant *Expectations* and the guidelines for *Circle*

    **Example**
    - One person speaks at a time.
    - Use the "talking piece" when speaking.
    - Use encouraging language.
    - Keep comments on point.

**Step Four:** Reflect with a Partner
- Share the prompt: *What's something that you love to do that we might not know about you?*
- Students reflect silently for a minute of think time.
- *Turn and Talk* with a partner.

Copyright ©2019 Engaging Schools | www.engagingschools.org | 800-370-2515

**Step Five:** Whole Group Share and Reflection

- Whole Group: Students share experiences in a Go-Round format: ask for a volunteer to begin and the speaking order moves to the left or right. This works for smaller groups of 15 to 20. In very large groups, have four-to-six *Turn and Talk* partners share highlights from their conversations or put the timer on for a certain number of minutes and let students share. In all contexts, make sure the speaker has the talking piece.

- Reflection: What questions or comments might you have about the thoughts shared in *Circle* today? Individuals interested in sharing can bring their voices in one at a time, using the talking piece.

**Step Six:** Optimistic Closure

- Always close the *Circle* in a hopeful, thoughtful and intentional way, leaving students continuing to think and feel like they belong. The closing can occur in a Go-Round, Popcorn or *Turn and Talk* format, depending upon time and the number of students.

    **Examples:**
    - In what ways might our *Circle* today support our class community?
    - What might be something you heard about today that you want to learn more about, or try yourself?
    - What's one thing you appreciated about *Circle* today?

**Examples of other Community *Circle* prompts:**

- Share a quote with the students and have them reflect and think about it: *"The quieter you become the more you can hear"* (Ram Dass). What does this quote mean to you? How might it be important for our class?
- Something about this class community you appreciate and one idea to make us a stronger group.
- Who is someone you trust? What are some of the things they do that make you trust them? What are the reasons trust is important in a class?
- What are the ways we can show respect to one another in our class?
- What are some things that help you work with another student or small group?

**Consideration:** If you are offering students more than one *Circle* prompt, repeat Steps 4 and 5.

# APPENDIX 4.8

# Problem-solving Circle Protocol

Problem-solving *Circles* are meant to help the group reflect on some of the challenges that surface in the class community or an incident within the class. Students use each other as resources to solve problems together. This *Circle* reinforces that students have the capacity and agency, with guided support, to work out problems that show up in the classroom. Students feel respected and empowered to work with fellow peers and the teacher to find resolution in community.

**Step One:** Circle Is About to Begin

- Using an auditory cue (bell, chimes, rain stick) signal that *Circle* is about to begin. Students will follow the procedure for arranging themselves and/or the physical space for *Circle*.

**Step Two:** *Gathering*

- Welcome your students with a two-minute *Gathering* to support the transition to *Circle*. The *Gathering* ensures all voices are engaged from the start.
- Example: Name a single word that captures the feeling you are bringing to *Circle* today.

**Step Three:** Agenda Check, *Expectations*/Guidelines, and *Circle* Topic

- Review the agenda.
- Review the topic.

  **Example:** Words and Actions That Help
  - I have noticed in the last couple of days, while you have been working in groups, that some hurtful words are being used between many of you. For example: You never help out here. Don't you know how to do that? You have the attention span of a flea…Words hurt and can have a lasting impression on the one that is being hurt, and also says something about the person using the words. *Circle* today is to explore how we can support each other when we work together.

- Review relevant *Expectations* and the guidelines for *Circle*

  **Example**:
  - One person speaks at a time.
  - Use the "talking piece" when speaking.
  - Use encouraging language.
  - Keep comments on point.

**Step Four:** Reflect

- Share the prompt: *Think about a situation in the classroom where you helped someone in need. What did you do or say that helped them?* This question enables students to tap into an act of kindness, and hear strategies and examples of what students can do when they see a fellow student who needs help.
- Students reflect silently for a minute of think time.
- *Turn and Talk* with a partner.

Copyright ©2019 Engaging Schools | www.engagingschools.org | 800-370-2515

**Step Five:** Whole Group Share and Reflection

- Whole Group: Students share experiences in a Go-Round format: ask for a volunteer to begin and the speaking order moves to the left or right. This works for smaller groups of 15 to 20. In very large groups, have four to six *Turn and Talk* partners share highlights from their conversations or put the timer on for a certain number of minutes and let students share. In all contexts, make sure the speaker has the talking piece.

- Reflection: What questions or comments might you have about the thoughts shared in *Circle* today? Individuals interested in sharing can bring their voices in one at a time, using the talking piece.

**Step Six:** Optimistic Closure

Always close the *Circle* in a hopeful, thoughtful, and intentional way, leaving students continuing to think and feel like they belong. The closing can occur in a Go-Round, Popcorn or *Turn and Talk* format, depending upon time and the number of students.

**Examples:**
- What's something you heard today that you want to try the next time someone needs help?
- In what ways might our *Circle* today support our class community?
- What's one thing you appreciated about *Circle* today?

**Examples** of other Problem-Solving *Circle* topics:
1. If students are struggling with meeting classroom *Expectations*, review the classroom expectations. What's one we are doing well on? What helps us to do this well? What's one we need to work on? What are some things we can do to support us in meeting this expectation?
2. If students are struggling with a classroom procedure review some of the reasons for doing it. What might be getting in the way of us doing this procedure? What are some things we can try?
3. If students are not taking care of the classroom materials, furniture, etc. What are you noticing about the condition of our classroom? What are the reasons it's important to make sure the classroom is clean and organized? What can we do to make sure we are taking care of our learning environment?

**Note:** In all of the examples above, make sure you bring specific observations to the group. Also, let the students know that you, with them, will be observing how things are going for a week. Make sure to share value-added feedback when you notice things are improving, and formally set a time in your lesson to share overall impressions.

**Consideration:** If you are offering students more than one *Circle* prompt, repeat Steps 4 and 5.

# APPENDIX 4.9

# Circle Facilitation

*Circles* require intentional preparation and facilitation. Planning for *Circle* will ensure student engagement, focus, and investment. The following checklist is offered to support your success setting the stage and facilitating *Circle* fluidly and seamlessly. Consider your context and use whatever on the checklist below feels supportive to you.

### Room Arrangement:
- Identify a space in the room that could accommodate a *Circle,* square, U-shape where everyone can see everyone else. If possible, try not to have furniture in the center, so everyone can see each other fully and be accountable to one another.
- Talking Piece: Find a talking piece such as a Koosh Ball, Glitter Wand, Pine Cone, or have some students create one, to regulate the dialogue of the students. It is passed from one student to the next around the circle/square. The person holding the talking piece has the floor, supporting others to focus on the speaker and listen.
- Agenda: Post an agenda for *Circle* in the same place that reviews the sequence of *Circle* and the topic for the *Circle*. This supports everyone to be on point and helps newcomers to the class.
- *Expectations* (See Chapter 7, p. 113) most likely will apply in *Circle*. You may want to add some additional guidelines for participating in *Circle*. Once the students get the feel of *Circle*, these could be co-constructed with the students. Post these in a place where students can see them and they can be easily reviewed.
- An auditory cue such as a bell, Tibetan singing bowl, or rain stick, signals that *Circle* is about to start, signaling students to set up. The cue can also be used to indicate that the *Circle* has ended, signaling again for furniture to be moved.

### Roles and Responsibilities:
- Students can help set-up and break-down the furniture arrangement. You will need a procedure for this so students can do this efficiently and in an organized fashion. Make sure to Model, Teach, Practice, and Assess how the procedure is going.
- Over time students can take on various roles as they become more comfortable with the structure of *Circle*. Sample roles: facilitate the *Circle Gathering*, review the agenda and *Expectations*/guidelines, the Reflection portion of the agenda, facilitate the Closing, or even facilitate the entire *Circle*.

### Facilitation Tips:
- Honor the right to pass and practice positive presupposition. If a student does not want to share, communicate that you want to hear his/her thinking and that you look forward to the student sharing when s/he is ready: "How about we give you some more time to think and hear from others, then come back to you in a few minutes." If the student demonstrates a pattern of passing, schedule a private time to check in with them to understand how you might support them in participating.
- Be mindful of commenting on students' responses during the Go-Round, so that some responses are not privileged over others.

Copyright ©2019 Engaging Schools | www.engagingschools.org | 800-370-2515

# APPENDIX 5.1

## Sample Learning Environment Layout

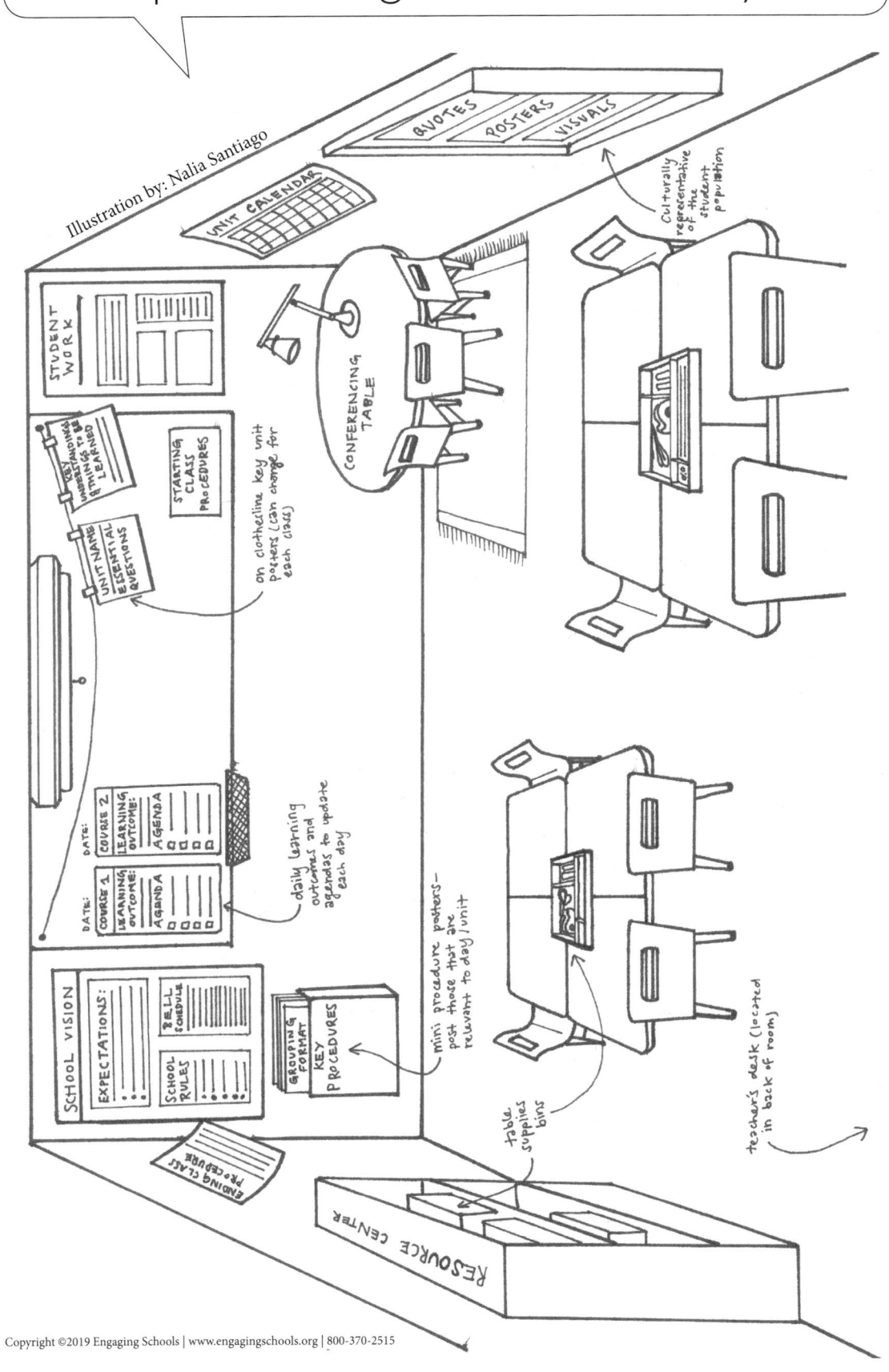

Illustration by: Nalia Santiago

# APPENDIX 6.1

## Interactive Notebook

An Interactive Notebook (IN) is a blank notebook used by students to organize course and content information in which one page of the notebook is reserved for incoming information from the teacher, and the other side is used for student processing of the incoming information and synthesizing thinking.[1] To ensure that students engage and are successful with the Interactive Notebook, it is important to strategically Model, Teach, Practice and Assess how to use one.

### The Interactive Notebook offers students opportunities to:

- Organize and manage information for easy reference, review and study.
- Create a structure that supports critical, reflective, and creative thinking.
- Revise and add to their thinking.
- Be creative and personalize their work.
- Monitor and self-assess their growth in skills and understandings over time.

### The Interactive Notebook offers teachers opportunities to:

- Formatively assess where students are in their understanding in the moment and over time.
- Have a comprehensive record of student learning to guide instruction, provide feedback, and individualize support.
- Develop meaningful and engaging ways for students to interact with the class content.
- Accommodate multiple learning preferences and provide opportunities for *Student Voice and Choice*.
- Teach an array of *Study Strategies*.
- Share demonstrations of student learning with the class, and parents/adult allies.

| |
|---|
| **Types of Notebooks:** Wire-bound notebooks, composition notebooks, pocket notebooks |
| **Options for Structuring Interactive Notebooks:** A personalized cover page; create a table of contents and number the pages; skip a page between units of study and write the title of the unit; create topic tabs to support easy reference; create a yarn bookmark to ensure that students are moving to the next blank page in the notebook; glue a notebook-size envelope to the back cover to store loose items. |
| **Common Interactive Notebook Components:** A letter to the students to outline the purpose of an IN; a set of expectations or rubric to support the student to meet; two-column notes; graphic organizers; sketches; storyboards; Reflect and Connects; written responses to prompts and questions; handouts; pre-assessments; formative assessments; self-assessments. |
| **Modeling and Teaching Interactive Notebooks:** Provide students with sample Interactive Notebooks to study; have a large model of an IN as an anchor chart that students can refer to; generate ideas with your students about how to structure their own IN. |

**Assessing Interactive Notebooks:** Consider an informal and formal grading system; spot check and offer formative feedback for self-correction on a daily basis by walking around and interacting with students; formally grade once per marking period (put it in your schedule) and consider grading when students are taking a unit test; incorporate a checklist or rubric that outlines expectations for the IN to make grading efficient; designate pages in the back to give feedback, and date the feedback; provide the students with two or three pieces of specific feedback for example: (1) a high-order skill they performed well (synthesis statements); (2) a high-order skill they could improve upon (vocabulary definitions); and (3) a low-order skill they performed well on (organization of Table of Contents, numbering pages, titling pages). Strategically schedule conferences with students who might need targeted support to help them set goals.

---

[1] Young, J. (2003). Science interactive notebooks in the classroom. *Science Scope,* 26(4), 44-46.

# APPENDIX 6.2

## Text Protocol Sentence Starters

**Purpose:** Support readers to practice key comprehension skills required for making meaning of text.[1,2]

Students can use sentence starters to interact with a text either orally (for example, "Silent Reading, Then Say Something" on p. 97) or by writing directly on a reproduced text, on sticky notes, or in their notes (see *Representing to Learn* p. 86).

| Activating Prior Knowledge | Inferring |
| --- | --- |
| Drawing connections to your own lived experience, another text, the larger society, or the world. | Using prior knowledge and informational clues to understand a text and make predictions about what might happen next. |
| <ul><li>This reminds me of …because…</li><li>This relates to…</li><li>I'm remembering…</li><li>Other:</li></ul> | <ul><li>I think this might mean…</li><li>Based upon…I predict/infer…</li><li>If…then…</li><li>Other:</li></ul> |
| **Questioning** | **Determining Importance** |
| Raising questions to clarify understanding or speculate about causes, meaning, or events. | Prioritizing key ideas in a text based upon the purpose for reading, textual features, and patterns. |
| <ul><li>I'm wondering…</li><li>What if…?</li><li>One question we haven't considered is…</li><li>Other:</li></ul> | <ul><li>Based upon… I think it's important to notice that…</li><li>One thing that stands out to me…</li><li>I'm not sure, but what seems to be important here is…</li><li>Other:</li></ul> |
| **Visualizing** | **Monitoring for Meaning** |
| Creating pictures in your mind that support your understanding of the text. | Keeping track of what you are understanding or using "fix-up" strategies like re-reading when you are confused. |
| <ul><li>I can picture…</li><li>When the text says…, I can see/smell/taste/hear/touch…</li><li>Other:</li></ul> | <ul><li>I need to re-read the part where…</li><li>I got confused here because…</li><li>Now I understand why…</li><li>Other:</li></ul> |

Copyright ©2019 Engaging Schools | www.engagingschools.org | 800-370-2515

| Synthesizing |
|---|
| Combining what you're reading with what you already know to form new ideas and connect to broader ideas. |

- I used to think… but now I think…
- One way this text might answer the Essential Question is…
- Other:

Adapted from: WeTeachNYC. https://www.weteachnyc.org/resources/collection/metacognitive-accountable-talk-stems/

---

[1] Pearson, D., Roehler, L. Dole, J., & Duffy, G. (1992). "Developing Expertise in Reading Comprehension." In Samuels, S. & Farstrup, A. eds. *What Research Has to Say About Reading Instruction*, 2nd Edition. Newark, DE: International Reading Association.

[2] Zimmerman, S. & Keene, E. (2007). *Mosaic of Thought*. Portsmouth, NH: Heinemann.

# APPENDIX 6.3

## Cooperative Learning Group Roles

**Purpose:** Group roles promote positive interdependence in a Cooperative Learning task.

Select and introduce roles that are a good fit for a particular task or roles that might work in a variety of Cooperative Learning tasks, so that students become increasingly more efficacious and skillful through practice.

**Note:** A Reporter role has not been included; it is suggested teachers increase individual accountability through a strategy like *Numbered Heads Together*™ (group members select a number from one to the maximum number in a group; teacher selects a number after the task is completed, and that student is the spokesperson for the group).[1]

| Role | Description |
| --- | --- |
| Facilitator | • Reads directions/task aloud to the group.<br>• Monitors the group's efforts to complete the task.<br>• Supports group members in listening and speaking respectfully. |
| Accuracy Checker | • Checks for accuracy and precision for the end product. |
| Questioner | • Asks questions of the group to seek clarity, more information, and alternative solutions and possibilities. |
| Resource Point Person | • Obtains, distributes, and collects resources.<br>• Checks with the teacher around questions the group might have. |
| Encourager | • Encourages individuals to participate.<br>• Makes supportive comments as group members say and do things that help the group meet its goal. |
| Summarizer | • Summarizes key information and discussion points at each step.<br>• Checks for agreement on key decisions. |
| Feedbacker | • Watches and listens.<br>• Jots down notes about how group is working together to meet its goal. |
| Recorder | • Records group responses and/or edits what group has written. |
| Timekeeper | • Keeps track of time.<br>• Provides reminders about remaining time for the task. |
| Other | |

[1] Kagan Publishing and Professional Development. (2018). https://www.kaganonline.com/

# APPENDIX 6.4

## End-of-Unit Assessment Choice

**Purpose:** Exercise choice among topics within a particular format in order to demonstrate learning of key unit knowledge/skills.

| ELA | Math | Social Studies |
|---|---|---|
| Design a storyboard that analyzes the archetypal hero's journey in a film of your choice. Vet your selection with the teacher by ____. | Survey the class on a topic (vet your selection with the teacher by ____). Use data to create four data displays from this unit that best represent the data. Reflect on each display's impact in a written paragraph and justify your reasoning.[1] | Choose one of the songs from the list about the Vietnam War. Write an analysis regarding the artist's message about the causes and impact of the war. Use at least five of our unit's key terms in your analysis. |

| Science | World Languages | Health |
|---|---|---|
| Take on the role of any part of a food chain. Identify a new, foreign plant or animal that is threatening your environment. Write a persuasive letter about why they must leave your environment.[2] | Write and perform a dialogue about planning a trip using ten unit vocabulary words. Work with your partner to decide on where you are going and the activities you plan to do. | Create a presentation for sixth graders to inform them of two human body systems, so they can use this resource to improve health and wellness. Include specific components and functions of each system and how they are interrelated. Provide information on how to improve or maintain the health of the specific systems.[3] Presentation will include a three-fold poster board and verbal talking points. |

| Art | Music |
|---|---|
| Create a self-portrait face collage and write an artist's statement that describes how you applied five of the ten principles of design. | Choose two musical excerpts and write a review that analyzes each for mood, meter, tempo, melody, and dynamics. |

---

[1] Webb, M. (2015). Data displays (6th grade). *Understanding by design: Complete Collection*, paper 234. http://digitalcommons.trinity.edu/educ_understandings/324.

[2] file:/// /Science-RAFT%20Example%20(3).pdf.

[3] Adapted from Washington State OSPI-Developed Health Assessment http://www.k12.wa.us/HealthFitness/CBAs/MiddleSchool/MSTouringTheSystems.pdf.

# APPENDIX 6.5

## Developmentally Informed Content

**Incorporate Authentic Assessments**

**Purpose:** Provide an opportunity for students to demonstrate learning in an authentic context to strengthen their sense of agency.

| ELA | Math | Social Studies |
|---|---|---|
| Write a persuasive speech on a school issue you would like to see addressed effectively for an invited audience of school leaders and staff. | The P.E. department is considering designing a ropes course outside. Work with your group to calculate measurements of the required structures and distances, and prepare a report that describes the landscape and evaluates the feasibility of the course. | Participate in a debate on whether or not the Electoral College should be eliminated. Debate will be judged by a local public official. |

| Science | World Languages | Health |
|---|---|---|
| Create a report on one aspect of the local watershed (identifying point sources of pollutants, water quality, the impact of local ecosystem on water quality) for local officials based upon your group's research. | Work with a partner to design one component of a Newcomers' Packet in the target language to orient students to your school. | Create a children's book that teaches the fundamentals of conflict resolution. Prepare to read it aloud at the local elementary school. |

| Art | Music |
|---|---|
| Paint a street scene in the style of one of the artists we have studied this unit. Paintings will be auctioned off to the highest bidder at Faculty Appreciation night to pay for art supplies. | Using your knowledge of music symbols and rhythms, compose and perform an eight measure melody that can be used to introduce morning announcements the week of _____. Student body will select the most compelling composition. |

## Inject Controversy through the Use of Multiple Perspectives on Real-World Issues

**Purposes:**
- Ramp up engagement by engaging students' hearts and minds.
- Practice critical thinking and civil dialogue.
- Explore divergent points of view.

| ELA | Math | Social Studies |
|---|---|---|
| Socratic Seminar on examining the use of 19th century colloquial language in Huckleberry Finn and its relevance to our current experiences. | Opinion Continuum Activator (Students position themselves along an imaginary line in response to a statement and *Turn and Talk* to partner.):<br><br>Elimination is the best approach to take in order to solve a linear system. | Fishbowl discussion in a unit on Rights at Risk in Wartime with the prompt:<br><br>In the war on terror, should foreigners (noncitizens) with allegiances to other countries be given the right to go into a U.S. federal court to challenge their imprisonment? |

| Science | World Languages | Health |
|---|---|---|
| On a mini-unit on the nature of scientific fraud, students read two cases and engage in a debate: Does actual harm have to occur in order for data fabrication to be ethically wrong? | *Turn and Talk*: Should students be required to study a World Language? | Debate: Is a healthier school lunch program a lost cause? |

| Art | Music |
|---|---|
| *Turn and Talk*: Should students be allowed to create a piece of art that communicates a message or belief that is politically controversial? | Fishbowl: Is '90s Hip Hop better than today's Hip Hop? |

---

[1] Annenberg Classroom. http://www.annenbergclassroom.org/page/habeas-corpus-the-guantanamo-cases.

# APPENDIX 6.6

## Activator Examples

### Card Sort

#### Mathematics Card Sort

**Math Foundations:** Match equivalencies (percentage, fraction, decimal).
**Algebra:** Sort examples into associative, commutative, and distributive properties.
**Geometry:** Match each picture of a geometric solid with its correct name, volume and surface area formulas.

*Credit: Geometric solids examples created by and used with permission from Winston Gayle, Queens Preparatory Academy, Queens, New York.*

#### Science Card Sort

**Earth Science:** Sort into renewable and non-renewable energy sources.
**Biology:** Match the cell organelles with their function, illustration, and city analogy.
**Chemistry:** Sort elements into metals, non-metals and metalloids.
**Physics:** Sequence the cards in the order of the electromagnetic spectrum.

#### Social Studies Card Sort

**U.S. History:** Categorize social, political, and economic effects of the Great Depression, then prioritize three that your group feels had the greatest impact on American society.
**World History:** Sequence the events leading up to World War I in the order of greatest impact to least impact on the start of the war.
**Geography:** Match the following: Country Economic and Developmental Indicator Terms + Definition + Examples (for example: GDP, Per Capita Income, etc.).

#### English Language Arts Card Sort

**Writing:** Sort the transition words into categories: similarity, contrast, sequence, examples, effect, conclusion.
**Reading Fiction:** Sequence five to seven key events in _____.
**Reading Informational Texts:** Sort claims that are supported by facts, reasons, and evidence and those that are not in Winston Churchill's "Blood, Sweat and Tears" speech.
**Speaking/Listening:** Sort qualities of debate vs. dialogue.
**Language:** Match Latin roots and affixes with their meaning.

#### World Languages Card Sort

Sort key vocabulary into themes: clothing, weather, food.
Sort correct conjugation of verb with appropriate sentences that have a blank space indicating a missing verb.
Match vocabulary to images.
Have students create their own Card Sorts using vocabulary related to the unit theme.

# Post-it-Up

### Math post-it-Up

**Geometry:** Review the standards that were included in this unit. Place a star sticker next to the standards that you would like to focus on during the review day.

1. Understand similarity in terms of similarity transformations.
2. Prove theorems involving similarity.
3. Define trigonometric ratios and solve problems involving right triangles.
4. Apply geometric concepts in modeling situations.
5. Apply trigonometry to general triangles.

**Algebra:** Place a dot on the method you would use to solve for this system of equations.

$$y = -3x - 7$$
$$-5x + y = 1$$

6. Graph them and find the point of intersection.
7. Make tables for both and look for the point of intersection.
8. Solve it algebraically using substitution.
9. Solve it algebraically using elimination.

Write out your solution on a sticky note and post it next to the letter that corresponds with your response. Be prepared to explain why your method is best.

## Science post-it-Up

**Earth Science:** Examine the different career options related to earth science. Put your initials by the one you would be most interested in. Be prepared to facilitate a discussion around the way the careers might relate to earth science.

- Lawyer
- Graphic Designer
- Engineer
- Writer
- Computer Programmer
- Chemist
- Forest Ranger
- Politician
- Meteorologist
- Oceanographer
- Fire Fighter
- Teacher

**Biology:** In table groups, on sticky notes, jot down five to seven individual food items you've eaten today. Afterwards, move the sticky notes around on your table to sort them into organic compound categories:

- Carbohydrates
- Proteins
- Nucleic acids
- Lipids

**Chemistry:** Place your dot sticker (or draw an X) on the continuum that represents your response to the following question:

*"We will be doing labs once a week in this course. How do you feel about doing lab activities and handling chemicals?"*

    Very confident and comfortable—————————Not at all confident and comfortable

**Physics:** Put a green dot sticker next to a concept you feel confident explaining to a neighbor and a red dot next to a concept you need further support in understanding.

- Circular motion
- Rotational inertia
- Torque
- Centripetal force
- Centrifugal force

## Social Studies post-it-Up

**Economics:** Supply and Demand graph – Place your dot sticker on the graph to show how much you would be willing to pay for one slice of chocolate cake right now. Next let students know that there are only 10 slices of cake and ask them to determine what each cake slice would probably cost, given their data.

**U.S. History:** Place your dot sticker on the continuum to indicate how skillfully you feel President Kennedy handled the Cuban Missile Crisis.

                Very Skillful———————————————Not Very Skillful

**World History:** Place a star sticker on the continuum to represent your response to the following question:

The consequences of China's industrialization and economic growth are:

                Mostly Positive————————————Mostly Negative

**Government:** Initial Post-It-Up:

Place a star sticker on the political compass chart to indicate where you think you might fall.

Follow-up Post-It-Up:

After students take a political spectrum quiz and you have explained the political compass chart: place your dot sticker on the chart based on your political spectrum quiz result.

(Search the internet to find a printable political compass charts and political spectrum quizzes.)

## English post-it-Up

**Writing:** Write your initials to an aspect of your persuasive speech you are feeling good about, and an exclamation point "!" next to an aspect of your persuasive speech you are feeling challenged by:

- Introducing precise claims.
- Establishing the significance of claims.
- Distinguishing claims from counterclaims.
- Supplying evidence for claims and counterclaims.
- Pointing out strengths and limitations of claims and counterclaims.

**Reading – Literature:** Put a sticky note next to the sign that represents your response to the following statement:

*The conflict in the novel 47 is unresolved at the end.*

True / True with Modifications / Not True / Unable to determine.

Credit: *True/Not True hold-up prompt adapted from The Language-Rich Classroom: A Research-Based Framework for Teaching English Language Learners* (Himmele & Himmele, 2009).

**Reading – Informational Texts:** Put a star or dot sticker next to the component that would be most helpful to you in reading a chapter in your textbook:

- Headings and subheadings.
- Italicized words.
- Summary at the end of the chapter.
- Review questions at the end of the chapter.
- Charts and graphs.
- Pictures and captions.

**Speaking and Listening:** Put a green dot sticker by one thing you did really well during today's conversation and put a blue dot by one thing you want to be more intentional in practicing next time:

- Using textual evidence to support ideas.
- Posing questions that connect our discussion to larger ideas.
- Actively engaging others in the conversation.
- Clarifying each other's ideas and conclusions.
- Verifying each other's ideas.
- Challenging each other's ideas respectfully.

**Language:** Draw an X along the strongly agree-strongly disagree continuum in a position that represents your response to the following statement:

"I can distinguish between when I need to use a semi-colon (;) and when I need to use a colon (:) in a sentence."

## World Languages post-it-Up

On the 3x5 size sticky notes, using a black marker, write down two to three vocabulary words (in English) that you think will be important to learn and know during our next unit on _____. Be sure you write them large and clear enough for students at the back of the room to read when we post these on the whiteboard.

Put your initials by the aspect of learning a language that you find most challenging:
- Vocabulary.
- Grammar.
- Speaking and pronunciation.
- Reading.
- Listening.

Put a dot sticker next to the career area in (the target language) you are most interested in.

# Four (or more) Corners

## Mathematics Four (or more) Corners

**Algebra:**

1. The following word problems are all modeled by the equation $y = .5x+3$ if x represents the number of weeks, or $y=2x+3$ if x represents the number of months. Choose one, move to the designated "corner" and solve with a partner:
   - On January 1st Melissa has $30 and earned $10 a week for delivering groceries to her neighbor. How much money does she have after four months?
   - Bob collects car magazines. He has three on January 1st and gets two more every month. How many does he have after 16 weeks?
   - Jamie collects jewelry and is currently obsessed with earrings. She has three pairs and buys a new pair every other week. How many pairs of earrings does she have after 16 weeks?
   - Alisa collects new iTunes albums. She has three albums and just started working for the Apple store. She is able to save up to buy a new album every two weeks. How many albums does she have after working there for four months?

2. Look at the functions around the room. Move to one and work with a partner to graph it without a graphing calculator and identify the type of function it is.
   
   a) $y = ½ x + 4$
   
   b) $y = -x$
   
   c) $y = x + 4$
   
   d) $y = x+3$
   
   e) $y = 2x - 5$
   
   f) $y = 7$
   
   g) $x = -2$

**Geometry:** Move to a corner that represents one of the geometric solids, and work with a partner to find its volume.

*Credit: Geometry examples adapted from Glencoe McGraw Hill Quick Review Math Handbook (McGraw Hill, 2010).*

### Science Four (or more) Corners

**Earth Science:** Pretend you are a resident of the country assigned to you. Stand next to one of the following factors that impact the climate in which you live: latitude, large bodies of water, elevation, mountain ranges, vegetation. Turn and Talk to a partner about the way this factor affects your climate. (Teacher assigns a country to each student.)

**Biology:** Think about a disease that you might want to research. Stand next to the human body system this disease impacts and talk to a partner about why you're standing there and what you'd like to find out.

**Physics:** Think about the law of inertia, stand next to the number representing one of the applications, and provide an explanation to a partner:

- Blood rushes from your head to your feet while quickly stopping when riding on a descending elevator.
- The head of a hammer can be tightened onto the wooden handle by banging the bottom of the handle against a hard surface.
- A brick is painlessly broken over the hand of a physics teacher by slamming it with a hammer (CAUTION: do not attempt this at home!).
- To dislodge ketchup from the bottom of a ketchup bottle, it is often turned upside down and thrust downward at high speeds and then abruptly halted.
- Headrests are placed in cars to prevent whiplash injuries during rear-end collisions.
- While riding a skateboard (or wagon, or bicycle), you fly forward off the board when hitting a curb, or rock, or other object that abruptly halts the motion of the skateboard.

*Credit: physics examples adapted from http://www.physicsclassroom.com/class/newtlaws/u2l1a.cfm.*

### Social Studies Four (or more) Corners

**Geography:** Which of the following do you think has had the greatest influence on your own socialization: family, religion, country, mass media, friends, school, other?

**US History:** Each of the six images represents life during the roaring twenties. Pick an image/topic to examine up close and then Turn and Talk with a partner/trio to identify three things you can infer from the image about what social changes were taking place during the 1920s. Be prepared to share out with the rest of the class.

(Use images of 1920s automobiles, women's clothing, household advertisements, movie stars, prohibition, etc.)

**Government:** Which political topic would be most important to you when deciding which political candidates to vote for: economy, foreign policy, immigration, women's issues, environment, education, other?

## English Four (or more) Corners

**Writing:** Stand next to a number that represents something you accomplished in the second draft of your narrative. Bring your draft and share with your partner what you accomplished.

1. A beginning that engages and orients the reader by establishing a context and a narrator.
2. Use of dialogue and description to develop characters.
3. Use of description to develop events.
4. Use of sensory details.
5. Transition words that signal shifts from one time frame or setting to another.
6. A satisfying conclusion that follows from and reflects on the narrated events.

**Reading – Literature:** Select a theme from In the Time of the Butterflies and talk with a partner about how this theme is developed in the novel. Choose from: courage, family, loyalty, power, religion, other.

**Reading – Informational Text:** Stand next to a sign representing one of the four freedoms included in Roosevelt's 1941 State of the Union address. Talk to a partner about Roosevelt's possible reasons for including this freedom in his speech.

- Freedom of speech and expression.
- Freedom of every person to worship God in their own way.
- Freedom from want.
- Freedom from fear.

**Speaking and Listening:** Think of a time when you changed the way you normally speak. Stand next to the sign that represents a reason why you might have adapted your speech in this situation:

- Your relationship with the listener.
- Your goal (what you wanted from talking to this person).
- The situation (where and when the conversation took place).
- The listener didn't belong to the same social group (basketball team, chess club, etc.) as you.

**Language:** Stand next to the number that you think best represents the meaning of the word _____ based upon sentence context.

## World Languages Four (or more) Corners

Move to the corner that represents what you feel should happen next in the story. Work as a group to craft the details of the ending in (the target) language using vocabulary you have learned over the course of the semester. Example story starter: *"A teenage boy was walking down a city street. (1) He gets a telephone call, (2) Something scary happens, (3) Something funny happens, (4) He is looking for something."*

Which verb on the upcoming quiz is the most challenging for you to conjugate? Go to that corner and practice conjugating the verb with a partner. Be sure to talk about what makes it so challenging and identify the mistakes you sometimes make.

# APPENDIX 6.7

## Skill Focused Discussion Protocol

**Purpose:** To practice a discrete skill needed to support a collaborative, learning-focused *Whole Group Discussion*.

### Set-Up

1. Identify a discrete skill for students to practice that will support them in participating successfully in more extended *Whole Group Discussion* protocols. Skills might include: pausing and paraphrasing, asking questions, providing reasons for agreeing or seeing things differently with a peer, elaborating on a previous response, using textual evidence.
1. Design an engaging prompt that will spark curiosity, challenge thinking, and make content relevant.
2. Ask students to arrange classroom furniture into a circle, "U" or square so that everyone can be seen.
3. Create a system for tracking student participation (notebook, chart, software template, etc.)
4. If the class is particularly large, use a Fishbowl format with some students acting as observers or consider breaking into two smaller groups that practice simultaneously.

| Step | Description |
| --- | --- |
| Model/Teach | 1. Elicit from students the reasons the discrete skill might be useful in school, work, and life.<br>2. Show students what the discrete skill looks like and sounds like by using the skill in a conversation with a student or asking two students to model in front of the class. |
| Establish Guidelines | 1. Explain that each student is encouraged to practice the skill once before any student speaks twice.<br>2. Use a Rotating Facilitator format (speaker calls on a student whose hand is raised) to identify the next speaker or another protocol for identifying speaking order.<br>3. Refer to relevant classroom *Expectations* or offer specific guidelines that might support a safe and productive conversation. |
| Quick Jot | • Project and read aloud the prompt and ask students to jot down a brief response to anchor their thinking for the conversation. |

| | |
|---|---|
| Practice | 1. A volunteer begins by sharing a response and calls on a student whose hand is raised.<br>2. The next student offers a response and practices the skill. Example: "So James is saying…I think that…" or "I agree with Shana because…" or I see it differently from Pilar because…" or "To build on what Alex said about…"<br>3. The teacher tracks student participation and notes effective use of the discrete skill.<br>4. If needed, the teacher pauses and provides *Feedback for Self-correction* (see p. 126) to support students in strengthening the skill. |
| Assess | 1. The students self-assess their use of the skill with a rating scale and a brief written reflection.<br>2. The teacher facilitates a Whole Group Reflection: On a scale of 1-10, how did we do as a group with practicing…? What were some effective examples of…? What was challenging? What are some ways you might address this next time? |
| Identify Next Steps | • Explain how the students will apply their use of this skill in a more extended *Whole Group Discussion* or give a heads up about what students will practice in the next Skill Focused Discussion. |

# Socratic Seminar Protocol

**Purpose:**

- To come to a shared understanding of a text, map, graph, or other type of visual
- To practice key skills that support the group in arriving at common ground and engaging in civil dialogue (e.g. pausing and paraphrasing, questioning, supporting ideas with evidence, elaborating on ideas)

| Prior to the Seminar | |
|---|---|
| **Select a Text/Visual** | • Choose a rich text or visual that encourages divergent thinking and sparks student interest.<br>• Limit the text to one page, so all students can access and reference it relatively easily. |
| **Select an Engaging Question** | • The teacher or student discussion leader identifies a question that is open-ended and invites multiple perspectives, e.g., "What might this text mean?" |
| **Students Read the Text/Examine the Visual** | • Students use a text protocol to read the text or annotate the visual in order to make meaning. This might happen in the same lesson as the seminar or the day before, depending upon the complexity of the text/visual. |
| **Identify a Participation Tracking System** | • Determine how you will track student participation in order to assess learning: e.g., chart, notebook, iPad. |

| Protocol | |
|---|---|
| **Establish Purpose and Guidelines** | • Elicit reasons for engaging in a dialogue in order to arrive at a shared understanding.<br>• Elicit or offer guidelines that might support a safe and productive dialogue. Key guidelines include:<br>  • Talk to each other, not just to the discussion leader or teacher.<br>  • Refer to evidence from the text to support your ideas.<br>  • Ask questions to understand.<br>  • Be mindful of how much/often you speak.<br>  • Listen responsively.<br>  • Explain that students direct the discussion without raising hands and the teacher steps back to observe. |

| Offer the Question | • Teacher or student discussion leader reads aloud a posted question. |
|---|---|
| Quick Jot | • Students do a Quick Jot in response to the question to anchor their thinking. |
| Engage in Dialogue | • Discussion continues anywhere from 15 to 30 minutes. |
| Track Participation | • Teacher tracks participation and jots down what students are saying/doing that moves the conversation forward and what might get the group off-track. |
| Reflect on Process | 1. Teacher offers questions for students to reflect on the seminar, for example:<br>(Refer to anchor chart with key *Whole Group Discussion* skills posted):<br>• What discrete skills did the group use today to support our seminar? What's your evidence? Or, What evidence did you see of people actively listening and building on others' ideas?<br>• In what ways has your understanding of this text been affected by the ideas explored in this seminar?<br>• What parts of the discussion did you find most interesting? In what parts were you least engaged?<br>• What might you like to carry forward in our next Socratic Seminar?<br>• What might you like the group to pay attention to in the next Socratic Seminar?<br>2. Students reflect individually in writing.<br>3. *Turn and Talk*: Students share a response with a partner.<br>4. Whole Group Reflection: Teacher facilitates a whole group reflection on the questions the group reflected on.<br>5. Teacher offers *Value-added Feedback* (see p. 51) and lifts up specific examples of what they saw/heard that supported the group in coming to shared meaning and what might have gotten the group off-track. |

## Variation:

Conduct the Socratic Seminar using a Fishbowl format (see 6 p. 103).

Adapted from Facing History (2018). https://www.facinghistory.org/resource-library/teaching-strategies/socratic-seminar

# APPENDIX 7.1

## Preparing for Five Kinds of Learners

Many factors influence students' experience of schooling and their mindsets about learning (ability, learning readiness and prior knowledge, language proficiency, personal interest, motivation, family background, developmental needs, race, gender, class, etc.). Assessing students' level of academic performance in your classroom can help you provide strategic instruction, social and academic support, and academic interventions to ensure success for every student. The categories below provide insight into five common student learning stances and suggestions for ways to support these different kinds of learners. It is important to note that these are not fixed states and a student might demonstrate different stances in different classes over the course of the school day or school year(s).

### 1 Help me PASS

Students in this learning stance have experienced little to no academic success for multiple semesters/years. As a result they feel a sense of defeat, discouragement, and failure. Their ability to organize to learn and demonstrate perseverance and resiliency with academic tasks is compromised. They are often unaware of the skills, behaviors and habits that will help them as a learner and don't know how to advocate for themselves. These students often perceive learning as ability-based (I'm either smart or dumb) and don't know how to engage in effort-based learning.

**These students benefit from:**
- Short, do-able tasks that build confidence to actually complete something successfully.
- A roadmap that clearly spells out what is required to pass your class.
- Checklists for breaking down steps to complete a task.
- Weekly *Progress Monitoring*.
- *Value-added Feedback*.
- Saturated messages that express your belief that they can succeed.

### 2 Help me IMPROVE

Students in this learning stance often have a mix of C's and D's and occasional B's. While their effort and skills are low, they are typically compliant and often "fly under the radar". As a result, their academic and subject area skills advance at minimal levels throughout middle and high school, and they fall farther and farther behind. They often lack the skills and or interest to self-advocate and self-start.

**These students benefit from:**
- Clear guides for what it takes to earn an A or B
- *Progress Monitoring* focused on academic behaviors that will help them improve their grades.
- Saturated messages that push for quality and express your confidence in student's capacity to perform at high levels
- *Value-added Feedback*.

### 3 Meet me HALFWAY

Students in this learning stance push back against following instructions exactly and are often non-compliant because of a) resistance to parental pressure and adult authority; b) honest boredom; c) a "not learn" stance that protects their sense of identity; or d) premature decisions they make about what is relevant and not relevant to their education and future plans. They may excel in one course while refusing to do most of the work in another. If you insist that they do it "your way", they may choose to do nothing.

**These students benefit from:**
- Options for identifying alternative ways to achieve the same learning outcome.
- Demonstrations of teacher flexibility, such as offering one-for-one trade-offs (i.e., student completes one standardized task successfully and gets to choose how to complete another task).
- Explaining how making a different choice comes with greater accountability.

### 4 Support my SUCCESS

Students in this learning stance are generally compliant, capable, "school smart" kids who do what it takes to earn As and B's. They are often "grade conscious" or see their grades as more important than the learning. They generally do what is asked of them and are able to advocate for themselves and seek help when needed. They are effort-based learners. Although they often self-identify as "good students", they may not yet have discovered personal and academic passions that will shape their future aspirations or drive them to truly excel.

**These students benefit from:**
- Self-assessment of what they know and can do accompanied by a push to move beyond their comfort zone.
- Tasks and assignments that offer rigorous, meaningful challenge level options that push for excellence.
- Conversations and tasks that invite students to consider and explore career options in this subject/discipline.

### 5 Push me to EXCEL

For these students, your class or subject is "their thing". They want A's and typically earn them. They welcome being pushed to excel, do more, move beyond their current knowledge, and use their skill sets to engage in advanced tasks and projects. They get excited about thinking like someone who practices your discipline and may already be assessing whether your discipline is a course of study that they want to pursue in the future.

**These students benefit from:**
- Honors level options for major summative assessments.
- Options to craft their own independent study project using a standardized template that includes required criteria and completion steps.
- Activities that help them explore what it is like to study and work is this field.

# APPENDIX 7.2

## Academic Reflection, Goal-setting, and Progress Tracking

NAME _____ GRADE _____

COURSE _____ TEACHER _____

EMAIL _____

**Setting My Learning Goal for the First Marking Period**

| A success, accomplishment, or something I'm good at in this class so far. | Something that is a challenge for me in class; something that is hard for me to do well. |
|---|---|
|  |  |

I want to earn a grade of _____ for this marking period.

---

My learning goal: The academic skill or target behavior I want to work on.

I want to…

---

Two specific action steps that will help me accomplish my goal and earn my target grade:

1.

2.

---

The first signs that I'm on track to achieve my goal will be:

1.

2.

---

| Something that might get in the way of achieving my goal: | A strategy for dealing with it is: |
|---|---|
|  |  |

Copyright ©2019 Engaging Schools | www.engagingschools.org | 800-370-2515

## Tracking My Progress in the Middle of the Marking Period

### Assessing My Progress

My current grade is _____.

Something that I am especially proud of that I have accomplished so far this marking period.

What is my biggest challenge at this point?

### Assessing My Learning Goal

I give myself a   5   4   3   2   1    for my efforts toward achieving my goal (target behavior or academic skill) (5 = a lot of effort and 1 = very little effort)

What evidence shows that I have made a good effort to work on my goal?

| I still need to continue working on this goal because… | I need to adjust my goal or write a new goal to say… |
|---|---|

### Moving Forward

Two action steps I will continue or new ones I will try out to achieve my goal and earn my target grade.

1.

2.

| A potential obstacle or distraction that might get in the way of achieving my goal: | A strategy for dealing with this obstacle: |
|---|---|

One thing my teacher can do to help me is…

## Tracking My Progress at End of the Marking Period

| Assessing My Progress |
|---|
| The grade I earned for the marking period is _____. <br><br> Something that I am especially proud of that I have accomplished this marking period: <br><br> One key skill I have steadily improved over the marking period: <br><br> One thing that continues to be a challenge for me: |

| Assessing My Learning Goal |
|---|

I give myself a   5   4   3   2   1   for my efforts toward achieving my goal (target behavior or academic skill) (5 = a lot of effort and 1 = very little effort)

What evidence shows that I have made a good effort to work on my goal?

| I still need to continue working on this goal because… | I need to adjust my goal or write a new goal to say… |
|---|---|

| Moving Forward |
|---|

Two action steps I will continue or new ones I will try out to achieve my goal and earn my target grade.

1.

2.

| A potential obstacle or distraction that might get in the way achieving my goal. | A strategy for dealing with this obstacle: |
|---|---|

One thing my teacher can do to help me is…

# APPENDIX 7.3

## Sample Obstacles, Learning Goals, and Action Steps Foldable

For directions on how to use this foldable, please see the Academic Turnaround Conference on page 132, and Appendix 7.10 – Academic Turnaround Plan.

### Obstacles that Get in the Way of My Learning

1. Coming to class with a negative attitude.
2. Too many absences, tardies, or cuts.
3. Sitting where I get distracted.
4. Losing my focus on the task and getting distracted easily.
5. Talking or goofing off with my friends.
6. Using my cell phone.
7. Saying things that are rude / disrespectful / inappropriate.
8. Fussing, arguing too much, or annoying others.
9. My relationship with the teacher.
10. Working after school.
11. Having to baby sit for my brothers/sisters.
12. Not feeling healthy.
13. Don't understand the content in the course.
14. Difficulty completing all parts of a learning task.
15. Difficulty writing meaningful notes.
16. Not fully participating in class activities every day (listening, speaking, doing something).
17. Not attending guided study or coaching sessions.
18. Difficulty organizing my school tools and work before I arrive at school.
19. Not re-reading directions, notes, or text.
20. Too many incomplete assignments.
21. Not comfortable asking for help – don't know how.
22. Not following directions or confused by directions.
23. Difficulty knowing and using study tools.
24. Fussing, arguing too much, or annoying others.
25. Giving up when I get frustrated.
26. Not using check lists to organize learning tasks.
27. Not proofing/correcting my work for accuracy/quality or don't know how to.

These are sample obstacles that might get in the way of your learning. What have I missed? What might be some others?

Copyright ©2019 Engaging Schools | www.engagingschools.org | 800-370-2515

# Sample Obstacles, Learning Goals, and Action Steps Foldable

| Learning Goal: Target Behavior I Want to Work On | Learning Goal: Academic Skill I Want to Work On |
|---|---|
| 1. Arrive to class on time and attend every day.<br>2. Manage my materials and organize for learning.<br>3. Focus my full attention on the learning task.<br>4. Read and re-read directions.<br>5. Use a range of study strategies.<br>6. Complete at least one learning task every day.<br>7. Improve the accuracy and quality of my work.<br>8. Follow rules, routines, and procedures.<br>9. Come to class with a positive mindset.<br>10. Express emotions skillfully.<br>11. Work silently and stay on task.<br>12. Accept help and feedback.<br>13. Cool down and re-focus when I am upset.<br>14. Work cooperatively with others in pairs, small and whole groups.<br>15. Use school appropriate language.<br>16. Other: | 1. Improve my reading comprehension.<br>2. Improve my vocabulary skills.<br>3. Improve my writing skills.<br>4. Improve my listening and speaking skills in pairs, small and whole groups.<br>5. Improve math fact automaticity (mental math).<br>6. Solve all parts of math or science problems.<br>7. Improve my quiz and test grades.<br>8. Improve how I take notes and capture important information.<br>9. Improve the accuracy and quality of my work.<br>10. Do advanced work and projects because I really like this subject and I am good at it.<br>11. Other: |

These are sample target behaviors and skills. What is something you want to work on that you are not seeing here?

## Action Steps that Will Help Me Achieve My Goal and Earn My Target Grade

1. Walk and talk with friends to arrive on time to class.
2. Organize my notebook and backpack at night to be ready in the morning.
3. Re-write directions to understand.
4. Identify a study partner and share study strategies.
5. Re-read my notes in study hall or at night and clean them up for review.
6. Change seats so I can improve my focus and complete my learning task.
7. Say, "Hey, I'm working. Talk with you after class" when someone is distracting you.
8. Use a check list to mark off fully completed tasks.
9. Review the expectations in this class and identify one to work on.
10. Divide complex tasks into 3 or 4 steps that will help me focus and stay on task.
11. Complete my "Connect and Reflect" within the first 5 min.
12. Ask a question or make an on-point comment every day.
13. Before I say it, write it on a post-it.
14. Ask for help when I get stuck.
15. Replace three inappropriate things I say or do in class with three new statements or behaviors.
16. Listen to feedback and correction before I respond.
17. Fiddle with something or doodle so I'm not bothering others.
18. Breathe slowly and write down one thing I can do to re-engage and focus when I am upset.
19. Agree on a signal with the teacher when you are feeling frustrated, so he/she can check in with you.

These are sample actions you can take to improve target behaviors and skills. I am sure you have ideas too, add to the list or ask your teacher for ideas, especially for academic skills.

# APPENDIX 7.4

## Student Checklist for Revising, Editing/Proofing for Expository Writing

This is a sample checklist for expository writing. We are confident that you will adapt this to your course, writing assignments, and the developmental needs of your students.

| Revising |
|---|
| ☐ **Requirements:** Does the writing fulfill assignment requirements? |
| ☐ **Purpose:** Is the purpose of the writing clear? |
| ☐ **Structure:** Does the writing include an introduction, main body, and conclusion? |
| ☐ **Opening Paragraph:** |
| ☐ Does the opening paragraph contain an introduction and sufficient background? |
| ☐ Is your thesis or big idea introduced clearly in the first paragraph? |
| ☐ **Paragraph Structure and Clarity:** |
| ☐ Does each paragraph include a topic sentence, one main idea, and a concluding sentence? |
| ☐ **Conclusion:** Does your conclusion align with your thesis or big idea? |
| ☐ **Coherence and Flow:** |
| ☐ Are all other sections or paragraphs aligned to your thesis to form an integrated whole? |
| ☐ Do your paragraphs (and sections) transition from one to another in a logical sequence? |
| ☐ **Detail:** |
| ☐ Is the subject covered fully with sufficient examples, facts, or data to support your thesis or big idea? |
| ☐ Are details sufficiently explained, so the reader understands clearly how they support the thesis or big idea? |
| ☐ What might be missing or incomplete? |

## Editing/Proofing

- [ ] **Prose:** Is your use of language convincing, compelling, and/or expressive?
- [ ] **Word Choice:** Does your choice of words match the subject, purpose, and audience. Is word choice precise?
- [ ] **Economical Language:** Where can you eliminate extra or unnecessary words? Where can you condense overlapping ideas into one sentence and eliminate wordiness?
- [ ] **Sentence Variety:** Does sentence length vary?
- [ ] **Style:** Is the tone, voice, and point of view consistent throughout and does it match the subject, purpose, and audience?
- [ ] **Sources:** Are your references integrated and cited accurately?

## Grammar and Usage:

- [ ] **Sentence Structure:** Do all sentences contain a subject and verb? Do all sentences contain subject-verb agreement? Have you eliminated all fragments and run-on sentences?
- [ ] **Verb Tense:** Do most of your sentences use strong verbs and active tense?
- [ ] **Language Conventions:** Have you eliminated informal language, contractions, and clichés?
- [ ] **Punctuation:** Are periods, commas, semicolons, colons, quotation marks, and apostrophes used correctly?
- [ ] **Capitalization:** Is the beginning of every sentence capitalized? Are all proper nouns capitalized?
- [ ] **Spelling:** Are all spelling and typing errors eliminated?
- [ ] **Formatting:** Have all formatting requirements been met?

# APPENDIX 7.5

## Responsive Listening

**Overview:** The goal of student conferencing is to provide a structure that allows students to reflect, problem solve, and think for themselves. When teachers demonstrate each of the skills below, they create the conditions necessary for students to practice and develop important Learning and Life Competencies: self-awareness, self-management, and social and academic efficacy.

Responsive Listening is surrounded by four components: Pause for Thinking, Ask Open-Ended Questions, Build Rapport, and Paraphrase for Understanding.

### Responsive Listening
Requires attending fully to the speaker, concentrating on what is being said, as well as being mindful of non-verbal communications.

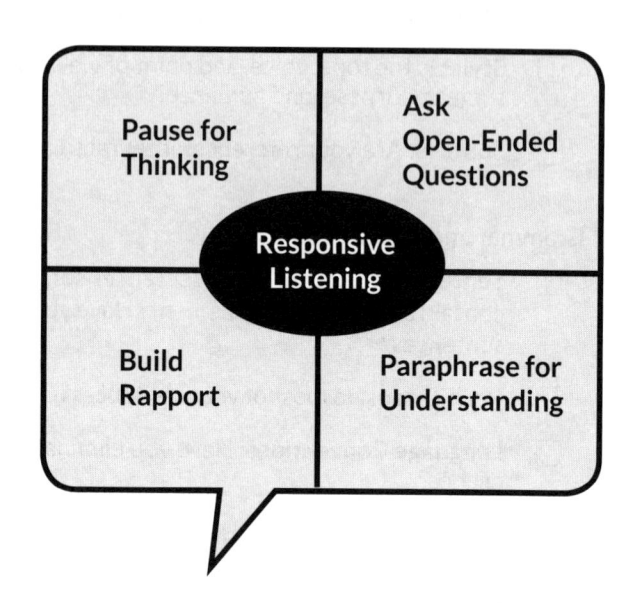

### Build Rapport
**Purpose:** When students feel safe and valued they are in an ideal emotional state for thinking and learning.

**How To:** Use both verbal and non-verbal communication to build rapport and establish relational trust.

| Nonverbal: | Verbal: |
|---|---|
| • Position yourself in a non-threatening way: side-by-side or kitty corner and at the same level as the student.<br>• Keep your facial expressions interested and friendly. | • Keep your tone light, positive, and calm.<br>• Make simple statements or ask questions that communicate you are tuned in to the student and care about their academic and personal success.<br>• Examples: "How is your day going so far, Jason?" "I appreciate you making time to meet with me, Selena." |

### Paraphrase for Understanding
**Purpose:** To make sure you accurately understand a student's thinking or reasoning while simultaneously communicating that you are listening and want to understand them.

**How To:** Make a statement that summarizes what you are hearing and observing. Use language, vocabulary, or phrasing that is different to help elevate the student's thinking.

## Pause for Thinking

**Purpose:** To provide "thinking time" for students so they can process, clarify, and develop their own ideas. To provide "thinking time" for you - sending the message that you respect what they have to say and to give yourself some time to consider before paraphrasing and questioning.

**How To:** After you ask a question, pause for 3-5 seconds allowing the student to respond. Resist the urge to fill the silence. Once the student has responded, take the opportunity to pause again to allow them to extend their thinking.

## Ask Open-ended Questions

**Purpose:** To support students to explore their thinking. To communicate to students that they are capable, and your belief they have something important to contribute.

**How To:** Ask a question that pushes the student to clarify his/her thinking, self-reflect, problem-solve, and/or plan next steps.

**Examples:** "What are some things you're thinking about…?"  "What might be some reasons for…"

# APPENDIX 7.6

## Academic Problem-solving and Planning Conference Protocol

**Goals:** (1) To share an academic skill/target behavior with the student that will support them as a learner and improve their grade. (2) To identify action steps the student can take to strengthen the academic skill/target behavior.

| Suggested Script | Interest |
|---|---|
| 1. Thank the student for meeting with you.<br>*Thanks, Pilar for meeting with me today. How are you doing?* | Thanking the student for meeting with you builds rapport before moving into the reason for the conference. |
| 2. Share the student's grade and academic skill/target behavior the student is struggling with.<br>*Pilar, right now you have a D in this course and I want to support you to improve on this grade. An area of difficulty that I have noticed, is your note-taking. I have collected notebooks three times now and I see that you don't have many notes to support you when you have to review and study.* | Sharing a discrete academic skill and a student work sample in a neutral way, depersonalizes the conversation and supports the student to lean into the conversation. |
| 3. Ask the student the reasons behind their academic challenge.<br>*Let's take a look at your notes. What are you noticing? What might be hard about taking notes? What might be getting in the way? How are you feeling about this?* | This question encourages the student to reflect on the observations and share his/her perspective. |
| 4. Identify the academic skill/target behavior you want the student to work on and invite the student to engage in a card sort (See Appendix 7.8 – Academic Card Sort: Sample Action Steps) to identify action steps they will take to strengthen the academic skill/target behavior. Take notes on the student's thinking on the Academic Problem-solving and Planning Template (see Appendix 7.7 – Academic Problem-solving and Planning Template).<br>*Let's take a look at some ways you can take organized, complete, and meaningful notes that will support you to remember information, to review, and to use when you are working in groups. What might be some actions steps you could take?* | The card sort of action steps will foster self-awareness and encourages the student to be self-directed in identifying actions he/she can take to strengthen the academic skill or meet the target behavior. |

Copyright ©2019 Engaging Schools | www.engagingschools.org | 800-370-2515

# Academic Problem-solving and Planning Conference Protocol

| Suggested Script | Interest |
|---|---|
| 5. Have the student review the actions steps he/she agreed to,<br><br>*I am going to (1) Use the sample note-taking sheet and set up my notebook. (2) Review my notes at the end of class/study hall/or for homework and fill in the holes using my text book/reading. (3)Work with Tracey as my note-taking partner, and check my notes with her notes in study hall twice a week.* | Asking the student to summarize their plan for getting back on track reinforces the steps they have decided to take to improve their grade and become more skillful. |
| 6. Introduce the *Progress Monitoring Tool* and have the student fill in the action steps. Let them know how it will work, and ask the student what you can do to help them. (Teacher fills this in.)<br><br>*You and I are going to monitor how you are doing on your note-taking skills. This tool will help us. Please fill in your action steps. What can I do to help you?* | Asking the student to fill in the action steps on the tool increases their investment in the process. Inviting the student to consider how the teacher can help communicates their commitment to assisting the student in improving their academic performance. |
| 7. Re-visit the grade with the student. Help the student make a connection to how their plan will support them as a learner and help them improve their grade. Student fills in the grade they would like to earn and how the academic skill or target behavior would help them be successful in class.<br><br>*So now that you have this plan, how might this help you be successful in class/as learner? What grade do you want to work toward?* | There is a positive presupposition that is embedded in the question that the student can do better.<br><br>When students predict a grade, it sharpens their focus on improvement. |
| 8. Thank the student again, and share an appreciation you have for the effort, thoughtfulness, or self-awareness the student demonstrated in developing a plan.<br><br>*Thanks again for meeting with me, taking this so seriously, and making a plan to be successful in this class. I really appreciate your effort.* | Closing with an appreciative comment continues to build rapport and communicates optimism about the student's capacity to meet the goal(s). |

# APPENDIX 7.7

## Academic Problem-solving and Planning Conference Template

**Note:** When you are facilitating an *Academic Problem-solving and Planning Conference*, the template below can be shared with the student to focus the conversation. The template becomes a third point in the conversation that the student and you are focused on, which can make many young people more comfortable. Ask permission to take notes on the student's thinking and ideas. Use the Academic Card Sort: Sample Action Steps (Appendix 7.8) to help the student identify actions steps that will support them in meeting their target behavior or academic skill. Have the student transfer this learning and plan to the Sample Progress Monitoring Tool (Appendix 7.9.)

| Name of Student: | Date: |
|---|---|
| Academic Skill or Target Behavior: | |

**Identify Action Steps to improve the academic skill or target behavior.**

**Grade:**

# APPENDIX 7.8

## Academic Card Sort: Sample Action Steps

**Note:** The cards below can be used during an *Academic Problem-solving and Planning Conference*. This card sort includes action steps that can support students in meeting **target behaviors**; for example, "I use a range of study strategies to remember and apply key knowledge, skills, and understandings" or strengthening **academic skills** like reading comprehension, speaking or mathematical fluency. Prior to the conference, narrow down the cards you put in front of the student in order to focus attention on action steps that best align with the target behavior or academic skill.

| Use Checklists | Connect Learning to What You Already Know |
|---|---|
| Organize your work into daily **Checklists** and check off tasks as you accomplish them to **complete quality work.** | **Daily Learning Connections** — in a study hall or after school, use a web graphic organizer to connect what you learned today to at least 3 things you already knew. |
| Organize Yourself Nightly | Study with a Partner |
| **Organize Nightly** by going through your backpack, binder, folders, and notebooks to **make sure you know where everything is and that you are ready for the next day.** | Identify a **Study Partner** and plan out two or more times a week to talk through what you are learning, review vocabulary, or study for assessments to **meet your target grade and build your relationship with a classmate.** |
| Ask a Question Once a Day | Summarize What You Learned |
| Write down and **Ask A Question Daily** about what you are learning in class. Keep track of these questions and review them at the end of each week to **reflect on what you are still wondering and what you now understand.** | Daily **Learning Summary**—in a study hall or after school spend 10 minutes jotting down everything you learned and remember from class on a 3x5 card. Keep and re-read all cards at the end of each week to **transfer your learning into your memory.** |
| Make a Study Card | Divide Large Tasks into Steps |
| **Make an evidence of study card** before a test by prioritizing and writing down key facts and concepts on a large index card that you anticipate will be on the test. | For all larger tasks, start by **dividing the assignment into 3-4 steps to make it easier to manage and stay on track.** |

Copyright ©2019 Engaging Schools | www.engagingschools.org | 800-370-2515

## Academic Card Sort: Sample Action Steps

### Use Vocabulary Flash Cards to Test Yourself

Create **flash cards with vocabulary words** on one side and sketches, definitions, synonyms and antonyms, or situations where you might hear/use the word on the back. Use flash cards to test yourself on vocabulary.

### Use Math Flash Cards to Test Yourself

Create **flashcards with key math vocabulary** on one side and explanations on another. Then use them to test yourself.

### Use Question Cards to Test Yourself

**Create index cards** with questions you think will be on a test on one side and answers on the other. Use the index cards to test yourself.

### Rehearse Complicated Concepts

**Rehearse complicated ideas/concepts** out loud as if you were teaching someone. Even better, ask a friend or family member if you can teach them, and invite the person to ask questions.

### Ask for Help

When you are confused or stuck, re-read what you are asked to do, circle where you are confused, and raise your hand to **Ask for Help.** While you are waiting for the teacher, jot down or sketch what you don't understand on a sticky note.

### Before Reading: Brainstorm

**Before reading: Brainstorm** everything you know about the topic.

### Before Reading: Make Predictions

**Before reading:** Use titles and headings in the text to **make predictions** about what you are going to read.

### During Reading: Make Connections

**During reading: Make connections** to your life, another text, society or the world to make meaning of what you're reading: *This reminds me of...because...*

### During Reading: Raise Questions

**During reading: Raise questions** to clarify your understanding or try to figure out what something in the text might mean: *I'm wondering...*

### During Reading: Determine Importance

**During reading: Determine what's important** by thinking about your purpose for reading and looking at textual features (for example, bold or underlined print, font size, graphics) and patterns: *Based upon...I think it's important to notice...*

### During Reading: Visualize

**During reading: Visualize** what you're reading by creating pictures in your mind that support your understanding: *I can picture...*

| During Reading: Monitor for Meaning | During Reading: Synthesize Your Thinking |
|---|---|
| **During reading:** Monitor for meaning by keeping track of what you're understanding and using "fix-up" strategies like re-reading when you're confused: *I got confused here because…Now I understand that…* | **After reading: Synthesize** your thinking by combining what you're reading with what you already know to form new ideas: *I used to think…Now I think…* |
| During Reading: Make Inferences | |
| **During reading:** Use what you already know and informational clues in the text to make inferences: *Based upon… I infer….* | |
| Speaking and Listening: Ask a Question | Speaking and Listening: Paraphrase |
| **Ask a question** to help you understand what a speaker has said: *"Could you explain what you mean by…"?* | **Paraphrase** a speaker to understand what they are saying and to demonstrate you're listening: *"So you're saying…"* |
| Speaking and Listening: Support an Opinion | Speaking and Listening: Ask to Hear Other's Ideas |
| Offer an **opinion** and support it with reasons: *"I see this similarly/differently, because…"* | Ask to hear **other people's ideas:** *"What do you think about…Ramon?"* |
| Speaking and Listening: Jot It Down | Speaking and Listening: Make Connections |
| **Jot down** a question you want to ask or a comment you want to make, when someone else is speaking, to avoid interrupting. | **Make connections** and elaborate on what others have said: *"To build on what Shauna just said…"* |
| Notetaking: Write Legible Notes | Notetaking: Synthesize Your Thinking |
| Write **legible notes.** Check by asking a peer to read them for you. | **Synthesize** your thinking when you take notes by connecting your notes to the Essential Question or learning outcome on the back of your notes, on an opposite page or on a sticky. |

| | |
|---|---|
| *Notetaking: Use Complete Thoughts*<br><br>**Use complete thoughts**, *meaningful abbreviations, symbols or sketches when you take notes. Check by asking a peer to read them for you.* | *Notetaking: Re-read and Clean-Up*<br><br>**Re-Read and Clean Up Notes** *every night by adding to them, highlighting key vocabulary, and making summary statements to get you* **ready for your next class.** |
| *Writing: One Paragraph Each Week*<br><br>Write **one paragraph each week** *that summarizes a specific argument, opinion, explanation, or narrative from a challenging text or brief article that you read in class.* | *Writing: Read Your Writing Out Loud*<br><br>**Read your writing** *out loud to yourself and insert periods when you hear your voice stop.* |
| *Writing: Write it At Least 3 Sentences*<br><br>**Write responses to class or homework assignments** *that are at least 3 sentences in length.* | *Writing: Re-Read and Underline/Highlight*<br><br>**Re-read your writing and underline/highlight** *the following (select from): a thesis, topic sentences, transition words, sensory details, supporting reasons/examples, other:* |
| *Writing: Edit/Proof*<br><br>*Before handing in a homework or class assignment,* **edit/proof** *your writing in a different colored pen for:*<br>_____ | *Mathematical Fluency: Get Fluent with Facts*<br><br>*Use math fact games, flash cards, puzzles, and exercises to reach a proficient level of* **math fact fluency** *through ten to twenty 15-minute self-directed sessions.*<br>*(See Fast Math (Houghton-Mifflin: Math Fact Fluency (Williams and Kling); and Developing Numerical Fluency (Kanter and Leinwand)* |
| *Mathematical Fluency: Use Card Sorts*<br><br>**Build proficiency working with fractions, decimals, and percentages** *using card sorts, games, manipulatives, and visual depictions to master equivalencies, and sequentially ordered number sets.* | *Mathematical Fluency: Be Strategic*<br><br>**Strategize before memorizing math facts** *by using skip strategies (2s, 5s, 10s); doubling; making 10 before adding or subtracting; creating number fact clusters; rounding up and subtracting; rounding down and adding.* |

| Mathematical Fluency: Solve A Problem Multiple Ways | Mathematical Fluency: Identify Problem Types & Thinking Errors |
|---|---|
| **Find multiple ways to solve for a specific answer** by printing out and using the cards at https://tinyurl.com/y7tvrrtd | **Correct problems in clusters that reveal similar errors** and then identify the problem type; identify the thinking error; re-do the problem; and circle where you corrected the error. |
| Mathematical Fluency: Make it Visual | Mathematical Fluency: Use Flashcards |
| **Draw a diagram or visual depiction to remember a formula**; write down the conditions for using the formula; then write an explanation (or create a story) that captures the big idea of the formula. | **Create flashcards** with common mathematical symbols and operations on one side and the meaning and a sample problem on the other. Then use them to test yourself. |

### Use A Check List for Unpacking Multi-Step Problems

- [ ] Jot down what are you being asked to do / solve / create / decide / identify.
- [ ] Re-read problem and circle key information you need to solve the problem.
- [ ] Ask yourself: Besides numbers, what other quantities, units, or elements need to be part of the solution?
- [ ] Ask yourself: What math operations are needed to solve the problem?
- [ ] Ask yourself: What rules, methods, formulae, or strategies will help you solve the problem? Make an equation if applicable.
- [ ] Predict your best numerical estimate for the solution.
- [ ] Solve the problem, writing neatly, separating each step, and showing your work
- [ ] Check for accuracy and correct errors. (Review steps; check solution with a buddy; get feedback from teacher.)
- [ ] Compare correct solution to your estimate. If estimate was way off, identify the mental math thinking error.

| Use Positive Self-Talk | Use a Strategy to Become Calm and Focused |
|---|---|
| Create a plan for using **Positive Self-Talk** to support your academic skill or target behavior (i.e., When I get overwhelmed, I am going to say to myself, *"Even though this is hard, I know I can do it. It is okay to struggle – that means I am learning."* | Use a **Breathing Strategy, Visualize a Place or Person You Love, or Count to Five** when you are feeling stressed or overwhelmed about a task to become calm and focused. |

## Create a Visual Reminder

Create an **Academic Skill/Target Behavior & Action Steps Reminder Visual** to insert in your binder or planner so you can refer to it **in order to motivate you:** (i.e., I want to… Because… This might be hard when… So I need strategies and they are…. And add images that inspire you.)

## Stay Focused

**Keep your focus** by changing your seat, jotting down key ideas or words in your notebook or on a sticky note, making on-point comments, or asking questions to **complete your learning task.**

**Other:**

**Other:**

## APPENDIX 7.9

### Sample Progress Monitoring Tool

**Student** _____

**Course** _____

**Teacher** _____

| Dates: _____ To _____ | Target Grade _____ |
|---|---|
| M \| T \| W \| TH \| F | Target Behavior or Academic Skill: |

|  |  |  |
|---|---|---|
| (Daily ratings grid) | ← Daily Student Rating | **Action Steps:** ☐ |
| (Weekly ratings grid) | ← Weekly Teacher Rating | ☐ |
| Circle Trend Line: ↑ ↔ ↓ <br> One thing student did well: | | ☐ |
| Next Week: One thing student can do to improve grade: | | |
| **How will this plan help you be successful in this class?** | | |

Copyright ©2019 Engaging Schools | www.engagingschools.org | 800-370-2515

## Considerations

1. Based on the timeline for monitoring, copy this sheet for the number of weeks, after the student has filled in their identifying information, target grade, target behavior or academic skill, action steps, and how the plan will them be successful.
2. Keep the packet in a folder, where the student can easily retrieve it at the start of class, fill it in at the end, and return it to the folder.
3. Leave a space at the bottom of the page for the student to write notes for you or for you to write a note to the student.
4. Some teachers want to and might have the time to engage in a daily rating.

## Rating Tool

The rating for each day goes in the small boxes below the days of the week, one set of boxes for student, and a space for the teacher to rate the target behavior or academic skill at the end of the week. Invite students to choose the rating scale they want to use:

**Option 1:** *When applicable…*
    (4) I did it consistently with no prompting
    (3) I did it most of the time with a little prompting
    (2) I did it sometimes with prompting
    (1) I didn't do it most of the time

**Option 2:** *When applicable…*
    Y or YES = I did it consistently.
    N or NO = I did not do consistently.

**Option 3:** *When applicable…*
    I did it 100% 90% 80% 70% 60% 50% 40% 30% 20% 10% 0% of the time.

# APPENDIX 7.10

## Academic Turnaround Plan

Name _____  Grade _____

Email _____

Course Name _____

Teacher _____

---

Fold your *Sample Obstacles and Learning Goals Foldable* so you are only looking at the obstacles:
**What are one or two obstacles that got in my way of passing or earning better than a D grade?**
1.
2.

---

Turn over the document and look at the *Sample Learning Goals*:
**What is a learning goal (target behavior or an academic skill) that I want to work on?**
1.
2.

---

Look at *Sample Action Steps*:
**What are two or three specific action steps I want to take to improve my grade?**
1.
2.
3.

I want to earn a grade of _____ for the next marking period.

---

**What can my teacher do to help me achieve my goal and earn my target grade?**

---

**What are some things that will indicate that I am becoming more successful?**

---

**So, what are some of your thoughts and feelings about this plan?**

Copyright ©2019 Engaging Schools | www.engagingschools.org | 800-370-2515

# APPENDIX 8.1

## Classroom Behavior Plan Template

| | My Classroom Behavior Plan | |
|---|---|---|
| Step 1 | Identify typical behavior to be ready for | |
| Step 2 | Identify Learning and Life Competency and desired Target Behaviors | Competency:<br><br>Target Behavior: |
| Step 3 | When the behavior occurs use First Response... | First *Depersonalize*.<br>Choose one or more from the options below:<br>• Use proximity and physical prompts<br>• Use a visual prompt or cue.<br>• Use an effective directive.<br>• Provide encouragement.<br>• Invite choice making.<br>• Invite problem solving.<br>• Postpone and revisit.<br>• Other: |
| Step 4 | When the behavior persists... | Facilitate a brief *Behavioral Check-in*. |
| Step 5 | When the behavior becomes chronic and seriously interferes with learning... | Consider the following:<br>*Behavioral Problem-Solving and Planning Conference* (see Chapter 8, p. 167).<br>Consult with grade level team, or student support specialist, or another colleague.<br>*Behavioral Coaching* (see Chapter 8, p. 167). |
| | What response(s) do I want to be mindful of avoiding when this behavior occurs? | |

- If there is a sizable group of students who engage in the same unskillful behavior, consider conducting a Problem-Solving *Circle*. (See Appendix 4.8– Problem-Solving Circle.)
- If it is a few students, consider a brief meeting, in which students unpack the issue and next steps.
- In some cases, the unskillful behavior may require a classroom procedure to support all students to meet the target behavior. In the example above, a procedure for *Getting Attention* and *Maintaining Silence* would be appropriate.

Copyright ©2019 Engaging Schools | www.engagingschools.org | 800-370-2515

# APPENDIX 8.2

## Behavioral Problem-solving and Planning Conference Protocol

**Goals:** 1) To share with the student a behavior that is interrupting his/her learning and potentially the learning environment. 2) To identify a target behavior and action steps the student can take to replace the unskillful behavior.

| Suggested Script | Interest |
|---|---|
| Thank the student for meeting with you.<br>• "Thanks Jamal for meeting with me today. How are you doing?" | Thanking the student for meeting with you builds rapport before moving into the reason for the conference. |
| Share the behavior the student is exhibiting.<br>• "I want to share a behavior that I have been noticing for several days now that I feel is interrupting your learning, and, I care about you learning and being successful in this class. At least three to four times in a 45-minute class you are talking with other students, and it's not on the topic." | Sharing a discrete behavior (data) in a neutral way *Depersonalizes* the conversation and supports the student to lean into the conversation. |
| Ask the student the reasons they might be engaging in this behavior<br>• "When you engage in sidebar talking what's going on for you? What are you thinking and feeling?" | This question encourages the student to reflect on the observations and share his/her perspective. |
| Identify the target behavior you want the student to work on and invite the student to engage in a card sort (see Appendix 8.4) to identify actions steps they will take to strengthen the target behavior. Take notes on the student's thinking on the Behavioral Problem-solving and Planning Template (see Appendix 8.3).<br>• "Let's take a look at some ways you can stop sidebar talking and stay focused and pay attention throughout the learning task. What might be some actions steps you could take? Or, let's take a look_____." | The card sort of action steps will foster self-awareness and encourages the student to be self-directed in identifying actions they can take to meet the target behavior. |
| Have the student review the actions steps he/she agreed to.<br>• "I am going to 1) Change my seat; 2) Look at you when directions are being given; and 3) Whenever I feel like I'm going to talk to someone that's not about what we are learning, I am going to put an x on a sticky note to remind myself." | Asking the student to summarize their plan for getting back on track reinforces the steps they have decided to take to improve their grade and become more skillful. |

Copyright ©2019 Engaging Schools | www.engagingschools.org | 800-370-2515

| | |
|---|---|
| Introduce the *Progress Monitoring* tool and have the student fill in the action steps. Let them know how it will work, and ask the student what you can do to help them.<br><br>• "You and I are going to monitor how you are doing on decreasing or stopping your sidebar talking. This tool will help us. Please fill this in. What might I do to help you?" (Teacher fills this in.) | Having the student fill in the action steps increases their investment in the process. Inviting the student to consider how the teacher can help communicates the teacher's commitment to assisting the student in turning around their behavior. |
| Ask the student how their plan will impact them as a learner. Have student fill this in on the *Progress Monitoring* tool.<br><br>• "So now that you have this plan, how might this help you be successful in class/as a learner?" (Optional): "What grade might you want to earn as a result of developing this plan?" | This question lets the student know you see them as a learner, and grows their understanding that target behaviors can help them engage academically. If it feels helpful for this student, consider asking what grade they might want to earn as a result of the plan they've developed. |
| Thank the student again, and share an appreciation you have for the effort, thoughtfulness, or self-awareness the student demonstrated in developing a plan.<br><br>• "Thanks again for meeting with me, taking this so seriously, and making a plan to be successful in this class. I really appreciate your effort." | Closing with an appreciative comment continues to build rapport and communicates optimism about the student's capacity to meet the goal(s). |

# APPENDIX 8.3

## Behavioral Problem-solving and Planning Conference Template

**Note:** When you are facilitating a *Behavioral Problem-solving and Planning Conference*, the template below can be shared with the student to focus the conversation. The template becomes a third point in the conversation that the student and you are focused on, which can make many young people more comfortable. Ask permission to take notes on the student's thinking and ideas. Use the card sort (Appendix 8.4) to help the student identify actions steps that will support them in meeting their target behavior. Have the student transfer their plan to the Sample *Progress Monitoring* Tool (Appendix 7.9.)

| Name of Student: | Date: |
|---|---|
| Unskillful Behavior: | |
| Target Behavior: | |

Identify Action Steps to meet the target behavior.

Target Grade (Optional):

Copyright ©2019 Engaging Schools | www.engagingschools.org | 800-370-2515

# APPENDIX 8.4

## Behavior Card Sort: Sample Action Steps

The cards below can be used during a *Behavioral Problem-solving and Planning Conference*. This card sort includes action steps that can support students in meeting target behaviors, for example, "I work silently without bothering others." Prior to the conference, narrow down the cards you put in front of the student in order to focus attention on action steps that best align with the target behavior.

---

**Create a Visual Reminder**

**Create a target behavior & action steps reminder visual** to insert in your binder or planner so you can refer to it in order to stay motivated. For example:
- "I want to…"
- "Because…"
- "This might be hard when…"
- "So I need strategies and they are…"

Add images that inspire you.

---

**Make a Positive Mindset Sticky Note**

**Review the posted expectations** and pick an **expectation to focus on** for the week, write it on a sticky note, and place it on your desk, so your teacher can see it and support you to have a positive mindset about the class and what you need to do to be successful.

---

**Agree on a Personalized Reminder Signal**

**Agree on a personalized reminder signal** (non-verbal or verbal) that your teacher(s) can use to remind you of your target behavior and action steps when you are struggling. (For example, the teacher rests their hand on the corner of your desk (non-verbal) or says, "Whose brain is working hard right now?")

---

**Apologize and Make It Right**

When you've said or done something that has upset someone you can say;
- "I'm sorry. I probably shouldn't have_____."
- "I didn't mean any disrespect. I won't say that again."
- "I can make it right by…"

---

**Use Positive Self-Talk**

**Create a plan for using positive self-talk** to support your learning goal (i.e., When I get frustrated with someone I am going to say to myself, "I am in control of myself and what I do next – I've got this.")

---

**Disagree Respectfully**

When you disagree with someone, **express yourself in a neutral way** by saying something like:
- "I see it differently. I think…"
- "It sounds like you think…The way I see it…"
- "I see your point. Here's how I see it:"

| **Use Your Hands to Get Focused** | **Use Three Before Me to Figure it Out** |
|---|---|
| **Use a silent fidget tool or doodle** instead of engaging in distracting behaviors to stay focused and complete your learning task. | When you are confused or stuck, use **Three Before Me:** 1) re-read directions 2) identify what is confusing/unclear 3) ask a student for help. Then, if you need to, raise your hand to Ask for Help. When called on, say something like:<br>• *I'd really like some help to _____.*<br>• *I'm confused. Can you tell me what to do?*<br>• *Could you please explain the directions again?*<br>While you are waiting for the teacher, jot down or sketch what you don't understand on a sticky note, so you can work silently without bothering others. |
| **Write it Down Before You Blurt** | **Use a Strategy to Stay in Control of Yourself** |
| **Write it down before you blurt** - keep a sticky note on the corner of your desk or binder and jot down the things that you want to say. Then ask yourself, "Is this the right time to say something? Will it add to or subtract from learning?" | **Manage your short fuse and emotions** by counting to three, taking a deep breath, visualizing a person or place you love, or using a mantra, for example, *"I don't want to pick a fight,"* in order to stay in control of yourself. |
| **Change Seats to Stay Focused** | **Identify a Way to Move When You Need To** |
| **Change seats** permanently or move to a different seat during certain types of activities to improve your focus, complete the learning task, and not distract others. | Work with your teacher(s) to identify a way to **Move when you need to** for those times when you have excess energy or are getting frustrated so you don't distract others in the class (i.e., an alternate seat you can move to, a task you can do for the teacher, or stand and review words on the word wall). |

### Accept Direction Without A Fuss

**Accept direction without a fuss by:**
- Asking yourself, "Is this worth arguing over?"
- Accepting the comment and saying, *"Okay."*
- Writing down how you feel and asking to discuss it later.

Any of these moves can help you develop a positive relationship with your teacher and stay on track during the lesson.

### Be a good group member

**Cooperate** by taking turns, doing your fair share of the work, listening to others in the group, and making encouraging comments that help get the work done.

### Be Assertive to Get What You Need

**Use assertive statements** to get what you need when you feel frustrated, angry, confused for example:
- *"I need your help please."*
- *"I am feeling frustrated about X. Please help me…"*

### Stay on Track with a Friendly Phrase

**Use a friendly phrase with peers** when they are distracting you from staying on track to make sure you finish the task.
- *"Hey, I really want to improve my grade in the class. Talk to you at lunch?"*

### Say It In a Neutral Way

**Turn negative statements into neutral statements.** Instead of saying *"This class sucks"* you might say, *"I want to learn more about…."* Or, *"I am confused about…"* Or *"I don't like____ because…"*

### Be Friendly

**Be friendly with your peers** by saying hello, offering to help, saying something nice about someone. This makes class a good place to learn, and helps everyone feel like they belong and are members of the class community.

### Commit to 100% in the First Five Minutes

Commit to spending the **first 5 minutes of class 100% on-task** by completing the Reflect & Connect, reviewing the agenda and lesson outcome, and coming up with a question or wondering about what you will be learning that day so you're ready to learn for the rest of the class.

### Write or Speak to Focus and Finish

**Jot down key ideas or words** in your notebook or on a sticky note, make on-point comments, or ask questions to stay focused and finish the task.

| **Be assertive when someone is bothering you** | **Use self-talk when you're angry** |
|---|---|
| • "Please don't bother me right now. I need to _____."<br>• "I don't like it when you _____. Please stop."<br>• "I know you didn't mean any disrespect, but that's how it felt. Thanks for stopping." | **Ask yourself three questions** to understand what you're feeling and cool down:<br>• "On a scale of 1-10, how angry am I? (10 = very angry; 1 = not angry at all)"<br>• "What am I angry about?"<br>• "What can I do to cool down and refocus?" |
| **Check Your Language** | |
| When you're tempted to use harmful or inappropriate language, **ask yourself:**<br>• "Will this bother others?"<br>• "Is it mean?"<br>• "Will this get me in trouble?"<br>Then choose:<br>• Not to say anything if it's hurtful.<br>• Replace the inappropriate language with school-appropriate language. | |
| Other: | Other: |

# APPENDIX 9.1

## Unit Planning Checklists

**CHECKLIST 1: Identifying Desired Results and Organizing Content**

### Key Knowledge & Skills

- ☐ Is this the most critical knowledge for students to walk away with from this unit?
- ☐ Are these the most critical skills for students to walk away with from this unit?
- ☐ Which college readiness skills might be most important for students to walk away with from this unit?

| Key Understandings | Essential Questions |
|---|---|
| ☐ Are these key understandings at the "heart" of the discipline and in need of uncovering?<br>☐ Will the synthesis of this unit's key knowledge and skills support students in reaching these key understandings? | ☐ Are my essential questions open-ended, thought-provoking and intellectually engaging? Will they spark discussion and debate?<br>☐ Do the essential questions support students in exploring the key understandings? |

### Key State Learning Standards

- ☐ Are these the essential, priority learning standards for students to demonstrate mastery in this unit?
- ☐ Have I chunked together similar standards into priority or "power" standards that support my own planning and student understanding of the unit standards?

### Learning and Life Competency Target Behaviors (Chapter 1)

- ☐ Are these the five to six target behaviors that will most support student success in meeting the outcomes of this unit (Appendix 1.3 – LLC Mini-Lesson)?

| Developmentally Informed Content (Chapter 5) | Culturally Relevant Content (Chapter 5) |
|---|---|
| Will my content:<br>☐ Draw connections to personal interests?<br>☐ Inject controversy through the use of multiple perspectives on real-world issues?<br>☐ Link course content to the real world? | Will my content:<br>☐ Explore the students' identities?<br>☐ Integrate students' cultures into the content?<br>☐ Solicit cultural perspectives within your discipline? |

## CHECKLIST 2: Determining Acceptable Evidence

### Formative Assessments (Chapter 7)

- [ ] Have I embedded formative assessments that will provide me with direct evidence of student knowledge, skills, or target behaviors corresponding to my listed outcome(s)?
- [ ] Have I planned ways to collect, track, and use this information once I have it to inform instruction, strategy selection, and interventions?

### Interim Assessments and Interventions (Chapter 7)

- [ ] Have I planned interim assessments that will provide me with enough evidence of student understanding to predict performance on the end of unit assessment?
- [ ] Have I identified the levels of understanding that would prompt additional levels of intervention?
- [ ] Have I identified what these interventions should be and built in time and systems into my unit plan to support students in need of additional interventions?

### End-of-Unit Assessments of Learning (Chapter 6)

- [ ] Have I identified *End-Of-Unit Assessments* that will provide me with enough evidence of student mastery of the unit outcomes?
- [ ] Will these assessments support students' continued growth and progress toward mastery?
- [ ] Have I incorporated *Student Voice and Choice* to increase commitment to and success with these assessments (Chapter 5)?
- [ ] Are these assessments *Authentic* (Chapter 6)?
- [ ] Have I designed ways for students who still haven't demonstrated mastery to continue to be supported toward mastery (e.g., *Revise, Edit/Proof, and Correct* Chapter 7)?


## CHECKLIST 3: *Anticipating and Planning for Learning Gaps* (Chapter 7)

### Anticipating Learning Gaps

- [ ] Have I identified the learning gaps in content that I have run into the most in my prior classroom experience (or if new to the profession: Are these the learning gaps my colleagues have encountered most often)?
- [ ] Have I planned to assess students' prior knowledge and skills that would support them in meeting the course outcomes?

### Planning Strategies & Interventions

- [ ] Have I identified the Tier 1 strategies will promote most students' success in acquiring this unit's key concepts, skills, target behaviors and avoid the learning gaps I have identified?
- [ ] Have I identified the Tier 2 interventions that will support some students to overcome learning gaps in this unit's key concepts, skills, and target behaviors?

# APPENDIX 9.2

## A Purposeful, Well-Paced Lesson

---

### A Purposeful, Well-Paced Lesson

**Lesson Purpose**
Clarifying the purpose of a lesson is a crucial first step to ensure that the lesson has a clear learning outcome that drives your choice of key strategies to support academic engagement. Below are several lesson purposes for you to consider in your lesson design:

- ☐ Introduction of new key knowledge or skills
- ☐ Deepened learning of key knowledge or skills
- ☐ Application of key knowledge or skills
- ☐ Direct experience of key knowledge or skill
- ☐ Independent practice

- ☐ Community Building
- ☐ Academic conferencing and coaching
- ☐ Academic discourse
- ☐ Research
- ☐ Reading and Writing Workshop
- ☐ Student performances and presentations

- ☐ Planning, creating, vetting, and finalizing major projects
- ☐ End of unit catch-up
- ☐ Preparation for assessments
- ☐ Interim and summative assessments
- ☐ Other

---

**Time Chunks**
- 3 minutes
- 7 minutes
- 10 minutes
- 15 minutes
- 20 minutes
- 30 minutes

**Grouping Formats**
- Whole Group
- Independent
- Pairs
- Trios
- Quads

**Voice Levels**
- Silence
- One Voice
- Low Partner Chat
- Medium: Multi-Group Conversations
- High Energy: Multi-Group Conversations

Copyright ©2019 Engaging Schools | www.engagingschools.org | 800-370-2515

## APPENDIX 9.3

# Domains of the Engaged Classroom

| Domains | Practices and Strategies | |
|---|---|---|
| **Positive Personal Relationships**<br><br>*How do I foster and sustain strong and supportive personal relationships?* | **1** Knowing Students and Making them Feel Known<br>☐ Student Names<br>☐ Meet and Greet<br>☐ Student Profile Data<br>☐ Personal Check-ins<br>☐ Value-added Feedback | **2** Creating Group Cohesion<br>☐ Gatherings<br>☐ Anchor Experiences<br>☐ Circle<br>☐ Student Feedback |
| **Organizing the Learning Environment**<br><br>*How do I purposefully organize my learning environment to support academic engagement?* | **3** Organizing the Learning Environment<br>☐ Visual Postings<br>☐ Furniture Arrangement<br>☐ Tools and Resources | **4** Foundational Procedures<br>☐ Starting Class<br>☐ Ending Class<br>☐ Getting Attention<br>☐ Maintaining Silence<br>☐ Clear Instructions<br>☐ Grouping Formats |
| **Content Design, Learning Tasks, and Protocols**<br><br>*How do I ramp up engagement and rigor in order to increase academic achievement?* | **5** Rigorous, Meaningful Learning Tasks<br>☐ Representing to Learn<br>☐ Problematizing a Learning Task<br>☐ Student Voice and Choice<br>☐ End-of-Unit Assessments<br>☐ Developmentally Informed Content<br>☐ Culturally Relevant Content | **6** Learning Protocols<br>☐ Text Protocols<br>☐ Activators<br>☐ Turn and Talk<br>☐ Cooperative Learning<br>☐ Whole Group Discussion |

Copyright ©2019 Engaging Schools | www.engagingschools.org | 800-370-2515

309

| Domains | Practices and Strategies | |
|---|---|---|
| **Academic Support**<br><br>*How do I target my academic practices and strategies to meet the range of learners in my classroom?* | **7 Academic Press**<br>☐ Setting and Monitoring Expectations<br>☐ Academic Reflection, Goal Setting, and Progress Tracking<br>☐ Anticipating and Planning for Learning Gaps<br>☐ Study Strategies<br>☐ Revise, Edit/Proof, and Correct<br>☐ Guided Work Period | **8 Formative Assessment**<br>☐ Academic Check-ins<br>☐ Walk-around Look-fors<br>☐ Feedback For Self-correction<br>☐ Five-minute Assessment Tools | **9 Academic Interventions**<br>☐ Academic Problem-solving and Planning Conference<br>☐ Progress Monitoring<br>☐ Academic Turnaround Plan<br>☐ Academic Coaching |
| **Restorative and Accountable Discipline and Behavior Support**<br><br>*How do I plan for, respond to, and manage behavior concerns and intervene in high-impact situations?* | **10 Planning for Behavior Concerns**<br>☐ Classroom Behavior Plan<br>☐ First Response to Behavior Concerns<br>☐ Behavior Check-ins | **11 Defusing Charged Situations**<br>☐ Depersonalization<br>☐ Responding to Disrespectful Behavior<br>☐ Defusing Students who are Upset<br>☐ Defusing Power Struggles<br>☐ Re-set Protocols<br>☐ Interrupting Physical Altercations<br>☐ Responding to Oppositional Behavior | **12 Behavioral Interventions**<br>☐ Restorative Conversations<br>☐ Behavioral Problem-solving and Planning Conferences<br>☐ Progress Monitoring<br>☐ Behavioral Coaching |

Domains of the Engaged Classroom | Appendix 9.3
Copyright ©2019 Engaging Schools | www.engagingschools.org | 800-370-2515

# APPENDIX 10.1

## Protocol for Identifying Implementation Look-fors

**Purpose:** Obtain teacher voice to inform the Look-for tool on the strategy

**Time:** 20 Minutes

**Participants:** Teacher teams (grade-level teams, departments, or course-alike cohorts)

### Instructions:

1. Independently (5 mins.): What impact on student learning and engagement have I noticed while purposefully implementing this strategy? Specifically, what am I doing? What do I see students doing in response to the strategy?
    a. On three individual sticky notes list three actions you do to implement the strategy.
    b. On three other individual sticky notes list three student responses to your actions.

2. Table Group(s) (9 mins.): Group members sort and cluster sticky notes and develop a T-Chart:

| When this strategy is implemented with fidelity and integrity: ||
|---|---|
| What specific actions might the teacher be doing and in what order (first to last)? | What specific responses/actions might students have in response to the implementation of the strategy? |
| | |

3. Table Talk (3 mins.): What might be some benefits of identifying Look-fors as a team?

4. Next Steps (1 min.):
    a. We will be using your brainstorm on these T-charts to develop a Look-for tool.
    b. We will share this tool with you prior to observing a randomized set of classrooms, and collecting and compiling implementation Look-for data.
    c. We will bring the data to you to analyze trends and patterns.
    d. We are doing this to support our learning to better solve our Problem of Practice.

5. Organize and Integrate (2 mins.): I came in thinking and feeling…I'm leaving thinking and feeling…

# APPENDIX 10.2

## Look-for Data Collection and Analysis

### Step 1: Prepare the Data Collection Team[1]

Look-for data collection and intentional dialogue are a powerful combination to support teachers' growth and development as practitioners. When instructional leaders are transparent about the role of Look-for data collection in the Professional Learning Cycle, teachers begin to lean in and trust the process. To support investment, focus, and commitment, consider the following:

**Teacher Voice:** Instructional leaders seek teacher voice to inform the Look-fors (teacher moves and student responses).

**Communication:** Instructional leaders share the tool, communicate and make transparent the purpose of Look-for data collection and how the data will be used to support ongoing professional learning.

**Formative Feedback — Not Evaluation:** Instructional leaders agree to use the Look-for data to support a collective understanding of grade-level, course-alike, departmental or schoolwide teacher practice, not as an evaluation of individual teachers for another purpose.

See Appendix 10.1 – Protocol for Identifying Implementation Look-fors about cultivating teacher commitment.

The goal of Look-for data collection paired with team dialogue is to support teachers in seeing the data as a structure for refinement and improvement. Developing and sustaining teacher trust in the process will be critical to the success of data collection.

### Step 2: Organize the Data Collection Team

**Who Collects Data:** This varies from school to school and often includes a combination of instructional leaders (i.e., assistant principals, instructional coaches, teacher leaders, or department heads). If possible, it is always helpful to travel in pairs to calibrate your use of the Look-for tool and learn together. That said, we are aware that resources can be limited in schools, and you may have to split up to visit a substantive number of teachers to have a representative sample of Look-for data.

### Step 3: Define Who and What

**Whose Classrooms Are Visited:** This depends entirely on the Problem of Practice and the teacher cohort tackling it. It could be schoolwide, grade-level teams, a course-alike team or a departmental team. The context will determine the teacher cohorts where Look-for data will be collected and the number of teachers involved, which is contingent on the size of the school. Thus, the group could be small or quite large. We recommend ten-minute classroom visits, knowing sometimes you will see the strategy in action and other times you may have missed it due to timing issues. When there are a large number of teachers to visit, it might be more viable to identify a smaller, representative group of teachers for this purpose. In this case, it is important to offer transparency around how teachers are identified for visits. One strategy is to randomize the list of teachers using a spreadsheet. Most spreadsheet programs will allow you to assign a random number to a list of teachers and then randomly sort the group. There are many tutorials available online on how to do this.

Copyright ©2019 Engaging Schools | www.engagingschools.org | 800-370-2515

**What to Collect Data On:** In advance of the Look-for data collection, a tool is constructed and informed by the teacher and student Look-fors brainstormed by teachers (See Appendix 10.1 – Protocol for Identifying Implementation Look-fors). We offer a sample below that instructional leaders can customize to suit the context of the data collection, the strategy, and the Problem of Practice.

| Cohort: | # of Classrooms Observed: | Date: |
|---|---|---|

**Problem of Practice:** Students are failing science courses disproportionally to other courses, due to the use of complex texts, unfamiliar terminology and concepts and substantive new and unfamiliar vocabulary required for success in the discipline.

Strategy #1: *Turn and Talk*

| Teacher Look-fors | Yes | No | N/A |
|---|---|---|---|
| 1. Teacher models the *Turn and Talk*, as needed | | | |
| 2. Teacher models the use of academic vocabulary | | | |
| 3. Teacher provides clear directions (written and oral) | | | |
| 4. Teacher circulates the room listening for academic vocabulary | | | |
| 5. Teacher provides feedback on the use of academic vocabulary to the group | | | |
| Additional Data (verbal/non-verbal) | | | |

| Aligned Student Look-fors | Yes | No | N/A |
|---|---|---|---|
| 1. Students *Turn and Talk* to one another | | | |
| 2. Students use academic vocabulary in their conversations | | | |
| 3. Students follow directions and reference written directions when needed | | | |
| Additional Data (verbal/non-verbal) | | | |

## Step 4: Compile the Look-for Data

Once the team has collected the direct evidence of the strategy being practiced in classrooms, a team member compiles the data into a one-page report. The data collection team gathers during their regularly scheduled meeting time to analyze the one-page report by moving through the protocol they will use with teachers (see below). This enables the team to rehearse the process, lift up their own learnings, and be prepared to lean in and listen when they meet with the teacher cohort involved.

## Step 5: Facilitate a Meeting for Teachers to Analyze the Data

The goal of analyzing the data is to support teacher teams to see trends and patterns across a grade, department, course-alike cohort or school in relation to the Problem of Practice. We offer the following protocol to support this process:

1. Distribute the one-page data report.
2. **Facilitate Go Rounds:** In two Go Rounds, each teacher will share his/her noticings and wonderings.
3. **Noticings:** Each teacher shares one noticing around the circle, without repeating what others have shared, until all noticings have been shared. These are charted by the facilitator.
4. **Wonderings:** Each teacher shares one wondering around the circle, without repeating what others have shared, until all wonderings have been shared. These are charted by the facilitator.
5. **Reflect on the Strategy and Problem of Practice:** The group holds an open discussion of what the noticings and wonderings communicate in relation to implementation fidelity of the strategy and academic engagement: "What are we learning? What do we want to continue to learn?" all the while keeping the Problem of Practice top of mind.

---

[1] Adapted from City, E., Elmore, R., Fiarman, S. & Teitel, L. (2009). *Instructional Rounds in Education: A network approach to improving teaching and learning.* Cambridge, MA: Harvard Education Press.

# APPENDIX 10.3

## Teaming Structures: Purposes & Benefits

Collaboration, in any team structure, strengthens teachers' capacity to engage in group problem-solving around a Problem of Practice to implement instructional practices and strategies that best support academic engagement and social and emotional development. Specific benefits for students within each grouping structure are listed below.

| Grouping Structure | Some purposes include... | Benefits are... |
|---|---|---|
| **Teacher-Initiated Collaborative Teams*** | • Collaborate to design a unit and share lesson plans. | • Shared language, protocols, and practices resulting in a safe and predictable learning environment across courses. |
| **Grade-Level Teams** | • Develop universal procedures, rituals, and strategies.<br>• Discuss individual student needs and interventions.<br>• Increase capacity to provide high social and emotional support. | • Strengthened key LLCs to meet students' developmental needs.<br>• Shared language, protocols and practices resulting in a safe and predictable learning environment across courses.<br>• Increased and more nuanced knowledge of students to better assess their strengths and challenges. |
| **Course-Alike Cohorts** | • Map curriculum to align with developmental and cultural needs.<br>• Develop common strategies in the course for all students.<br>• Standardize formative, interim, and summative assessment practices.<br>• Collaborate to design units.<br>• Anticipate and plan for learning gaps. | • Strengthened key LLCs to meet students' developmental needs.<br>• Increased student knowledge, skills, and understanding and improved course grades. |
| **Departmental Teams** | • Map curriculum to align with the developmental and cultural needs of students.<br>• Develop common strategies in the discipline for all students.<br>• Increased curricular coherence horizontally across grades and vertically within the department. | • A more seamless transition from one year to the next within a particular discipline.<br>• Strengthened key LLCs to meet students' developmental needs.<br>• Increased student knowledge, skills, and understandings and improved course grades. |
| **All Staff Schoolwide Cohorts** | • Review data and implement a core set of universal strategies and interventions to be used by all staff.<br>• Encourage an ongoing school-wide conversation on best practice. | • Strengthened key LLCs to meet students' developmental needs.<br>• Increased student knowledge, skills, and understandings and improved course grades. |

*Increased academic engagement and equity of outcomes for all students.*

*2 or more teachers who work with the same students.

# APPENDIX 11.1

## Sample Introductory Letter

Consider these suggestions for your one-page letter.

### Salutation:

*Dear Families, Guardians, and Adult Allies,*

### Paragraph 1: Introducing Yourself

Opening welcome: *"My name is _____ and I teach your son/daughter in _____ (name of course). I would like to take this opportunity to introduce myself, the course I teach, and some expectations I have for students in this course."*

- Your experience as a teacher.
- Your history at your current school.
- One or two things appropriate to share about yourself personally.

### Paragraph 2: Introducing Your Course

- Brief statement that explains what the course is about.
- Two or three key topics or learning units.
- Key knowledge and skills students will learn during the course (no more than four).
- Any special projects, activities, products, or presentations that students will experience this year.

### Paragraph 3: Hopes and Expectations for Students

- Two or three of your expectations that will support students' success in your class.
- Any specific school supplies and materials that students need for your class.
- Explanation of what families can expect you to do when students are struggling academically or behaviorally in class.
- A big hope for what students will take away from your class.
- Closing sentence: *"I value all of the ways that you can encourage and support your son's / daughter's academic progress this year. I look forward to teaching and supporting each and every student to have a successful year in this class."*

### Other Information (if applicable)

- Office hours (day and time) and phone number or email where parents can reach you.
- Blank line where a parent signs the copy of the letter that students return to you.
- Blank lines for any information or responses you would like parents to send back on the signed copy of the letter (best contact phone number, preferred communication mode, etc.)
- Blank lines for something the parent would like to share about their child that they want you to know and understand.

# APPENDIX 11.2

## Informational Update Formats

Identify a couple of ways you might systematically communicate with families over the course of the year. Creating a viable format and venue (e.g., email, Website, letter home, team dashboard) for sharing information will support timely communication with parents.

### Sample One: Quarterly Memo

- What we've been working on…
- What's next…
- Important dates and deadlines…
- Unit topics for the quarter…
- Ask your student about…

### Sample Two: Reminder

- Families: Please remind your child to rehearse their two-minute speech and bring in their speech preparation cards to class on Monday. We are looking forward to everyone's first performance. Thank you!

### Sample Three: Special News Blast

- You did it! Everyone turned in their completed unit projects. Families, give your students a shout out and ask them all about it.
- Families, I want you to know that every student in 5th Period _____ worked very hard to meet a challenging benchmark on _____. Invite them to show you their work.
- Families, ask your children about their fabulous performance in the mock trial this week.

# APPENDIX 11.3

## Student-Led Conference Check Lists

### Preparation for All Conferences

Decide on all of the materials and work samples you need to share your progress report or project. Make sure the materials provide evidence of key knowledge, skills, and understandings you have learned.

Place all materials in a paper or electronic folder that is easy to access.

Prepare an agenda so that your role and your parent/guardian/adult ally's role are clear.

Create note cards with key points for your presentation.

Review your cards with at least one adult.

Rehearse your presentation with a partner.

| Agenda for Progress Report Conferences | Agenda for Project Conferences |
|---|---|
| ☐ **Student welcomes parent, guardian and/or adult allies** to the conference.<br>☐ **Student summarizes what she is going to share** (my grades, samples of my work from two different courses, and goals for next term).<br>☐ **Student shares specifics from two courses:**<br>　☐ Progress report grade.<br>　☐ Work samples that show what you have learned including a "best effort" work sample.<br>　☐ Something you learned or experienced that you found particularly interesting, enjoyable, and meaningful.<br>☐ **Adults are invited to ask questions** and make comments after the student has presented her information.<br>☐ **Student reflects on overall progress for the term.** "I made the most progress (or my best effort) in_____ course. Here is what I did." and "My biggest challenge this term was _____ in_____ course. Here's why."<br>☐ **Adults are invited to ask questions** and make comments.<br>☐ **Student shares other personal accomplishments and milestones** achieved during the last several months inside and outside of school.<br>☐ **Student shares goals for next term.** "I want to earn a grade of _____ in _____ course next term. This is what I plan to do to improve." OR "I want to really improve my _____ skills, and this is what I plan to do to get better at this."<br>☐ **Adults share appreciations** about what the student has accomplished. | ☐ **Student welcomes** parent, guardian and/or adult allies to the conference.<br>☐ **Student summarizes what he is going to share** (the course, name of the project, the topic or problem focus).<br>☐ **Student shares specifics about the project that include some, most, or all of the following:**<br>　☐ Standards that the project met.<br>　☐ Requirements that the project needed to meet.<br>　☐ The steps that explain the process for completing the project from the development of the idea until final formatting and submission or presentation.<br>　☐ Explanation of summary of project findings.<br>　☐ Things that made the topic or problem interesting or meaningful for them.<br>☐ **Adults are invited to ask any questions** they have so far.<br>☐ **Student shares his big learnings from the project experience:**<br>　☐ Key knowledge and understandings gained.<br>　☐ Key skills improved or refined.<br>　☐ A challenge they experienced while completing the project.<br>　☐ Any topics or ideas from the project that they want to explore further.<br>　☐ Feelings upon completion of the project.<br>☐ **Adults share appreciations** about what the student has accomplished. |

# APPENDIX 11.4

## Family Conference Protocol

**Purpose:**

The goal for most parent calls or conferences is to describe the situation that prompted the call or conference; share the plan you and the student have developed to address the current situation; and solicit the parent's support in implementing the plan.

**Protocol:**

1. Introduce yourself and the course for which you are the student's teacher. Ask the parent if it is a convenient time to talk for a few minutes. *"Hello Ms. Green, my name is _____ and I teach Delvin in my 3rd period _____ class. Is this a convenient time to speak for a few minutes?"*

2. Share something that indicates that you know the student—a positive quality that she or he brings to the classroom, something he or she does well, something unusual that she or he knows about, etc. *"First, I want to say that I'm glad to have Delvin in my class. He is energetic and likes to participate. He has also told me about his interest in_____."*

3. Get right to the point and state the problem simply. Be clear about the behavior or skill gap that prompted the call. Share how it impacts the student (and the classroom if applicable). *"Here is the situation I would like to discuss. Our class has been working hard on learning when to work silently and when it is okay to talk. Delvin's chatter and blurting out during times for silence or silent work keep him from focusing on the task and makes it difficult for other students to focus. I am very interested in helping him maintain silence to support him to learn."*

4. Inform the parent of the plan for improving behavior and academic performance and invite the parent to respond to the plan. *"Delvin and I have spoken, and we have a plan for getting him back on track. Delvin has agreed to change seats, so he is sitting at the front of the room and is less distracted. He has also agreed to post his "Help" card when he needs to ask a question during silent work time. We have both agreed to monitor his behavior during silent times for three weeks using a daily progress card, and I will call you to let you know how he is doing at the end of every week. How does that sound?"*

5. Invite the parent to talk to their son/daughter about the situation and the plan for improvement. Reassure the parent you are calling so that the student can practice behaviors and habits that will improve the student's performance. *"I would really appreciate it if you could speak with Delvin about this and let him know that you will be expecting to see improvement on his progress card. I am calling now because learning when and how to be silent in class will help Delvin be a better student. And, I want him to have a great year in this class."*

6. Invite the parent to share information or ask questions. *"What questions do you have about the situation or plan? What are your thoughts? What might you recommend?"*

7. Thank the parent for their support and pause to invite any last words. *"Ms. Green, thank you so much for your support. I will let you know how Delvin is doing at the end of the week."*

8. Note: If the parent is upset, acknowledge their feelings and try to find a common concern or hope that you share about their daughter/son. *"I appreciate your concern, and I hope we can work together on this."* or *"It sounds like this is upsetting to hear, do I have that right?"; " I have confidence that Delvin can correct this."*

Copyright ©2019 Engaging Schools | www.engagingschools.org | 800-370-2515

# APPENDIX 11.5

## Calls and Conferences at the Request of a Parent

**Purpose:** The goal of this call or conference is to resolve the situation in ways that support the parent and the student; ensure that the parent's concerns are understood and their feelings about the situation are acknowledged; and agree on next steps that will help move forward.

### Protocol:

1. **First, thank the parent** for taking the time to speak with you. *"Ms. Grey, I want to thank you for making time to talk with me. I appreciate it."*

2. **Invite the parent to share exactly what the concern is.** *"I understand that you want to discuss_____. Tell me about your concern."*

3. **Paraphrase what the parent said to communicate your understanding.** *"So it sounds like_____; So you're thinking/wanting_____."*

4. **Ask open-ended questions** to help clarify the parent's thinking and your own. *"What else should I know about_____?; "How has this affected your child?"* Continue to paraphrase what parent says.

5. **Support the parent in problem-solving and offer support.** *"What might a good solution look like?"; "What are some specific ways I might help?"*

6. **Reach agreement on action steps** and ask parent, *"What feels important to discuss when I conference with your child tomorrow?"*

7. **Summarize the plan** of what you will do and how you will follow-up with the parent (phone call, text, email, etc.). *"So tomorrow, I will_____. Then I will call you on_____ and let you know how it's going."*

8. **Thank the parent for the conversation**, express your appreciation for the parent's concern, and express your confidence that the situation can be resolved positively. *"Thank you so much for bringing your concern to me. I have a clearer sense of what you want and what I need to do to support your daughter. I'm confident that this plan can make things better for her. Please stay in touch and call me with any other thoughts or questions you might have."*

**Note:** If the parent is extremely upset or agitated, continue to reflect her/his feelings and paraphrase concerns to help the parent reach a calmer state.

# INDEX

## A

abilities, validating, 22

Academic and Goal-setting Conference, 116

Academic Check-ins, 124–125

Academic Coaching, 133–134

Academic Conferencing, 115

academic efficacy, 13
    academic interventions, 130
    academic press, 113
    academic support, 112
    classroom practices to learn/strengthen, 225–228
    formative assessment, 124
    organizing the learning environment, 64
    practices supporting, 31, 115–116
    Value-added Feedback, 51

academic engagement, 17
    conditions for, 4 (*See also* Six Conditions for Academic Engagement)
    defined, 18
    to keep students in school, 26
    to support academic success, 25

academic interventions (practice #9), 129–134
    Academic Coaching, 133–134
    Academic Problem-solving and Planning Conference, 130
    Academic Turnaround Plan, 132–133
    Progress Monitoring, 131

academic mindsets, 17, 20
    building, 18 (*See also* Six Conditions for Academic Engagement)
    commitment related to, 23
    growing, 34
    negative, 24, 26

academic optimism, 200

academic press (practice #7), 113–123
    Academic Reflection, Goal-Setting, and Progress Tracking, 115–116
    Anticipating and Planning for Learning Gaps, 116–118
    Guided Work Period, 122–123
    Revise, Edit/Proof, and Correct, 121–122
    Setting and Monitoring Expectations, 113–115
    Study Strategies, 118–120

Academic Problem-solving and Planning Conference, 130
    Card Sort: sample action steps, 286–291
    protocol, 282–283
    template, 284

Academic Reflection, Goal-setting, and Progress Tracking, 115–116, 272–274

academic success
    core beliefs related to, 17
    engagement supporting, 25
    long-term indicators of, 185

academic support
    defined, 109
    link between academic outcomes and, 110
    in Multi-Tiered System of Supports, 111

academic support domain, 31, 33, 109–135, 309. (*See also individual practices*)
    academic interventions (practice #9), 129–134
    academic press (practice #7), 113–123
    adult mindsets aligned to, 234
    big ideas informing, 110–112
    formative assessment (practice #8), 124–129

Academic Turnaround Conferences, 132

Academic Turnaround Plan, 132–133, 294

accountability
    in discipline (*See* restorative and accountable discipline and behavior support domain)
    in Professional Learning Cycle, 185
    as reciprocal process, 185

achievement
    and involvement of parents, 203
    racial gaps in, 22

Activators, 99–100
    Card Sort, 258
    examples of, 258–265
    Four (or more) Corners, 263–265
    Post-it-Up, 259–263

*The Adaptive School* (Robert Garmston and Bruce Wellman), 188

Adelman, Howard, 52

adolescent development, 21–22, 221–224

adolescent experience, benchmarks of, 7

adult mindsets
    for academic support, 112
    aligned to domains, 234
    for content design, learning tasks, and protocols, 84
    for organizing the learning environment, 63
    for positive personal relationships, 46
    for restorative and accountable discipline and behavior support, 145
    for teacher-family partnerships, 206

adults
    adolescents' emotional connections with, 43 (*See also* positive personal relationships domain)
    mediated conversations with, 20

agency, 83. (*See also* personal agency)

aggression
    common factors in, 223
    student to student, 149
    student to teacher, 149

aggression/conflict aversion bias, 145

amygdala, 221

Anchor Experience(s), 54–55
    Building the Tallest Tower, 54, 242–243
    Lava River, 54, 239–241
Anticipating and Planning for Learning Gaps, 116–118
anticipating and planning for learning gaps (stage 3 unit planning), 177–178, 305
Anticipation Guide, 97
Appreciations, 54, 57
Appreciative Feedback, 57
Approachable teacher voice, 36
Aronson, J., 22
assessments. (See also Model, Teach, Practice, and Assess (MTPA))
    of academic readiness and performance, 110–111
    authentic, 93, 256
    Five-minute Assessment Tools, 127–129
    formative (See formative assessment (practice #8))
    Implementation Assessment phase (Professional Learning Cycle), 188
    of Interactive Notebooks, 251
    unit, checklist for, 177
    Unit Name, Essential Question(s), Key Understandings and Skills, 65
attachment, sense of, 45
attention
    as condition of academic engagement, 21–22
    Getting Attention, 73–74
    in responding to oppositional behavior, 163
auditory cues, for getting attention, 73
authentic assessments, 93, 256
authoritarian teachers, 223
authoritative teachers, 35–36
authority, questioning/challenging of, 223
autonomy, need for, 90

# B

Barth, Roland, 186
becoming, as benchmark of adolescent experience, 7
behavioral biases, 143–144
Behavioral Coaching, 167–168
behavioral engagement, 18
behavioral interventions (practice #12), 164–168
    Behavioral Coaching, 167–168
    Behavioral Problem-solving and Planning Conference, 167
    Progress Monitoring, 167
    Restorative Conversations, 165–166
Behavioral Problem-solving and Planning Conference, 167
    Card Sort: sample action steps, 299–302
    protocol, 296–297
    template, 298

behavioral settings, 61

Behavior Check-ins, 152–153

behavior concerns
    Behavior Check-ins, 152–153
    categories of, 148–149
    in charged situations (*See* defusing charged situations (practice #11))
    chronic, sources of, 164
    Classroom Behavior Plan, 146–150
    First Response to Behavior Concerns, 151
    planning for (*See* planning for behavior concerns (practice #10))

behaviors
    Classroom Behavior Plan, 146–150, 295
    difficult (*See* behavior concerns)
    habitualized in adolescence, 221
    Immature, 156
    Inappropriate, 156
    normal range of, 223
    Responding to Disrespectful Behavior, 156–157
    Responding to Oppositional Behavior, 162–163
    target, 11–14, 112–114, 131
    Unskillful, 156

behavior support. (*See* restorative and accountable discipline and behavior support domain)

being, as benchmark of adolescent experience, 7

beliefs
    about intelligence, 22
    about teachers' individual efficacy, 200
    related to academic success, 17
    that drive behavior (*See* mindset(s))

belonging. (*See also* creating group cohesion (practice #2))
    as benchmark of adolescent experience, 7
    sense of, 45

biases of teachers, 37
    formation of, 144
    influence on teaching and student treatment, 144–145
    and students with challenging behaviors, 143–144

Bill & Melinda Gates Foundation, 26

biological clocks, 222

brain
    during adolescence, 21–22, 221
    corpus callosum development, 222
    and "full-body" classroom experiences, 84

brainstorming, 96, 98

*Bridging the Gap Between Standards and Achievement* (Richard Elmore), 185

Building the Tallest Tower Anchor Experience, 54, 242–243

# C

calls, at request of a parent, 215, 319

Card Sort, 99
    for Academic Problem-solving and Planning Conference, 286–291

for Behavioral Problem-solving and Planning Conference, 299–302
for curriculum areas, 258

caring
    impact of, 140
    sense of, 45

Check-ins
    Academic, 124–125
    Behavior, 152–153
    Personal, 50

*Checklist Manifesto* (Atul Gwande), 174

checklists, 174
    academic Card Sort, 286, 290
    anticipating and planning for learning gaps, 178, 305
    determining acceptable evidence, 177, 305
    expository writing, 278–279
    identifying desired results and organizing content, 176, 304
    Student-led Conferences, 317
    unit design, 174
    unit planning, 304–305

Check-off Agenda, 65

choice, 83
    in End-of-Unit Assessment, 92, 255
    in responding to oppositional behavior, 163
    Student Voice and Choice, 90–91

Circles, 55–56
    Community, 55, 244–245
    facilitating, 248
    Problem-solving, 56, 246–240

Clarifying Instructions, 75

Classroom Behavior Plan, 146–150

Classroom Behavior Plan template, 295

classroom culture, 39

classroom design. (*See* organizing the learning environment (practice #3))

classroom discipline. (*See also* restorative and accountable discipline and behavior support domain)
    about, 130
    approaches to, 141–142
    in Multi-Tiered System of Supports, 143

classroom management, 62, 139

Clear Instructions, 76–77

Closing a lesson, 71

Coaching, 130
    Academic, 133–134
    as academic intervention, 130
    Behavioral, 167–168
    toward self-awareness and self-management, 20

coding, 97

coercive compliance, 23

cognitive biases, 143–144

cognitive engagement, 18

cohesive community, 18

collaboration, 183
    competencies, skills, and mindsets for, 198
    critical role of, 183
    teacher capacity supported by, 200

collaborative efficacy, 189

collaborative teaming, 183–200
    building collaborative efficacy, 198–199
    course-alike cohort example, 194–195
    grade-level example, 189–191
    interdepartmental example, 192–193
    literature and research on, 200
    Problem of Practice, 184–185
    Professional Learning Cycle, 185–189
    schoolwide example, 196–197

commitment
    as condition of academic engagement, 24–25
    for Maintaining Silence, 75
    of teachers to teaching, 45

committed compliance, 23

communication
    after Family Conferences, 214–215
    in cultivating trust, 19, 20
    to facilitate participation, 20
    Gatherings as practice in, 52
    for getting attention, 73
    Good News Communications, 210
    nonverbal, 36, 73
    respectful and caring, 140
    Restorative Conversations, 165–166
    between school and families, 205 (*See also* teacher-family partnerships)
    through voice and physical presence, 36

community, 52. (*See also* creating group cohesion (practice #2))

Community-Building Circles, 55

Community Circle Protocol, 244–245

competency(-ies)
    classroom practices to learn/strengthen, 225–228
    for collaboration, 198
    defined, 11
    in Learning and Life Competencies, 11–14 (*See also* Learning and Life Competencies (LLC))

competitive classrooms, 20

compliance, coercive vs. committed, 23

comprehension strategies, for studying, 119

conferences. (*See also individual types of conferences*)
    Academic and Goal-Setting, 116
    Academic Problem-solving and Planning, 130
    Academic Turnaround, 132
    Behavioral Problem-solving and Planning, 167
    Family, 214
    at request of a parent, 215, 319
    Responsive Listening in, 280–281
    Student-led, 210–211

Conferencing, Academic, 115

conflict. (*See also* defusing charged situations (practice #11) and aggression/conflict aversion bias, 145)
    effective teams' management of, 199

Conley, David, 118–120

connecting with all families, 207–211
    Course and Personal Introductions, 207–208
    Good News Communications, 210
    Informational Updates, 208–209
    Student-led Conferences, 210–211

connections
    emotional, 43, 222
    with families, 207–211
    to personal interests, 93
    planning for, 174
    school-home (*See* teacher-family partnerships)

consequences, 141, 164

content
    choice in, 91, 92
    linked to real world, 94
    organizing, 175–176, 304

Content
    Culturally Relevant, 95
    Developmentally Informed, 93–94, 256–257

content design, 31, 32

content design, learning tasks, and protocols domain, 81–104, 308. (*See also individual practices*)
    adult mindsets aligned to, 234
    big ideas informing, 82–84
    learning protocols (practice #6), 96–103
    rigorous, meaningful learning tasks (practice #5), 85–95

controversy, injecting, 93, 257

cooperation, within groups, 20. (*See also* group cohesion)

cooperative classrooms, 20

Cooperative Learning, 101–102

Cooperative Learning roles, 254

core beliefs, 17

core classroom documents, 68

Cornell Notes Plus, 86

corpus callosum, 222

Correct tasks, 121–122, 278–279

course-alike cohort collaboration, 194–195

course-alike cohort teams, 314

Course and Personal Introductions, 207–208

Course Feedback, 57

creating group cohesion (practice #2), 52–58
    Anchor Experiences, 54–55
    Circle, 55–56
    Gatherings, 52–54
    Student Feedback, 56–58

creative thinking, 82, 83
Credible teacher voice, 36
critical thinking, 82, 83
Cuban, Larry, 184
cultural biases, 144
cultural competence, 37
Culturally Relevant Content, 95
Culturally Responsive Classrooms, 7. (*See also* Equity-Centered Classrooms)
*Culturally Responsive Teaching* (Geneva Gay), 140
cultural perspectives, exploring, 95
culture(s)
    of classroom, 39
    integrated into content, 95
    of school, identifying with, 23
    study culture, 119
    work culture, 122

# D

daily rituals, 181
Darling-Hammond, Linda, 93
Data Collection and Analysis Look-for, 187, 311–313
Data Review and Analysis phase (Professional Learning Cycle), 188
decision-making, 184, 200
defusing charged situations (practice #11), 154–163
    Defusing Power Struggles, 158–159
    Defusing Students who are Upset, 157–158
    Depersonalization, 155
    Interrupting Physical Altercations, 161
    Re-set Protocols, 159–160
    Responding to Disrespectful Behaviors, 156–157
    Responding to Oppositional Behavior, 162–163
Defusing Power Struggles, 158–159
Defusing Students who are Upset, 157–158
departmental teams, 314
Depersonalization, 155
desk arrangements, 66
determining acceptable evidence (stage 2 unit planning), 176–177, 305
developmental delays, biases related to, 144
Developmentally Informed Classrooms, 7. (*See also* Equity-Centered Classrooms)
Developmentally Informed Content, 93–94, 256–257
differentiated learning, 90
disabilities, biases related to, 144
discipline. (*See* classroom discipline; planning for behavior concerns (practice #10))

disrespect, 154
    identifying, 156
    Responding to Disrespectful Behaviors, 156–157

distributed leadership, 200

diversity, knowledge, recognition, and appreciation of, 37

domain, defined, 30

Domains of the Engaged Classroom, 4, 29–39, 308–309. (*See also individual domains*)
    academic support domain, 31, 33
    adult mindsets aligned to, 234
    content design, learning tasks, and protocols domain, 31, 32
    effective teaching characteristics underlying, 30
    and empowered teacher presence, 34–38
    organizing the learning environment domain, 31, 32
    positive personal relationships domain, 31, 32
    reasons for incorporating, 34
    restorative and accountable discipline and behavior support domain, 33, 34

Do-Nothing approach to discipline, 141–142

Double-entry Journal Plus, 86

Doyle, Sir Arthur Conan, 188

dropout rate, 26

Dweck, Carol, 22, 119

# E

Ecological Approach to Classroom Management, 62

Edit/Proof tasks, 121–122, 278–279

educational equity, 4, 5. (*See also* Equity-Centered Classrooms)

effective teaching, characteristics of, 30

efficacy, sense of, 45

effort-based learning and growth mindsets, 22–23

elaboration, in studying, 120

Elffers, Joost, 53

Elmore, Richard, 185

emotional connection, 43, 222. (*See also* positive personal relationships domain)

emotional engagement, 18

emotional escalation, 154

emotional learning. (*See* social and emotional learning (SEL))

emotions
    during adolescence, 221
    causal relationship between learning and, 21
    and hormonal changes, 222
    intense and sudden expressions of, 154

empathy, in parent-teacher connections, 212

empowered teacher presence, 34–38

empowerment, personal, 23

Ending Class, 71–72

End-of-Unit Assessment, 92

End-of-Unit Assessment Choice, 255

*Enhancing Adult Motivation to Learn* (Raymond Wlodkowski), 187

enhancing family engagement through teaming, 216

equity, taking a stance for, 37

Equity-Centered Classrooms, 4–8
    about, 3
    culturally responsive classrooms, 7
    developmentally informed classrooms, 7

Evertson, C. M., 30

Exiting the Classroom, 71, 72

Exit Tickets, 129

Expectations, 61
    aligned with target behaviors, 113–114
    Setting and Monitoring Expectations, 113–115
    Visual Postings of, 64

explicit biases, 37

# F

families
    adolescents' aspirations influenced by, 204–205
    connecting with, 207–211
    enhancing engagement pf, 216
    home visits with, 215
    involvement in student interventions, 211–215
    partnerships with (See teacher-family partnerships)
    understanding kinds of, 204

Family Conferences, 214

Family Conferences Protocol, 318

Feedback
    Appreciative, 57
    Course, 57
    Group Process, 56
    Lesson, 57
    for Self-correction, 126–127
    Student, 56–58
    Unit, 57
    Value-added, 51

First learning unit, planning, 178–180

First Response to Behavior Concerns, 151

Fishbowl, 103

Five-minute Assessment Tools, 127–129

fixed mindset, 22

formative assessment (practice #8), 124–129
    Academic Check-ins, 124–125
    defined, 124
    Feedback for Self-correction, 126–127

Five-minute Assessment Tools, 127–129
in Multi-Tiered System of Supports, 8
Walk-around Look-fors, 125–126

formative student data, 184

Forming stage (group development), 198

foundational procedures (practice #4), 68–78
Clear Instructions, 76–77
Ending Class, 71–72
Getting Attention, 73–74
Grouping Formats, 77–78
Maintaining Silence, 74–75
Starting Class, 69–70

Four (or more) Corners, 100, 263–265
English, 265
mathematics, 263
science, 264
social studies, 264
world languages, 265

frameworks supporting engaged classrooms, 3–15
Equity-Centered Classrooms, 4–8
Learning and Life Competencies, 11–14
Multi-Tiered System of Supports, 8–10

Freymann, Saxton, 53

frontal cortex, 221

Fullan, Michael, 198

Furniture Arrangement, 66–67, 71

# G

gaming-up content, 89

Garmston, Robert, 188

Gatherings, 52–54

Gay, Geneva, 140

gender biases, 144

gender gap, among high school graduates, 26

Getting Attention, 73–74

goals
Academic and Goal-Setting Conference, 116
Obstacles, Learning Goals, and Action Steps Foldable, 276–277
professional, 34

Goal-Setting, 115–116

Good News Communications, 210

goodwill, as condition of academic engagement, 18–20

grade-level collaboration, 189–191

grade-level teams, 314

graphic organizers, 87

group cohesion
	among students, 20
	creating (See creating group cohesion (practice #2))

group developmental stages, 198

group dialogue, 20

Grouping Formats, 77–78, 180

Group Process Feedback, 56

group roles
	choice in, 91
	for Cooperative Learning, 254
	in problem solving, 102

group supplies caddies, 67

growth mindset, 22

Guided Work Period (GWP), 122–123

Gwande, Atul, 174

# H

*Handbook of Classroom Management* (C. M. Evertson and C. S. Weinstein), 30

Hargreaves, Andy, 198

Hattie, John, 25

high-impact practices and strategies, 30
	academic press, 113
	for academic support, 112

high school, keeping students in, 26

home groups, 78

home visits, 215

hormonal changes, 221, 222

How are you feeling?, 53

*How are You Peeling?: Foods with Moods* (Joost Elffers and Saxton Freymann), 53

How is your day going?, 53

# I

identifying desired results and organizing content (stage 1 unit planning), 175–176, 304

identity
	developed through social interactions, 20
	group-based, 20

Immature Behaviors, 156

Implementation Assessment phase (Professional Learning Cycle), 188

Implementation Look-for, protocol for identifying, 310

Implementation Practice and Reflection phase (Professional Learning Cycle), 187

implicit biases, 37

impulse control, 148

IN (Interactive Notebook), 87, 250–251

Inappropriate Behaviors, 156

Individualized Comment or Acknowledgment, 50

Informational Updates, 208–209

Informational Updates formats, 316

Instructions
    Clarifying, 75
    Clear, 76–77
    Verbal and Written, Presenting, 75

intelligence, students' beliefs about, 22

intentional group formats, 78

Interactive Notebook (IN), 87, 250–251

interdepartmental collaboration, 192–193

interest, as condition of academic engagement, 23

interpersonal skills, 43

Interrupting Physical Altercations, 161

interventions
    Academic, 112 (*See also* academic interventions (practice #9))
    behavioral (*See* behavioral interventions (practice #12))
    classroom, 9, 10
    Classroom Behavior Plan, 150
    defined, 141, 164
    intensive, 9, 10
    involving families in (*See* involving families in student interventions)
    in Multi-Tiered System of Supports, 9, 10
    Red Flags prompting, 118
    restorative and accountable discipline and behavior support, 145
    teacher-family partnerships, 206

Introductory Letter, 207

Introductory Letter sample, 315

Introductory Video, 207

involving families in student interventions, 211–215
    Family Conferences, 214
    Parent Requests a Call or Conference, 215
    Progress Monitoring After a Family Conference, 214–215
    Tell Me More Interviews, 213

# J

Jigsaw, 101

# K

knowing students and making them feel known (practice #1), 46–51
    Meet and Greet, 48
    Personal Check-ins, 50
    Student Profile Data, 48–50
    Student's Name, 47
    Value-added Feedback, 51

knowledge, social construction of, 222

Kudos, 57

## L

Landmark Method Plus, 86

Lava River Anchor Experience, 54, 239–241

Learner Profile, 49

learners, kinds of, 270–271

learning
    causal relationship between emotions and, 21
    emotional connection in, 222
    engagement in, 17
    link between academic support and, 110
    merging concrete and abstract in, 222
    planning for (*See* planning for student learning)
    Problem of Practice around, 184–185
    Professional Learning Cycle, 185–189
    secondary schools' focus on, 109
    students' evaluation of new learning situations, 17

Learning and Life Competencies (LLC), 11–14
    about, 3
    and academic interventions, 130
    and academic press, 113
    and academic support, 110, 112
    and behavioral interventions, 164
    in classroom practices, 225–228
    and creating group cohesion, 52
    and defusing charged situations, 155
    and formative assessment, 124
    and foundational procedures, 69
    and knowing students and making them feel known, 46
    and learning protocols, 96
    and organizing the learning environment, 64
    and planning for behavior concerns, 146
    and rigorous, meaningful tasks, 85
    sample mini-lesson, 230–231
    self-assessment and reflection tool, 232–233
    and Value-added Feedback, 51

learning biases, 144

learning environment layout, 249
    behavioral settings, 61
    organizing (*See* organizing the learning environment (practice #3))

learning gaps
    Anticipating and Planning for Learning Gaps, 116–118
    defined, 116, 177
    hardening of, 222
    sources of, 117

learning mode, choice in, 91

Learning Outcomes for the Lesson, 65

learning protocols (practice #6), 96–103
    Activators, 99–100
    Cooperative Learning, 101–102
    as multisensory and incorporating movement, 84
    Text Protocols, 96–98

        Turn and Talk, 100–101
        Whole Group Discussion, 102–103

learning readiness, 110–111

learning tasks, 31, 32
        balance of meaning and rigor in, 83 (*See also* rigorous, meaningful learning tasks (practice #5))
        movement in, 84
        multisensory, 84
        passive and active, 222
        Problematizing a Learning Task, 88–90

Learning Wall, 65

Lee, V., 113

Lesson Feedback, 57

lessons
        Closing, 71
        Feedback on, 57
        Learning Outcomes for, 65
        LLC sample mini-lesson, 230–231
        Purposeful, Well-Paced Lessons, 178–180, 307

listening
        Gatherings as practice in, 52
        Responsive Listening, 280–281

LLC. (*See* Learning and Life Competencies)

Look-for Data Collection phase (Professional Learning Cycle), 187

Look-fors
        Data Collection and Analysis, 187, 311–313
        Implementation, protocol for identifying, 310
        Walk-around, 125–126

## M

Maintaining Silence, 74–75

marking period rituals, 181

McTighe, Jay, 174

meaningful learning tasks, 83, 85. (*See also* rigorous, meaningful learning tasks (practice #5))

media, choice among, 92

medium, choice within, 92

Meet and Greet, 48, 70

memory
        and feeling-learning connection, 21
        nature of, 23
        procedural, 62–63, 68, 96

Metaphor Object Bag, 53

*Mindset* (Carol Dweck), 22

mindset(s)
        academic (*See* academic mindsets)
        of adults (*See* adult mindsets)
        for collaboration, 198
        defined, 14

    effort-based, 22–23
    of empowered teachers, 35
    fixed, 22
    growth, 22
    of students, 14

mini-whiteboards, 128

MIP (Most Important Point), 128

Model, Teach, Practice, and Assess (MTPA)
    classroom procedures, 63
    cooperative learning, 101
    end-of-class procedure, 71
    foundational procedures, 68–69
    getting attention, 73
    Guided Work Periods, 122
    Interactive Notebook, 250
    learning protocols, 96
    representational systems, 87
    social skills, 222
    target classroom behaviors, 14

monitoring
    Progress Monitoring, 130, 131, 167, 214–215, 292–293
    Setting and Monitoring Expectations, 113–115

Most Important Point (MIP), 128

movement in learning tasks, 84

MTPA. (*See* Model, Teach, Practice, and Assess (MTPA))

MTSS. (*See* Multi-Tiered System of Supports)

multisensory approaches
    learning tasks, 84
    study strategies, 118

Multi-Tiered System of Supports (MTSS), 4, 8–10
    about, 3
    academic support in, 111
    classroom discipline and student support in, 143

My Name, Getting it Right, 47

My Personal Story, 49, 237

# N

name
    My Name, Getting it Right, 47
    Name Tents, 47
    The Story of My Name, 47, 235
    Student's Name, 47

Name Tents, 47

negativity bias, 145

News Blasts, 209

Noddings, Nel, 140

non-cooperation, 148

non-participation, 148

nonverbal communication, 36, 73

normative compliance, 23

Norming stage (group development), 198

norms, effective teams' use of, 198

Note-Catcher, 87

note-taking methods, choice in, 91

# O

Obstacles, Learning Goals, and Action Steps Foldable, 276–277

ODD (Oppositional Defiant Disorder), 162

One Sentence, One Phrase, or One Word, 98

1 Student / 5 Actions / 5 Days, 238

openings, of classes, 69–70

oppositional behaviors
    characteristics of, 162
    Responding to Oppositional Behavior, 162–163

Oppositional Defiant Disorder (ODD), 162

optimism
    about students, 23
    academic, 200
    in parent-teacher connections, 212

organization strategies, for studying, 119

organizing the learning environment (practice #3), 64–68
    Furniture Arrangement, 66–67
    Tools and Resources, 67–68
    Visual Postings, 64–65

organizing the learning environment domain, 31, 32, 61–79, 308. (*See also individual practices*)
    adult mindsets aligned to, 234
    big ideas informing, 62–63
    foundational procedures (practice #4), 68–78
    organizing the learning environment (practice #3), 66–67

Organizing Your Space, 71, 72

# P

Parent Requests a Call or Conference, 215, 319

parents. (*See also* families)
    holding positive presuppositions about, 212
    as resource in dealing with student issues, 212

Parent-Teacher Home Visits Project, 215

participation, as condition of academic engagement, 20

participative decision-making, 200

peers, emotional connections with, 43. (*See also* positive personal relationships domain)

Performing stage (group development), 198

Perry, Theresa, 23

personal agency
    and meaningful, rigorous tasks, 83
    for students, 23
    for teachers, 35

Personal Check-ins, 50

Personal Contact Card, 49, 236

personal distress, 148

personal interests, 23, 93

Personalized Questions, 50

perspectives, differing, 198–199

Physical Altercations, Interrupting, 161

physical escalation, 158

physical presence, of empowered teachers, 36

Pianta, Robert, 114

planning for behavior concerns (practice #10), 146–153
    Behavior Check-ins, 152–153
    Classroom Behavior Plan, 146–150
    First Response to Behavior Concerns, 151

planning for student learning, 173–182
    planning first learning unit, 178–180
    Purposeful, Well-Paced Lessons, 178–180
    ritualizing days, weeks, units, and marking periods, 181
    unit planning, 174–178

Pluses and Wishes, 58

Poplin, M., 45

positive personal relationships domain, 31, 32, 43–58, 308. (*See also individual practices*)
    adult mindsets aligned to, 234
    big ideas informing, 44–46
    creating group cohesion (practice #2), 52–58
    knowing students and making them feel known (practice #1), 46–51

Post-it-Up, 99

Post-it-Ups, 259–263
    English, 262
    math, 259
    science, 260
    social studies, 261
    world languages, 263

power struggles
    defined, 158
    Defusing Power Struggles, 158–159

practice(s). (*See also* Prevention practices/strategies; Promotion practices/strategies)
    culturally responsive, 37
    defined, 30
    high-impact, 30
    reasons for incorporating, 34
    to support academic engagement, 29–30 (*See also specific practices*)

practice strategies, for studying, 120

Practicing Silence, 75

praise, of students' effort, 22

Preparing for Five Kinds of Learners, 270–271

Presenting Verbal and Written Instructions, 75

prevention, in Multi-Tiered System of Supports, 9, 10

Prevention practices/strategies
    academic support, 112
    Classroom Behavior Plan, 150
    foundational procedures, 63
    learning protocols, 84
    organizing the learning environment, 63
    positive personal relationships, 45–46
    restorative and accountable discipline and behavior support, 145
    rigorous, meaningful learning tasks, 84
    teacher-family partnerships, 206

Previewing, 97

Principle of Reciprocity, 185

Problematizing a Learning Task, 83, 88–90
    in ELA, 89
    in Science, 90
    in Social Studies, 89
    in world languages/ELL, 89

Problem of Practice, 184–186
    in course-alike cohort collaboration, 194
    in grade-level collaboration, 190
    in interdepartmental collaboration, 192
    in schoolwide collaboration, 196

problem-solving
    Academic Problem-solving and Planning Conference, 130, 282–284, 286–291
    Behavioral Problem-solving and Planning Conference, 167, 296–302
    group roles in, 102
    practices supporting, 31
    Problem-solving Circles, 56, 246–240

Problem-solving Circle Protocol, 246–240

Problem-solving Circles, 56

procedural infractions, 148

procedural memory, 62–63, 68, 96

procedures
    in organizing learning environment (*See* foundational procedures (practice #4))
    students' uncertainty around, 21
    Visual Postings of, 64, 65

*Professional Capital* (Andy Hargreaves and Michael Fullan), 198

Professional Learning Cycle, 185–189
    in course-alike cohort collaboration, 195
    Data Review and Analysis phase, 188
    in grade-level collaboration, 191
    Implementation Assessment phase, 188
    Implementation Practice and Reflection phase, 187
    in interdepartmental collaboration, 193
    Look-for Data Collection phase, 187
    Professional Learning Sessions phase, 186
    resources required for, 189
    in schoolwide collaboration, 197

Professional Learning Sessions phase (Professional Learning Cycle), 186
professional sustainability, 45
Progress Monitoring, 130, 131
    After a Family Conference, 214–215
    for behavioral concerns, 167
    sample tool for, 292–293
Progress Tracking, 115–116
promotion, in Multi-Tiered System of Supports, 9, 10
Promotion practices/strategies
    academic support, 112
    Classroom Behavior Plan, 150
    foundational procedures, 63
    learning protocols, 84
    organizing the learning environment, 63
    positive personal relationships, 45–46
    restorative and accountable discipline and behavior support, 145
    rigorous, meaningful learning tasks, 84
    teacher-family partnerships, 206
protective factors, 8
protocol(s), 31, 32. (*See also* content design, learning tasks, and protocols domain; learning protocols (practice #6))
    Academic Problem-solving and Planning Conference, 282–283
    adult mindsets for, 84
    Behavioral Problem-solving and Planning Conference, 296–297
    Community Circle, 244–245
    for identifying Implementation Look-for, 310
    Problem-solving Circle, 246–240
    Raised Hands, 73
    Re-set, 159–160
    Skill Focused Discussion, 102, 266–267
    Socratic Seminar, 103, 268–269
    Text, 91, 96–98, 252–253
punishment, 141–142, 223
Purposeful, Well-Paced Lessons, 178–180, 307

# Q

quarterly memo, 208

# R

racial and ethnic groups
    commitment to learning among, 22
    dropout rate for, 26
    graduation rates for, 26
    stereotype threat for, 22
racial biases, 144
racism, 22
Raised Hands Protocol, 73
randomized group formats, 77

Reader's Club, 118

real world content, 94

real world problems, 90

Reciprocity, Principle of, 185

Recognitions, 57

Red Flags, 118

Reflect and Connect, 69, 70

reflection
    Academic, 116
    in Anchor Experiences, 54
    Learning and Life Competencies, 232–233

reflective practitioners. (*See also* Academic Reflection, Goal-Setting, and Progress Tracking)
    LLC self-assessment and reflection tool, 232–233
    maximizing capacity to become, 34

reflective thinking, 82, 83

rehearsal strategies, for studying, 120

relationships
    positive (*See* positive personal relationships domain)
    power of, 43
    Restorative Conversations, 165–166
    teacher-student, 20

relaxed alertness, 21, 221

remediation, 130

Reminders, 209

Representing to Learn, 86–87

*Research-Based Strategies to Ignite Student Learning* (Judy Willis), 84

Re-set Protocols, 159–160

resilience, 7
    fostering, 8
    presence and availability of adults for, 46

Resource Center, 67, 68

resources, for Professional Learning Cycle, 189

respect, 18, 19
    and disrespect, 154, 156–157
    impact of, 140
    sense of, 45

Responding to Disrespectful Behaviors, 156–157

Responding to Oppositional Behavior, 162–163

Responsive Listening, 280–281

restorative and accountable discipline and behavior support domain, 33, 34, 139–169, 309. (*See also individual practices*)
    adult mindsets aligned to, 234
    behavioral interventions (practice #12), 164–168
    big ideas informing, 140–145
    defusing charged situations (practice #11), 154–163
    planning for behavior concerns (practice #10), 146–153

Restorative Conversations, 165–166

Revise, Edit/Proof, and Correct, 121–122, 278–279

*The Right to Learn* (Linda Darling-Hammond), 93

rigorous, meaningful learning tasks (practice #5), 81, 85–95
    Culturally Relevant Content, 95
    Developmentally Informed Content, 93–94
    End-Of-Unit Assessment, 92
    as multisensory and incorporating movement, 84
    Problematizing a Learning Task, 88–90
    Representing to Learn, 86–87
    Student Voice and Choice, 90–91

rigorous learning tasks
    criteria of, 85
    defined, 82

risk factors for students, 223

rituals, 181
    for ending class, 71
    Goal-Setting, 115
    Meet and Greet, 48
    ritualizing days, weeks, units, and marking periods, 181

role plays, 89

*Run School Run* (Roland Barth), 186

# S

safety
    emotional, 45
    feelings of, 18
    Interrupting Physical Altercations, 161

*Scandal in Bohemia* (Sir Arthur Conan Doyle), 188

school culture, 23

school-home partnerships. (*See* teacher-family partnerships)

school improvement initiatives, 188

school rules, 65

school schedule, 65

school vision, 65

schoolwide collaboration, 196–197

schoolwide teams, 314

SEL (social and emotional learning), 3, 11. (*See also* Learning and Life Competencies (LLC))

self-assessment, for Learning and Life Competencies, 232–233

self-awareness, 12
    academic press, 113
    academic support, 112
    behavioral interventions, 164
    coaching toward, 20
    creating group cohesion, 52
    defusing charged situations, 155
    effective teams' support of, 199
    organizing the learning environment, 64
    planning for behavior concerns, 146

practices supporting, 31
Value-added Feedback, 51

self-confidence, communicating, 36

self-control, communicating, 36

Self-correction, Feedback for, 126–127

self-esteem, 83

self-management, 12
- academic interventions, 130
- academic press, 113
- academic support, 112
- behavioral interventions, 164
- as behavior concern, 148
- classroom practices to learn/strengthen, 225–228
- coaching toward, 20
- creating group cohesion, 52
- defusing charged situations, 155
- formative assessment, 124
- organizing the learning environment, 64
- planning for behavior concerns, 146
- practices supporting, 31
- Value-added Feedback, 51

Sentence Starters, Text Protocol, 252–253

Sergiovanni, Thomas, 18

Setting and Monitoring Expectations, 113–115

Silence
- auditory signal for, 73
- benefits of, 74
- Maintaining, 74–75
- Practicing, 75

*The Silent Epidemic* (Bill & Melinda Gates Foundation), 26

Silent Reading, Then Say Something, 97

simulations, 89

situational interest, 23

Six Conditions for Academic Engagement, 4, 17–26
- attention (I'm ready), 21–22
- commitment (I should), 24–25
- effort (I can), 22–23
- goodwill (I trust), 18–20
- interest (I want to), 23
- participation (I belong), 20

size effect, 30

sketches, 87

skill(s)
- for being on teams or in groups, 52
- classroom practices to learn/strengthen, 225–228
- for collaboration, 198
- defined, 11
- interpersonal, 43
- in Learning and Life Competencies, 11–14
- Progress Monitoring for, 131
- Study Strategies, 118–120

Skill Focused Discussion Protocol, 102, 266–267

sleep, 222

small groups, for Academic Coaching, 134

Smith, J., 113

social and emotional learning (SEL), 3, 11. (*See also* Learning and Life Competencies (LLC))

social biases, 143–144

social capital, 200

social efficacy, 12–13
    academic interventions, 130
    academic support, 112
    behavioral interventions, 164
    classroom practices to learn/strengthen, 225–228
    creating group cohesion, 52
    defusing charged situations, 155
    formative assessment, 124
    organizing the learning environment, 64
    planning for behavior concerns, 146
    Value-added Feedback, 51

Socratic Seminar Protocol, 103, 268–269

speaking, Gatherings as practice in, 52

Stand in the Same Place, 73

Starting Class, 69–70

Steele, C., 22

stereotypes, formation of, 144

stereotype threat, 22, 23

sticky notes, 97

Storming stage (group development), 198

storyboards, 87

The Story of My Name, 47, 235

strategy(-ies)
    in course-alike cohort collaboration, 195
    defined, 30
    in grade-level collaboration, 191
    high-impact, 30
    in interdepartmental collaboration, 193
    for purposeful, well-paced lessons, 180
    reasons for incorporating, 34
    in schoolwide collaboration, 197
    to support academic engagement, 29–30 (*See also under specific practices; specific strategies*)

structured dialogue, 20

structured processes. (*See* learning protocols (practice #6))

Student Contact Card, 49, 236

Student-Developed Questions, 98

Student Feedback, 56–58

Student-led Conferences, 210–211, 317

Student Profile Data, 48–50

Student Reflections, 209

Student's Name, 47

student to student aggression, 149

student to teacher aggression, 149

Student Voice and Choice, 90–91

student work folders, 67

study culture, 119

study skills, 118

Study Strategies, 118–120

# T

table arrangement, 66

Table Topics for Teens, 53

Tallest Tower Anchor Experience, 54, 242–243

target behaviors
    in academic support, 112
    defined, 11
    Expectations aligned with, 113–114
    in Learning and Life Competencies, 11–14
    Progress Monitoring for, 131

Taylor, Linda, 52

teach by walking around, 156

teacher-family partnerships, 203–216
    big ideas informing, 204–207
    connecting with all families, 207–211
    enhancing family engagement through teaming, 216
    involving families in student interventions, 211–215

teachers, beliefs about efficacy of, 200

teacher-student relationships, 20, 43. (*See also* positive personal relationships domain)

teaching
    effective, 30
    Professional Learning Cycle, 185–189

teaming
    collaborative (*See* collaborative teaming)
    enhancing family engagement through, 216
    structures for, 314
    and student performance, 200

technology, 39

Tell Me More Interviews, 213

text, choice in, 91

Text Protocols, 91, 96–98

Text Protocol Sentence Starters, 252–253

Think Like a Practitioner, 89

Tier 1 (MTSS), 9, 10
    academic supports in, 111
    connecting with all families, 207–211

Tier 2 (MTSS), 9, 10
    academic interventions, 129–130
    academic supports in, 111
    behavioral interventions, 164
    involving families in student interventions, 211–215

Tier 3 (MTSS), 9, 10, 111

time
    for family engagement efforts, 206–207
    for purposeful, well-paced lessons, 180

*Tinkering Toward Utopia* (David Tyack and Larry Cuban), 184

Tools and Resources, 67–68

topic, choice in, 91, 92

touch points, 114

trust, 18–20, 45

Try Three Before Me, 75

Tuckman, Bruce, 198

Turn and Talk, 70, 100–101

Two-Column Notes, 86

Tyack, David, 184

## U

unanxious anticipation, 21, 221

Unit Feedback, 57

Unit Name, Essential Question(s), Key Understandings and Skills Assessments, 65

unit planning, 173–178
    anticipating and planning for learning gaps (stage 3), 177–178
    checklists, 304–305
    determining acceptable evidence (stage 2), 176–177
    for first learning unit, 178–180
    identifying desired results and organizing content (stage 1), 175–176

University of Chicago Consortium on School Research, 17, 26

Unskillful Behaviors, 156

## V

Value-added Feedback, 51

values of schooling
    and commitment, 23
    self-identification with, 14

verbal cues, for getting attention, 73

verbal escalation, 158

*Visible Learning* (John Hattie), 25

vision
    "family-driven, youth-guided," 211
    school, 65

visual cues, for getting attention, 73
Visual Postings, 64–65, 67
voice, of empowered teachers, 36
volume level, for purposeful, well-paced lessons, 180

## W

Walk-around Look-fors, 125–126
Weather cards, 53
weekly rituals, 181
Weeres, J., 45
Weinstein, C. S., 30
Wellman, Bruce, 188
What It Looks Like, 98
Whole Group Discussion, 102–103
    Skill Focused Discussion Protocol, 102
    Socratic Seminar Protocol, 268–269
Wiggins, Grant, 174
Willis, Judy, 84
Wlodkowski, Raymond, 187
Wood, J. Luke, 22
work culture, 122

## Y

*Young Gifted and Black* (Theresa Perry), 23

## Z

zone of proximal development, 20
zones of discomfort, 143–144

# ABOUT THE AUTHORS

**Carol Miller Lieber** got the call to teach as a teenager and never stopped. Exploration of the art, craft, and science of teaching and learning has been her driving passion for over forty-five years as an urban educator in the roles of middle and high school teacher, school founder, principal, curriculum writer, and clinical professor in teacher education. She is a national leader in integrating principles of personalization, schoolwide and classroom discipline, and youth development into everyday practices and structures for middle and high schools. Carol is the author of many books and publications including *The Advisory Guide, Making Learning REAL: Reaching and Engaging All Learners* and *Getting Classroom Management Right*, and a co-author of *Shifting Gears: Recalibrating Schoolwide Discipline and Student Support*. She is a longtime professional development consultant and program designer for Engaging Schools. Carol lives in Lancaster County in rural Pennsylvania.

**Michele Tissiere** has extensive experience as a classroom teacher and senior administrator in secondary schools. As director of program for Engaging Schools, she oversees the implementation of the Engaged Classrooms Program. Michele has extensive experience partnering with district leaders, school leaders, and teachers on aligning their vision, mission, and core beliefs with their policies, systems, structures, and processes to support effective and sustainable change. Michele is committed to co-constructing strategic and differentiated professional learning opportunities to maximize adults' capacity to carry out the complex work of school change, helping to shape healthy faculty, peer, school, and classroom cultures. Michele is co-author of *Shifting Gears: Recalibrating Schoolwide Discipline and Student Support, Getting Advisory Right: Tools for Supporting Effective Advisories*, and several articles. Michele lives in Denver, Colorado.

**Sarah Bialek** is Engaging Schools' director of district and school partnerships, facilitating the collaborative development of Professional Services contracts that support the interests, needs, and vision of school and district leaders and maintaining relationships with those leaders. Previously she served as an Engaging Schools consultant, facilitating schools' effective implementation of Engaged Classrooms, Schoolwide Discipline and Student Support, and Advisory Plus. For a decade, Sarah was a science teacher in culturally and economically diverse urban schools in Denver, and spent a year as an assistant principal working with students, teachers, and parents around school discipline issues. Sarah lives in Golden, Colorado.

**Donna Mehle** spent more than 15 years as a teacher, mostly in New York City public high schools, before joining Engaging Schools. In addition to her work in the classroom, Donna served as a literacy coach, advisory program coordinator, school leadership team member, New York City Writing Project seminar coordinator, and English Department facilitator. As Engaging Schools' Engaged Classrooms specialist, Donna supports districts, schools, and teachers around the country with student-centered teaching and learning, advisory program design and development, classroom management, and building restorative school cultures. She co-authored *Activators: Classroom Strategies for Engaging Middle and High School Students*. Donna lives in Corpus Christi, Texas.

# ABOUT ENGAGING SCHOOLS

Founded in 1982, Engaging Schools is a national nonprofit organization that collaborates with educators to create school communities where each and every student develops the skills and mindsets needed to succeed and make positive contributions in school, work, and life. We partner with schools and districts to address the particular challenges of middle and high schools, with a focus on the integration of academic, social, and emotional learning and development. Engaging Schools is well-known for providing research-based professional learning and resources with practical strategies. We support a shift in systems, policies, and practices and foster classrooms and schools that are safe and supportive, engaging and inspiring, and challenging and equitable. Our services and resources address:

- instructional practice and classroom management
- discipline and student support
- climate and culture
- advisory programs

## Engaged Classrooms Service

*The Engaged Classrooms Institute and Professional Learning Cycle*

Our students come to school influenced by social, cultural, and environmental factors that impact their engagement in school, their academic success, and their relationships with their peers and adults. Understanding and supporting them, with their myriad complexities, is essential to their healthy growth and development. The Engaged Classrooms Institute and Professional Learning Cycle prepares teachers, and the staff who support them, to create developmentally informed and culturally responsive classrooms where students feel safe, cared for, engaged, and challenged to think, create, and perform.

## The Engaged Classrooms Institute

This four-day institute engages teachers in dynamic experiences with high-impact practices and strategies that contribute to increases in equity in the classroom, social, emotional, and academic efficacy, engagement in learning, and support for every student. The learning experiences will deepen their ability to:

- Foster and sustain strong and supportive personal relationships with and among students;
- Purposefully organize the learning environment and establish procedures to support academic engagement;
- Ramp up engagement and rigor through meaningful learning tasks and foundational learning protocols to increase academic achievement;
- Target academic press, formative assessment, and academic intervention strategies to meet the needs of the range of learners in the classroom; and
- Use a restorative and accountable approach to promote positive behaviors; prevent unnecessary problems; plan for, respond to, and manage behavior concerns, and; intervene in high impact situations.

### The Professional Learning Cycle

The Professional Learning Cycle equips teacher teams and instructional leaders to address a collectively held problem of practice. It supports teams to become more highly effective, where teachers grapple with the question, "What is it that we do not yet know how to do effectively and how are we going to learn it?" The Cycle supports mutual accountability amongst peers by providing sustained professional learning that employs a core set of norms, strategies, and protocols, helping teachers discover and plan for solutions that improve student outcomes.

### Engaging Schools
www.engagingschools.org
800-370-2515